D1593601

Ethics of Our Fighters
A Jewish View on War and Morality

MAGGID

Shlomo M. Brody

ETHICS
OF OUR
FIGHTERS

**A JEWISH VIEW ON
WAR AND MORALITY**

Maggid Books

Ethics of Our Fighters:
A Jewish View on War and Morality

First Edition, 2024

Maggid Books
An imprint of Koren Publishers Jerusalem Ltd.

POB 8531, New Milford, CT 06776-8531, USA

& POB 4044, Jerusalem 9104001, Israel
www.korenpub.com

The publication of this book was made possible
through the generous support of *The Jewish Book Trust.*

ISBN 978-1-59264-676-0, *hardcover*

Printed and bound in the United States

Dedicated to the memory of my beloved father

Prof. Baruch Brody z"l

ברוך אלתר בן הרב אליעזר זאב ומרים גיטל

whose thought inspired this book
and whose memory accompanied the writing of each page

Dedicated to the memory of

Dr. Baruch Brody *z"l*

Distinguished Ethicist
Communal Leader
Cherished Friend

Wesley & Carole Ashendorf
Sheldon & Debbie Bootin
Howard & Beverly Feldman
Danny & Barbara Gold
Rick & Dorit Guttman
Nancy Beren & Larry Jefferson
Basil & Doreen Joffe
Roger & Evelyn Medvin
Gideon & Nava Miller
Ira Mitzner & Riva Collins
Irving Rotter
Wayne & Laura Yaffee

Contents

Chapter 22: Legitimate Military Targets: Military Necessity and Discrimination in Gaza and Lebanon

Chapter 23: Proportionality and the Great Missed Opportunity

Chapter 24: Justifying Collateral Damage in Serbia and the Middle East

Introduction

A STORY ONE HUNDRED YEARS IN THE MAKING

Several years ago, I invited one of Israel's most eminent philosophers to speak to a group of students in Jerusalem about the Israel Defense Force's code of ethics. At the end of his talk, one of the women asked how Jewish thought might impact military behavior. The philosopher, himself not religiously observant but quite knowledgeable in Jewish sources, sharply responded, "What could Judaism possibly teach us about military ethics? The laws of *eshet yefat to'ar*, regulating how to take a captive foreign woman as a wife? We're better off without it."

This book is my response to my student's question.

In fairness, the philosopher was onto something. Classic Jewish sources do not speak at great length about the ethics of warfare. After all, because of their political situation, Jews were not active in military affairs for many centuries. We have extensive literature about proper moral behavior. But books like *Ethics of our Fathers* contain nothing about the ethics of our fighters. And when you dig back deep into the Bible and antiquity, the military behavior can sometimes be quite ferocious, indistinguishable from other nations in those times.

Nonetheless, over the last one hundred years, rabbis and other Jewish thinkers have developed profound thoughts about war and ethics. That legal and theological corpus takes in a range of issues – from conscription, to the ethics of going into battle, to military tactics, to the making of territorial compromises for peace, and more.

Yet these writings are not so well known. They are generally written in Hebrew for a rabbinic audience. It almost always does not relate to the broader ethical categories found in general philosophical literature. And it displays limited interest in contributing to global discourse. That is quite regrettable. For many of these scholars were implicitly in conversation – or in debate – with others writing about similar developments in geopolitics, international law, and ethics.

Judaism, it turns out, has much to say about these topics. It just never joined the conversation. This book is meant to change that.

Yet as much as this is a book about ethics, it is also a story. It tells the tale of how Jews were confronted anew with the moral challenges of warfare. After many centuries of not fighting, Jews were once again on the battlefield. This confrontation forced them to articulate a Jewish political worldview that protected communal interests but also reflected Jewish beliefs. These values drew in part from teachings of classical Jewish texts but also drew lessons from the experiences of Jewish history. Following many centuries of powerlessness, Jews needed to ask: What does it mean to fight as a Jew?

The answers given to this question would help shape, and be shaped by, the pivotal historical moments of the last one hundred–plus years: World War I, the creation of the League of Nations and the United Nations, the bombing of Hiroshima, Nagasaki, and Dresden, the Holocaust, the establishment of Israel, multiple Israeli-Arab wars, intifadas, 9/11, the "war on terror," and so forth. Some of the events discussed in the book are well known, others less so. Yet they all played a critical role in helping Jews, and Judaism, to formulate an ethical worldview on military dilemmas.

This book draws from philosophical, historical, and rabbinic literature to articulate a holistic perspective on the ethical dilemmas of warfare. It is the first attempt in Hebrew or English to present a systematic Jewish perspective on military ethics. It is rooted in traditional sources of Jewish ethics yet remains intelligible to a general reader. For this reason, the chapters are organized thematically in a way that will be familiar to any reader of the many contemporary works on military ethics. The events depicted are largely in chronological order, but we'll sometimes jump back and forth in history to sharpen the argument.

The insights are relevant not only to Jews and to Jewish thought but to key issues facing contemporary military strategists in general. The worldview emerging from Jewish sources can help guide anyone thinking about military ethics today.

Throughout, I've tried not to force Jewish thinking into compliance with standard models in the discipline of military ethics. The sources must be studied on their own terms before drawing broader conclusions. Instead, by placing rabbinic writings in dialogue with secular philosophical discourse, I hope to present a systematic worldview that is at once distinctly Jewish and more broadly insightful.

The positions taken in the coming chapters draw deeply from the insight of rabbinic luminaries and Jewish thinkers. Yet this book is not a summary of their positions. Instead, it's the story of how these thinkers grappled with new moral dilemmas and my attempt to utilize their insights toward building a holistic worldview about military ethics. Different readers, looking at the very same sources and stories, will undoubtedly come to different conclusions on particular issues. I hope, however, the general moral framework proposed to tackle ethical military dilemmas will be compelling. At the very least, it should spark a conversation about how Judaism can speak to the pressing moral dilemmas facing Jews and all peoples around the world.

A BRIEF OUTLINE

The first part of the book will focus on the responses of rabbinic writers to some of the major ethical concepts that arose during the period between World War I and World War II and its immediate aftermath. Those issues include pacifism, total war, international legal governance, civilian immunity, and contractarianism. These initial rabbinic writings addressed the complex moral legacy left by the Bible and a broader discussion as to whether conventional military norms can hold up to ethical scrutiny. We'll try to show that Judaism offers a sophisticated moral framework that takes into account several central values in approaching ethical dilemmas.

The rest of the book, covering events from 1940 to 2014, depicts and analyzes Jewish perspectives on the classical distinctions within just-war theory that dominate contemporary discourse on military ethics:

namely, the conditions that justify going to war (known in philosophical literature as *jus ad bellum*) and behavior in war (known as *jus in bello*).

In part 2, we'll focus on salient incidents in early Zionist military history that discuss the classic criteria necessary to go to war: just cause, probability of success, competent authority, and so on. In these debates, legends of ancient Jewish history like Masada and the Bar Kokhba rebellion suddenly come back to life.

Part 3 will discuss whether self-defense wars require the other side to take the first shot, or whether countries can launch preemptive or preventative strikes. Examples here will be drawn from pivotal decisions Israeli leaders made to go to war between the years 1956 and 1982. We'll also draw on the more recent experience of the United States and other countries, with a particular focus on the invasions of Iraq and Afghanistan within the broader "war on terror."

Part 4 will concentrate on how we are supposed to fight once the war has started. These issues have gained prominence in recent years as bloody scenes from Gaza, Lebanon, Iraq, Afghanistan, and elsewhere raise questions of "proportionality" and "civilian immunity." We'll show how these terms have been misused and stress how balancing different moral values is the only way to fight well and act nobly.

Most books today on military ethics draw on examples from warfare conducted by the Jewish state. One hundred years ago, that possibility would have been unfathomable to our story's protagonists. For our first protagonist, in fact, it would have been a nightmare. Let the story begin.

Part I

Judaism Confronts War

Chapter 1

World War I and the False Promise of Pacifism

WAR AS IDOL WORSHIP: RABBI TAMARES AND THE HORRORS OF WORLD WAR I

In 1920, a rabbi of the small village Milejczyce, today located in Poland, looked back on the alleged progress made in Europe since the Enlightenment. Reason and wisdom had advanced to remove many evil beliefs, superstitious idiocy, and immoral idolization. Yet one idolatrous idea survived and had ruined everything: war. Europe had left in place "that idol that is known as 'The Homeland' together with its worship known as 'War.'"[1] This false god had now desolated the world's most advanced continent and left its national homelands in tatters.

Rabbi Aaron Samuel Tamares (1869–1931) was certainly not the only person who, looking back upon World War I, would reject utterly the morality of warfare. Tens of millions had been killed or wounded in a great conflict whose causes were not entirely clear and that had dramatically failed to fulfill its promise to become, in a phrase popularized by the American president Woodrow Wilson, "the war to end all wars." Beyond the geopolitical chaos, the war had also left behind a moral shambles as many grappled with what had been done to them – or by them.

Winston Churchill, who served Britain as both a military officer and a government minister during the war, mordantly itemized the material and civilizational wreckage:

> The wounded died between the lines: the dead moldered into the soil.... Bombs from the air were cast down indiscriminately. Poison gas in many forms stifled or seared the soldiers. Liquid fire was projected upon their bodies. Men fell from the air in flames, or were smothered, often slowly, in the dark recesses of the sea....
>
> When all was over, Torture and Cannibalism were the only two expedients that the civilized, scientific, Christian states had been able to deny themselves, and these were of doubtful utility.[2]

Neither faith nor reason, but only usefulness, had restricted the means of Europe's self-mortification.

How did a civilization built on the great principles of both reason and faith descend into such depravity? The injuries of the war had fallen on all Europeans. Yet Jews were also the objects of specifically antisemitic actions and frequently accused of supporting the "other" side, whichever that might be. Already in early 1915, with the advance of the Russian army on the Eastern Front, Jews had been ordered from their homes in Polish, Ukrainian, and other specified areas within the Russian "Pale of Settlement." By 1917, as many as one million Jews had been expelled and left to the mercies of rapacious soldiers and citizens.[3]

In 1915, the Yiddish writer and demographer S. Ansky (Shloyme Zanvl Rappoport) was sent from Petrograd by the Relief Committee of Russian Jewry to distribute aid to Jewish refugees. He reported that hundreds of thousands of Jews in the Galician region (today in Western Ukraine) were "enclosed within a ring of fire, blood, and steel. They were cut off and at the mercy of frenzied and violent soldiers and Cossacks who attacked them like packs of wild animals."[4] Some seventy-five hundred Jews lived in the town of Sadigure. All of the women, except for a group hidden by a non-Jewish pharmacist, had been raped over three days in September 1914.

In a battered synagogue now serving as an infirmary for Russian soldiers, An-sky found a Christian icon occupying the place in the holy ark normally reserved for Torah scrolls. "I couldn't tear my eyes from the sight of this terrible sacrilege, this desecration of both religions," he wrote. "The brutal hand of a crazed soldier had exacted the same revenge from God that he had from man."[5]

JEWISH SOLDIERS FIGHTING FOR COMPETING HOMELANDS

To be sure, many Jews were far from passive observers in this war, with unprecedented numbers serving as active soldiers on both sides in World War I: more than a million in Allied forces and 450,000 in the armies of the Central Powers.[6] Some, particularly from places like Turkey (Central Powers) or Russia (Allies), had been impressed into service by rulers they didn't like. Elsewhere, like in Austria-Hungary, Jews fought out of patriotic gratitude for their relatively safe position in that monarchical realm. Internal factors also played a role among Jewish soldiers, as many sought to wreak vengeance on the Russians, who earlier in the century had committed pogroms in places like Kishinev and Odessa.

In some places, military service was deemed an act of religious duty. Rabbi Moshe Shmuel Glasner of Hungary denounced draft dodgers who claimed that service in the army would preclude a religious lifestyle. To his mind, the obligation to follow the laws of the state demanded not only paying taxes (*damim* in Hebrew) but also risking one's blood (also *damim*). If such national service entailed violating Shabbat and other commandments, so be it.[7]

Rabbis in Allied countries agreed. Rabbi Joseph Hertz, the chief rabbi of Britain, praised Jewish servicemen and regularly condemned those who shirked their combat duties, especially if they did so in the name of religion.[8] A French rabbi declared in April 1915:

> Ah! my brothers, we glorify the martyrs of faith, those who have suffered all the tortures and have sacrificed their lives for the integrity of their religious belief. Love of the homeland: is that not also a religion? To die for one's homeland, is that not the same as to die for one's God?[9]

Such rabbinic declarations no doubt also served to rebut the claim of many antisemites that Jews were mere fair-weather residents of their countries.

Mass Jewish enlistment in World War I marked a turning point in a two-hundred-year rabbinic debate regarding the moral status of warfare among nations and the particular issue of Jews soldiering for their host countries. The question emerged after the French Revolution when Jews were first allowed to join their host forces. Partly because of the difficulty of observing ritual laws while serving, many rabbis were opposed to such participation. Yet recognizing that it was often not a matter of choice, like in Czarist Russia, they frequently confined themselves to advising enlisted soldiers in the observance, to the extent possible, of dietary and Shabbat laws. Later, one well-known scholar, Rabbi Yisrael Meir Kagan (1839–1933), would even write a popular handbook for Jewish soldiers that included, inter alia, ethical urgings to avoid the trap of sexual temptation.

More fundamentally, and long before World War I, many rabbis spoke out against the wanton bloodiness of warfare, particularly when not undertaken out of self-defense. Proactive belligerence, in their view, especially but not solely when directed against civilians, flagrantly violated the commandment "thou shalt not murder."[10] To this was added the fear that Jewish soldiers on one side might be killing Jewish soldiers on the other side, a trope common in Jewish literature throughout the nineteenth and early twentieth centuries.[11]

During World War I, this predicament became particularly salient. The dilemma highlighted conflicting duties as Jews perforce asked themselves: Which are the true brethren whom I'm willing to die for? Or to put it another way, who are emphatically not my brethren so that I'd be willing to kill them?

One rabbi, struggling to find a legal precedent for such killing, took refuge in general counsel: "The obligation devolves upon every God-fearing individual to labor on behalf of world peace so that innocent blood not be spilled throughout the world and that warfare will desist."[12] That's fine advice, but of little help to a young Jew deliberating whether to enlist or to flee.

As we've seen, however, other authorities did not confine themselves to such well-meaning but bland remedies. In addition to Rabbi

Glasner in Germany and Rabbi Hertz in England, many, particularly but not only in the Reform movement, positively embraced army service as a path toward integration. Within traditionalist Orthodox circles, an earlier major figure, Rabbi Samson Raphael Hirsch of Frankfurt (d. 1888), praised those who in general fully dedicated themselves to their "Fatherland." Beyond following the laws of the state, R. Hirsch wrote, it was a religious precept (mitzva)

> to be loyal to the state with heart and mind, loyal to the kings, to guard the honor of the state with love and pride, to strive with enthusiasm wherever and whenever you can so that the nation's institutions shall prosper so that every aim which your country has set as its national goal shall be achieved and furthered.[13]

This obligation, R. Hirsch asserted, held true even when the state made harsh demands, including sacrificing one's life to defend it. In the nineteenth century, many Jews applied this approach to military service, just as many more would do in the following century with regard to fighting in World War I.

KILLING IN THE NAME OF GOD? THE CASE FOR PACIFISM

After the Great War, patriotic talk of the "Fatherland," clothed in religious rhetoric, was seen by many as gravely misguided. One critic, a friend of Rabbi Tamares, was the philosopher Hillel Zeitlin (1871–1942). Zeitlin grew up in a hasidic community in Russia but later abandoned his observant life for the world of philosophy, ultimately becoming a popular writer with a superior reputation in Jewish literary circles.

Then, after World War I, Zeitlin re-embraced religion and became an innovative mystic and theologian. In a treatise written "to the nations of the world," he lambasted all of the warriors who, in his words, had taken the name of the Lord in vain:

> Nations fight nations, brothers spill blood like water, and in the hour of killing and bloodletting they shout out in the name of God! They desire God to help them stab in the heart their

> brethren and fellow human beings, to denigrate and decimate
> His creatures![14]

Nothing, to Zeitlin's mind, was more antithetical to the divine will than this wholesale destruction.

In truth, even during the war, many Europeans already recognized that it was uniquely horrible and completely unnecessary. Why didn't it stop earlier? [15] R. Tamares had his own answer to the much-debated question. Europe was spiritually decrepit. The great political ideas of the late nineteenth and early twentieth centuries, including nationalism and socialism, had birthed bloody revolutions and oppressive new regimes. R. Tamares had little faith that new institutions like the League of Nations and the Hague tribunals could prevent the false gods of nation and war from demanding human sacrifices on the altar of their cause.

What the world needed, R. Tamares concluded, was nothing less than a spiritual counter-revolution, one that would fill the earth with the knowledge of the Lord and His central teaching that all human beings were created in His image. Only thus could humanity be brought to understand that war was never justified, thereby fulfilling Isaiah's prophecy that "nation shall not lift up sword against nation."[16]

To Rabbi Tamares, then, there was only one answer: pacifism. Broadly speaking, pacifism affirms that war is always wrong and that there is always a better alternative: no solid moral grounds exist on which to justify war, and mass killing for political reasons can never be condoned. In support of their cause, proponents of pacifism usually adduce three major arguments:[17]

1. The negative *consequences* of fighting always outweigh the benefits (the "consequentialist" argument).
2. War violates the *basic duty of justice*, which is not to kill humans (the "intrinsic" or "deontological" argument).
3. Wartime *behavior* is a vice that contradicts established norms of human excellence (the "virtue" argument).

If many pacifists combine more than one of these arguments in their thinking, R. Tamares, for his part, invoked all three. First, he believed that violence, even for the sake of justice, would ultimately lead to more violence (the "consequentialist" argument). Citing the history of European political revolutions, he asserted:

> The strategy of these revolutions, the answering of evil with evil, is questionable. It may succeed, but on the other hand, it is just as likely to aggravate the original evil. And even when it does succeed, it is only a short-lived palliative. This we have seen clearly in every land where freedom was seized forcibly by nationalist revolutions: In no time at all the plague of despotism erupted in the flesh of the body politic – just as before.[18]

Violence is self-normalizing. Even when undertaken for a seemingly just cause, violence creates a world in which the political order legitimizes the use of force, which will ultimately be employed in an unjust cause or executed unjustly.

More integrally, R. Tamares writes, the Bible expresses a fundamental repulsion to the very idea of murder (the "deontological argument"). It's just wrong to shed blood, the soul of man. Bloodshed also corrupts our own souls, for when we use our fists or our weapons, even in self-defense, we ultimately transform our character, rendering ourselves incapable of distinguishing right from wrong (the "virtue" argument).[19]

Thus, warfare, wrong in its own right, further corrupts both society and its members. Indeed, after having participated in the Fourth World Zionist Congress in 1900, R. Tamares soon left the movement on the grounds that Zionism would ultimately become just another form of nationalism that would distort Judaism's core message. The one true territory of the Jews was the kingdom of the spirit.

To his philosophical and theological reasoning, R. Tamares added a psychological motivation for his pacifism: his experience, as a child, observing a non-Jewish neighbor mourning the loss of her son in the Russo-Turkish war. "The fallen soldier's mother wept bitterly at the news – and the little Jewish boy wept with her. From that moment on, the boy's consciousness was consumed by an awareness of the depravity of war."[20]

Such experiences, we might pause to note, have done more than any intellectual argument to inspire pacifists over the course of centuries. After the horrors of World War I, several American Reform rabbis flirted with the idea of adopting a principled, movement-wide pacifist position.[21] And their example can be multiplied many times over. Although some ultra-Orthodox anti-Zionists shared his disdain for Jewish militarism,[22] R. Tamares is the Orthodox rabbinic figure who espoused pacifism most clearly.

THE BIBLICAL CASE AGAINST PACIFISM: KILLING IS SOMETIMES A MORAL DUTY

R. Tamares's worldview is seductive but not compelling; in fact, it's even dangerous. There can be no doubt that Judaism aspires to a world in which warfare will cease; such is the eschatological vision in the prophecies of Isaiah, Micah, and others. These prophecies, along with other passages in the Bible, have inspired many peace initiatives in history. Nonetheless, it would be very hard to argue that the Bible condemns all warfare.

Central biblical heroes, from Abraham through Moses, Joshua, and David, led or fought in battles ordained or blessed by God. To soldiers going to war, the high priest would give a rousing invocation: "Let not your courage falter! Do not be in fear…. For it is the Lord your God who marches with you to battle for you!"[23] Biblical prophets also foresaw the occurrence of great armed clashes before justice and peace would descend on the world.

Indeed, the prophet Micah, while envisioning an era of peace in which people "shall beat their swords into plowshares, and their spears into pruning hooks," also anticipated the violent downfall of the enemies of the Jews: "For I will give you horns of iron and provide you with hooves of bronze – and you will crush the many people."[24] Warfare will be eliminated by the end of days, but it remains necessary to bring that utopia to life.[25]

Pacifists argue that it is an intrinsic duty not to shed blood – "thou shall not murder" [means "thou shall not kill," with no exceptions]. The philosopher Elisabeth Anscombe notes that pacifists fail to distinguish between shedding *innocent* blood and shedding *any* human blood.[26] It may be wrong to spill wantonly and with malice the blood of those who have done nothing to forfeit their right to live; but guilty aggressors are in another category altogether, having committed acts so heinous as to warrant, and demand, retribution. The Talmud teaches this point regarding a biblical verse about an intruder: "If the thief is seized while tunneling, and he is beaten to death, there is no bloodguilt in his case. If the sun has risen on him, there is bloodguilt in his case."[27] The talmudic Rabbis, reading the two sentences in reverse order, explain the passage as follows: if it is as clear as daylight that the thief intends no violence, one may resist the burglar but not kill him; otherwise, he may be killed with impunity, following the legal principle "If one comes to slay you, kill him first."[28]

Philosophers offer their own formulations of this same principle, but the underlying logic is similar and clear: it is both unreasonable and unfair to deny to victims of aggression the ability to protect their liberty through the use of counterforce; to the contrary, aggressors forfeit their rights against the violence of others.[29]

This same idea is applied to national conflicts in a biblical passage about the warrior Jephthah. Rehearsing the history of relations between the Israelites and the Ammonites, Jephthah exclaims that, whereas Israelites previously fought Ammonites in a legitimate struggle over territory, the current Ammonite king has crossed the line into an aggressive war against Israel. "I have done you no wrong," Jephthah asserts, "yet you are doing me harm and making war on me. May the Lord who judges decide today between the Israelites and the Ammonites."[30]

Leading seventeenth-century thinkers on the morality of war like Hugo Grotius and John Locke cited this verse to ground a right and even a duty of national self-defense.[31] Of course, humans will not always agree on who is the victim and who the unjust aggressor; the biblical passage cited above leaves God as the ultimate arbiter. Yet the moral principle is unmistakable: victims of unjust aggression are not only entitled but morally obligated to defend themselves, even at the cost of killing their attackers.

NOT BY MIGHT AND NOT BY POWER? STRENGTH AS A VIRTUE

To be fair, R. Tamares's argument that violence is a vice was extreme but has some roots in post-biblical rabbinic thought. Some sages sought to promote alternative notions of courage and bravery in the era after Jews lost sovereignty and became far removed from the battlefield. Already in biblical times, Moses himself warned against victorious Israelite warriors arrogantly declaring, "My own power and the might of my own hand have won this wealth for me," instead of assigning ultimate credit for military success to God's special providence for His people.[32] Declares the psalmist:

> Through You we gore our foes; by Your name we trample our adversaries. I do not trust in my bow; it is not my sword that gives me victory. You give us victory over our foes![33]

Similarly for the prophets: "Not by might and not by power, but through the spirit of the Lord" are salvation and redemption earned.[34] Thus, when David slays Goliath without the aid of sword or spear, he proclaims not himself but God to be the Lord of the battlefield and the deliverer[35] – even as the Bible informs readers of David's adulatory welcome home by the fawning masses.[36]

In later rabbinic literature, however, bravery is modeled mainly through examples of self-restraint and the rescue of others, rather than traditional martial prowess. Thus, in midrashic lore, King David is quoted as defining courage in terms of saving a person drowning in a river or fallen at the bottom of a pit.[37] Elsewhere, in collections of proverbs and aphorisms, rabbinic Sages answer the question, "Who is brave?" by naming one who controls his passions, turns his enemy into his friend, or, again, saves a person from drowning. "The true warriors are warriors in Torah," they declare.[38] *Ethics of our Fathers* doesn't just ignore the ethics of our fighters but seems to downplay fighting altogether.

Taking another tack, the Rabbis suggest that biblical references to weapons can be reinterpreted symbolically as allusions instead to the power residing in, and unleashed through, the wisdom of scholars. This image they apply to David himself, called in the Bible a man of valor and war but now reenvisaged as one who excelled in the give-and-take of religious intellectual discourse. By contrast, actual warfare is the way not of the virtuous but the wicked, encapsulated for the Rabbis in the figure of Esau, the Bible's archetypical nemesis.[39] As R. Tamares would put it, "We strive for [real] manhood…the study of Torah."[40]

Early secular Zionists scorned this rabbinic notion of virtuous passivity as rendering Jews easy prey to their oppressors. The Ukrainian-born writer Micha Yosef Berdichevsky (1865–1921) mocked the ignominy of a nation that, priding itself on a lofty ethical culture, was wholly unable to defend itself from marauders.[41] In the wake of a shattering 1903 pogrom in the Bessarabian capital of Kishinev, the towering Hebrew poet Hayim Nahman Bialik (1873–1934) penned "In the City of Slaughter," a searing condemnation of the local Jewish men, putative "heirs of the Hasmoneans," who hid in latrines and pigpens rather than defend their families from rape and pillage. "Crushed in their shame, they saw it all; they did not stir or move.… Perhaps, perhaps, each watcher had it in his heart to pray: a miracle, O Lord – and spare my skin this day!"

In truth, Bialik himself had privately documented several cases of resistance and self-defense in Kishinev, complicating his portrait of male cowardice.[42] In general, moreover, the broader historical record is more complex than his or other Zionists' narrative of Jewish submissiveness in exile.[43] In medieval Europe, for example, crusaders and others came up against occasional acts of resistance and Jewish self-defense. In Iberia, the outstanding poet and scholar Shmuel (Samuel) HaNagid, also known by his Arabic name of Ismail ibn Nagrela (993–1055), served as vizier to the caliphs Habbus and Badis of Granada and saw battlefield action as the commander of a Muslim army. "If you lack the power to pay back the cruel," he wrote in one short poem, then try to "forget what they did to your image; but perhaps you're a hero and *can* get revenge; then atone for their sins with your courage."[44]

Still, Diaspora Jews often suffered from their relative powerlessness and dependency on the mercy of others. Even if the rabbinic virtues of scholarship and peace did not always lead to passivity, much Jewish lore remained dominated by stories of martyrs. Traditionalists saw them as exemplars of self-sacrifice, but Zionists saw them as models of vulnerability. In reaction, Zionists looking to Jewish history for confirmation of their own activism sought models in antiquity other than those elevated by the Talmud.

For instance, the talmudic Rabbis do not mention the Maccabean rebellion against the second-century BCE Seleucid empire in their account of the Hanukka holiday. They assert that the festival was established to commemorate the rededication of the Temple and the miracle of a cruse of oil lasting eight days. For the Zionists, by contrast, Judah Maccabee and his brothers were military heroes. Similarly lionized were both the fighters who took their own lives in the siege of Masada (73 CE) rather than submitting to Roman captivity, and the participants in the failed Bar Kokhba rebellion against Rome (132–135 CE).

As none of these stories had been elaborated upon in classical rabbinic literature, Zionists turned instead to the Greek writings of the Jewish-Roman historian Josephus, and especially to the much-reworked Hebrew version of his *Wars of the Jews* in the tenth-century *Yossipon*. Reprinted over the centuries in many languages and forms, that medieval retelling was mined by proto-Zionist figures like Rabbi Yehuda Alkalai, Berdichevsky, and others for exemplars of how Jews once did and should once again comport themselves in the world. One of those early Zionists, the Polish-born David Grün (1886–1973), would change his family name to Ben-Gurion after a central protagonist in that book.[45]

The core argument advanced by Zionists like Ben-Gurion and many others – that when Jews are vulnerable to attack, powerlessness is not a virtue but a vice – was and remains irrefutable. But does this mean that physical power and might must inevitably become idolized, as in Greek mythology, or turned into supreme values? The danger of feting warrior culture motivated R. Tamares's argument that the real heroes of the Bible were the prophets, not the kings.[46] The truth is more complex, however: kings who fought just wars are praised in the Bible as loyal servants of God; those who defended their people against the Goliaths of the world are called virtuous.

Missing from R. Tamares's and later pacifists' worldview, in short, is the possibility of incorporating physical strength and courage into a broader moral framework, thereby enabling an understanding of how, in what circumstances, and with which safeguards power can be rightly and even heroically used to forward a just cause.[47]

THE EVIL CONSEQUENCES OF PACIFISM: GANDHI, BUBER, AND THE NAZIS

Nazi persecution of the Jews tested commitments to the consequentialist argument for pacifism: that violence just begets more violence. Is violence always just a temporary cure that will lead only to more violence? Certainly it would be a blessing if everyone in the world would abandon warfare. Yet, as was repeatedly the case in the twentieth century, inaction in the face of evil is not only a grave moral failure of protecting the innocent; it also rewards aggression and invites further despotism. Sometimes one must utilize power to stop violence.

In the 1930s, this essential moral principle lay buried or repressed as many citizens and leaders of Western democracies, still traumatized by the horrific carnage of World War I, preferred appeasing Hitler and ignoring his expansionist aims.[48]

One Jew who did learn the moral value of resistance, albeit tardily, was the famed German philosopher Martin Buber (1878–1965). In the early days of World War I, he celebrated the outbreak of hostilities as an opportunity for Germany to manifest its "historic mission" by exporting its superior values to a benighted world. He also saw an opportunity for Jews to reinvigorate their Judaism by displaying self-sacrifice for this great cause and thus becoming fully integrated into the German people (*volk*). It was regrettable, Buber thought, that individual Jews would be enlisted on opposite sides of the battlefield. Nonetheless, it was better to fight for one's convictions than look on passively. We Jews, he wrote, "will no longer need our motto, 'Not by might but by spirit,' since force and spirit shall now become one for us. *Incipit vita nova!* [The new life begins!]"[49]

Buber was strongly criticized by some of his friends for overly stressing values like manliness and sacrificial courage in the face of the war's already rampant violence. But he, putting his words into deeds, even tried, unsuccessfully, to volunteer for the German army.

By 1916, Buber had become disillusioned with the war. Afterward, while remaining a Zionist, he demonstrated his newborn fear of the violent tendencies of nationalism by helping to found Brit Shalom (Covenant of Peace), a group advocating for a binational state in

Palestine. Forced to leave Germany following increased Nazi hostilities, he ultimately emigrated to Palestine in 1938 where he continued to advocate for Jewish-Arab coexistence.

Yet despite his pacifist leanings, even Buber recognized that sometimes force is necessary for self-defense. In 1938–39, as Hitler's tanks were already rumbling in Europe, a few Zionists sent a letter begging Mahatma Gandhi to support their quest for a Jewish state as a haven from the Nazis. Gandhi greatly disappointed them. While acknowledging Hitler's "wanton" antisemitism, Gandhi insisted on a pacifist response:

> If there ever could be a justifiable war in the name of and for humanity, a war against Germany, to prevent the wanton persecution of a whole race, would be completely justified. But I do not believe in any war.

What then should the Jews do? Gandhi suggested that each of his correspondents stand tall and practice civil disobedience, challenging his German persecutors to "shoot me or cast me in the dungeon." As for the Jews in Palestine, they should try to convert the Arab heart through passive nonviolent resistance (*satyagraha*, in Gandhi's coinage) and "offer themselves to be shot or thrown into the Dead Sea without raising a little finger against [the Arabs]."

One can imagine the alacrity with which both Nazis and many Arabs would have accepted this offer to dispose freely of the Jews. Buber undertook to rebut Gandhi's assertions directly. Describing his activism for peace, he nevertheless emphasized that absolute pacifism would necessarily allow evil to triumph:

> I cannot help withstanding evil when I see that it is about to destroy the good. I am forced to withstand the evil in the world just as the evil within myself. I can only strive not to have to do so by force. I do not want force. But if there is no other way of preventing the evil destroying the good, I trust I shall use force and give myself up into God's hands.[50]

Pacifism, in effect, allows the strong to defeat the good. Its belief in the *absolute* evil of war, to the point where counterforce of any kind, in any circumstance, is utterly shunned, allows evil to triumph. Rabbi Tamares was fearful that nationalism had become a form of idolatry, sacrificing all other goods and values for the sake of the nation. Absolute pacifism, too, can become a form of worship that sacrifices the just on the altar of its ideals.[51]

That little was done to initially resist Hitler and defend Europe from his terror poignantly proves Buber's conclusion. Among the victims of the Holocaust was the philosopher Hillel Zeitlin, the friend of R. Tamares whom we met early on, killed in the Warsaw Ghetto while, it is said, wrapped in his prayer shawl and phylacteries. R. Tamares himself died in 1931. His wife and two of their daughters were murdered in Treblinka, but four other children had fled to Palestine before the war and survived, thanks to the Zionism that their father scorned. One daughter, Rikva Perelis, became a leading researcher of the Jewish resistance movements in the Warsaw Ghetto and elsewhere.

Jews had learned the high cost of being defenseless.[52]

Chapter 2

Total War, Religious Fundamentalism, and the Ghosts of Canaan

THE WARTIME MESSIANIC DREAMS OF RABBI KOOK

From a small Swiss village during the first months of World War I, Rabbi Abraham Isaac Kook looked upon the Great War and saw something very different than what R. Tamares saw: the heralding of the Messiah and the eradication of evil.

> When there is a great war in the world, the power of Messiah is aroused. The time of song has come, the pruning of tyrants, the wicked perish from the Earth, and the world is invigorated as the voice of the turtledove is heard in our land.[1]

R. Kook (1865–1935) and R. Tamares had both studied in the famed rabbinic academy in Volozhin, the former alongside Berdichevsky and the latter with Bialik. At the turn of the twentieth century, the two rabbis embraced Zionism but then took deeply different directions. R. Tamares stayed in his small village to write antinationalist treatises and rebuke those who saw great wars as the harbinger of the Messiah.[2]

R. Kook immigrated to Palestine in 1904 to become the rabbi of Jaffa and ultimately the first Ashkenazic chief rabbi of Mandatory Palestine. On the last days of July 1914, R. Kook traveled from Palestine to Frankfurt for a rabbinic conference with the hope of rousing support for Zionism. The war broke out on August 1. Managing to make it to St. Gallen, Switzerland, R. Kook sheltered there for the next eighteen months. He eventually got to London, where he served as a congregational rabbi until returning to Jerusalem in 1919. Stranded in Europe for the war's duration, R. Kook had a front-row seat to the "global tempest," as he called it, "and the horrors in its storm."

THE PROMISES AND PERILS OF NATIONALISM

Rabbis Kook and Tamares testified to the same horrors of the Great War. Their contrasting views on what might emerge afterward stemmed from differing views on the promise and perils of nationalism. Like R. Tamares and many others at the turn of the twentieth century, R. Kook had been deeply engaged in thinking about the purpose of different countries in general and the Jewish nation in particular. [3] His treatise on the topic was aptly called "Israel's Mission and its Nationhood." In R. Kook's analysis, the individualism and atomism of the Enlightenment movement had left people lonely and disillusioned; secular Zionists, like other nationalists, were seeking a healthy collective identity. [4] Religious Jews must embrace the nascent nationalist Jewish movement because the national spirit, left dormant for many centuries, was central to both Torah and human nature. He thus sharply criticized religious anti-Zionists, like R. Tamares, who deemed Zionism a foreign implant grafted onto Judaism; in fact, the religious life and human spirit can never be separated from nationhood.

Yet R. Kook also recognized that nationalism, when seen as an end in itself with no greater purpose, can easily degenerate into a nasty chauvinism. [5] Divorced from the divine spirit, nationalism leads to brutality.

> Nationalist feeling is a sentiment exalted in its honest naturalness, but when it is not properly directed and does not turn to the higher goal of the absolute happiness of general perfection, it will eventually burst the bounds of morality when it oversteps its

boundaries by *raising a hand to capture castles that do not belong to it,* without righteous judgment and with no holy goal or purpose.[6]

Such expansionism to capture 'foreign castles' is caused by one nation not respecting the unique contribution of other peoples. Nationalists begin to see others as uncivilized barbarians against whom one may legitimately attack aggressively.[7] The horrors of World War I confirmed to R. Kook how unfettered nationalism leads to cruel wars. Atonement for this bloodshed, he believed, will only come through the "total dismantling of all the foundations of contemporary civilization, with all of their falsity and deception, with all their poison and venom."[8]

R. Kook asserted that Jews may have been denied political power for two millennia precisely to avoid running a country in such a corrupt international order.

> We left the world of politics by force of circumstance that [nevertheless] contains an inner desire, until a fortunate time will come, when it will be possible to conduct a nation without wickedness and barbarism – this is the time we hope for.… It is not worthwhile for Jacob to engage in statecraft when it must be full of blood, when it requires an ability for wickedness.[9]

After the madness of the Great War, however, a new world order can emerge. The antidote to immoral nationalism is the biblical doctrine that all individuals were created by God and in His image. One does not quickly kill or conquer others when one internalizes that all humans possess inherent dignity.

Yet R. Kook warned that Jews must not blindly imitate the aggressiveness that taints many nationalist movements.[10] Unlike R. Tamares, who believed that Zionism would fall into the same pitfalls as other nationalist movements, R. Kook hoped that a refined Jewish nationalistic movement would set the tone for a new era in international affairs.

TOTAL WAR AND THE ERA OF UNRESTRAINED WARFARE

R. Kook was a visionary but not a prophet. His lofty hope for a refined world remains uplifting even as in retrospect it seems remarkably unfulfilled. World War I, in many ways, was the turning point in military history in which notions of "total war" dominated strategic planning.[11] Historians characterize total wars as conflicts with two major features: (1) the mobilization of armed forces and civilian populations, with all of its economic and technological resources, in order to destroy the other side, and (2) the disregard of restraints imposed by law, custom, or morality to allow for intended (and not just inevitable) harm to noncombatants.[12] When statecraft operates without moral or material constraints, barbarism reigns.

It takes a lot to mobilize a country for total warfare. The historian James Turner Johnson identifies a few necessary components.[13]

1. Ultimate Cause: First, winning the war is tied to preserving the ultimate values of society or protecting the very existence of the nation. During the American Civil War, Abraham Lincoln asserted that the Union must be preserved at all costs, thereby justifying the war methods used to achieve unconditional surrender by the Confederacy. Woodrow Wilson argued in 1917 that America should enter World War I since the "world must be made safe for democracy." Accordingly, "America is privileged to spend her blood and her might" to achieve these great principles.

2. Propaganda: Second, fiery propaganda helps whip the people into action. In an infamous speech in February 1943, German Propaganda Minister Joseph Goebbels, standing under a banner proclaiming "Total War – Shortest War," cried out,

> Do you believe with the Führer and us in the final total victory of the German people? Are you and the German people willing to work, if the Führer orders, ten, twelve, and if necessary fourteen hours a day and to give everything for victory? Do you want total war? If necessary, do you want a war more total and radical than anything that we can even imagine today?

Such rhetoric, of course, might be utilized for more honorable causes. Thus, *mutatis mutandis*, Winston Churchill, in his famous 1940 "Blood, Toil, Tears, and Sweat" inaugural speech to inspire an embattled Britain to fight on, concluded with the following declaration:

> You ask, what is our policy? I will say: It is to wage war, by sea, land, and air, with all our might and with all the strength that God can give us; to wage war against a monstrous tyranny, never surpassed in the dark and lamentable catalogue of human crime. That is our policy.
>
> You ask, what is our aim? I can answer in one word: Victory. Victory at all costs – Victory in spite of all terror – Victory, however long and hard the road may be, for without victory there is no survival.

Obviously, Churchill's side had a noble cause, but the important point is that common to both speeches was the passionate call for all citizens to contribute to the ultimate cause.

3. "All-In" Capabilities: Third, the country must possess the economic, military, and human resources to attack the enemy's soldiers and citizens. Technological advances in the modern era have made widespread destruction more feasible. Many cite, for example, the advent of airpower toward expanding the scope and scale of twentieth-century warfare. Without it, we would not have the images of the German assault on Guernica during the Spanish Civil War or the bombardments of London, Dresden, Hiroshima, and Nagasaki during World War II.[14]

Military historians debate whether conflicts like Napoleon's wars or the American Civil War began the "total war" era. Yet they agree that such warfare certainly continued beyond World War I and into the interwar period conflicts. It culminated with World War II, which featured naval blockades to cause civilian starvation, indiscriminate bombardment from the air, and premeditated genocide. The threat of nuclear warfare since the Cold War has kept the possibility of total warfare alive and well. Suffice to say, R. Kook's hopeful predictions for a new world order did not come true.

RICHARD DAWKINS, AMALEK, AND THE SEVEN CANAANITE NATIONS

The bigger challenge for R. Kook's religious vision is that the Bible seems to mandate not only the expansionist wars that he bemoaned but also total war and genocide. King David, arguably Israel's greatest military and political leader, enlarged his borders to places like Aram-Damascus (in contemporary Syria). Such wars to "conquer foreign castles" were standard throughout history and seem to be acknowledged in the Bible with equanimity.

Admittedly, rabbinic literature expresses some misgivings about David's conduct. They were bloody affairs that cost many lives, including those of Israelites, and further distracted David from essential tasks like uprooting enemies closer to home.[15] His excessive bloodshed was mentioned elsewhere in the Bible as an explanation for why he was not worthy to build the Temple, whose rocks could not be hewn by metal – the raw material of warfare – let alone built by a man who excessively used his sword. Nonetheless, in classic Jewish law, expansionist wars by the monarch were permitted as "discretionary" (in Hebrew, *reshut*, i.e., nonobligatory) wars, even for the sake of enlarging the monarch's territory or prestige. If you allow for warfare "to extend the borders of Israel or to enhance [the king's] greatness and prestige," then it becomes hard to imagine, as Michael Walzer noted, what is left to prohibit.[16]

An even greater challenge for R. Kook's vision emerges from two biblical commandments, one to wipe out the Amalekite people and the second to eradicate the seven Canaanite nations that occupied the Land of Israel. In the former case, the assignment is sharing in God's work, since "the Lord will be at war with Amalek throughout the ages" (Ex. 17:16). There is no greater ultimate mission than fighting the Lord's battles.

Elsewhere, the rationale given for this eternal battle is that these people attacked the weary Israelites, entirely unprovoked, following the Exodus from Egypt. "Remember what Amalek did to you...undeterred by fear of God, he surprised you on the march, when you were famished and weary, and cut down all the stragglers in your rear.... You shall blot out the memory of Amalek from under the heavens. Do not forget!" (Deut. 25:17–19). Their ancestors violated the standards of war – now kill them all!

This commandment was codified in Jewish law to comprise the various aspects of total wars. It includes an eternal obligation for all Jews to utilize their resources in killing all inhabitants of Amalek – men, women, children, and even animals. The commandments also mandate national propaganda ("Do not forget!") about how the Amalekites represent the antithesis of God's values. Keeping these memories fresh ensures that the zealousness toward fulfilling this order will not abate over the generations. The seriousness of the obligation is emphasized in a later biblical narrative when King Saul destroys almost all of the Amalekite people. Nonetheless, the prophet Samuel strips him of his throne because he spared one person, the Amalekite king, and some sheep.

The biblical commandment to wipe out the seven nations of Canaan relates to the territorial conquest of the Land of Israel. Moses adjures the people that when God delivers victory to the Israelites, they "must doom them to destruction: grant them no terms and give them no quarter."[17] Cleanse the territory of Israel's borders from all idolatry, he urges, alongside the immoral cultic practices that come along with it.[18] Moses's successor, Joshua, was fairly successful in beginning the process of wiping out the Canaanite nations. Yet his people did not complete the mission. The remaining Canaanites led the Israelites astray into unethical, idolatrous practices that led to Israel's political downfall.[19]

In truth, the Bible even mandates destroying an *Israelite* city that is engulfed in idol worship. This follows a general biblical theme that only God-fearing nations who behave ethically, including the Israelites, can merit living in the Holy Land. Pious behavior is a necessary condition for dwelling there. Hence, when God promises Abraham that his descendants will inherit the land of Canaan, He asserts that they will need to wait for four generations until the current inhabitants will be sufficiently iniquitous to deserve annihilation. The war for the Holy Land, as such, is cultural, not ethnic. The territorial aspirations of the Israelites are dependent on a certain type of behavior. Those who don't meet those standards, Jew and non-Jew alike, must die.[20]

Taken literally, these commandments and narratives have served as fodder in more recent centuries for antireligious critics of the Bible. Take, for example, the accusation of a prominent "new atheist," Richard Dawkins:

> The Bible story of…the invasion of the Promised Land…is morally indistinguishable from Hitler's invasion of Poland or Saddam Hussein's massacres of the Kurds and the Marsh Arabs. The Bible

may be an arresting and poetic work...but it is not the sort of book you should give your children to form their morals.[21]

Religious believers like R. Kook require an explanation for how they can seek world peace while affirming the morality of The Book.

"HOLY WARS"?: LIMITS IN WARS AND THE LIMITS OF APOLOGETICS

Some scholars refer to the quest against Canaan and Amalek as "holy wars,"[22] but this label is not particularly helpful. The term does not appear in the Bible or subsequent Jewish literature. Within rabbinic literature, these biblical wars are called "commanded wars" or "obligatory wars," in contrast to the "discretionary" expansionist wars discussed earlier. Yet the wars of self-defense are also characterized as "obligatory wars." One might have a religious obligation to fight for the nation, making the war a holy cause, but that doesn't necessitate unrestrained battlefield tactics or imperial crusading.

Additionally, as with all other scriptural norms, different rules developed regarding these "obligatory wars." The most important of them was the requirement, attributed by the Sages to Joshua, to preemptively offer the Canaanite nations to make peace or to leave the land.[23] When the adversary has the right to surrender and war is seen as a last resort, the mandate loses some of the thunder of genocidal "holy wars."

According to some traditions, the requirement of offering peace before all wars was boldly initiated by Moses himself. He sought to avoid battles that kill the innocent alongside the guilty. Amazingly, God acceded to Moses's ethical sensibilities. Here's one version of this development.

> The Holy One had said that he would destroy them, as stated, "You shall utterly destroy them." However, Moses did not do so. Rather he said: Am I to go and smite them? I do not know who has sinned and who has not sinned. Instead, I will come to them in peace....
>
> The Holy One said to Moses: I myself told you, "No, you shall utterly destroy them." Now you have come to them in peace.

By your life, just as you have said, so will I do. Thus it is stated: "When you draw near to a city to fight against it, you shall offer terms of peace unto it" [Deut. 20:10].[24]

As the text makes clear, Moses brazenly delayed fulfilling God's command. He wanted to avoid killing those who did not deserve to die. God conceded that peace should always be pursued. The text concludes by citing this story as evidence of the proverb, "The Torah's ways are ways of pleasantness, and all her paths are peace."[25]

For some thinkers, this rabbinic tale shows that despite the Bible's plentiful descriptions of warfare, Judaism views it as the option of last resort. We, like Moses and Joshua, should take the initiative to avoid unnecessary bloodshed.[26] Nonetheless, the passage also makes clear that if the peace offer is rejected, the biblical mandate can include wiping out an entire nation ("So they smote him, his children, and all his people"), raising again the ethical qualms with "total wars."

Various strategies were taken throughout the centuries to explain or defend these commandments.[27] One approach, which we'll dub "legitimation," seeks to justify the morality of the action. A few commentators pointed to the utter depravity of the Amalekites and Canaanites, making them – and their descendants – worthy of destruction. The ethnic nature of this explanation is problematic because it implies some form of intergenerational depravity or guilt passed from one generation to the next. The Torah does speak of punishing children for the sins of their fathers. Within the Ten Commandments, God declares, "I the Lord your God am an impassioned God, visiting the guilt of the parents upon the children – upon the third and fourth generations who reject Me."[28] Ezekiel, however, later rejected the principle when he avowed, "The person who sins – he alone shall die. A child shall not share the burden of a parent's guilt, nor shall a parent share the burden of a child's guilt."[29] This sentiment challenges the continued validity of punishing Amalekites based solely on their heritage.

Others adopted a "restrictive reinterpretation" approach to interpreting a law anew in a way that makes it so narrow that it is no longer applicable. For starters, they point to a talmudic tradition that allowed individuals from these nations to repent, adopt the Seven Noahide Laws, or even convert. If that is the case, the commandment to kill would focus on a person's merits, not ethnicity. Another line of thought asserted that the identity of the Canaanites and Amalekites has long been lost, thereby making these commandments inapplicable.[30] Yet another interpretation asserted that these commandments apply only in the Messianic Era, leaving them dormant for the foreseeable future. Taken together, the various interpretations might neutralize the threat of someone asserting, today, that the Bible has commanded them to commit genocide or other barbaric wartime acts found in the Bible, including plunder, booty taking, and rape.

The late contemporary theologian Rabbi Lord Jonathan Sacks cited this method of restrictive interpretation as the ultimate antidote to fundamentalism. Fundamentalists, he argued, "go straight from revelation to application without interpretation. In many religions, including Judaism, this is heretical." Jews have never read a text simply. Prophets or sages interpret and apply the text in their given era based on overarching values like the quest for peace and the dignity of all human beings. Concerning Amalek, this means severely limiting the commandment to render it inapplicable. In this respect, R. Sacks argued, religious fanatics and strident atheists like Dawkins both commit the same sin: reading holy texts without interpretation. In the Jewish interpretative tradition, the texts "speak of then, not now; of ancient nations, not contemporary ones."[31] At a stroke of the pen, the biblical commandments become inoperative.[32]

R. Sacks's strategy inspires but does not entirely solve the problem. The challenge is not just the technical legal commandment but the broader ethos. The actual Canaanites and Amalekites may have repented or no longer exist, yet new enemies emerge who can be treated in the same fanatical manner. Throughout the ages, Christians have applied the moniker "Amalek" to their enemy nations.[33] Pope Urban II, for example, told crusaders in 1095 to fight the Muslims "like dauntless warriors against Amalek." Centuries later, the Puritan preacher Cotton Mather labeled Native Americans as Amalek infidels for refusing to convert to Christianity. Powerful religious figures can utilize this biblical model to justify indiscriminate mass killing against those who refuse to accept their religion. When defeating the "new Amalek" becomes the ultimate cause, restraints get easily discarded.

Jews have also applied the term to various agitators throughout the centuries of their exile – crusaders, Inquisitors, Cossacks, and others. Mostly this was a metaphorical label thrown against those imperiling the Jewish people. At times, it was meant as homiletic rhetoric to remind Jews of our important duty to uproot evil from the world.[34] For a few, however, this was taken on a literal level. A handful of recent radicals have even applied it to the Arab-Israeli conflict, with dangerous results.[35] For all of its innovativeness, restrictive reinterpretations seem insufficient to address the biblical ethos that would allow unrestrained warfare.

THE QUALMS OF MOSHE SEIDEL AND THE EVOLUTIONARY ETHICS OF RABBI KOOK

Moshe Seidel (1886–1970) was deeply bothered by the morality of these and other biblical commandments. Seidel was a young prodigy who studied with some of the greatest rabbinic scholars in Lithuania, including R. Kook, who not only entrusted him to teach in his school in Boisk (Bauska), Latvia, but also utilized him as the personal tutor of his son, Tzvi Yehuda. R. Kook encouraged Seidel to pursue academic training in realms that were seen as threatening within the rabbinic world, such as biblical studies. He believed that scholars of Seidel's piety could address modern intellectual questions for traditional believers.[36] Seidel ultimately received his doctorate in biblical studies at the University of Bern in Switzerland. Yet he was left with many misgivings regarding his faith. The pupil Seidel turned to his teacher R. Kook, by then in Jaffa, with a series of queries relating to the major issues of the day.[37]

One of Seidel's queries related to the morality of biblical commandments.[38] How can the Bible endorse slavery, or command wiping out Amalek and Canaan? These seem to be calls for indefinite cruelty. Will the world ethically progress while Judaism remains behind?

R. Kook responded, somewhat radically, by asserting that biblical laws should not always be seen as the Jewish ideal; instead, they reflect a divine attempt to lead a process that will lead the world toward greater moral perfection. There's a gap between the ideal and the real, or as R. Kook puts it, "how it is and how it ought to be."[39] The morals found in the Torah are not always ideal or idyllic. Instead, they address the actual moral state of the world and serve as a "precious vessel" meant to direct society toward greater improvement. The Torah's laws regarding slavery, for example, reduced how the powerful exploited the weak since the master had to care for the welfare of the slave. Slavery was not ideal, but the Torah's regulations helped improve the way that people were treated in that historical period. The goal was for people to act "beyond the letter of the law" and treat their fellow humans as equals.

This brings R. Kook to address the alleged cruelty of biblical warfare.

> Regarding wars, it was impossible, at a time when all of our neighbors were truly wolves, that Israel alone would not wage war, for then they would have gathered together and wiped out their remnant, God forbid. On the contrary, it was very necessary to place fear in the hearts of the wild ones, even through cruel acts, with the hope of bringing humanity to the point where it is supposed to be, but not before its time.[40]

According to R. Kook, given the vicious nature at that time of Israel's enemies, these tactics were necessary measures to defeat our brutal neighbors. This cruelty was required to establish the Israelite presence in the Promised Land and defeat its immoral enemies. Even then, however, it was not the only model of behavior, but merely a legitimate option in the context of a larger process fitting for that period. As such, we find that many Jewish kings in the Bible did not take such measures against unethical idolatrous nations because they were not necessary.

Probed further about this position, R. Kook remains unapologetic about biblical warfare and these concessions to the failings of that era. The world would have been a worse place if those nations had not been significantly weakened, he argues.[41] He further criticizes early Christianity for adopting a pacifistic perspective that would not permit doing what it takes to address such evil.[42] Yet he adds that not everything which was done by our ancestors was flawless. We certainly do not have to emulate these actions in our times. The Torah made concessions to accommodate the deficient social norms of earlier periods, but it did not embrace them.

One might label this approach as "evolutionary" because it acknowledges that once ethics evolve, the law follows suit. Herein lies the subtle but very significant difference between the hermeneutical methods of R. Kook and R. Sacks. For R. Sacks, while a restrictive reinterpretation may have been motivated by our ethical qualms with the law, the norm itself remains, at least theoretically, on the books. Contemporary circumstances make the biblical mandates of genocide inapplicable because we are lacking certain necessary conditions. Since we can't truly identify an Amalekite, the law is inapplicable in our times. For R. Kook, these commandments were only designed for earlier eras. Once humanity advanced in a certain way, the laws became nonoperative because the ethos behind them was no longer necessary, whether fighting an Amalekite or any other people. For R. Sacks, these biblical commandments do not apply in today's circumstances; for R. Kook, the law was never meant for today's circumstances.[43]

Interestingly, R. Kook would utilize both the reinterpretation and evolutionary techniques when addressing the dispensation given for "discretionary" expansionist wars. While writing from Switzerland, he highlighted a talmudic rule (discussed more in chapter 13) that a king must get permission from the Great Court (Sanhedrin) before engaging in such expansionist warfare. This requirement provided an important check-and-balance, moral and political, to the monarchy. R. Kook further contended that the court would only allow such offensive warfare, as a matter of exigency, if it was truly needed for the nation's physical and spiritual welfare. Most significantly, he concluded that such offensive warfare was not permitted since the Great Court ceased to function many centuries ago.[44] The law, under this interpretation, could not apply in his era.

This is a surprising conclusion since in the same correspondence R. Kook argued that the elected leaders of the people can fill the formal role of the defunct monarchy to represent the polity and fight licit commanded wars. Why can't they do the same for the defunct Sanhedrin? It's not entirely clear. The answer, it would seem, is that R. Kook was not interested in replacing the institution necessary to "capture foreign castles."[45]

Yet elsewhere R. Kook applied his "evolutionary" approach to this question of "discretionary wars." In diary entries written about the same time that he wrote "Israel's Mission and Its Nationhood," R. Kook expressed hope that the world would reject undertaking such expansionary battles and understand that "it was illegitimate to spill blood for the sake of achieving political goals."[46] The expression he used bears echoes of the famous phrase usually attributed to the theorist Carl von Clausewitz (d. 1831): "War is the continuation of diplomacy by other means." This expression is frequently cited to argue that violence is a legitimate means to achieving political or strategic goals. It's impossible to know if R. Kook knew of the maxim, but what is clear is that he didn't like this notion. Utilizing the same strategy, R. Kook similarly asserted that we would no longer accommodate taking a captive enemy woman for a wife (*eshet yefat to'ar*), as permitted in Deuteronomy. Indeed, it was about this law that the Sages asserted that the Bible was merely "accommodating the evil instinct." Some biblical practices, it seems, were not meant to last forever. [47]

How could R. Kook justify such legal innovation? The case of intergenerational punishment provided a precedent for how biblical ethics may evolve. As noted earlier, Ezekiel rejected the notion that the sins of one generation would be paid for by the next generation. Under what authority could the prophet boldly reject this biblical belief? R. Kook, in a different letter to Seidel, gave the following explanation.

> When the nation declined, Ezekiel saw that spiritual separateness was good for her so that the past sins would not factor into their judgment... this is what the situation required. When a righteous person decrees a decree, Heaven upholds it... and the new path is paved... to judge each individual separately.[48]

Different eras, it would seem, require changing moral principles to govern matters of collective responsibility and punishment. R. Kook also suggested that with its return to the Land of Israel, an authoritative rabbinic body ("Sanhedrin") could be reestablished that would solve these types of problems with creative interpretations of the biblical text.[49]

However R. Kook worked out his legal philosophy, the upshot seems clear: just as we should not own slaves today or punish children for the sins of their father, so too we do not have to fight like Joshua.[50] Our enemies are not Amalekites or Canaanites, and Jewish mores are not the same as those of the Israelites.[51]

While R. Kook doesn't mention this, it seems that the initial criticism of total warfare already appears in the Bible. Beyond the battles of the Israelites, the Bible also documents the bloody wars of many other nations. God does not judge them kindly. The prophet Amos condemns several empires for the decimation they wrought. The Gazans "exiled an entire people," the Edomites "rejected all pity and kept their wrath forever," and the Ammonites "ripped open the pregnant women of Gilead to enlarge their own territory." This military treachery was executed with no limits, and God promises to decimate them in kind.[52]

Following this theme, a rabbinic text asserts that the Kingdom of Judah itself was also exiled for military cruelty. King Amaziah's soldiers, the Bible tells us, killed ten thousand children of Edom by casting them off the top of a cliff: "They cast them down from the top of the rock and they were all broken in pieces."[53] God, according to rabbinic legend, never mandated such excessive cruelty. For this sin, the Kingdom of Judah was exiled.[54]

The Bible might provide pragmatic guidance in an era of unrestrained warfare. That doesn't mean God likes it. R. Kook's revolutionary teaching was that if efforts emerge to limit the totality of warfare, Jews have a responsibility to embrace and encourage these developments, even as that means accepting different norms than their Israelite ancestors. This assertion is the ultimate refutation of fundamentalists and antireligious critics alike.

Did R. Kook's answers satisfy Seidel's angst? It's not entirely clear. A later letter written by R. Kook indicates that Seidel continued to struggle with these qualms, even as his teacher reiterated the utility and importance of the "evolutionary" strategy.[55] Did Seidel find R. Kook's explanation overly apologetic? Perhaps too radical? We don't know. Yet Seidel stayed loyal to his faith and his teacher. After receiving his doctorate, he taught at Yeshiva University in New York where he headed the Bible department. There he helped gather support for a short-lived Zionist organization, *Degel Yerushalayim* (The Banner of Jerusalem), which R. Kook founded in 1918 with the hopes of better demonstrating a refined Jewish nationalism. Seidel ultimately moved to Palestine and reunited with his teacher. Among his many scholarly writings, his most lasting contribution is a commentary on the book of Micah, published in a series produced by academic scholars committed to Orthodox Jewish doctrines.[56] It includes an extended comparison of the peace prophecies in Micah, Isaiah, and other works.

WHAT IF BRUTAL TACTICS ARE SOMETIMES NECESSARY?

Jewish law, then, does not mandate fighting war without restrictions. Yet there are other incentives, beyond religion, to fight that type of war. The "total war" era emerged precisely in a period when religion played a lesser role in international politics. The Bible cannot be blamed for such brutal warfare. Religion did not inspire Hitler, Stalin, Mao, Pol Pot, or many other despicable despots of the twentieth century. Religion *can* inspire total war. Yet as we have seen and will continue to note, it may also inspire placing limits on war. Conversely, secular ideologies can equally lead to brutality or humanitarianism. Religions do not have a monopoly on fundamentalists.

Of course, not all total warfare is waged by the likes of Ammonites, Napoleon, or Hitler. We also have figures such as Lincoln and Churchill, whose larger causes were undoubtedly just. They felt that some measures of total war were necessary to respond to the unrestrained warfare that they faced or to defeat the vicious evil they confronted. Some may retort that everyone always thinks that *their* instance is exceptional. Yet it may be that the Civil War and World War II were different. On limited occasions, as we'll see in chapter 4, one might be able to argue that the ends justify the means. The Bible shows how warfare is regularly barbaric and immoral but may sometimes be required and justifiable, given the nature of the era and the tactics of the enemy.

This brings us to another principle that emerges from the battles against Canaan and Amalek: occasionally defeat is unfathomable, and all measures must be taken to ensure victory. Evil, the Bible teaches us, must be identified and uprooted. It is morally hazardous to deem an enemy nation as a "modern Amalek," and we should be very wary of using such labels. Yet it's even more dangerous to entirely avoid calling out wickedness for what it is, and utterly perilous to allow evildoers to be victorious.

These cases, however, must be seen as moral aberrations in extreme circumstances, not the norm. The rejection of the models to defeat Canaan and Amalek means that standard war tactics can be – and must be – limited within a compelling moral framework. Indeed, R. Kook indicated that the Jewish people would need fighters of both great physical and spiritual strength before their ultimate redemption.[57] The question remained whether they could fight in a way that would be different from the way of their own ancestors and the nations of the world.

Soon after the war, however, it would be the nations of the world that would declare that warfare must change. Could they deliver on that promise?

Chapter 3

The League of Nations and the Dashed Hope of International Law

JEWISH INTERNATIONALISTS AND DREAMS OF A NEW WORLD ORDER

On November 12, 1917, while the Great War continued to rage, R. Kook sent a letter to his son R. Tzvi Yehuda: God's light has finally pierced into our dark world. The redemption has begun.[1]

What inspired this proclamation? Ten days earlier, the British foreign minister issued the Balfour Declaration establishing support for the "establishment in Palestine of a national home for the Jewish people." The British soon afterward conquered Palestine from the Turks, ending four hundred years of Ottoman control of the Holy Land and raising the hopes of Zionists around the world.

R. Kook had been waiting for this moment. Now dwelling in London, he had been delivering Bible-laced sermons praising British patriotism and their fight against Germany.[2] With the declaration of the world's great power, he wrote to Seidel, the messianic process has begun! The Lord, who is "master of battles and sprouts salvations," had delivered.[3] It's true, he conceded, the bloody war had revealed the depravity of modernity and its European delegates. God, however, had now made it possible for people of uplifted spirit to bring about a new era.

A few years later, the Balfour Declaration was incorporated by the newly established League of Nations into its broad mandate system that would govern territories of collapsed empires. Belgium controlled Rwanda and Burundi, the French oversaw Syria and Lebanon, and the British governed Palestine and Transjordan, to name a few prominent examples. The goal of the mandate system, at least as proclaimed by its founders, was to end the colonialist era of exploitation. At the base level, this would entail protecting the rights of the local inhabitants through a system of international law. More ambitiously, the mandate system would facilitate the founding of new states. Concomitantly, various treaties were enacted to ensure minority rights in all nation-states, new and old. Taken together, a new world order was sought to preserve peace among states and prevent persecution of minorities within them.

Many Jews, including some avowed Zionists, were deeply involved in these movements.[4] One such figure was a rising academic star and legal activist, the Polish-born Hirsch Tzvi Lauterpacht (1897–1960). In the days after World War I, Lauterpacht had witnessed the horrible November 1918 pogrom in Lemberg, a contested city within the newly independent Poland. The war was over, yet Jews continued to be slaughtered.[5]

As borders were getting drawn anew across the globe, Lauterpacht dedicated his life to providing protections for minorities in these new states. He believed that Britain could use its imperial power to bring lasting peace, including support for both Jewish nationalism in Palestine and rights for Jews and other minorities throughout Europe.[6] Lauterpacht would become a leading law professor at Cambridge and later a judge on the International Court of Justice. He is credited with establishing that international law prohibited territorial conquest through warfare; that's precisely the expansionist "discretionary wars," to use rabbinic terms, that R. Kook wanted to end. Lauterpacht also helped establish that those who waged aggressive warfare could be placed on trial. His advocacy directly led to the Nuremberg trials against Nazi figures after World War II. This was a deeply personal case for Lauterpacht. His parents, siblings, and extended family were all killed in the Holocaust.[7]

Another prominent international jurist who escaped Europe before the war and worked with Lauterpacht on the Nuremberg trials was Jacob Robinson (1889–1977). Robinson was born in a small village in the Russian empire to an Orthodox Jewish family from distinguished rabbinic lineage. Like many others, he sought solutions to the "Jewish problem" after the antisemitic violence in Kishinev and elsewhere. After earning his law degree, he was drafted into the Russian army in 1914. He was captured by the Germans and spent the next three years in eight different German POW camps. Somehow surviving, he returned home to the newly independent Lithuania where he not only led a Hebrew-language school but was also elected to the Lithuanian parliament. Robinson became a renowned advocate for national minority rights, playing critical advocacy roles in the Congress of European National Minorities and at the League of Nations. Throughout the 1920s, he promoted a "pan-Europa" transnational community that would allow minorities to peacefully live within whatever national borders they found themselves.[8] At the same time, he was also the de facto leader of Lithuanian Zionism. Ben-Gurion even deemed him "the most important man in Lithuania."[9]

For many Jews, international governance presented an enticing alternative to pacifism toward achieving the prophetic visions of a new world order. We don't need to naively declare that violence is never justified. Instead, we can work to create an institutional system that will find alternative methods for conflict resolution. If peace efforts fail, then these bodies will act to ensure that any belligerent aggressors face justice. The world can together agree upon what military actions are acceptable. They will provide direction for moral dilemmas alongside clarity for determining which sides were right or wrong. For many, this was, and is, an alluring vision of prophetic proportions.[10]

Yet could international governance deliver on these high hopes? Could world powers, in fact, now provide justice for the Jewish people and other persecuted groups?

TWO EXCOMMUNICATED RABBIS AND THE CHANGING SELF-IMAGE OF THE JEW

In August 1920, a book ban was issued by the leaders of the ultra-Orthodox community of Jerusalem. The author of the prohibited book was none other than Rabbi Abraham Isaac Kook, who had recently returned from London to assume the position of the chief rabbi of Jerusalem. Once the family had settled in, R. Tzvi Yehuda published his father's major treatise, *Orot* (Lights), which included his reflections on the Great War from Switzerland and his hopes for a new era in international relations.

What raised the ire of his critics to ban this book? R. Kook had equated the spiritual merits accrued by youthful physical training to those gained by piously reciting Psalms or mystical enchantments. This was not the first time R. Kook had aroused controversy for praising the ethos of self-defense. In the first years of the twentieth century, Jews – usually immigrants fleeing the pogroms in Russia – founded different groups to build character based on physical toil and exercise. "Muscular Jews" could work the land and fight for themselves. R. Kook wrote enthusiastically about the importance of Jewish self-defense, viewing the phenomenon as "heartwarming."[11] While recognizing that these groups were led by secular Jews, he embraced their efforts. He mourned the loss of two who were killed in 1911, designating them "holy martyrs" despite the fact that both had abandoned the religious lifestyles of their upbringing.[12] For R. Kook, physical strength was a sign of renewed Jewish vigor to develop the homeland and instill fear in its enemies.

Yet his latest expression of praise for profane labor and physical strength – comparing it to a classic religious act of beseeching God for assistance – was too much for those who viewed the Jewish hero as pious, pensive, and passive. They wanted R. Kook out of Palestine. The controversy quickly spread throughout the Jewish world, with competing images of Jews and Judaism at stake.[13]

Unlike several of R. Kook's apologetic defenders, one of his most strident supporters felt that R. Kook didn't go far enough. What's the benefit, he asked, of simply reciting Psalms as a protective charm or incantation?

> It is unquestionable that to strengthen Jewish boys to enable them to defend themselves against their pursuers (with God's help) is a greater mitzva (religious deed) than reciting Psalms.... Reciting Psalms is the task of the indolent; calisthenics is the task of the industrious.

Prayer, he added, can have a valuable role, but only alongside self-defense training. He further accused R. Kook's critics of timidity and suggested they instead go back to Europe. Among the Jewish residents, their cowardice was only causing fear of antisemitic Arabs who looked upon their diffident Jewish neighbors as "dead meat."[14]

R. Kook's defender, Rabbi Hayim Hirschensohn (1857–1935), knew something about rabbinic bans. He himself had left Jerusalem two decades earlier following controversies over his own publications. Unlike most of the prominent Zionists of this era, R. Hirschensohn was born in the Land of Israel. His parents were proto-Zionists (*hovevei Tziyon*) who had immigrated from Pinsk in 1847. They helped develop Jewish settlement in the cities of Safed and Jerusalem before Herzl was even born. The younger Hirschensohn followed in their footsteps by organizing the acquisition and development of properties around the country. He later became a founding member of the religious Zionist movement, Mizrachi.

As a scholar, R. Hirschensohn aroused the ire of traditionalists in Jerusalem. This was partly because of his outspoken advocacy for reviving Hebrew as a spoken language, including his founding, with Eliezer Ben-Yehuda, of an organization toward that goal. (His and Ben-Yehuda's were the first two families to enforce Hebrew-speaking in their homes.) He also displayed openness toward analyzing classic rabbinic texts from a critical historical lens. These factors, among others, led to his formal excommunication by the old-school rabbis of Jerusalem. Needing to make a living, R. Hirschensohn was forced to leave his birthplace.

So in 1904, the same year that R. Kook immigrated to Jaffa, R. Hirschensohn made it to Hoboken, New Jersey, where he served as a rabbi for the rest of his life. During World War I and its aftermath, he attests, he was deeply engrossed in pastoral work with veterans and their families, for which he received a letter of commendation. R. Hirschensohn remained active in various Zionist organizations and maintained correspondence with the great rabbinic figures in Palestine. Yet he died in relative obscurity, with his writings becoming well-known only in the past couple of decades. His works remain particularly important because in the wake of the horrors of World War I and the excitement of the Balfour Declaration, he wrote several books dedicated to establishing the legal groundwork for a democratic state within Jewish thought, including addressing the dilemmas of war and conquest.[15]

THE JEWISH LEGION AND THE HASMONEAN SPIRIT OF SELF-DETERMINATION

The 1920 excommunication controversy was not the first time that Rabbis Kook and Hirschensohn had supported Jews taking up arms. Both men had endorsed enlistment during World War I in the so-called Jewish Legion, battalions within the British army composed of Jewish volunteers from England, North America, and other countries to fight in Palestine. They were created upon the initiative of Joseph Trumpeldor and Vladimir Jabotinsky. Trumpeldor was a veteran of the Russo-Japanese War in which he lost his left arm and received four medals of bravery, making him the most decorated Jewish veteran of the Russian Army. Jabotinsky was a Russian writer who made Bialik's poem on the Kishinev pogrom famous by translating it into Russian. More significantly, he had been an organizer of Jewish self-defense organizations and an advocate for minority rights in Europe, seeking to protect the Jewish people with both law and shield.[16]

During World War I, Trumpeldor and Jabotinsky sought British permission for Jews to fight the Ottomans in Palestine. After protracted negotiations, including those of Chaim Weizmann, the Legion finally formed and played a minor role in completing the British conquest of Palestine in 1918. Its fighters included David Ben-Gurion, later Israel's first prime minister, Eliyahu Golomb, the founder of the pre-state Haganah defense force, and Berl Katznelson, a future labor leader.

The Legion did not accomplish much and soon disbanded, yet it transformed the image of the Jew into someone who could fight for himself and his homeland. The chaplain of the Legion was Reverend Leib Falk (1889–1957), who grew up in Boisk and studied in the school of R. Kook and Seidel. In a Hanukka holiday sermon, Falk reflected on the significance of the first Jewish military corps that had fought in nearly eighteen hundred years:

> The whole world was watching [and] were looking on us, but they see now the Maccabean spirit revived, they see now that Israel is

not only powerful with his voice, but he has also a mighty arm....
The Jewish soldier upholds now the honour of our nation. The
Jewish warrior saved our national honour which was at stake.[17]

While the troops were still in England, R. Kook visited Falk and his
men. Previously, R. Kook had opposed the enlistment of yeshiva students (frequently new immigrants from eastern Europe) into the British
army because of their inability to maintain a religious lifestyle.[18] Yet he
bestowed Jewish Legion fighters with blessings of strength while deeming them the bearers of the beginning of salvation.[19] Years later, when
the Jewish Legion's flag was brought to Palestine for a grand ceremony,
R. Kook compared it to the banners that the Israelites used in the desert
on their way to conquering the Land of Israel.[20]

Yet it was R. Hirschensohn who penned the most extensive treatise in support of the Legion. Even though Jews were fighting within
a foreign army, he nonetheless deemed fighting in Palestine as within
the category of an "obligatory war" for the liberation of the homeland.
Earlier rabbinic Zionist figures were concerned that military activity may
violate talmudic oaths that prohibited the Jews during their exile period
from "rebelling against the nations" or "rising up together in force."[21]
They thus advocated for a peaceful settlement through land acquisitions.
R. Hirschensohn was not deterred by this talmudic prohibition; it
applied, in his mind, only to rebellions in foreign lands, not to conquering the Holy Land. This was especially true since the British had recognized the right of the Jews to establish a state in Palestine. This was
not treason, but rather a deeply honorable fight by soldiers for their
homeland which had been taken from their people centuries beforehand. Most significant about his declaration was the negation of the
talmudic impulses against militarism, discussed in chapter 1, as binding
on the Jewish people in the current era. It was a holy deed, in his mind,
not just to settle the land, but to fight for it.[22]

A TEMPLE OF PEACE WITHOUT SACRIFICES?

Renewed Jewish warfare naturally meant that Jews would need to think
about the legacy of biblical warfare. Like R. Kook, R. Hirschensohn
sought to neutralize the ethos behind the Bible's total wars, albeit more

radically. First, he contended, any remnant of these nations has long been lost, thereby making the commandments irrelevant. Second, while the commandment to conquer the land is eternal, the clause to "leave no one alive" among the land's inhabitants was only applicable to Joshua's generation, when such military tactics were necessary to conquer the land and remove the fears of the Israelite people. Once completed, however, no such clause existed; as such, we don't find Kings David or Solomon fighting total wars against the local inhabitants.[23]

Even if we could identify the seven Canaanite nations, he further argued, we would not wipe them out because such behavior is morally unacceptable in our era. "It is prohibited to violate international law that regulates the conduct of war by charter. God forbid that Israel be regarded by the nations as barbaric murderers who violate international law and the norms of civilization."[24] The continued history of biblical warfare – alongside our moral intuitions – proves that this biblical verse was a temporary provision, not a permanent commandment.

Given his embrace of the norms of civilization to reject this biblical model of warfare, one might expect that R. Hirschensohn would be enthusiastic about the postwar treaties to prevent armed conflicts. Yet R. Hirschensohn expressed doubts that these proposals to resolve international conflicts would be more successful than earlier treaties.[25] Those rules, which governed hostile conduct, seemed utterly ineffective during the Great War. R. Hirschensohn was skeptical that the efforts of American president Woodrow Wilson and the League of Nations, meant to prevent the outbreak of war, would be any more effective. Ultimately, these bodies were subject to the political interests of powerful nations which would thwart any real attempt at justice.

Indeed, an early glimpse of this problem emerged in the aftermath of the post-war Lemberg pogrom. Wilson initially pushed hard for strict provisions of minority rights as a condition for Polish sovereignty. He pulled back when a related measure was proposed that would possibly condemn racial segregation in America.[26] Protecting minority rights was important, but only if it didn't endanger American interests.

Instead of a politicized court, R. Hirschensohn desired to build, in the spirit of the prophets, a new house of worship on Jerusalem's Temple Mount. It would feature song and prayer but leave out the animal sacrifices mandated in the Bible. The Temple would serve as a "House of Peace" to advocate for each nation to thrive within its own borders without succumbing to the evil excesses of nationalism. He penned an extensive essay to resolve how Jews could walk onto the Temple Mount in light of heavy ritual restrictions against treading on its sanctified grounds. R. Hirschensohn sought to ensure that Zionism would have a center for religious and moral development that would guide Jewish nationalism. It would also serve as a model for nationalist movements around the world.[27]

Yet he also had a political agenda: if the Jews did not develop the Temple Mount, it would not remain closed to all. Instead, it would be controlled by foreigners and Arab Muslims. The Jews would be left standing, as they had throughout centuries of exile, by the Dung Gate, with all that this name entails.

R. Kook rejected this proposal. While agreeing that Jewish nationalism must be rooted in a religious spirit, he disallowed stepping on the Temple Mount, let alone building on it. He further criticized R. Hirschensohn for eliminating the use of animal sacrifices. R. Hirschensohn had written that the restoration of the sacrifices "would make us the object of ridicule before all the nations of the world. Instead of being a light to the nations, they would think of us as an unenlightened people who walk in darkness."[28] In R. Kook's mind, this was a religious reform corrupted by the ideals of European philosophy. We should leave the Temple Mount alone and instead build a synagogue next to the Western Wall that could serve as a house of prayer and peace.[29]

R. Hirschensohn, in reply, accused R. Kook of making a religious and political error that was equivalent to the 1903 "Uganda plan" to grant the Jews a state in Eastern Africa. Just as you can't temporarily replace the Holy Land with some other territory, you can't replace the heart of the Temple Mount with its outer western wall! Either Jews settle their territory or someone else will. As for R. Kook's jibe that he was overly influenced by Western norms, R. Hirschensohn replied that there is no doubt that the Great War had shown the failings of European culture. Nonetheless, the prophets repeatedly asserted that God did not truly desire animal sacrifices.[30] With all the failings of Western culture, knowledge and wisdom would not recede backward, or as he put it, that "which is uncivilized will not suddenly become civilized!"[31] In any case, the mission of the hour was to purchase all holy sites toward ensuring our political and spiritual future.[32]

THE VALUE OF TREATIES

R. Hirschensohn's idyllic visions for a "Temple of Peace" are stirring yet fantastical. He also does not offer a sufficient answer as to how it would avoid the politicization that plagues other international bodies. It's possible that this was more a theoretical exercise than an actual plan.[33]

Nonetheless, his writing reflects a deep ambivalence on the potential success of international bodies to execute justice in a world of competing nationalistic claims. On the one hand, there is a genuine desire to promote humanistic values that will avoid a repetition of the unnecessary bloodshed of the Great War. On the other hand, R. Hirschensohn recognizes that political interests will dominate international bodies. Therefore, to achieve equity, Jews need to take hold of what belongs to them, such as the Temple Mount, based on their own values and interests. Otherwise, someone else will decide based on their interests, not justice.

This weariness toward international political bodies is also reflected in R. Hirschensohn's extended 1926 treatise on the standing of international treaties. Nations should be careful before signing treaties, he believed, because once they commit, they are liable to punishment for breaking their word. This is why the Israelites were punished by God for violating the covenant at Sinai and breaking His law. So too, he asserted, Germany got its due in World War I because Kaiser Wilhelm had treated the 1839 Treaty of London that granted sovereignty and neutrality to Belgium as "a scrap of paper."[34] The Allies were justified in resisting Germany since treaties are only binding when they are reciprocally observed.[35]

Yet treaties are not the only obligations that are binding on the Jewish people. So too are the ethical practices of "civilizations."[36] While he doesn't fully translate that term, it seems that he has in mind the widespread moral sentiments of modern civilized nations.[37] Violating these standards, in his mind, constitutes a grave desecration of the reputation of God and His people. Considering these beliefs, we can further understand his rejection of the models of fighting against Amalek and the Canaanite nations. Whether or not there is a treaty against total war or genocide, Jews must hold themselves to the highest standards of morality and build a stellar reputation.[38]

So what would a Jewish state do in this era of treaties? R. Hirschensohn argued that it should make accords with as many foreign nations as possible – in Europe, America, and Africa. Like R. Kook, R. Hirschensohn asserted that imperialist excursions beyond Israel's borders had no place in contemporary Jewish law and that all wars required moral justification.[39] Nations must stick to their own borders. As such, there was a confluence here between the religious value of international peace and Jewish national interests.

What about Arabs living within Palestine? R. Hirschensohn claimed that permanently ceding territory in the Holy Land would violate the biblical mandate to conquer the land. He also believed that Jews should not quickly initiate negotiations that would put them in a position of weakness.[40] Yet he recognized that despite the Jewish historical claim to the land and the Balfour Declaration, there was an Arab population who had legitimate conflicting claims to the same territory. This was primarily because they were residents in the land. At the end of the day, the strongest claim to any territory is based on settlement. Given these competing legitimate claims, he suggested that Jews form long-term peaceful accords with their neighbors. One day, he hoped, the Jews could peacefully get full control of the territory. In the meantime, it was in the interests of all parties involved to have peaceful relations.[41]

Independent of one's assessment of R. Hirschensohn's particular strategy, the framework of his analysis is particularly striking. On the one hand, he embraces positive developments in international mores. Judaism is a peace-promoting religion that should support all initiatives to reduce animosity and bloodshed, even with those competing for hold of the Holy Land. This entails integrating new values – including democracy, minority rights, and conventions to limit the horrors of war – by finding support for them in traditional Jewish texts.

On the other hand, he understood that it was far from clear that international institutions will have the ability to promote and enforce these values. There are too many national interests at stake to make this possible.[42] Thus Jews must wisely develop a strategy that will endorse refined values while actively promoting their own political interests. In his time, this meant taking hold of their homeland through the purchase of holy locations and the settlement of the Land of Israel.

ARAB RIOTS IN PALESTINE AND THE TRIUMPH OF BRITISH POLITICAL INTERESTS

The most pressing question, however, was whether force would also be necessary to reestablish Jewish sovereignty in Palestine. Both Rabbis Kook and Hirschensohn hoped that a combination of Jewish political initiatives and international diplomacy would be sufficient. Yet this was not meant to be. In March 1920, Trumpeldor was sent to help protect Tel Hai, an upper Galilean settlement that ended up under French control in the unstable period after World War I, leaving those Jewish settlers suddenly outside of British auspices. In a chaotic confrontation with Arab Bedouins from Syria, Trumpeldor was killed, alongside five other Jews, including a couple of other Jewish Legion veterans. His alleged dying words became immortalized as the fighting spirit of the new Jew: "No matter, it is worth dying for the country."[43]

Trumpeldor would become lionized by Zionist writers like Hayim Yosef Brenner, who eulogized this "symbol of pure heroism" for teaching that it is good to die for the national cause. R. Tamares the pacifist had opposed the Jewish Legion and saw Trumpeldor's legacy as the embodiment of force and ultranationalism, but his views were hardly noticed.[44] The self-image of Jews was being transformed. A few years later, Jabotinsky would break away from the Zionist Organization and establish the revisionist Zionist organization "Betar." The name commemorated the last fighting ground of the Jewish people in the second century, but also paid homage to the fallen hero of Tel Hai, with the letters of Betar standing for "the covenant of Joseph Trumpeldor."

Jewish-Arab tensions were also rising in Jerusalem. Jabotinsky warned the local British military governor of an upcoming slaughter, this time by Arabs against their Jewish neighbors. Jabotinsky and other founders of the Jewish Legion had been busy training the Jews in calisthenics and self-defense; it was their group, among others, for whom R. Kook's praise in *Orot* had earned him the scorn of the local ultra-Orthodox leaders just a few months later. When the riots started in Jerusalem's Old City, however, Jabotinsky's men were not around. Several Jews were killed and over two hundred more were wounded. Two sisters were raped.

Long aware of the self-defense groups, the British governor nonetheless arrested Jabotinsky and his men for carrying illegal weapons, with Jabotinsky receiving a fifteen-year jail sentence. R. Hirschensohn, from afar, would cite the case as an example of the ways in which a civilized justice system can become corrupt.[45]

R. Kook joined others in demanding Jabotinsky's release as he and his comrades threatened to go on a hunger strike. R. Kook saluted their brave efforts but warned that Jewish law strictly prohibits taking such drastic protest measures.[46] Jabotinsky stopped the hunger strike. Soon afterward, his sentence was commuted, alongside those of many of the Arab rioters. R. Kook protested to the British high commissioner that the Arabs should be punished politically for the violence, but to no avail.[47]

For now, the international community stayed the course with British plans for Palestine and affirmed the Balfour Declaration in the San Remo conference a month later. Yet Arab-Jewish tensions remained high and in May 1921, riots broke out again, this time in Jaffa. Forty-seven Jews were killed and over 140 more wounded. Among the dead was the writer Brenner, who had been busy editing the letters of Trumpeldor.

Yet the biggest turning point was 1929. Arab-Jewish tensions over control of the Western Wall had existed for several years but escalated after a march in Jerusalem's Old City on Tisha B'Av, Judaism's annual day of mourning for the Temple's destruction. R. Kook, who had protested restrictions on Jewish access to the wall for several years, supported the march, telling a local newspaper that the youth had demonstrated "national pride and Maccabean zealousness" toward defending Jewish rights to the holy site.[48] Arab riots soon broke out in Jerusalem, Hebron, Safed, and other locations.

The riots left the Jewish community particularly vulnerable since most of its leadership was in Zurich for the sixteenth Zionist Congress. Beyond working with the remaining Zionist authorities to secure British protection for the Jewish settlements, R. Kook sent a brief letter through the head of the Jewish Telegraphic Agency. "To the entire Jewish world: All of the Jewish community in the Land of Israel is in danger. Act to save us in any way you can as fast as you can."[49] The sense of urgency was palpable.

Robinson and other activists organized mass rallies, sent urgent telegrams, and penned editorials to get the League of Nations to act. They called on the mandate's commission to protect the Jewish people, noting their centuries-long connection to the Holy Land. They further demanded the removal of British officials who had not come to their rescue. No response came. In the end, more than 130 Jews were killed over two hot August weeks.

Lauterpacht, the rising jurist now teaching at University College of London, lamented the tepid British response and its failure to ascribe full blame to the Arab side. Why did the British fail to protect the Jews? Lauterpacht's answer was telling: even the mighty British empire had to cower before the prospect of a religious war with all of Islam. Britain cared about minority rights. But it had to take into consideration its own political interests in placating the feelings of the millions of Muslims who lived within its empire.[50]

Lauterpacht's conclusion was reached after the publication of the findings of the Shaw Commission that investigated the riots. The Muslim mufti, Haj Amin al Husseini, blamed the Jews for provoking the rioters. R. Kook forcefully rebutted these claims and accused Husseini of incitement. While expressing hope and belief that most of the Arabs wanted to continue to live in peace with the Jews, he insisted on Jewish rights to their holy sites and encouraged their settlement.[51] A similar sentiment was expressed by R. Hirschensohn, who further encouraged Jews to learn Arabic so that they could build personal relations with their Arab neighbors and thereby circumvent the incitement of their leaders.

After their investigations, the Shaw Commission concluded that the Arabs were the guilty instigators. Nonetheless, they argued that the broader cause of the violence was Jewish immigration. How could the British recognize that the Arabs were guilty of violence yet punish the Jews politically? Many in Britain had concluded that the Balfour Declaration was a mistake and against their interests. The solution came in the White Paper issued by Colonial Secretary Passfield in October

1930. Britain must restrict Jewish immigration and land purchases to ensure that the Jews remain a minority and do not negatively impact the Arab economy – or broader Arab support for Britain. R. Kook, for his part, condemned Britain for its treachery. He wondered aloud if His Majesty's government had abandoned its esteemed role in the world's redemption. Deliverance, he asserted, would come in other ways.[52]

It certainly didn't come from Britain. Ultimately, after another extended period of violence later in the decade (discussed extensively in the next chapters), the British would issue, on the eve of the Holocaust, an even more restrictive immigration policy (the 1939 "White Paper") which essentially undermined the Balfour Declaration and their entire mandate. Weizmann appealed to the League of Nations, but to no avail.

Stung by the betrayal of the British, Zionists learned what R. Hirschensohn had declared several years beforehand: when it comes to international politics, interests will trump justice.

"THE GENERATION IS NOT READY": THE EDUCATION OF JACOB ROBINSON

If the mandate failed to protect Jews in Palestine, it did little better in Europe. The idea behind the minority rights treaties was a sense of reciprocity between different states: "I protect your minority, you protect my minority." Yet as the interwar period progressed, it became clear that attempts to protect minority rights in Europe were no guarantee to help the stateless Jews. Jewish loyalty was regularly suspect in these new ethnic states, with Jews suffering discrimination and persecution in Hungary, Poland, Romania, and elsewhere. As Robinson darkly quipped about the interwar period, European reciprocity meant "I hit my Jews, you hit your Jews."[53] Recognizing the failure of the interwar treaties to protect Jews or other minorities, Robinson concluded that the only real solution for European Jewry was to emigrate to Palestine, or as in his case, to flee to America.

While Lauterpacht would continue to promote international legal protections as a judge on the International Court of Justice, his colleague Robinson became more skeptical of its potential efficacy. After Israel's founding, Robinson served as a leading adviser on diplomacy and international law to the Israeli delegation at the United Nations. He was wary of the prospects of the UN providing real solutions to human rights problems. Its Genocide Convention, developed in the wake of the Holocaust, was too vague and lacked any enforcement mechanism that would make it efficient. Moreover, it and other UN initiatives would be manipulated by Israel's Arab neighbors and minorities to attack the Jewish state, even as these countries would do nothing to respect the human rights of minorities in their own lands.

While he remained a prominent albeit somewhat reluctant international jurist, Robinson understood that national interests and politics would forever play a problematic role in international law. Toward the end of his life, he would assert that while local protections for minorities remained important, the globalized system had failed. Recalling his childhood yeshiva education, he cited the talmudic expression *lo ikhshar dara* (the generation is not prepared) to assert that the world had been insufficiently ready to weave minority rights into its social fabric.[54]

In the coming decades, rabbinic scholars would collectively take a similarly ambivalent but increasingly critical view of such international bodies.[55] Many were thankful for the essential role of the UN in the eventual establishment of the State of Israel after World War II. This was despite it coming way too late to save the six million Jews killed in the Holocaust and not preventing the Jews from still having to go to war to gain what the international community had been promising for over thirty years.[56] Going beyond particular Jewish interests, others appreciated the attempt by international organizations to reduce warfare and limit the atrocities committed when war occurs. They further noted that despite the imbalance of power between strong nations and weak ones, the United Nations and other bodies still promoted the important idea that even the smallest of nations have basic rights that should not be trampled upon.[57]

One scholar, Rabbi Shaul Yisraeli, whose theories we'll treat more thoroughly in chapter 7, even went so far as to assert that Jewish law would obligate Israel to observe all international treaties limiting warfare – including a total ban on war – provided that all parties equally respect these obligations. In the meantime, he noted, *lo ikhshar dara*, the generation is not ready to reciprocally implement such measures.[58]

Aspirations are not a measure of success. The criteria must be whether treaties are loyally followed by their signatories and if international bodies prevent moral mayhems. In the years after R. Hirschensohn wrote, these institutions were entirely ineffective in preventing the continued pogroms in Europe after World War I, the horror of the Holocaust, and the forced migration of 850,000 Jewish residents from Arab countries in the 1950s and '60s, to name just a few egregious examples. When preparing to attack Israel in May 1967, the Egyptian army demanded that UN peacekeeping forces immediately leave the Sinai area; the UN forces hastily left without even an appeal by the UN secretary-general to Egyptian leaders.[59] In 1975, the UN General Assembly passed a resolution declaring that "Zionism is a form of racism," with the support of the USSR, Arab- and Muslim-majority countries, and many African countries, essentially rejecting, again, the justice of the Balfour Declaration. (The resolution was only repealed in 1991.) Many observers also accuse these bodies of unfairly singling out Israel for censure in its complex and protracted struggle with Palestinians while ignoring many travesties around the world.[60] This alleged bias has, in part, led many rabbis and Zionists to severely question whether these international bodies can ever provide justice in the Middle East and around the world.[61]

RWANDA, SYRIA, AND THE EDUCATION OF SAMANTHA POWER

The "failure to protect" critique against international bodies has extended well beyond Jews and Israel. It has also been leveled after Pol Pot's terror in Cambodia, Saddam Hussein's destruction of the Kurds in northern Iraq, the Bosnian Serbs' eradication of non-Serbs, the Rwandan Hutus' systematic extermination of the Tutsi minority, and the systematic killing of ethnic Darfuri people in Western Sudan. There are many reasons given for these failures. Some assert that the diffusion of responsibilities to prevent war crimes absolves too many specific international players of taking the lead.[62] Yet it's also clear that the politics of these bodies regularly prevents them from acting. To take the most obvious example, the UN Security Council, with veto power given to its five permanent members, is helpless in addressing Chinese human rights abuses or the 2014 Russian invasion of Crimea and its subsequent invasion of all of Ukraine. As historian Paul Kennedy has documented, the granting of additional privileges to great powers is inherent to the UN system and, more fundamentally, to any international body that is dependent on its member-states to provide its funding and soldiers.[63] Despite its improvements over the League of Nations, the UN cannot circumvent the political nature of any international body.

There was no greater critic of the Western response to these twentieth-century atrocities than Samantha Power. Her award-winning, best-selling book *"A Problem from Hell": America and the Age of Genocide* extensively documented these cases, including the 1994 ethnic cleansing in Rwanda. Power showed how political considerations led the Clinton administration to ignore the plight of the hundreds of thousands of Tutsis who were killed and raped over four months. US officials, for example, purposely avoided utilizing the "G-word" (genocide) in describing the atrocities because that might obligate them – morally, if not legally – to intervene under the 1948 Genocide Convention. This treaty, whose potential effectiveness was doubted by Robinson, as we noted, was the culmination of years of work by Lauterpacht and especially Raphael Lemkin, another European Jew who had fled Europe and become a leading international jurist. They believed it would succeed in committing countries to prevent and punish "crimes against humanity," a term coined by Lauterpacht.[64] It was signed and affirmed by well over a hundred nations, including leading superpowers. None of those signatures helped when the Hutus began their slaughter.

Power singled out senior administration officials like National Security Adviser Anthony Lake, who had written a well-known critique of immoral realpolitik considerations in previous eras of American foreign policy yet had now fallen into the same trap. Power's book helped inspire the 2005 "Responsibility to Protect" declaration of all UN member states to prevent genocide, war crimes, ethnic cleansing, and crimes against humanity.

Two decades later, Power became the American ambassador to the United Nations under President Barack Obama. A civil war was raging in Syria, with the UN Security Council unable to act because Russia vetoed any measures against the Syrian government. Then Syria used chemical weapons against her own citizens. Such weapons have long been banned under international law with a nearly universal and unprecedented endorsement from countries around the world. This had been a declared "red line" of Obama, even as he was wary of an unpopular excursion of American troops into another bloody Middle East conflict. According to one aide, Obama even noted, "People always say never again, but they never want to do anything."[65]

Yet Power wanted to act. She declared in the UN that the international system had broken down in Syria, with one side being gassed and the other feeling it could get away with it. Claiming that all alternative options were exhausted, she called for limited military strikes. "If violation of a universal agreement to ban chemical weapons is not met with the meaningful response, other regimes will seek to acquire or use them to protect or extend their power."[66] At stake, in other words, was whether treaties had teeth or were just another scrap of paper.

In the end, Obama called off airstrikes, instead electing to work with the Russians to get the Syrians to give up their chemical weapons. Subsequently, Obama's aides have testified about the many political and strategic considerations that led the White House to abandon this limited military action. Some have further asserted that Obama did not want to risk ruining negotiations with the Iranians over their nuclear ambitions.[67] Whatever the reason, America, followed by others, backed away. Syria, with Russian support in both the UN and on the battlefield, continued to commit atrocities in places like Aleppo, including the repeated use of chemical weapons it hid from international inspectors.

Power, for her part, was left to Twitter to share her indignation while delivering scathing speeches at the Security Council against the Russians. "Aleppo will join the ranks of those events in world history that define modern evil, that stain our conscience decades later. Halabja, Rwanda, Srebrenica, and now, Aleppo.... Are you truly incapable of shame?" Powerful words, but international treaties were meant to be backed by more than speeches and 140-character tweets. The Russian ambassador responded by calling her Mother Teresa and called it a day. Since then, critics of American policy have labeled Power a hypocrite and questioned whether she should have resigned.[68]

In her memoir, aptly titled *The Education of an Idealist*, Power admirably lays out her conflicting feelings. Perhaps American intervention would have failed and uselessly endangered American soldiers. Or perhaps the administration, and the entire system, simply failed.

The ultimate result was pretty bad: the Syrian regime, with Russian and Iranian support, massacred hundreds of thousands more while causing a flood of homeless refugees who have in turn helped create political instability in Europe. Western inaction also left the roughly 30 million Kurds quite vulnerable to the whims of the despotic leaders of four countries in which they reside, one hundred years after the 1920 Treaty of Sèvres, signed between the Allies and the defeated Ottomans, called for an independence referendum in their territory. Despite all the treaties and promises they were given over the century, they have neither a state nor minority rights.

These examples only strengthen R. Hirschensohn's basic claim: international laws and treaties provide no guarantee that justice will be executed or that the innocent will be protected. Sometimes they will help, but many times they will not. Even people with the best of intentions like Lake and Power fall into the trap of allowing power and politics to color, if not shape, international legal bodies.

This sad but important truth does not mean that we should simply dismiss the ethics that international law aspires to implement. While displaying great skepticism about the efficacy of the system, R. Hirschensohn affirmed many of the values of "civilized society." He sought to prove how Judaism may incorporate concepts like democracy and minority rights in order to make them valuable to Jews on their own terms, independent of their enforcement in broader international society. If, for example, forsaking total war tactics is an upright decision, then Jews should integrate and implement those values for integral reasons, and not just for the sake of preserving our reputation as an ethical people.[69]

At the same time, Jews should not be naive about the prospects of international bodies providing them with support or protection. In practice, self-help is the prevailing rule of world affairs. Jews cannot wait for others to deliver justice. In an international order deeply impacted, if not driven, by interests, Jews need to proactively do what it takes to gain what they deserve.

DOES TERROR PAY?

Yet there was another lesson that the Jews might learn from the British response in 1929: violence pays. The Arabs also suffered many casualties during the 1929 riots, almost all at the hands of the British police. Yet at the end of the day, many of their jail sentences were commuted, and the British rewarded them politically. In the absence of adequate British protection, the Jews were left to debate whether they should adopt tactics similar to those of their Arab enemies. Within the Haganah, the Jewish defense organization, disagreements over its failure to adequately protect the Jewish community led to the founding of the Etzel (short for *Irgun Tzvai Leumi*, the National Military Organization). This breakoff defense group had an activist orientation more akin to the ideology of Jabotinsky, who himself was permanently exiled from Palestine by the British.

What would Rabbis Kook and Hirschensohn have said about this? No one knows, as they both died in 1935, a year before the next round of Arab riots and the beginning of a fierce ethical debate about whether Jews should fight terror with terror.

Chapter 4

Reprisal Killings, "Purity of Arms," and the 1936–1939 Arab Riots

BLACK SUNDAY AND THE "RESTRAINT VS. RESPONSE" DEBATE

On October 31, 1937, Alan Alkazitz, 32, was walking in Jerusalem's Old City after praying at the Western Wall when he was shot dead by Arab terrorists. Two other Jews were wounded. This murder followed the shooting of Rabbi Eliezer Gerstein on September 3 at a nearby spot. Then on November 10, a group of five Jewish field workers, recent immigrants from Poland, were gunned down on their way to tilling the land in Kiryat Anavim outside of Jerusalem.[1] One might have viewed this as simply the next attack on Jews since the start in 1936 of Arab riots in response to increasing Jewish immigration or, for that matter, the latest episode in centuries of antisemitic violence.

Yet something different happened this time. The next day, while World War I Jewish Legion veterans were commemorating Armistice Day (November 11) alongside Brits on Mount Scopus, a bomb was hurled at a bus near the central post office, killing one Arab and wounding five others.[2] Three days later, on a day later known as Black Sunday, the Etzel group, in a series of coordinated attacks in Jerusalem and Haifa, killed seven Arabs, including three women, and injured eight more. For centuries Jews had nonviolent responses to antisemitic murders. Now, an organized group of Jews had taken revenge by indiscriminately killing members of the perceived enemy nation.

Over the next couple of years, similar reprisal killings would take place in Arab cafés, buses, and markets. These attacks would drive the Yishuv into the first significant debate over the renewal of Jewish power and its deadly implications which, as we'll see, continued to reverberate over the coming decades and still resonates today.

How could a Jew randomly kill innocent civilians? This was the question that many Jews in Palestine asked following Black Sunday. Critics deemed these attacks as vengeful acts that were unethical and counterproductive. The Etzel was immorally fighting terror with terror while endangering further Jewish settlement in Palestine, since the British would see the Jews as no different from petty terrorists.

Figures in the Jewish Agency and Haganah, like Katznelson and Ben-Gurion, favored a policy of self-restraint (*havlaga*) against Arab violence. It was in response to this ethical challenge that they developed a larger vision of "purity of arms" (*taharat haneshek*) opposing the use of force beyond self-defense.[3] At the funerals of the five field workers, attended by fifty thousand people, Moshe Shertok (Sharett), then head of the Jewish Agency's political department and later Israel's second prime minister, stressed the same point. "Although we are deeply stirred, let us nevertheless realize that retribution by attacks on innocent and law-abiding Arabs will not affect the terrorists nor will it prevent terror." He called upon the British government to fight Arab terrorists and provide arms to Jews for self-defense, a request that was only partially fulfilled. More critically, he asserted, "Our reprisal will be intensive continuation of our peaceful work" to strengthen Jewish immigration and settlement.

Undoubtedly, targeting civilians in retaliation is a horrifying prospect. Yet perhaps this is the type of self-interest calculation that would make terrorists think twice about their killings? For some Jews, whose ancestors had suffered from centuries of powerlessness in the face of crusades, pogroms, and inquisitions, the ability to avenge the killing of the faithful while deterring future attacks was (and is[4]) a tempting prospect. Indeed, in the same years, Betar members in Poland were making similar arguments about how to defend Jews in Europe against the increasing numbers of antisemitic attacks.[5]

The Etzel commander was David Raziel, who had been a student of Rabbi Tzvi Yehuda Kook before cofounding the underground movement.[6] He clearly articulated the rationale behind their actions: "He who saw the faces of the Arabs on 'Black Sunday' and in the days following is able to describe for himself what fear fell on them. All of their insolent heroism that in the past year and a half pierced their eyes disappeared suddenly at once." This brought him to the following conclusion: "He who does not want to be defeated has no choice but to attack… He needs to charge his enemy and to break his force and his will."[7]

Any response (*teguva*) was preferable to restraint (*havlaga*). Given the utilization of indiscriminate terror by antisemites against Jews, whether in Europe or Palestine, perhaps it was necessary – and therefore justified – to respond in kind to that type of immoral behavior.

BELLIGERENT REPRISALS IN THE TOTAL WAR ERA

This debate, in truth, was a variation of a long-standing question among just-war theorists who appreciated the impetuses and dangers of reprisal killings. The first modern attempt to codify military norms was the 1863 Lieber Code, drafted by the German-American legal scholar Franz Lieber on behalf of President Abraham Lincoln. The Lieber Code captured the dilemma of belligerent reprisals. On the one hand, it proclaimed, "A reckless enemy often leaves to his opponent no other means of securing himself against the repetition of barbarous outrage." On the other hand, reprisal killings may not succeed in deterring future acts; in fact, they may be done simply as acts of vengeance for past actions and can lead to a cycle of violence. Thus the code goes on to insist:

> Retaliation will, therefore, never be resorted to as a measure of mere revenge, but only as a means of protective retribution, and moreover, cautiously and unavoidably…. Unjust or inconsiderate retaliation removes the belligerents farther and farther from the mitigating rules of regular war, and by rapid steps leads them nearer to the internecine wars of savages.[8]

The idea of limiting reprisals was also shared by General Henry Hallack, head of the Union forces during a period of the Civil War. He argued that while we generally only retaliate against the individual offender, sometimes there are exceptions in which a city, army, or an entire community is punished for the illegal acts of its rulers or individual members. Yet, he warned, these actions must not exceed the "punishment in all civilized governments and among all Christian people – it must never degenerate into savage or barbarous cruelty."[9]

That line between "protective retribution" and un-Christian savage cruelty can get quite fuzzy. In any case, the code certainly did not prevent many retaliatory acts in the coming decades which today are widely seen as barbarous. Many warn that the true impetus behind reprisals is frequently revenge, a natural emotional response that unleashes the worst in the retaliating soldiers.[10]

The Lieber Code began a process which accelerated after World War I to utilize legal codes as a better way of preventing "savage" reprisal attacks. Thus a 1929 convention prohibited reprisal attacks on prisoners of war. Yet it was only after World War II in the 1949 Geneva convention that reprisal attacks against civilians were prohibited, albeit only against those interned or located in occupied territories.[11]

Despite the growing awareness of its moral hazards, belligerent reprisals continued to be the way of the world in the interwar period. Reprisal killings against noncombatants as a form of collective punishment were features of the Spanish Civil War, the Mexican Revolution of 1910–20, the conflict in Nicaragua between 1927 and 1933, El Salvador in 1932 and 1944, the Russian Revolution, and of the British Empire in India, Ireland, and most significantly, Palestine.[12]

ORDE WINGATE AND THE SPECIAL NIGHT SQUADS

British reprisals commenced in July 1937 after the Peel Commission proposed to partition the Palestinian mandate into two states, one for Arabs and the other for Jews. The Arab reaction was fierce, with renewed attacks not only against Jews (like the five field workers in Kiryat Anavim) but also against British targets, including the assassination of the district commissioner of the Galilee.

In response, the British established a counterinsurgency force, the Special Night Squads (SNS). The force was comprised of British soldiers and Haganah members who would become future IDF generals such as Moshe Dayan and Yigal Alon. They were led by Orde Wingate, a deeply-religious Christian who became an ardent Zionist and friend of Zionist leaders like Weizmann and Shertok. The northern village of Ein Harod served as the SNS base. Ein Harod was symbolically signifi- cant since this was the home of the biblical warrior Gideon who, like Wingate, utilized guerrilla warfare tactics and other unorthodox methods to defeat the local enemies.[13] Wingate strongly supported training and arming Jewish fighters. Yet he had little sympathy for the Etzel attacks which, beyond its vigilantism, targeted random civilians. Instead, he favored a two-pronged strategic approach that aimed not only to defend against attacks but also to root out the Arab gangs from their villages.[14]

Wingate's aggressive approach unquestionably utilized collec- tive punishment against Arab villages that harbored terrorists. While not quite the same as an Etzel member aiming at any random passersby, the SNS strategy did place collective responsibility on all tribe mem- bers who may (or may not) have directly or indirectly supported the killers.[15] This line between culpable villagers and random Arabs could easily get blurred. In one dramatic incident, a Jewish settlement leader and friend of Wingate, Chaim Sturmann, was killed when his car went over a land mine. Sturmann was a strident opponent of collective pun- ishment. Wingate would write about him, "A great Jew, a friend of the Arabs, who was killed by Arabs." Upon hearing of Sturmann's death, Wingate entered the Arab section of Beit She'an and wreaked havoc in several shops. In some reports, two or three Arabs were killed.

While having lost control on this occasion and crossed the line on others, it seems he recognized the moral dilemma of collective punishment. His aide, Zvi Brenner, described Wingate's agony over the matter, including his misdeeds. "On the one hand, he demanded that the innocent not be harmed. On the other hand, he knew that he faced a dilemma: Can one observe this rule in battle against gangs which receive assistance from the residents of the villages?" Or as two of his biographers put it, Wingate, who carried a Bible around with him, understood that he could not behave like an avenging Old Testament warrior.[16] Significantly, two weeks after the Beit She'an incident, Arabs attacked the Jewish quarter of Tiberias and killed nineteen Jews, including eleven children. Was this a counter-reprisal attack? Likely not, but either way, it shows how drastic tactics bring no guarantee of stopping terror attacks, at least in the short term.

In truth, even among the Revisionists, there were deep divisions over their reprisal attacks. Avraham Tehomi, one of the Etzel's founders, opposed such indiscriminate violence. So did, at least initially, Vladimir Jabotinsky, who served for many Etzel members as an ideological figurehead. Jabotinsky told a group of Revisionist leaders in 1937, "I see nothing heroic about shooting an Arab peasant in the back for bringing vegetables on his donkey to Tel Aviv."[17] Even as late as June 1939, Jabotinsky was writing private letters to Etzel leaders to protest attacks that targeted women, children, or the elderly.[18]

In public, however, Jabotinsky came out in support of the more militant leanings of figures like Raziel. His tone particularly shifted after the British executed Shlomo Ben-Yosef in the summer of 1938 for his failed reprisal attack on an Arab bus. Restraint, the Etzel asserted, had proven to be a political miscalculation of the Haganah. Jews were continuously killed with no reprieve, while repeated British concessions to limit Jewish immigration, like after the 1929 riots, had taught the local Arabs that terror paid. Indeed, later in 1938, the Woodhead Commission was sent to explore the implementation of the Peel partition plan in light of the Arab protests. Peel proposed that the Jews should be given a state, albeit on a very small strip of land between Tel Aviv and Haifa. In the face of Arab violence, the British government concluded soon afterward that partition was no longer possible under the circumstances.

For Jabotinsky and others, the moral imperative in 1938 was to defend the Jewish people and free the homeland at all costs. Under the circumstances this meant, in their words, that "a hitting fist must be answered by two hitting fists. A bomb explosion has to be replied to with two bomb explosions."[19] Not surprisingly, Jabotinsky, known for founding the Jewish Legion that fought with the British, cited the British reprisal bombings of German cities toward the end of the Great War as moral precedent for this attitude. Ultimately, he asserted in a July 1938 speech in Warsaw, "The greatest enemy of equality for Jews is he who says that the means used by the Arabs in their war against us must not be used by us against them."[20] Any brutal tactic used against Jews may be utilized in response.

THE MORAL DEBATE OVER REPRISALS

Many ethicists, both then and especially today, disagree with Jabotinsky's claim: tactics of indiscriminate killing are always wrong, even when the other side violates such rules. This sentiment guided the Additional Protocols (AP/1) to the Geneva conventions signed in 1977, which prohibit reprisals against an enemy's civilian population, even when there is no occupation.[21] What's inherently wrong with belligerent reprisals? Michael Walzer, among others, has argued that reprisal killings raise deep ethical questions because of their radical utilitarianism: in the name of deterrence, we kill innocent people.[22] Reprisals do not target those guilty of the egregious action, like the biblical "eye for an eye"; instead, they punish random members of the enemy state in a form of collective punishment. In the words of one early-twentieth-century advocate of reprisals, J. M. Spaight, "For every offense punish someone; the guilty, if possible, but someone." Such a notion, however, violates the very concept of individual responsibility.

Moreover, beyond problems of collective punishment, such an attitude can lead to a cycle of violent reprisals, invoking the pious maxim "violence breeds violence." Or as Gandhi allegedly asserted, "An eye for an eye leaves both sides blind." Walzer himself defends reprisal attacks in very limited conditions against military targets and civilian property – to the chagrin of some fellow progressive theorists – yet strictly proscribes targeting civilian lives or any other basic rights of the innocent. Indiscriminate killing is *malum in se*, an evil in itself that cannot be permitted because of its disregard of individual human rights.[23]

Beyond the moral claim, many advocates of international humanitarian law argue that military commissions and international courts can now provide retributive justice in the case of war crimes, thereby making collective reprisals both obsolete and indefensible. As Frits Kalshoven, the widely-cited historian of belligerent reprisals, has argued, "The balance and demerits of belligerent reprisals has now become so entirely negative as no longer to allow their being regarded as even moderately effective sanctions of the laws of war."[24] For him and others, the new world of international legal order makes reprisals anachronistic. This was the argument made by Justice Robert Jackson at the opening of the Nuremberg trials. "That four great nations, flushed with victory and stung with injury stay the hand of vengeance and voluntarily submit their captive enemies to the judgment of the law is one of the most significant tributes that Power has ever paid to Reason."[25] Justice, it was argued, is the best reprisal.

The turn to individual criminal responsibility, however, seems less compelling when terrorists and nonstate actors continue to thrive with no effective reprieve from international courts or bodies. Did the trials of Nazi war criminals at Nuremberg and Bosnia genocide prosecutions in the Hague prevent ethnic cleansing around the world? Has the prosecution of any terrorist in the United States deterred any actions by Al Qaeda operatives? Have the convictions of thousands of Hamas and Islamic Jihad terrorists in Israel prevented additional bloodshed in the streets of Jerusalem or Tel Aviv? Positive answers to these questions are far from clear. War crimes trials have many merits and remain necessary, but they seem *insufficient* as a deterrent, whether in the midst of full-fledged battlefield warfare or following "peacetime" belligerent actions.

The potential continued necessity of reprisals was already perceived in 1977 by many countries, including the United States and Israel, both of which did not sign the new AP/1 conventions. These countries feared that those conventions would prohibit reprisal actions that may occasionally be necessary when enemies violate the protocols of war, such as using unconventional weapons.[26] Indeed, the premise of the famed "mutually assured destruction" doctrine during the Cold War was that each side would retaliate in kind to a nuclear attack. This is somewhat of an extreme scenario, yet these countries felt that it was critical not to take options off the table for other occasions as well. If you want to make the other side play by the rules, so to speak, you may need to make them pay a price by hitting back in a way that will deter them from utilizing an unjust method. Thus the United States struck Libyan airfields in April 1986 in the name of self-defense after a terrorist bombing by Libyan agents in West Germany killed an American serviceman. Many condemned the strike as an immoral reprisal attack.[27] Such retaliation inevitably harms those beyond the limited group of individuals who committed the initial crime, bringing us back to the deep moral dilemmas of reprisals and the 1936–39 debates.

SHECHEM AND JEWISH HISTORY: THE CASE FOR INDISCRIMINATE REPRISALS

The rabbinic leadership of the Yishuv did not stay out of the debate. In fact, Ben-Gurion even demanded their response: "Where are the wise men of the Jewish religion?" These figures sought to provide traditional Jewish sources to back their moral positions. This was a challenge, given that Jews had not developed their own teachings on the ethics of fighting for many centuries. What emerged in this tense period were a series of public declarations, policy speeches, and newspaper op-eds laced with biblical and talmudic references that would tease out inchoate notions of Jewish military ethics.

The interpretation of traditional Jewish sources was also impacted by each figure's understanding of the meaning of the history of Jewish powerlessness. In this respect, the initial formulation of Jewish perspectives was no different from other moral traditions in which, as James Turner Johnson put it, "one encounters the values that shape moral decisions through reflection on history, and historical events shape human understanding of what is morally valuable."[28] History impacts morality. In the Jewish case, conflicting perspectives on the meaning of Jewish history greatly impacted how various rabbis approached the new moral dilemmas.

Rabbi Yehuda Leib Maimon (1875–1962) was one of the founders of the Mizrachi religious-Zionist movement and its representative in the Jewish Agency Executive. He would later sign Israel's Declaration of Independence and serve as a minister in the first two Israeli governments. Ordained in Russia by leading rabbinic scholars, he also became a Zionist activist, for which he was arrested on several occasions. He immigrated to Palestine in 1913, but alongside many other Russian citizens was kicked out by the Turks during World War I. He continued his Zionist activities in America, and upon his return to Palestine in 1919 helped found many of Mizrachi's educational institutions. Additionally, he assisted R. Kook in establishing the Chief Rabbinate in Palestine. Yet R. Maimon refused to join R. Kook's short-lived alternative religious-Zionist party because he believed it would cause unnecessary fractionalization. The Jewish political condition demanded greater unity. He further believed one could influence the Zionist movement only from within its mainstream institutions.[29]

For similar reasons, during the early debates over reprisal activities, R. Maimon publicly called upon people to refrain from such killing, as he feared the discord created by offshoot groups like the Etzel. Yet within internal meetings of the Jewish Agency, he wondered whether, on a fundamental level, reprisal attacks were not justified.[30] After the killing of the five workers in 1937, he attributed partial blame for their deaths to the Jewish leadership while further asserting that promoting "self-restraint" was teaching Jewish youth to be cowards. R. Maimon, in fact, even indicated to his colleagues that if he were a younger man, he would commit reprisal killings himself!

Looking to the Bible, he noted that after the leader of the city of Shechem took Dinah captive, her brothers, Levi and Simeon, sought revenge by wiping out the entire town. "Simeon and Levi, brothers of Dinah, took each his sword, came upon the city unmolested, and slew all the males. They put Hamor and his son Shechem to the sword, took Dinah out of Shechem's house, and went away" (Gen. 34:22–23). Against the protests of their father, who feared retaliation against his small family, the brothers responded, "Shall our sister be treated like a whore?" (34:31). On a practical level, Jacob's fears were not realized since a "terror of God was upon the cities…and they did not pursue Jacob's sons" (35:5). Yet how could Simeon and Levi morally validate their actions? This collective punishment was justified by the medieval jurist Maimonides, who argued that the townspeople were responsible for not establishing a judicial system that would prevent such crimes. In this spirit, R. Maimon concluded, Arab civilians may be held responsible for the breakdown of their society as "responsible bystanders," as some philosophers put it.[31]

R. Maimon wasn't the only one who invoked this story to protest the self-restraint strategy. The secular poet Shaul Tchernichovsky penned a poem, "The Dinah Affair," in which Dinah, who is utterly silent in the biblical narrative, praises her two courageous brothers while condemning her other siblings as cowards. This literary ventriloquism contrasts with the Bible's final depiction of the affair, in which Jacob gets the last word and strongly condemns his sons for their violence (Gen. 49:6).[32]

Alongside other executive members who angrily rejected R. Maimon's position, Ben-Gurion shot back by questioning whether one could rely upon medieval rabbinic statements as the basis for contemporary moral assessments. "Maimonides didn't live in our period – he didn't witness the Balfour Declaration or the mandate, nor did he see the condition of the Jews in the Diaspora or the factors motivating the Zionist enterprise today." Ben-Gurion, as such, rejected the notion that one can take a rabbinic statement from earlier centuries and simply apply it to a later time period. The authority to make moral statements must rest on one's evaluation of the current situation and not rely upon the authority of the ancients.

R. Maimon, in any case, reiterated this line of thought again in June 1939, but this time by invoking a historical argument. Zionist leaders passionately debated how to react to the British White Paper issued in May 1939 that severely limited Jewish immigration and settlement. The Arab leadership was not placated by this generous proposal and instigated a new round of violence. While the Jewish Agency supported increased measures toward self-defense against the Arabs alongside a policy of civil disobedience toward the British, the Etzel had other ideas. In the subsequent five weeks, that group, now led by Hanoch Kalay (Raziel had been arrested), carried out over twenty-one attacks, including four indiscriminate bombings of crowded public places, resulting in the killing of forty Arabs and the wounding of dozens more.[33]

At a meeting of the Zionist General Council, Menahem Ussishkin, its head, denounced the Etzel's action as terror attacks that went against "Jewish ethical and historical sentiments." R. Maimon retorted that while the ethical concerns were real, Jewish history tells a different narrative. The nature of warfare doesn't allow for distinguishing between good and evil among our enemies. This lesson, he added, was well understood by the talmudic Sages, who asserted, "Once permission is granted to the destroyer to kill, it does not distinguish between the righteous and the wicked."[34] The same Bible which proclaims, "Thou shall not murder," he reminded the Zionist leader, also commands to utterly wipe out the seven Canaanite nations (as discussed in chapter 2). While affirming that this latter commandment was not normative in the current era, R. Maimon utilized it to argue that doing "what it takes" to effectively respond to the murder of Jews, even if it involves killing, is not the moral equivalent of murder.

Then, in a remarkable moment, he referenced a famous verse of the New Testament. "You have heard that it was said, 'Eye for eye, and tooth for tooth.' But I tell you, do not resist an evil person. If anyone slaps you on the right cheek, turn to them the other cheek also" (Matthew 5:38–40). This pacific sentiment has been rejected by Judaism, R. Maimon asserted. Therefore, he concludes, "if they kill us, we'll kill others," tellingly leaving open the identity of the "others." It would appear that he didn't think it really matters, thereby turning the "eye for eye" commandment into a mandate that insists on exacting some form of forceful reaction to the killing of Jews. This was not "terror," in his mind, but rather "a response." If done by the official Jewish agencies in a controlled, disciplined manner, R. Maimon reasoned, it would not only be justified killing, but it would have the further benefit of preventing Jewish vigilante acts. Ultimately, he argued, Jews must take the initiative. As we've tragically learned from many painful moments in Jewish history, not responding is not an option.

WAR DOES NOT DISTINGUISH BETWEEN THE RIGHTEOUS AND THE WICKED

R. Maimon made a number of logical assumptions in his claims. By invoking the talmudic teaching about warfare, he assumed that Jews in Palestine were actually engaged in battle. Given the sporadic nature of the violence, this hypothesis was certainly not clear to everyone in the late 1930s, even as Jewish casualties would climb to over five hundred killed. Etzel figures regularly reiterated this claim: if hundreds of Jews have been killed or wounded, then we are at war, and in war one does not have the luxury of targeting only those specific individuals (whether citizens or soldiers) who have threatened you.[35] As Jabotinsky put it,

> In war, any war, each side is innocent. What crime has he committed against me – that enemy soldier who fights me – and is as

poor as I, as blind as I, as much a slave as I, who has been recruited against his will?... There is no war which is not conducted against the innocent, just as there is no war which is not fraternal strife. Therefore every war and the tribulations it brings is accursed, whether offensive or defensive, and if you do not wish to harm the innocent – you will die. And if you do not wish to die – then shoot and stop prattling.

War is a collective enterprise, and therefore even individuals who have no specific desire to harm you, whether elderly citizens or forcibly conscripted soldiers, become legitimate targets.

On a closer look, however, the talmudic passage cited by R. Maimon about the indiscriminate nature of bloody combat mourns that reality and certainly does not advocate directly targeting the innocent. As the passage reads,

> Once permission is granted to the destroyer to kill, it does not distinguish between the righteous and the wicked. And not only that, but it begins with the righteous first, as it is stated in the verse: "And will cut off from you the righteous and the wicked" (Ezek. 21:8).
>
> R. Yosef cried and said: Are all these righteous people also compared to nothing when calamity strikes? Abaye said to him: It is goodness for the righteous that they die first, as it is written: "The righteous is taken away because of the evil to come" (Is. 57:1) (i.e., so that he will not have to endure the suffering that will befall the people).

The Sages cry over the fact that the innocent die (first!) and certainly do not justify targeting them.

On a moral level, furthermore, there's a difference between targeting a uniformed soldier (even if he has been forcibly conscripted) who represents the enemy side who threatens your well-being, and assaulting a random, uninvolved, noncombatant enemy citizen. The latter is not a proximate threat or an official representative of the belligerent collective. While it can be quite difficult, in practice, to separate the innocent from the guilty in general warfare, these reprisal killings could hardly be deemed collateral damage when they directly targeted noncombatants.[36] As we'll note in the coming chapters, sometimes civilians might be engaged in the war efforts and lose their non-combatant status. Nonetheless, a random fruit stand in a crowded market can never be perceived as a military target.

Ultimately, then, R. Maimon seems to be left with the following argument: Jews can no longer be passive and must respond. If they cannot punish the attacker, they must direct the response elsewhere. We are at war, and once in battle, the Bible teaches that this struggle is of a collective nature.

Jabotinsky made a similar point, also in July 1939. Given that it was impossible in most cases to punish the actual perpetrators,

> the choice is not between retaliating against the bandits or retaliating against the hostile population: the choice is between these two practical possibilities – either retaliating against the hostile population or not retaliating at all. The question is not new. All peoples have faced it and especially if a war were to break out now, they will be faced with the same question every day....
>
> Where it is a question of war you do not stand and ask questions as to what is "better," whether to shoot or not to shoot. The only permissible question in such circumstances is on the contrary: "what is worse," to let yourself be killed or enslaved without any resistance, or to undertake resistance with all its horrible consequences? For there is no "better" at all. Everything connected with war is bad, and cannot be "good"....
>
> If you start calculating what is "better," the calculation is very simple; if you want to be good let yourself be killed; and renounce everything you would like to defend: home, country, freedom, hope.
>
> I do not treat this lightly and I suggest that nobody treat lightly a situation where there is horror on every side. But the worst of all horrors known to history is called *galut*, dispersion; and the blackest of all the characteristics of *galut* is the tradition of the cheapness of Jewish blood.[37]

Here, in his last line, Jabotinsky articulates the ultimate moral justification for reprisal killings: after eighteen hundred years of Jewish powerlessness, Jewish blood can no longer be cheap. Primary moral consideration must now be Jewish survival, even if this entails tragic moral decisions.[38]

"YOU SHALL NOT MURDER!" THE RABBINIC CASE AGAINST INDISCRIMINATE REPRISALS

At the 1939 meeting, Shertok did not let R. Maimon's claims pass without comment. He argued the prohibition of murder and the commandment to wipe out the Canaanite nations cannot be easily reconciled and possibly reflect different perspectives. Subtly referencing talmudic outlooks on how to reconcile such differences, he noted, in a pluralistic vein, that each may be "the living words of God," i.e., legitimate perspectives. One could argue that such conflicting tendencies make it impossible to utilize Jewish texts as a source of clear moral authority. Shertok, however, claimed that there was a third rule to reconcile the dispute,[39] which establishes the principle of self-defense. "If they come to slay you, rise up and kill," asserts the Talmud. Self-defense, Shertok exclaimed, is perfectly legitimate. Yet had the indiscriminate killing of the Etzel saved any Jewish lives? At this point in 1939, he asserted, we have a significant amount of evidence to test the efficiency of the Etzel's terror over the past three years. As far as he could tell, it had only led to greater bloodshed and had not stopped any attacks on Jews.

Shertok undoubtedly knew that much of the rabbinic establishment was clearly on his side of the debate. R. Maimon, by his own admission, was in the distinct minority within broader rabbinic circles.[40] As Eliezer Don-Yehiya has shown, the rabbinic majority deemed indiscriminate killing a violation of the commandment "Thou shall not kill." This was certainly true of non-Zionist rabbinic figures like Rabbi Moshe Blau, head of the Agudat Israel Party in Israel. After the reprisal attacks following the Kiryat Anavim killings in 1937, Blau mourned the innocent blood spilled on both sides. He denounced the Etzel for violating the centuries-old principle of not committing murder out of revenge, even against non-Jews.[41]

Yet the Etzel were also condemned by religious Zionist figures who were more sympathetic to taking up weapons in self-defense. "Rise and kill first" is a principle of self-defense enshrined in Jewish law, but only when that person is threatening you. In the absence of self-defense, Sephardic Chief Rabbi Ben-Zion Uziel asserted, murder was an absolute prohibition. Whatever the intent of the Etzel and others, he declared, Judaism believes that the ends do not justify the means. This is especially true when it comes to settling the land, as Moses warns, "Blood of the innocent will not be shed, bringing bloodguilt upon you in the land that the Lord your God is allotting to you."[42] This admonishment points to a collective responsibility of preventing innocent bloodshed in order to merit possession of the Land of Israel. The claim, part metaphysical and part ethical, highlights the special connection seen between the Jewish people and the land. Yet as opposed to similar types of nationalistic claims, which may justify killing for the homeland, R. Uziel asserts that this verse demands a heightened ethical awareness of preventing innocent bloodshed. Israel must deserve national redemption, and that will not be achieved through unethical behavior.[43]

For additional support, R. Uziel cited rabbinic traditions that depicted the biblical forefathers Abraham and Jacob as entering battles while being equally fearful of getting killed or unintentionally slaying an innocent member of the enemy party.[44] Their goal was to stay alive without killing immorally. God had pledged the Promised Land to them, but nonetheless they did not feel entitled to kill innocents toward that goal. R. Uziel added that throughout the generations, Jews have repeatedly refrained from revenge killings of innocents in spite of untold horrors that have been committed against the Jewish people. This, he believed, was the Jewish definition of courage and the moral legacy of Jewish history.[45]

Isn't the killing of innocents a part of all rebellions and insurgencies, let alone warfare, throughout the ages? This, as we'll recall, was one of R. Maimon's claims. Yet for the Ashkenazic chief rabbi, Isaac Herzog (1888–1959), it was precisely the duty of Jews to avoid following the wars of the nations. R. Herzog was born in Poland but moved to Leeds, England, in his childhood. Unique among the rabbinic figures in this time period, he was educated at the Sorbonne and ultimately received a doctorate from the University of London. R. Herzog served as a communal rabbi in Ireland during its revolutionary period against the

British, and later was its chief rabbi, giving him many contacts that he'd ultimately use to promote the Zionist cause.[46] While he supported Irish independence, he also saw firsthand the cruelties of warfare. He urged the Jews of Palestine not to fall into the trap of immoral fighting. The policy of "self-restraint," he argued, was a sanctification of God's name (*kiddush Hashem*) and exemplified the greatness of Jewish morality. After so many years of not being able to protect themselves, Jews were obligated to engage in self-defense without crossing moral boundaries. R. Herzog even instructed that if he should be killed, the people should not avenge his murder! As Anita Shapira and Ehud Luz have documented, the defensive ethos that dominated much of the broader Zionist movement was bolstered by the self-image of Jews who hated violence, as opposed to their bloodthirsty neighbors.[47] Indeed, in his public eulogy for the five workers killed in 1937, R. Herzog called on the British to provide greater means for self-defense, while urging Jews to refrain from retaliatory attacks. At the same time, he wondered aloud if "such a cry could also be heard on the other side, from the leaders of Islam, against the spilling of innocent blood."[48]

Be that as it may, R. Herzog's detractors not only derogatorily called him the "reverend of Belfast," but also derided, à la Jabotinsky, the entire notion of Jews holding themselves to higher moral standards. Indeed, other underground figures would cite the Irish example as showing that securing a homeland could be achieved only through sacrifice and armed struggle, no matter what means were necessary to achieve those ends. As for R. Herzog's claim that indiscriminate violence would bring dishonor to God, others retorted that the greatest desecration of God's name (*hillul Hashem*) is the continued suffering of the Jewish people in the Land of Israel. Only the political redemption of the Jewish people, the prophet Ezekiel stated, can restore God's honor.[49] The tragedy of Jewish exile must come to an end.

This, in fact, was the belief of the founders of the Hasmonean Alliance (*Brit HaHashmona'im*), a group of yeshiva students who joined forces with the Etzel during this period.[50] For many supporters of the Etzel, the Maccabees represented model Jews not only for their bravery in fighting against a mightier enemy, but because they employed the uncompromising guerrilla tactics necessary to achieve victory.[51] The

Jews must have a secure state, at any price. To paraphrase Moses, "What will the nations say when you bring the Jews to the Land of Israel and they get slaughtered by the Arabs?"[52] Under that perspective one could argue that the most important thing for God's honor – and that of His people – is victory, at all costs.[53]

This utilitarian argument – contending that the goal of sovereignty justifies all means – was countered by the most strident opponent of reprisal killings, Rabbi Moshe Avigdor Amiel, chief rabbi of Tel Aviv. While a passionate Zionist, R. Amiel was deeply concerned that nationalistic movements could easily sacrifice individuals for the sake of the greater good. This, he believed, was the hallmark of Bismarck and Hitler. They would carelessly declare war and send citizens and enemies alike to their deaths, all in the name of the national good. Jewish history, R. Amiel asserted, went against this immoral version of nationalism. With its deep ethical principles, Judaism could prevent the excesses of nationalist utilitarian calculations because it valued the inherent worth of each individual, Jew and non-Jew alike, as created in the image of God. For this reason, we disallow collective punishment. As Ezekiel asserted, "The person who sins – he alone shall die." R. Amiel rejected the term *havlaga*, restraint, to describe the policy of the Yishuv, since it had utilitarian connotations; the proper term for the policy should be *lo tirzah* (you shall not murder), the sixth commandment, which created an unconditional prohibition against murder. Indiscriminate killing was nothing more than murderous terror.

Thus was established the first principle of a Jewish just-war theory: we don't target noncombatants. All humans were created in the divine image and we are therefore obligated not to kill indiscriminately.

Yet is this an absolute principle? Or might there be extreme circumstances when this severe prohibition may be overridden to "do what it takes," as R. Maimon put it, to save the Jewish people?

Chapter 5

Supreme Emergencies and the Ethical Imperative of Survival, 1938

AN ALTERNATIVE DEFENSE OF THE ETZEL'S REPRISAL KILLINGS

Rabbis Uziel, Amiel, and others condemned the Etzel attacks because the "ends don't justify the means." How far did this anti-utilitarianism go? During the heated debate after the execution of Shlomo Ben-Yosef in 1938, R. Amiel asserted that even if we could save a thousand people, we wouldn't kill someone innocent. He then went even further:

> Even if we knew for certain that we could bring about the Final Redemption [by indiscriminate killing], we should reject such a "Redemption" with both hands, and not be redeemed through [innocent] bloodshed.[1]

R. Amiel's absolutist, anti-utilitarian position recalls an old Latin adage: *Fiat justitia ruat caelum*, translated as "Let justice be done though the heavens fall," i.e., whatever the consequences, stick to your moral commitments.

Yet is there no ethical obligation for political leaders to think of the practical consequences of their moral stances? R. Amiel's rhetoric is passionate and powerful – but is his moral absolutism compelling? Ben-Gurion, for one, did not think the moral argument was sufficient.

At the 1938 Jewish Agency directorate meeting in which Rabbis Amiel and Herzog articulated the "biblical perspective" on the self-restraint debate, Ben-Gurion contended that while he agreed with their ethical sentiments, members of the Yishuv would need to see that this policy was also pragmatically wise.[2] This was, in part, because other religious figures could selectively cite other biblical verses to support belligerent reprisals. Ben-Gurion, who studied the Bible carefully and knew its narratives well, was conscious of other biblical stories that might portray a different military ethic. Yet Ben-Gurion went further to argue that people ultimately act based on interests, not morals. Cooperating with the British on both defense and diplomacy had to be seen as the better political option. The moral argument, in other words, must be coupled with a pragmatic case for the strategic effectiveness of restraint. A moral triumph seems inadequate – and ultimately illusionary – if your people continue to get slaughtered with no reprieve.

"DIRTY HANDS" AND THE ETHICS OF RESPONSIBILITY

In truth, however, the dilemma may not pit morals against interests, as Ben-Gurion claimed, but rather involve two competing moral claims or obligations. This can happen, for example, when fulfilling an "absolute" moral obligation (a fundamental "Thou shall not," so to speak, like not murdering innocents) brings with it horrific consequences or results for the greater collective. The Yishuv leadership, as a political entity, had a moral obligation not to target innocent noncombatants. But no government or leadership can put the very life of its community at risk if there are actions, even immoral ones, that would avoid such a risk. Power and sovereignty imposed, as the philosopher Max Weber put it, an "ethic of responsibility" for the nation's freedom. This approach does not disregard moral restraints (what Weber calls the "ethics of moral conviction") but rather argues that they are not absolute. A countering moral claim for protecting or saving one's own people may, at times, challenge or even trump other ethical considerations.

"Ethics of responsibility" does not mean that the reality of warfare – and all international relations for that matter – dictates that countries should be guided by their interests alone. Such a "realist" attitude, attributed to figures like Thucydides or Machiavelli, readily acknowledges the hellishness of war and then concludes that "all is fair" to win this hell fight. Given the ethical sentiments against unnecessary bloodshed already cited by various rabbinic figures, it would be foolish to make such a claim within the Jewish tradition.

Instead, this moderate approach acknowledges the necessity of moral considerations in international affairs, yet asserts that either (a) national self-interest and partiality have moral weight to counter some ethical constraints, and/or (b) such moral constraints may be waived (as in the case of reprisals) to provide self-defense when one's opponents fail to abide by them.[3] A balance must be made between conflicting values, which can include choosing between two bad options.

One prominent philosopher called this a "moral blind alley," but the metaphor is misleading.[4] The test of leadership lies in making difficult decisions precisely in such circumstances. The best action to take – and therefore the moral one – might be something which would normally be seen as very wrong. This conundrum, known as the "dirty hands" dilemma, confronts leaders when they realize they might need to take an ostensibly immoral action (i.e., to get their hands dirty) because they are ethically obligated to prevent a greater harm to the larger collective.

Such considerations were already in discussion among rabbinic figures. R. Kook, in a somewhat theoretical epistolary debate in the midst of World War I, argued that some of the Torah's gravest prohibitions, like murder and suicide, are mandated if necessary to save the larger collective.[5] In limited circumstances, sinful behavior is not a sin. One may *feel* guilty afterward for that action, since it produced regrettable results, but one is not actually guilty or wrong for making that decision.[6] One might even argue, like the philosopher Michael Stocker, that is correct to *feel* regret in such circumstances because it shows that the person understood the gravity of the action.[7] Nonetheless, the path taken remains fully justified under the given circumstances.

As proof for his broader contention, R. Kook cited a well-trodden talmudic tradition that permits violating the law, as it were, for the sake of God (*aveira lishmah*). The talmudic Sages, he noted, had pondered that maybe God loves His Torah (i.e., the law) more than His people, but they taught otherwise: in extreme circumstances, the people take precedence over norms.[8] One of R. Kook's primary disciples, Rabbi Yaakov Moshe Charlap, even went so far as to assert that we learn this message from the biblical commandment to annihilate Amalek. This genocidal commandment, he suggested, was sinful behavior that was mandated as a temporary, emergency measure (*horaat shaa*).[9] Acting with dirty hands might sometimes be a divine command.

"DIRTY HANDS" AND THE LIMITS OF HUMAN RIGHTS

"Dirty hands dilemmas" greatly challenge many modern philosophers because much of contemporary discourse on military ethics stresses principles based on rights. Individuals are entitled to life and liberty, while states have rights of self-determination and territorial integrity. Using force against individuals or states is thus wrong because it violates their rights, unless they have previously forfeited those rights through their own illicit actions (i.e., an unethical act of aggression). Similarly, it is wrong to target civilians, because they have done nothing to abnegate their right to life and merit such treatment.

This process of thinking is sometimes called a "rights-based casuistic" method. Ethicists examine each case and determine which rights claims are most relevant or compelling in the given scenario. This approach now dominates philosophical discourse and "international humanitarian law" by placing human rights as its primary consideration.[10] This has meant, most significantly, that the laws were designed not just to reduce or minimize suffering "as far as possible" while each side attempted to win the war and protect their national interests. The new legal framework dictates that protecting the rights of civilians would override other considerations, including military interests. Indeed, as we'll explore in later chapters, many of these theorists assert that we must endanger our own soldiers in order to protect enemy noncombatants. Just-war theory demands of soldiers to take extra risks on themselves for the sake of limiting the scope of war.[11] Wavering on our absolute moral requirements on the basis of national interests and utilitarian calculations will easily lead to excusing mass killings, or as one prominent theorist put it, "a certain number of charred babies."[12]

The shift in just-war theory to prioritize individual rights was crystallized in the AP/1 protocols signed in 1977. Here's how one leading jurist described the change:

> The Protocol places primary emphasis on humanitarian demands and, indeed, in many respects subordinates military exigencies to such demands. On this score, the Protocol markedly departs from the customary law, which in general tends to put military necessity on the same footing as humanitarian demands.[13]

Many have shown that in earlier decades, humanitarian considerations were secondary to military exigencies. The laws of war acknowledged that the primary obligation was to win by overpowering the opponent and protecting one's own citizens and soldiers. As we'll see in the coming chapter, the classic set of priorities also dominates Jewish thought.

Yet even right-based theorists do not advocate for national suicide in the name of protecting human rights. On very limited occasions – when the heavens are going to fall, to invoke the Latin adage – they are willing to make exceptions to the rule of civilian immunity. In recent years, this argument is regularly invoked over torturing prisoners plotting a terrorist attack. How far can we go to procure information that can prevent a mass terror attack?[14]

The "ticking bomb" dilemma is just one of many scenarios known as "supreme emergencies." Michael Walzer, in a well-known essay, justified the British reprisal aerial bombings of German cities before 1942, even though there was little chance for the bombs to hit military targets, because the threats to Britain's very existence were too great to rule out that option. At times, political leadership entails choosing the lesser of two evils in order to protect the future of the collective. They have a moral obligation to get their hands dirty, so to speak, and choose between starkly competing moral claims. Yet not any threat qualifies as supreme emergency. A "special emergency" scenario requires the following conditions: (a) a group faces the grave threat of an evil such as massacre or enslavement; (b) conventional means, diplomatic or military, are unable to counter the threat; and (c) unconventional means normally absolutely forbidden can prevent the otherwise inevitable catastrophe.[15]

WAS 1938 A CASE OF "SUPREME EMERGENCY"?

Using this framework, let's think about the dilemma of the Jews in 1938 when they were regularly under attack in Palestine and Europe. It's obvious that the threat of the Holocaust fulfills condition (a) and that following the onset of World War II, there were no conventional means readily available to Jews to successfully thwart the Nazi threat, fulfilling condition (b). Did the Jews have an unconventional means (c) to prevent their catastrophe? Walzer, in a later essay on the ethics of terrorism, made the following remark regarding Jews in Germany:

> In rare and narrowly circumscribed cases, it may be possible, not to justify, but to find excuses for terrorism. I can imagine myself doing that in the hypothetical case of a terrorist campaign by Jewish militants against German civilians in the 1940s – if attacks on civilians had been likely (in fact they would have been highly unlikely) to stop the mass murder of the Jews.[16]

Thus Walzer concedes that on a theoretical level, Jewish terrorist attacks on German citizens would have been excusable under those circumstances. Yet he quickly notes that such Jewish attacks would have likely failed, and that in general, he has never found, in practice, a justified case of terrorism.

Let us now think of the situation of Jews in Palestine in 1936–39. In the "self-restraint" debate, the purported clash, at least in the political analysis of the Etzel, was between killing innocent Arabs or endangering one's own people by failing to respond at all. In such a circumstance, one must obviously first try to devise a strategy to save one's own without killing innocents. Yet in the face of no good alternatives, choosing the lesser evil, whatever one might deem that to be, is the correct choice – but only if it can effectively avert the greater evil (condition c).

Jabotinsky didn't see the Holocaust coming, but he had been warning for years about an impending disaster from rampant antisemitism in Europe. He even devised an extensive "evacuation plan" for mass immigration of Polish Jews to Palestine.[17] He procured the initial agreement of the Polish government to send hundreds of thousands of Jews to Palestine, a plan which was being thwarted by British refusals to increase immigration quotas alongside skepticism about the plan's viability from mainstream Zionist leaders.[18]

In July 1938, on Tisha B'Av, nine years to the day in which he had supported the march on the Western Wall in Jerusalem that preceded the 1929 riots, Jabotinsky began his aforementioned speech to a crowd in Warsaw with the following warning:

> For three years I have been imploring you, Jews of Poland, the crown of world Jewry, appealing to you, warning you unceasingly that *the catastrophe is nigh…* for my heart is bleeding that you, dear brothers and sisters, do not see the *volcano which will soon begin to spew forth its fires of destruction.* I see a horrible vision. *Time is growing short for you to be spared.* I know you cannot see it, for you are troubled and confused by everyday concerns…. Listen to my words at this, the twelfth hour. For God's sake: let everyone save himself, so long as there is time to do so, for time is running short.[19]

Three months later, the Nazi persecution of the Jews began with Kristallnacht on November 9, 1938. It was the same day in which the Woodhead Commission would release its findings and effectively table any plans to grant the Jews a state. In 1939, Jabotinsky even concocted a plan with Etzel leaders to try to take Palestine by force from the British and open the gates to Palestine for refugees fleeing Europe.[20]

In the same July 1938 speech, Jabotinsky also made a more interesting claim regarding the morality of reprisal killings. On the law books, he notes, it is illegal for someone to steal bread, even if the thief is poor and the victim is rich. Yet during a famine (i.e., a supreme emergency), when the thief steals the bread to survive, the law might still say this is a crime, yet a judge will nonetheless declare, "not guilty." So too, he asserted, there are times in which our high ethical conscience must go against the written law. Those who break the absolute "thou shall not murder" restraint policy will be deemed, at least by Jewish history, as "not guilty." This, at the very least, would be the opinion of the supreme divine Judge. Under these circumstances, as Jabotinsky would now argue, one must choose between bad options. He preferred to shoot, anyone, rather than be shot.

In this context, one understands why Ben-Gurion and Shertok thought it was so critical to prove that the reprisal killings were not effective. First, they harmed relations with the British, who remained the best source for defense and the only political option for achieving sovereignty. Second, there was no evidence that reprisal terror attacks would stop the Arab onslaught. Given these factors, at least in their minds, one could not argue that this was a necessary tactic of last resort or that it had a reasonable probability of success. Supreme emergency actions could not be justified.

WHO WAS RIGHT? THE "RESTRAINT VS. RESPONSE" DEBATE IN RETROSPECT

Who was right in the debate over the restraint policy? On a tactical level, it's hard to say. When it came to political strategy, this debate ultimately became moot with the outbreak of World War II. Jews felt that it was wise to minimize agitation in Palestine and joined the British efforts against the Germans. Raziel, as we'll see, was killed in Iraq while on a mission for the British army. Jabotinsky, for his part, traveled to America to campaign for a Jewish force to fight the Nazis. He died from a sudden heart attack in 1940 at a Betar self-defense camp in New York. When Menachem Begin renewed Etzel activity in 1944, his targets were British symbols of power. He explicitly stated that the goal was to avoid human casualties, and especially not to target civilians.

Thus it's difficult to know if the reprisal killings of Arabs between 1936 and 1939 did anything to protect Jews in Palestine during that period or expedite their gaining sovereignty. One could always argue that they would have been more effective had the Haganah joined the efforts as well. In a recent wide-ranging study on rebel groups, or freedom fighters, one scholar has argued that guerrilla attacks on military targets are much more effective than targeting civilians.[21] One of his many proofs, in fact, is the effectiveness of Etzel strikes on British military targets after World War II compared to the negative impact on the Zionist campaign from attacks that harmed civilians. For rebels, targeting military or political targets is critical; killing civilians is not effective. The broader findings will undoubtedly be disputed. Yet the very claim serves as a poignant reminder that responding to terror with morally questionable tactics may not always be a good or necessary strategy, let alone an ethical one.

Such cautionary claims are particularly important to remember since the claim of "supreme emergency" can be widely abused and utilized even when other options are available. Indeed, apologists for terror groups have utilized this argument to justify many barbaric actions. Those sympathetic to the tactics of the Etzel should also remember that a similar line of reasoning could be manipulated to justify Arab terror attacks on Jews and Brits during the same time period or, for that matter, Palestinian bombings today from the Gaza Strip.[22] Palestinian terrorism on civilians has also not proven to be particularly effective, as Israelis regularly respond with greater fortitude and a willingness to fight back. As Michael Gross has argued, "Terrorism has done little to advance the Palestinian cause, publicize their grievances, or delegitimize their opponent. Just as civilians in World War II were not demoralized by terror bombing but, in fact, resolved to fight on, Israeli citizens overcome terror attacks."[23]

Nonetheless, the category of supreme emergency highlights the argument that saving the larger collective, in fact, may, on very rare occasions, override some of our deeply-held moral commitments. Yet this is only if it is truly an option of last resort and has a reasonable chance for success. Such calculations require a keen strategic assessment along with a dose of humility.

A LESSON FROM JEWISH HISTORY: JEWISH BLOOD CANNOT BE CHEAP!

Whatever one's take on the *havlaga* strategy, all agree that Jews must respond to attacks on them, in one form or another. Nations cannot react passively to attacks on their people. The historical experience of Jewish powerlessness created another moral imperative in Jewish thought: Jewish blood cannot be cheap! This message can be extracted from classical texts but was ultimately internalized through the lesson books of

Jewish history. For if there is anything that the exilic experience teaches it is that Jews must be willing to do what it takes to protect themselves.

This lesson was dramatically articulated by an American Zionist theologian, Rabbi Joseph B. Soloveitchik, a few years after Israel was founded.

> When God smote the Egyptians, He sought to demonstrate that there will always be accountability for the spilling of Jewish blood. At present, it is necessary not only to convince the dictator of Egypt [Nasser], but the self-righteous Nehru, the Foreign Office in London, and the sanctimonious members of the United Nations, that Jewish blood is not cheap.[24]

The question then becomes what means Jews will employ to prove that Jewish blood isn't cheap. Sovereignty brings with it responsibilities both toward one's own people and their enemies. The "dirty hands" dilemma does not simply disappear. How dirty are Jews willing for their hands to get? The dilemma, as we saw, is particularly acute when their enemies seem to play by no rules, raising the specter of bloody reprisals.

The dilemma gets further complicated when dealing with cases that are not supreme emergencies. The question of reprisal killings reemerged in the 1950s, and it was in this context that R. Soloveitchik made his claim about Jewish blood not being cheap. This time, however, it was not with respect to Jewish underground fighters, but rather regarding the Israeli national armed forces protecting their sovereignty. While the moral issues were somewhat like those in the 1930s, the stakes were different now because the Jewish fighters were not just rebels or insurgents. They were official representatives of the State of Israel protecting their people's sovereignty. As we'll see in the next chapter, the IDF was acting from a place of greater power and without the constraints of British rulers. They now had to make the moral decision if they'd behave differently from the standards set – but frequently not followed – by the community of nations.

Chapter 6

Must Jews Fight with Higher Moral Standards? The Debate over Kibiyeh

KIBIYEH AND THE RETURN OF REPRISAL ATTACKS

On the morning of October 13, 1953, a grenade was lobbed into a home in Yehud, Israel, killing a thirty-two-year-old mother, Susan Kanias, and her two children, aged four years and eighteen months. This was only the latest terror attack in Israel's young history. Arab *fedayeen* (irregular) fighters were constantly raiding Israel from the porous borders of Gaza, then controlled by Egypt, and the West Bank, then controlled by Jordan. In the previous six months alone, twenty-nine civilians and two soldiers had been killed by infiltrators from Jordanian territory.[1] The Israeli public was fed up. Diplomacy and defensive measures against these raids were not working. Despite their newfound sovereignty, Jewish blood still felt cheap.

The IDF responded by creating an elite commando force, Unit 101, that would launch reprisal raids against the infiltrators. Its leader was Ariel Sharon, a bold army commander who was recruited out of a short-lived retirement. After the murder in Yehud, Sharon marched his men into the village of Kibiyeh, which the IDF had deemed as a frequent infiltrator base. The result was gory: roughly seventy dead Arabs, with approximately two-thirds of them women and children.

It's undisputed that the commandos were ordered to kill all members of the Home Guard and any army reinforcements as well as blow up major buildings and houses in the town.[2] The revisionist historian Benny Morris claims that the orders, in fact, were to carry out maximum killing to drive the inhabitants out of the village.[3] Others, however, assert that the civilian casualties were a result of the houses not being properly searched before being blown up. There was never intent to harm civilians.[4] If that's the case, the alleged moral error of not taking proper precautionary measures would be less egregious. As the legal scholar William V. O'Brien put it, "The means employed in the raid were indiscriminate, not because there was intention to kill noncombatants but because there was a failure to take reasonable measures to assure that they would not be killed."[5] This was certainly the claim made then in public Israeli discourse.

The policy of reprisal attacks was meant to deter cross-border raids and push the Arab states to control their side of the border. Moshe Dayan, appointed as IDF chief of staff in December 1953, acknowledged this approach in a 1955 essay for foreign audiences. He compared the response to Arab riots in the 1920s and 1930s with recent Israeli responses.

> In these conflicts [i.e., in the 1920s and '30s], it was the policy of the Jewish authorities, upheld by the bulk of the community, to abstain from retaliation. The same restraint was maintained when after the establishment of the State of Israel, the old guerrilla attacks and marauding expeditions were resumed. Tension in the border areas, however, has of late become so acute as sometimes to result in a breakdown of that traditional attitude.[6]

While purposely cryptic in this statement, it seems clear that Dayan himself was one of the leading military figures who supported the "breakdown of this traditional attitude," both before and after his appointment as chief of staff. According to Yigal Alon, Dayan expressed his strategy in the following way.

We cannot save each water pipe from explosion or each tree from being uprooted. We cannot prevent the murder of workers in orange groves or of families in their beds. But we can put a very high price on their blood, a price so high that it will no longer be worthwhile for the Arabs, the Arab armies, for the Arab states to pay it.[7]

Dayan, as we'll recall, served in the 1930s under Orde Wingate in the Special Night Squads and was greatly influenced by his tactics and tutelage, a point which comes through in this quote and many others. He firmly believed that such tactics of targeted collective punishment were effective. While some have questioned their efficacy, many historians have contended that they had some success in getting the Jordanians to better control their side of the border, at least in the short term.[8]

The policy, according to one of Ben-Gurion's assistants, was pithy and simple: An "eye for an eye."[9] Beyond deterrence, the strategy also sought to placate Israeli fears that Jews could still be killed with no one held accountable. Rabbi Soloveitchik, in his 1956 speech cited at the end of the last chapter that Jewish blood is not cheap, would later make this point:

> For the first time in the annals of our exile, Divine Providence has amazed our enemies with the astounding discovery that Jewish blood is not cheap! If the antisemites describe this phenomenon as being "an eye for an eye," we will agree with them. If we want to courageously defend our continued national and historical existence, we must, from time to time, interpret the verse of an "eye for an eye" literally. So many "eyes" were lost in the course of our bitter exile because we did not repay hurt for hurt.... With respect to the Mufti and Nasser I would demand that we interpret the verse in accordance with its literal meaning – the taking of an actual eye!
>
> Pay no attention to the saccharine suggestions of known assimilationists and of some Jewish socialists who stand pat in their rebelliousness and think they are still living in Bialystok, Brest-Litovsk, and Minsk of the year 1905, and openly declare that revenge is forbidden to the Jewish people in any place, at

any time, and under all circumstances. "Vanity of vanities!" (Ecclesiastes 1:2).

> *Revenge is forbidden when it is pointless, but if one is aroused thereby to self-defense, it is the most elementary right of man to take his revenge.*[10]

Once again, the question remained whether such a revenge (or reprisal) policy could deliver security. This, in part, depended on whom the IDF would now target, particularly when the actual infiltrators were not known.

Unfortunately, beyond the murkiness of what exactly happened in Kibiyeh, responses to the incident at the time were also somewhat skewed by the official Israeli response. The embarrassed Ben-Gurion would not admit that this was an official IDF action and blamed Jewish inhabitants of border settlements for the raid. Thus MK Rabbi Yitzhak Meir Levin went on the Knesset floor to condemn border residents for not living up to the standards of Jewish ethics, even as he censured the world for their hypocritical condemnation of Israel that overlooked the background to the attack.[11]

ABRAHAM VERSUS JOSHUA? CONFLICTING VALUES IN BIBLICAL STORIES

The leader of the Mizrachi political party, Haim-Moshe Shapira, did not accept such excuses. While publicly toeing the government line, Shapira was privately outraged by the Kibiyeh attack. Shapira sharply censured the military actions in a cabinet meeting, contrasting this approach to the restraint shown in the 1930s when the Haganah refused to fight terror with terror.

> Throughout the years we were always against this. Not just today. Even when there were murders of Jews in the Land of Israel, which was quite common before the founding of the State of Israel, we know how many were killed week after week, month after month. Yet we have never said, "Let the innocent be swept away with the guilty" (Gen. 18:23).[12]

Shapira buttressed his claim by citing the argument that Abraham had with God before the destruction of Sodom. The innocent should not be killed in an act of collective punishment.

Remarkably, this biblical reference led to a spirited exchange between secular government ministers over the lasting value of biblical stories. In response to Shapira's claim that Jews cannot act this way, the health minister, Yosef Serlin, interjected, "In the times of Joshua we didn't act this way?", referring to destruction of Canaanite cities, as discussed in chapter 2. Sharett, then foreign minister, replied, "Are we living in the times of Joshua?" Ben-Gurion tried intervening, "Don't try to compete with biblical verses – there are all sorts of verses." While known as a lover of the Bible and inspired by the book of Joshua in particular,[13] Ben-Gurion did not think it could be invoked to resolve such moral disputes, a theme which we saw in the last chapter regarding his dispute with Rabbi Maimon.

Shapiro, in any case, retorted that we wouldn't do things today that we did in the times of Joshua. "In the times of Joshua, we had the story of Achan – would we do that today?"[14] Yet he then conceded, "Let's not bring proof from Israelite history – all of us could bring different types of proofs." Shapira, it seems, was willing to grant that Jewish sources could be garnered toward different approaches. He preferred for the IDF to follow in the ways of Abraham at Sodom and not Joshua in Canaan.

The cabinet debate points to a central dilemma in formulating Jewish military ethics: if each side can invoke a countering biblical verse or rabbinic source, does Judaism add much to this debate? As we saw in chapter 5, this was the broader challenge raised by Ben-Gurion in his reply to Rabbis Amiel and Herzog in 1938 and now reiterated in 1953. Shapira presented a model, albeit somewhat inchoate, to resolve the tensions between competing ethical trends in Jewish sources. One needs to decide which ideas are the dominating moral polestars and which concepts can be deemed dormant, or at the very least, of secondary importance. Some values, he argued, are more compelling than others. The Jewish people need to choose which Jewish values they'll live by.

YESHAYAHU LEIBOWITZ AND THE HYPOCRISY OF
WORLD CONDEMNATION

While the cabinet members argued over biblical verses, Israeli religious intellectuals were debating a more fundamental question: must Israel behave differently than any other nation in the world? The reprisal attack on Kibiyeh, the philosopher Yeshayahu Leibowitz noted, followed common international practice. International leaders could easily criticize the Jewish state because they didn't bear the responsibilities of defending her, while they hypocritically ignored their actions to defend their own countries. After all, at Hiroshima and Nagasaki, the Americans took vengeance for the horrors of Pearl Harbor in order to suppress a ruthless enemy and end a seemingly endless war. In Leibowitz's words:

> We can, indeed, justify the action of Kibiyeh before "the world." Its spokesmen and leaders admonish us for having adopted the method of "reprisal" – cruel mass punishment of innocent people for the crimes of others in order to prevent their recurrence, a method which has been condemned by the conscience of the world.
>
> We could argue that we have not behaved differently than did the Americans.... America saw herself in the fourth year of a war she had not initiated, and after the loss of a quarter of a million of her sons, facing the prospect of continued war in the style of Iwo Jima and Okinawa for an unforeseeable period of time...
>
> We, too, are now in the sixth year of a war that was forced upon us and continues to inspire constant fear of plunder and murder. No wonder that border settlers and those responsible for their life and security overreacted and reciprocated with cruel slaughter and destruction.[15]

Even if the IDF soldiers had premeditatively killed everyone, we could justify this action. And yet, he concludes, "Let us not try to do so."

If the raid on Kibiyeh was indeed justifiable by international standards, then why not defend it? Leibowitz's answer seems to be that even if one can rationalize or excuse a certain violent action, it may ultimately be corruptive behavior that will lead to accursed behavior.

Excessive Jewish violence, he argues, occurred because Jews have come to sanctify the state. This allows them to justify any actions done for the greater good. How else, he wonders, can you explain how a generation of soldiers "felt no inhibition or inner compunction in performing the atrocity when given the inner urge and external occasion for retaliation?" Nationalist militarism, even when justifiable, corrupts our soul and our sword.[16]

For Leibowitz and others, this would be a telling moment: could Jews successfully utilize power without falling into the moral trappings that led Christianity and Islam into many centuries of bloody warfare? As the philosopher Ernst Simon noted then, this challenge was already highlighted by the twelfth-century philosopher Rabbi Judah HaLevi. In his imagined dialogue between a rabbi and a gentile king, the former criticized religions that originally preached "turning the other cheek" yet ultimately utilized horrific warfare. The king, however, rejected this critique, and shot back, "If you had power, you too would slay!"[17] Indeed, as we saw in the last chapter, Rabbi Maimon asserted that Jews never had any pretensions to "turn the other cheek," if we only had power.

For Leibowitz, the challenge for Israel was to find the right balance between necessary defense and militarism. "Ethical postulates" were necessary to help Israel use its newfound power both wisely and morally. In his mind, such ethical guidelines would not necessarily come from the sources of Judaism since morality is universal and not subject to adjectives like "Jewish." Only a profound sense of ethical commitments will prevent us from taking God's name in vain and using the Bible to justify such bloodshed.

This call for holding ourselves to higher standards, however, was rejected by other religious thinkers.[18] Rabbi Shlomo Zalman Shragai, for example, argued that Israel simply had no choice but to respond to Arab belligerence. All Israelis, he argued, regretted "the blood that they were forced to shed in Kibiyeh."[19] Yet ultimately responsibility lay with the *fedayeen* infiltrators and their Arab sponsors who utilized these raids for their own political purposes.

More fundamentally, the blood of the Arab victims was "not redder" than that of the hundreds of Israelis killed in recent years by *fedayeen* infiltrators. Shragai was invoking a well-known talmudic passage that addresses the following dilemma: if you are told at gunpoint to murder someone innocent or be killed, you must be killed rather than violate the prohibition of murder. After all, "Who says that your blood is redder than that of the other person?"[20] The logic in the Talmud is that you can't save yourself by doing the same heinous act – murder – that someone would do to you. It's ironic for Shragai to cite this principle. The premise of reprisal killings was that on the collective level, one may kill the innocent in retaliation, with the goal of preventing the further killing of one's own people. In national conflicts, it seems, your own people's blood is redder than others.

Kibiyeh, in his mind, was not revenge, but rather an act of self-defense and deterrence that followed international practices. Western powers condemned Israel but conveniently ignored the fact that they offered no true alternative. Advocates of international humanitarian law, as we saw in chapter 3, argue that the creation of international bodies of justice makes the need for reprisal attacks archaic. Yet in practice, the UN and other institutions were at best powerless or unwilling to act. Indeed, as the legalist O'Brien noted, the pristine model of international resolution to such disputes was utterly divorced from reality, and certainly in the 1950s.[21] In the eyes of R. Shragai, reprisal attacks were the only reprieve. Jews need to protect themselves in the same way that everyone else does.

Yet one may ask: don't Jewish sources teach, contra both Leibowitz and Shragai, that Jews must behave differently? After all, Judaism traditionally portrays itself as an exemplar to the world that can serve as a light unto the nations. Does Judaism have a unique moral teaching about war? It's to this question that we'll turn in the next chapter.

Chapter 7

Moral Standards: Ethics or Conventions?

RABBI SHAUL YISRAELI: ISRAEL IS BOUND ONLY TO INTERNATIONAL CONVENTIONS

In the wake of Kibiyeh, one prominent decisor declared that the standards of international behavior alone are precisely what Jewish law demands of Jewish soldiers. No less, but no more. This provocative thesis was suggested by Rabbi Shaul Yisraeli (1909–95), who penned the most influential rabbinic essay to be written on Jewish military ethics.[1] He concluded with a startling thesis: Judaism does not have a unique moral teaching about how to behave in war.

The early life of R. Yisraeli was deeply shaped by the political tumult of the interwar years in Belarus. His father, a distinguished rabbi, was exiled to Siberia by the Communists for teaching Torah. He was never heard from again. The young son followed in his father's footsteps and studied in secret "underground" academies, going from one to the next as the Communist authorities continued to suppress Jewish learning. In 1933, he attempted to flee the Communist regime but was caught by Polish border guards. The elder Rabbi Kook, however, was able to intervene and secure R. Yisraeli a visa to emigrate to Palestine. R. Yisraeli would become one of R. Kook's last students; a few decades later, he was appointed as the head of the seminary founded by his teacher and became a member of Israel's Supreme Rabbinic Court.

R. Yisraeli purposely doesn't address the specific actions taken in Kibiyeh, perhaps because of the murkiness of the details.[2] Instead, he speaks to the larger ethical issues of reprisal attacks. In contrast to Leibowitz, R. Yisraeli believed that reprisals, even if motivated by revenge, are legitimate acts of self-defense. He cites a fascinating biblical passage (Numbers 31) in which Moses led the Israelites in a war of *nekama*, usually translated as "revenge" or "retribution" but perhaps best understood here as "reprisal." The Midianites were blamed for enticing the Jewish people to engage in illicit relations and causing a plague; in response, they were wiped out. According to a late midrashic statement, this war serves as a paradigm for the general need for collective self-defense. "If one comes to slay you, rise and kill first."[3] Vengeance – which is normally seen as a vice – is mandated to defend the entire people.[4]

Wartime norms also permit other behavior which would normally be viewed as problematic. In war, we accept the inevitable (even if unintentional) killing of enemy citizens who are not directly threatening you, something which we would not tolerate in a protean case of individual self-defense. In truth, he notes, some of the Kibiyeh residents could be treated as combatants for supporting and aiding organized *fedayeen* raiders. Yet this legal reasoning certainly would not support targeting children (who are unambiguously noncombatants) or punishing them after the cessation of hostilities. R. Yisraeli further notes that one cannot easily treat town residents as belligerents. After all, their assistance to the *fedayeen* may stem from coercive social pressure. So why does Judaism permit such inevitable bloodshed?

R. Yisraeli's answer is quite surprising: the international community allows it. Since the earliest periods of the Bible, the nations of the world have agreed that warfare, despite its violence, is an acceptable manner of dispute resolution. Jewish law does not have an independent teaching regarding the laws of wartime behavior (what philosophers call *jus in bello*). Instead, it relies on the international norms in the given period. Agreement by the nations of the world, after all, is what allows such collective bloodshed in the first place. Consequently, Jews may act in warfare just as everyone else does. The test for Kibiyeh is whether other nations behave similarly. As he writes,

> In war there is no need to be meticulous and differentiate between righteous and wicked because the nature of war does not make it possible to be meticulous. Moreover, war [conducted] in this way is permitted as long as this conduct [in war] is accepted among the nations.
>
> Therefore, with regard to the matter under discussion (i.e., reprisal attacks), one must examine if a [military] response of this kind is supported and accepted among the nations, because [if it is accepted] one would have to view it as [something agreed upon by] a consensus on behalf of all those [nations] involved in the matter [of war], and there would be nothing about it involving the [prohibition against] the shedding of blood.[5]

Accordingly, he goes on to say, if all nations would agree to ban war and follow that regulation, it would be forbidden according to Jewish law to declare war. The current state of geopolitics and international law, however, shows that the "generation is not ready" for such a declaration (a point discussed in chapter 3). In the absence of such a declaration, however, warfare remains permissible which, by its nature, will lead to the loss of innocent life.

WHY DON'T WE TARGET ENEMY CHILDREN? THE WEAKNESS OF CONVENTIONS

R. Yisraeli's thesis is attractive because it forces Israel to maintain international standards as a matter of religious obligation, without the difficulty of trying to determine the source for such values. The debate over the implications of competing biblical sentiments becomes largely moot. Jews must follow international standards just as they obey, in their civil lives, the law of the land. Moses and Joshua followed the standards of their times, and so should the IDF.

Yet the thought that Jewish law has no independent regulations on wartime behavior remains deeply troubling. Judaism sees itself as being a leader, not a follower, in ethical standards. Moreover, it implies

that Jewish law would permit targeting noncombatants, including children, if international norms allowed such behavior, or at the very least
tolerated it in practice.

R. Yisraeli pulls back from this conclusion by rejecting the war
with the Midianites as an unequivocal precedent. In that war, Moses
insisted that the Israelites should kill all male children and adult women.
Is this a paradigm for Jewish military ethics? What if the world would
now adopt the methods used against the Midianites as its operating
standard – would Jewish law then permit it?

R. Yisraeli deems this as unfathomable. While the Bible elsewhere
does mandate wiping out an entire idolatrous Israelite city (as discussed
in chapter 2), this is not meant to set an example for wartime behavior. The Midianite war was legitimate, but not all the tactics should be
emulated. As he writes,

> There is room for [military] operations of retaliation and revenge
> against those who assail Israel and an operation of this kind is
> in the category of mandatory war. And whatever disaster and
> harm is inflicted on the [enemy] perpetrators [of violence], their
> associates, and their children, it is their very own responsibility,
> and they will bear their sin. And there is no obligation to avoid
> [military] operations of retaliation because of the concern that
> the innocent will be harmed, for it is not we who are the cause [of
> this harm], but they themselves [i.e., the enemy]; we are guiltless.
>
> However, *regarding the intention to harm children from the
> outset, this is something we have not found [in the Jewish tradition]*
> except with the sin of idol-worship. Therefore, one should take
> care not to harm them.[6]

Children should never be targeted, he concludes, even as we recognize
that they sometimes are tragically killed during the process. The same
principle would prohibit targeting any adults who were not complicit
in any enemy activity, even as it may be at times difficult to define what
makes someone a combatant or noncombatant, as R. Yisraeli noted
in the case of Kibiyeh.[7] In any case, R. Yisraeli thinks Jewish law has
declared targeting children as inherently illegitimate. Yet it's unclear

how he derived this principle of "child immunity" beyond postulating that there is no precedent for killing children, especially since the Bible provides ample examples of it.

THE MISTAKEN TEMPTATION OF MORAL CONVENTIONS

R. Yisraeli was not the only thinker to struggle with the suggestion that wartime ethics derive from widely accepted norms. In the mid-1970s, the philosopher George Mavrodes similarly claimed that the legal obligation not to target noncombatants is dependent on conventional behavior, not ethical imperatives.[8] Many theorists, he noted, treated the immunity of noncombatants as a moral fact, based on a Judeo-Christian ethos that condemns those "whose feet are swift to shed innocent blood."[9] Yet are combatants always "guilty" and noncombatants so "innocent"? Take, for example, the case of two neighbors. John is a patriotic, enthusiastic backer of the war who also works in an industry that supports the war effort and profits handsomely from it. Bruce is poor with little curiosity about the politics of the war and no real interest to kill or die for its cause. Yet John is both fifty and physically impaired, so he cannot fight on the battlefield. Bruce is eighteen and mighty so the army drafts him into a combat unit. Why is Bruce more morally culpable than John? Some will reasonably retort that willy-nilly, Bruce wears a uniform that designates him as an official representative of a warring collective. He also carries a rifle, and however reluctant he might be to use it, that makes him a more proximate threat than your regular citizen. Yet it's also true that John, even without wearing a uniform or bearing a weapon, is also participating in the war effort and contributes toward the threat against the opposite side. The same could be argued of civilians who work in critical war-industries, such as manufacturing guns or supplying food for the front lines. (The status of such workers will be discussed at length in later chapters.) The line, then, between civilian and soldier is blurry, raising the question of how strong the moral distinction remains between combatant and noncombatant.

Mavrodes, nonetheless, contends that the norm of civilian immunity should be maintained because it helps reduce the hellish costs of warfare. This is a positivist rule that has moral grounding but is ultimately obligatory because civilized countries have developed a convention for maintaining this distinction. International agreement makes it wrong. The law might be based on disputable moral grounds. Yet we should uphold it for its useful benefits in reducing the destruction of warfare. Should countries agree upon different conventions of warfare, then those would become binding, and the old rule would no longer be obligatory because its moral basis was always shaky.

WHAT HAPPENS WHEN ONE SIDE BREAKS THE RULES? THE CHALLENGE OF RECIPROCITY

The problem with this approach, however, is that the agreements are quite susceptible to being broken by one side, thereby removing all restraints – legal and moral – from the other party. For if we admit that the ethical claims are tenuous and the legal agreement is dependent on reciprocity, little is left to prevent unmitigated bloodshed.

Mavrodes suggests that one side might undertake unilateral restraint for a time to try to cajole their opponent to reciprocate and form (or reaffirm) a new conventional restraint. If that fails, however, then the side is entitled to "reevaluate" their policies. As critics have argued, Mavrodes seems to invite that party to no longer uphold non-combatant immunity, thereby undermining a central aspect of just-war theory's restrictions on wartime behavior.[10]

This challenge for contractarian theorists has only become more acute in the twenty-first century, because the rise of asymmetric warfare has accentuated two troubling phenomena. First, the line between civilians and noncombatants is purposely blurred by terrorists, especially when acting for national liberation movements. Second, the stated unwillingness of terrorist groups to follow rules of wartime behavior, including respect for noncombatant immunity, has broken down any hope for the reciprocal adoption of traditional restraints. In the absence of reciprocity, it's not clear why the other side should also follow those rules.[11] As one leading theorist put it, "It is rational for each side in a conflict to adhere to them only if the other side does. Thus if one side breaches the understanding that the conventions will be followed, it may cease to be rational or morally required for the other side to persist in its adherence to them."[12] These dilemmas created by the lack of reciprocity, of course, were already understood within Israel during the 1950s.

Some proponents of international law will claim that it was precisely these types of dilemmas that the Geneva AP/1 protocols came to resolve. Even when the other side acts illegitimately, reprisals against all civilians are illegal. Yet as one leading proponent of international law has noted, such expectations are unrealistic. As he put it, "What do the framers of the Protocol expect State B to do? Turn the other cheek? That is a religious tenet rather than a serious military or political proposition."[13] The entire system of international law, he feared, will collapse if countries find their standards to be unfair or unrealistic. For this reason, some philosophers have suggested that it would be justified for a country to respond "in kind" to egregious violations. By giving them a taste of their own medicine, so to speak, you might restore good behavior on all sides. The Israeli philosophers Daniel Statman and Yitzhak Benbaji, two leading advocates of the contractarian model, even suggest that when one side targets noncombatants, the other party may relax the conventional rules of civilian immunity by targeting "involved civilians" such as politicians.[14] Yet children and the elderly remain off-limits. But why? Ultimately, one must go back to some form of base morality.

Conventions thus seem too tenuous as a sole basis for military ethics. Their underlying logic is not always compelling, and they lose much of their force when aggressive parties refuse to play by the rules. That being the case, we must return to fundamental moral values, not positive law or conventional practices, to explain why we must avoid targeting noncombatants even though our enemies will not reciprocate.

ETHICAL REASONS TO NEVER TARGET CIVILIANS

There are three fundamental rationales why, barring a supreme emergency (discussed in chapter 5), soldiers should never target uninvolved noncombatants:

1. *Personal virtue and martial honor:* Soldiers refrain from horrific acts not because of treaties or human rights but because of obligations that we have to ourselves. For many, this includes the idea that soldiers, for the sake of their own conscience or the honor of their country, do not indiscriminately kill noncombatants for no purpose. Virtue has always played an important role in military culture. The eminent military historian John Keegan, in fact, goes so far as to say that this is the

only true factor of restraint on the battlefield. "There is no substitute for honor as a medium of enforcing decency on the battlefield – never has been and never will be."[15]

Such a notion draws from an admonition given to soldiers in the book of Deuteronomy. "When you go out as a troop against your enemies, be on your guard against anything untoward." The Sages understood this verse as a warning for soldiers to avoid acts of murder, sexual immorality, blasphemy, and even gossip. One prominent medieval commentator, Nahmanides, noted that military men will perform all sorts of immoral abominations, with even the most righteous figures donning the traits of cruelty and rage when they fight their enemies. It's precisely at this moment when we need to instill within ourselves the moral stamina to avoid the evil excesses of wartime behavior.[16]

Indeed, the failure to maintain this virtuous character led to the downfall of the greatest military general in Israelite history. Joab was a bold and courageous warrior who saved King David's reign on multiple occasions while leading many glorious battle victories. Yet he and his sons lacked the self-discipline to stop killing when it was no longer necessary. They took bloody vengeance against allies for whom they held personal grudges. At the end of his days, King David himself would condemn Joab as a firebrand who "sheds blood of war in peacetime, staining the girdle of his loins and the sandals on his feet with blood of war."[17] The once-glorious military leader would be killed while grabbing onto the corners of the sacrificial altar. The House of God does not provide sanctuary to anyone who unnecessarily spills blood.

2. *National exceptionalism*: A related claim asserts that we cannot fight against evil in a way that makes us lose our own exceptional identity and principles. That's not "who we are," so to speak. Thus, US Senator John McCain, who was a POW during the Vietnam War, would argue, "When the principle of reciprocity does not apply, we must instead remember the principles by which our nation conducts its affairs…. Were we to abandon the principles of wartime conduct to which we have freely committed ourselves, we would lose the moral standing that has made America unique in the world."[18] Even when our enemies show no such inhibitions, our code of honor calls for a higher standard, including

to refrain from attacking noncombatants. This is critically important for how we see ourselves, let alone how others see us.

In previous chapters, we have seen how the notion of preserving God's reputation was central to Jewish conceptions of national honor. Figures like R. Shragai, R. Herzog, R. Maimon, R. Uziel, and Leibowitz argued about how *exceptional* our standards must be compared to our enemies. Yet there remains a clear aspiration for highest *possible* standards, even in complicated periods when circumstances might force us to get our hands dirty and commit morally complex actions. On this basis, one might argue that it is unfathomable to target children and other noncomplicit civilians, even as a reprisal. Nahmanides, in his above-cited comments, takes this type of argument to another level: we are worthy of God's support only when we behave distinctly. Once the Israelites stoop to the level of their enemies, they will no longer merit to dwell in the Holy Land.

3. *Inherent human dignity*: The ultimate antidote to killing uninvolved citizens is to remember that all human beings were created in the image of God. This is a theological tenet, as we saw in chapter 4, which has direct ethical implications. The military figure who emphasized this is none other than the IDF's first head chaplain, Major General Rabbi Shlomo Goren.

RABBI SHLOMO GOREN AND THE DEVELOPMENT OF JEWISH MILITARY ETHICS

R. Goren was born in Poland toward the end of World War I. His parents, fleeing both hunger and pogroms, moved to Palestine when he was a young boy. R. Goren fought with the Haganah and later the IDF during the War of Independence and developed close relationships with many of Israel's political and military leaders. He served for twenty years as chief military chaplain in the IDF before becoming the State of Israel's Ashkenazic chief rabbi. In his multivolume work on Jewish military law, *Response to War: Responsa on Matters of the Military, War, and Security*, he asserted, in contrast to R. Yisraeli, that one could determine definitive teachings from Jewish sources on a broad range of issues like universal conscription, applying the death penalty to terrorists, laying sieges to cities, and civilian immunity.[19]

When it came to the issue of targeting noncombatants, R. Goren argued that the Torah commands us to be merciful to all, and especially not to target noncombatants and certainly innocent civilians like "women and children." Tellingly, in contrast to Rabbi Maimon, who cited the biblical story of destroying Shechem to justify the Etzel's actions in the 1930s, R. Goren asserted that we should draw the opposite conclusion from this story.[20] The Bible, he notes, gave the final word to Jacob, who many years later still denounced the vengeance of his sons, not just for endangering them, but also for its moral decadence.

> Their weapons are tools of lawlessness. Let not my person be included in their council, let not my being be counted in their assembly. For when angry, they slay men; and when pleased, they maim oxen. Cursed be their anger so fierce, and their wrath so relentless.[21]

Their lack of self-control, Jacob asserted, makes them unfit to serve as the virtuous leaders, for indiscriminate violence, even in reprisal for a vicious act like the rape of Dinah, cannot be condoned. As for the commandment to wipe out the seven Canaanite nations, including their families, R. Goren contends that this was a onetime commandment which does not represent a model for later generations.[22]

These statements were a part of a larger methodological approach which highlighted certain humanistic tendencies while minimizing other passages that could be understood as expressing indifference to deaths on the enemy side. The overarching principle is set by verses like "And he was merciful on all His creatures." God desires the victory of the Jewish people but does not celebrate the death of any of His creatures. Jewish law values all lives, even as some enemies must be regretfully killed to achieve military success. He went so far as to assert that biblical commandments like "Do not stand idly over your neighbor's blood" impose a moral requirement on military commanders to avoid causing unnecessary harm on enemy territory. He thus systematically understood certain verses or stories to establish general principles while relegating others to yesteryear, or at the very least, to specific circumstances.[23]

This approach helps explain the feelings that he had for his own paramilitary experience. In the period after World War II, R. Goren left the Haganah to join the Lehi movement in Jerusalem. His small apartment, in fact, was used to hide weapons. His brother, by his own admission, carried out attacks that killed Arabs. While supportive of the Lehi attacks on the British (the focus of their activities in this period), he held grave reservations about attacks on random Arabs who had committed no crimes. As he wrote in his autobiography,

> Truth be told, I did not agree with all of the Lehi's actions. I was against the murder of Arabs just because they were Arabs. I objected to the murder of people who had committed no crime against the Jews. We had many ideological arguments. After all, I was a rabbi, and we had our moral standards, the Torah's moral standards, according to which every person is created in God's image. Therefore, I believed we must be merciful and respect every person's life, as long as he is not a danger to us and is not fighting us. To me, the main struggle was against the British government, which had closed the gates of Eretz Yisrael to the immigrants who had wanted to escape the Holocaust in Europe.[24]

R. Goren here beautifully articulates the restraints he believes are imposed by the Torah on belligerent reprisals in particular and nationalistic movements in general: even in times of conflict, one cannot forget that all humans are created in the image of God. R. Goren invokes this notion to establish an important rule of Jewish military ethics: in the midst of a collective battle, we should avoid targeting uninvolved nonbelligerents, because they too were created in the image of God.[25]

This fundamental moral stand, built on religious humanism, highlights a crucial aspect of the relationship between religion and nationalism. Many fear, as did Leibowitz, that the combination of these two powerful social forces can unleash unfettered violence. Yet in our case, it shows how religion can provide a powerful shield against the excesses of nationalism. By affirming the prohibition of "You shall not murder," even against citizens of our enemies, Jewish law provides a sharp reminder that there are limits to the steps we take toward nationalist goals. It's not only a reminder that sometimes the ends don't justify the means, but also that the Torah may help bridle the forces of national liberation and sovereignty to achieve its lofty – and ethical – goals.

Chapter 8

The Jewish Multivalue Framework for Military Ethics

DOES JUDAISM HAVE A MORAL TEACHING ABOUT WAR?

The varying Zionist perspectives on reprisals, made in the name of Judaism, raises the question of how successfully Jewish wisdom can provide definitive answers to complex dilemmas. As we saw, Ben-Gurion didn't think the Jewish tradition could provide conclusive answers about fighting. This was not only because these classic Jewish sources originated in very different eras and contexts, but also because they are full of conflicting notions. Does the sixth commandment "Do not murder" guide our deliberations? Or the paradigm of Amalek? Until now, we've seen a lot of values invoked: the divine image found in all human beings, self-defense, the standards necessary for dwelling in Israel, sanctifying God's name and the nation's honor, international conventions, and the collective nature of warfare. These values are all rooted in classical Jewish sources and represent a legitimate Jewish value. Given the ways in which they might lead to very different conclusions, one might assume that Jewish sources cannot offer too much advice with contemporary relevance.

Some might even claim that the religious texts are essentially invoked in order to consecrate previously held ideological beliefs. Choose whatever answer you want, and you can find a Jewish source to defend it. Jewish values aren't driving people's behavior; instead, Jewish texts are being used to support political decisions. At the very least, the relationship between religion and politics is complex, with one supporting the other and leading to very different perspectives all speaking in the name of religion.[1]

In fact, the plurality of voices and values is precisely the strength of Jewish ethical discourse. As the protagonists in the reprisal debates understood, Jewish wisdom can instruct about contemporary military dilemmas. Yet Judaism does not speak in one voice, and more significantly, out of one principle. Multiple voices and values are found within the biblical canon, talmudic discourse, and later Jewish legal and ethical writings. Jewish military ethics draws from several types of moral appeals found in earlier Jewish literature. These include the following factors, as seen in the preceding chapters:

1. *Dignity of mankind*: All humans, friend and foe alike, were created in the image of God.[2] This demands us to generally grant basic dignity to any person and not to cavalierly treat people as a means toward some desired end.

2. *Inherent wrong of illicit bloodshed*: The commandment "Thou shall not kill" is reflective of this deep theological principle and demands that we do not take a life lightly. In fact, the ability to avoid unnecessary bloodshed is one of the factors that make the Jews worthy of settling the Land of Israel.[3]

3. *Individual responsibility*: Individuals bear primary responsibility for their actions and should ideally bear the sole weight of responsibility for their actions.[4]

4. *Vision of world peace*: The ultimate biblical vision is for the cessation of all warfare and is a goal toward which humanity must aspire.[5]

5. *Warfare in pursuit of justice*: Until the Messianic Era, the Bible calls upon its followers to take up arms for the sake of justice. This can be:
   - to defend oneself,[6]

- to settle the Homeland, or[7]
- to rid the world of evil.[8]

6. *Warfare, by its nature, is a collective affair.* This entails citizens and soldiers endangering themselves for their nation alongside a willingness to kill individual members of the enemy nation. Accordingly, warfare creates a form of communal identity and responsibility.[9]

7. *National partiality*: The primary responsibility of political leaders and citizens is to protect their own people. Israel goes to war even to redeem one captive.[10] This is part of a general ethos that people have particularistic obligations to their family, comrades, community, or nation. These "associative commitments" create a moral obligation not to shirk one's responsibility to fight on behalf of the collective.[11]

8. *Bravery and courage*: In warfare, bravery is a virtue and fearfulness is a vice.[12] It is virtuous to worry about killing someone illicitly, like Abraham and Jacob. Nonetheless, one must still fight courageously.

9. *National honor*: As with all actions, the honor of both God and His people is a factor. This includes:
   - not acting in an unethical manner that will disgrace our reputation and
   - not becoming a downtrodden people subjugated to mass ridicule.

It pays to take a second read of this list. All of these values are readily comprehensible and will undoubtedly appeal to many people in various contexts. But do you think that one should always take precedence over another? Or might you answer that it depends on the situation?

This is a critical question because one can quickly imagine how these values can conflict with each other. We prefer a world in which individuals alone are responsible for their sins but recognize that warfare is a collective enterprise. National honor is a double-edged sword as we seek to be a proud and free nation without utilizing the means that will disgrace us. Peace is our ultimate aspiration, yet warfare may sometimes be unavoidable. And so on. Some situations make certain values incompatible with each other.

The challenge for ethicists and leaders is to determine which of these moral appeals are most relevant for a given case. The method of sorting this out is sometimes called "casuistry." This is a case-based process to utilize ethical principles to resolve moral dilemmas. In the Jewish framework, we are dealing with what my late father, the ethicist Baruch Brody, called "pluralistic casuistry," i.e., the attempt to determine which of the plural or multiple values should be most prominent in the given circumstance.[13] Some philosophers utilize this framework to "balance," so to speak, different values and determine which moral claim should outweigh other ideals in this particular circumstance. Other ethicists cast doubt on whether we can create a hierarchy between the competing values; after all, they are difficult to measure. Instead, after intense deliberations, we need to make a judgment call which value should determine our behavior in this specific case. Either way, the key point in "pluralistic casuistry" is that one will take *all these moral claims into consideration* when making an ethical assessment of the given case, as opposed to prioritizing a single factor, like national victory, or some metavalue, like human rights.

Here lies the key distinction between a "pluralist" system and systems that prioritize a single factor, what philosophers call a "monist" system. The latter appreciate that there are multiple values but contend that one *overrides* all other considerations. A human rights-based, just-war account, for example, asserts that one major principle, namely rights, trumps other values like military utility or partisan allegiance. By contrast, pluralists, as the philosopher John Kekes has argued, believe that there is *no absolute hierarchy* of principles.[14]

All of these important values are conditional. No matter how precious a given value might be, it may be violated when it conflicts with some other value that has a stronger claim in *that particular situation*.

The alleged weakness of "pluralistic casuistry" is that it does not supply a golden rule or principle to address cases of conflicting moral appeals. This makes it hard to provide *the* definitive ruling desired in complex cases. After all, people may strongly disagree about how one should factor or weigh the different values in each circumstance. Yet the truth is that even proponents of more monolithic theories, like the rights-based model, concede that other values must occasionally (albeit rarely) take precedence. As discussed in chapter 5, in "dirty hands" cases or supreme emergencies, one essentially admits that military utility sometimes takes precedence. It acknowledges that competing moral principles and particularistic responsibilities may, at times, trump metavalues like human rights.

"Pluralistic casuistry" asserts that every case, not just extreme circumstances, requires taking into consideration multiple values. The moral life is too complex to be resolved by one overriding principle. The complexity of the dilemmas forces us to consider a variety of legitimate moral factors that we intuitively recognize. We need to embrace the reality that there will always be multiple factors to consider, and that sometimes these values will be incompatible with each other.

In this book, we'll use the term "Jewish multivalue framework" (JMF) to describe the system of considering the plural values found in classic Jewish sources.

JMF provides a framework for understanding how decent and thoughtful people are so deeply divided over these issues even when they share the same moral tradition or religion. It allows us to reasonably debate with each other as we debate which values should take priority. Decisions will be deemed legitimate or reasonable, even if not compelling, as long as they take into consideration the full *set of values*.[15] Rabbi Amiel and Rabbi Maimon, for example, can continue to work together because they remain committed to preserving the common system of values.

To highlight the value of "pluralistic casuistry" and JMF in particular, it pays to examine a controversial reprisal raid that occurred between the two greater Zionist controversies over reprisal raids in 1936-1939 and 1953: the 1945 Allied bombings of Dresden toward the end of World War II. This is a great test case because, as we'll see, followers of a monolithic system have an easy time praising or condemning the raid, while many others recognize that matters are not so simple.

Chapter 9

The Bombing of Dresden

A CASE EXAMPLE FOR THE JEWISH MULTIVALUE FRAMEWORK

On the night of February 13, 1945, the Bomber Command of the British Royal Air Force carried out orders "to destroy built-up areas and associated rail and industrial facilities" in the historical German city of Dresden. Initial target indicator bombs successfully lit up the centrally located soccer stadium. This provided perfect illumination for the first wave of 244 bombers that would drop incendiary bombs throughout the city. Aided by strong westerly winds, the maelstrom was already so great that by the time the second round of 550 heavy bombers entered Dresden airspace, they had to bomb blindly through the thick fire and smoke. By the time they left at two in the morning, the flames were visible from over a hundred miles away.

The next day – Ash Wednesday, in multiple senses – a fleet of 311 American B-17s dropped another payload of 771 tons of bombs, some on the Dresden railway marshaling yards, but most, because of smoke inhibition, on scattered points around the city. (Forty B-17s also accidentally targeted Prague seventy miles away, killing seven hundred civilians.) On February 15, another 210 B-17s bombed Dresden as a secondary option after they failed to reach their primary target. By the time they were done, flames could be seen two hundred miles away.

Within Dresden, the fire was so hot that those who did not perish from their burns suffocated from the lack of oxygen in the city. Those taking cover in the sparse city shelters suffocated from carbon monoxide, and those above ground perished in collapsed buildings. Germans fleeing in the streets were struck by flying roof tiles and metal sheets that peeled off scorching rooftops as burning embers showered onto the ground.[1]

Kurt Vonnegut was an American POW who had been imprisoned to work in a Dresden slaughterhouse. He survived by taking refuge in a cool meat locker three stories underground. The safest place for cover that night was hiding with meat carcasses.

Afterward, he and other prisoners were forced to clear corpses from the destroyed buildings. That experience inspired his antiwar science-fiction novel, *Slaughterhouse Five*, published during the Vietnam War.

Another famous survivor was the humanist Victor Klemperer, the son of a Reform rabbi in Berlin. Klemperer had converted to Protestantism in 1912 a few years after marrying a Christian woman. He patriotically fought for the Germans in World War I and became a distinguished professor. Yet his Jewish roots doomed him to suffer under the Nazi regime. Because he was married to an "Aryan," he avoided deportation, but he and his wife were moved to a "Jew house" at the beginning of the war.

On the afternoon of February 13, he witnessed some of the two hundred remaining Jews living in Dresden receiving deportation notices. They were to be sent to the concentration camp Theresienstadt in three days. When the air-raid sirens surprised the house residents, one of his companions bitterly said, "If only they would smash everything." He had no idea what was coming.

That night, Klemperer and his wife Eve managed to stay alive but had become temporarily separated from each other in the chaos. While searching for Victor, she tried to light a cigarette on something glowing on the ground, only to realize it was a burnt corpse. Taking advantage of the chaos, he ripped his yellow star from his coat and they managed to survive until the ultimate German surrender eighty-four days later.

MALCOLM GLADWELL AND THE STATUE OF "BOMBER" HARRIS

Nearly eighty years later, popular opinion continues to be divided over the morality of the Dresden bombing and other raids by Allied forces in Europe. At the time, many justified it as a legitimate reprisal following the German bombardment of cities like Warsaw, Rotterdam, Amsterdam, London, and Coventry. On the day after the Dresden raids, a *New York Times* editorial asserted, "The Allied triumph is being achieved with the very weapon that was to win the world for Hitler." It blamed the führer for the German blood spilled because of his stubborn resistance.

Yet the reprisal excuse is complex for at least two reasons. First, many historians cite documents and statements which indicate that the British believed in the targeting of German cities even before the *Blitzkrieg* had begun over England. At the European war's outbreak, US President Roosevelt asked the British and Germans to promise not to employ the "inhuman barbarism" seen in World War I of attacking civilian centers, echoing an earlier 1938 League of Nations statement condemning "intentional bombing of civilian centers." For many critics, the ultimate breaking of this pledge by the Allies highlighted how they had lost their moral compass in the vortex of total war. Second, as we saw previously, rights-based ethicists believe that reprisals may not legitimately target civilians. German terror may not be fought with terror.

In any case, it's clear that the Allied motivation hovered over the shady line that differentiates reprisal attacks from revenge killing. As Sir Arthur "Bomber" Harris, head of the Royal Air Force, famously asserted, paraphrasing the prophet Hosea, "The Nazis entered this war under the rather childish delusion that they were going to bomb everyone else, and nobody was going to bomb them. At Rotterdam, London, Warsaw, and half a hundred other places, they put their rather naive theory into operation. *They sowed the wind, and now they are going to reap the whirlwind.*" In Hosea, however, the revenge is executed by God, not by mortal and flawed men. Moreover, revenge might be biblical, yet as we've previously argued, that doesn't necessarily make it the most strategic decision or the most moral choice of various options on the table.

In fact, in England, some activists have recently tried to remove a public statue of Harris. They see the bloodshed of German noncombatants as an indelible moral stain on the country. Their voice has been emboldened by Malcolm Gladwell, the best-selling author of *The Bomber Mafia: A Story Set in War*. Gladwell labeled Harris a "psychopath" whose bombing campaign was inspired by vengeance. Gladwell himself opposes taking down his statue, but only so society can be reminded of the mistakes of its past. Harris's defenders, by contrast, have condemned Gladwell and other critics as "armchair air marshals" who do not appreciate the strategic value of the raids or the complex moral decisions necessary to defeat the Germans.[2]

The debate over Dresden is overshadowed only by the US air force bombing of Tokyo alongside the nuclear bombs dropped on Hiroshima and Nagasaki. Public opinion continues to be divided over the morality of the latter decisions. In the United States, for example, 56 percent of Americans still believe that the nuclear bombings were justified, in large part because they feel it was necessary to bring the war to an end. That's down from the 85 percent approval rating in 1945, but still a distinct majority.[3]

But while the public continues to debate these actions, the vast majority of rights-based theorists believe that these area bombings were entirely unjustified, even under the claims of supreme emergency. The philosopher Igor Primoratz declared that "the bombing was an unmitigated moral disaster," especially since the British had no reason to think such raids would succeed in damaging German morale.[4] The prominent British thinker A. C. Grayling similarly condemned the Dresden raid as both unethical and ineffective.[5] Douglas P. Lackey took the claim to an entirely different level. His outrageous article title, "Four Types of Mass Murderers: Stalin, Hitler, Churchill, Truman," says it all.

Many respond to these rights-based theorists by arguing that area raids hastened the war's end and ultimately saved lives on both sides. This was one of the many defenses that were offered during the war and immediately afterward. The archbishop of York, Dr. Cyril Garbett, who already in 1942 was urging Britain to do more to prevent the "deliberated and cold-blooded" extermination of the Jewish people, had this to say after a similar earlier raid:

The real justification for continuing this bombing is that it will shorten the war and may save thousands of lives. Those who demand the suspension of all bombing are advocating a policy *which would condemn many more of our soldiers to death, and would postpone the hour of liberation which will alone save from massacre and torture those who are now in the power of the Nazis.*

Garbett went on to skillfully depict the dirty-hands dilemma:

Often in life, there is no clear choice between absolute right and wrong; frequently the choice has to be made, of the lesser of two evils, and it is a lesser evil to bomb a war-loving Germany than to sacrifice the lives of thousands of our own fellow-countrymen who long for peace and to delay delivering millions now held in slavery.[6]

Priority must be given to salvaging the greatest number of lives, especially those of his fellow countrymen and the victims of German aggression.

Michael Walzer, advocating the primacy of rights, rejects such utilitarian calculations, even using religious terms. As he writes,

To kill 278,966 civilians (the number is made up) in order to avoid the deaths of an unknown but probably larger number of civilians and soldiers is a fantastic, *godlike*, frightening, and horrendous act.... It is the acknowledgment of rights that the destruction of the innocent, whatever its purposes, is a *kind of blasphemy* against our deepest moral commitments.[7]

For Walzer, the greater duty is to preserve our moral civilization by protecting rights and shunning utilitarian calculations that consider body counts.

The same arguments also apply to the bombing of Japan. Many historians argue that had the war extended longer, "many more people of all nations – and especially Japan – would have lost their lives than perished at Hiroshima and Nagasaki."[8] Indeed, in the battle of Okinawa that concluded less than two months before the nuclear bombings, roughly

240,000 people on both sides were killed. American forces also suffered great losses in Iwo Jima. Any ground incursions on the Japanese mainland would have been costlier in term of casualties and general suffering.

Such utilitarian calculations are illegitimate to thinkers like Walzer, who assert that the civilians of these cities did nothing to forfeit their rights to allow them to be targeted by air raids. This was not a case of "supreme emergency," since the Japanese no longer posed an imminent threat to America's survival. The American demand for unconditional surrender that delayed the cease-fire, he further argued, might have been "morally justifiable because of the character of Japanese militarism." Yet he concluded it was not worth the human costs that it entailed.[9] The problem, it should be clear, was not the use of atomic bombs as opposed to more conventional bombing, but rather the indiscriminate nature of the killing. Thus, in Walzer's mind, the raid on Tokyo in March 1945 represented the immoral adoption of the "British policy of terrorism" displayed in its attacks on places like Dresden (twenty-five thousand estimated killed) or two years earlier in Hamburg, when a weeklong series of raids killed an estimated thirty-five thousand people. That operation was aptly named "Operation Gomorrah" after the biblical city that was decimated.

GETTING THE FACTS CORRECT

To provide a more nuanced assessment of these air raids, it's critical to (a) get the historical facts correct and (b) understand the moral arguments made then by the protagonists. Many have criticized these philosophers for relying on inaccurate historical claims regarding the inevitability of the Allied victory. Walzer, for example, cites a quote from Churchill to assert that by the summer of 1942 the Allies knew that the Germans could not win. (He also mistakenly claims that one hundred thousand people were killed in Dresden, largely relying upon the bestselling book of David Irving, who later was exposed as a distortionist and Holocaust denier by Professor Deborah Lipstadt.[10] It is a shame that Professor Walzer has not corrected this error in more recent editions of his now-classic work.) Primoratz cites those who think that the German war effort was essentially lost in February 1943 at Stalingrad, after the British aerial campaign had begun but well before many of the infamous area raids. Grayling thinks that the war was clearly won by the summer of 1944.

Such assessments display the certainty of hindsight and ignore that the unexpected is expected in war. New weapons by the Axis powers (such as the V-2 rockets), strategic errors by the Allies (especially in the poor winter weather), or a breakdown of the tenuous Anglo-American alliance with the Russians could have led to a catastrophic reversal. These assessments also forget the counteroffensives that Hitler launched after these dates, including Operation Spring Awakening (March 1945) on the Eastern Front and, most significantly, the Battle of the Bulge (December 1944–January 1945) on the Western Front. The tremendous losses incurred by the Americans (19,000 killed, 23,000 missing, 45,000 wounded) shows how costly the continued campaign would be in military causalities, let alone the civilians who would continue to suffer. *Time* magazine reported that February 1945 was one of the deadliest months for US soldiers on both fronts: 49,689 killed, 153,076 wounded, 31,101 missing, and 3,403 taken prisoner.[11] The Battle of the Bulge was also particularly significant because it was an attempt by Hitler to conquer the port city of Antwerp and thereby put himself in a better strategic position to avoid unconditional surrender on the Western Front. Should anything but total victory have been an option against Nazism?

We should also not forget all the Jews who continued to be slaughtered in concentration camps, even as this tragically was not a major priority of the Allies. To get some perspective, 350,000 German civilians are estimated to have been killed from all Allied air raids; some seventeen times that number of Jewish noncombatants alone were killed by the Nazis.[12]

More nuanced historical analysis, including the important work of Frederick Taylor and others, shows a series of complex goals regarding the air raids on Dresden and their effectiveness. These include: (1) an attempt to break down German morale and prevent further resistance on both the Eastern and Western Fronts; (2) destroying the significant war-related industry in Dresden and dislocating those civilians whose status as "noncombatants" was made complex by their critical industrial work; and (3) disrupting the German movement of troops, since Dresden sat in the middle of important east-west and north-south traffic routes. The Allies were not targeting civilians, but they also didn't have the technological tools to engage in precision bombing of military targets, especially without losing a significant number of fighter planes and pilots. They were engaged in "strategic indiscriminate bombing." The hope was to hit military targets while accepting the large amount of damage to noncombatants.[13] This wasn't just collateral damage to civilians, but an appreciation that harm to civilians would help achieve a military goal.

Yet the indiscriminate nature of the bombing wasn't just because of the technological limitations on aerial bombardment accuracy, but also an inevitable result of the "total war" strategy launched by the Germans. Precisely two years beforehand, Goebbels, as we discussed in chapter 2, called on civilians to participate in an all-out mobilization to push back against Allied advances. Since that time, almost all of Dresden's 127 factories had been turned over to war work, making the city more conspicuous to British intelligence trying to stop the Nazi war machine.[14] It also complicated the "civilian" status of some of the city's inhabitants working in military production, even as many residents, children, and refugees would certainly be categorized as uninvolved "noncombatants."

THE RAID ON DRESDEN IN THE JEWISH
MULTIVALUE FRAMEWORK

With this nuanced historical understanding, we can also now appreciate the arguments made to justify the Allied raids beyond their desire to quickly end the war. In leaflets dropped on the German people in 1942 and 1943, bluntly titled "Why We Bomb You" and signed by Harris, the British argued that they were not emulating the terror attacks of the Nazis. Instead,

> we are bombing you and your cities, one by one, and ever more terribly, in order to make it impossible for you to go on with the war.... Obviously we prefer to hit your factories, shipyards, and railways. It damages your Government's war machine most. But nearly all these targets are in the midst of the houses of those of

you who work in them. ... Therefore we hit your houses – and you – when we bomb them. We regret the necessity for this. But this regret will never stop us; you showed the world how to do it.[15]

The leaflet nicely sums up a range of justifications for bombing cities: destruction of a war machine, the location of military targets within civilian centers, the breakdown of morale, and poetic justice. We regret what needs to be done, but we are acting justly.

Even then, some senior Allied leaders worried about the morality of these raids. Churchill warned Harris afterward that he feared that the Dresden raid was done "simply for the sake of increasing the terror." General George Patton, who led American troops in Germany, worried in his wartime diary that "indiscriminate bombing has no military value and is cruel and wasteful."[16] Thoughtful historians will continue to debate the motivation behind and efficacy of such raids. This is no small task. As one historian who has questioned the usefulness and morality of the raids has readily admitted, "War is always easier to fight looking backward."[17] The critical challenge then becomes creating an ethical framework to examine these complex strategic decisions. As I've argued, the universalist, rights-based model or the nationalistic model of "all is fair in war" are too monolithic to sufficiently consider the ethical intuitions that people reasonably bring into consideration when debating Dresden.

Now let us examine the claims under the Jewish multivalue framework that I've proposed. On the one hand, because of the value of human dignity, we should not treat lightly the loss of any innocent life, even in the context of collective warfare. Indiscriminate bombing, even when it may have military benefits, is highly problematic for the toll it takes on noncombatants. Yet precisely because we value the dignity of all human beings, minimizing the total number of lives lost must also be a consideration. Making such calculations might be "godlike," as Walzer asserts. Yet it is sometimes necessary in order to maximize the number of God's creatures created in His image who get to stay alive in these collective struggles. The ground battles of Okinawa and Iwo Jima were more conventional attacks to achieve military goals. Yet if those bloody clashes could have been avoided by first bombing Tokyo and Nagasaki, a good argument could have been made to justify such a decision.

"ASSOCIATIVE OBLIGATIONS": WHAT WE OWE TO OUR OWN

Beyond calculating the sum of casualties on both sides, one cannot ignore the ethical obligation to give moral partiality to one's own countrymen. We prioritize those with whom we have special obligations, such as family members, comrades, community, and nation. Philosophers call these commitments "associative obligations." Our associations with these people generate unique responsibilities to them. The fact that soldiers are warriors does not take away our responsibility to them as citizens or as bearers of human dignity; to the contrary, as representatives of the collective who endanger themselves for the sake of the nation, they deserve equal amounts of protection. Warfare is taken on behalf of a collective that seeks victory and safety for their members. The state, therefore, must come up with a compelling reason to endanger the lives of their soldiers. It therefore may choose to adopt a strategy, such as air power over a ground attack, that will reduce risks to its own soldiers even as it will likely increase the number of casualties, including those of civilians, on the other side.

This partiality for one's own people is not unlimited, however. Because we recognize the divine element in all humans, we don't carpet bomb every enemy town to exterminate our enemies, soldiers and civilians alike, in order to avoid any risks to our soldiers. A sensitive balance must be drawn between the internal obligations to our own people and our external obligations to others, as we'll discuss in later chapters. Yet sometimes one may justifiably act in a way that prioritizes protecting one's own soldiers over the civilian lives of enemies.

Take, for example, the case of battlefield triage. Sometimes medics may have to choose between providing immediate health care to a wounded soldier or a wounded enemy civilian. We should try to help both. Yet we prioritize the former, for the simple reason that the primary obligation of leaders and commanders is to protect their citizens, which includes their citizen-soldiers. This may seem intuitively obvious to some. Yet it's far from clear to some contemporary philosophers who, following language from the 1949 Geneva conventions, insist that wartime medical care should be impartial to the patient's identity and based on medical considerations alone. Such ethicists fail to recognize the "associative obligations" that we owe to our compatriots.[18]

ERADICATION OF EVIL

Finally, we get to the biblical value of eradicating evil through the Allies achieving an absolute victory against the Axis powers. Some ethicists worry that calls for "unconditional surrender" take on a crusader-like vengeance which demands – or at least easily tolerates – the utter destruction of the enemy. This slaughter is undertaken in the name of justice – the survival of a civilization, the preservation of liberty, the future of democracy, or some other supreme ideal. The concern that such idealism will lead to the zealous killing of many innocent people is real, as we noted regarding total wars in chapter 2. It is important to place moral limits on our actions and establish limited goals for our wars.

Yet our concern for not violating the rights of noncombatants might also hold us back from delivering sound defeat to ruthless enemies and relentless tyranny. There is vile evil in the world. Brutal practices must stop, and pernicious ideas must be repudiated.

When facing such an enemy, victory should include, when possible, the following conditions: (1) the replacement of the evil regimes, whether by killing or capturing and trying its leaders; (2) the rollback of any political gains achieved by the evildoers' aggression; (3) some form of protections or guarantees against repeated hostilities, including, when necessary, the rehabilitation and reconstruction of the guilty society. This process may include demilitarization, admission of guilt, and reparations to victims. This should be a forward-looking process that seeks to bring greater peace to the world. None of this means that the victors should cause noncombatants to suffer as a goal for its own sake. Yet it does mean that the war should end under the best conditions that will facilitate the implementation of these conditions. Achieving that goal may entail morally complex military decisions regarding the collective enemy. It is good to fear, like the biblical forefathers Abraham and Jacob, making moral mistakes in warfare. Such concern should lead to prudence and caution, but not prevent one from getting their hands dirty for a noble goal.[19]

General George S. Patton articulated this well when it came to achieving victory against the Germans. Writing to the men of the Third Army, he stated, "We are now entering the final stage of a great war, of a great victory! The victory can only be attained by maximum use of all weapons, both physical and spiritual. It is the duty of all commanders to see that their men are fully aware of the many vile deeds perpetrated upon civilization by Germans, and that they attack with the utmost determination, ferocity, and hate."[20] Such rhetoric may rightfully scare people. Yet a greater fear is the prospects of Nazism not being fully eradicated on the battlefield and repudiated for its utter moral repugnance.

Some ethicists are willing to agree with this sentiment against Nazism but find it more difficult to make such a declaration against Imperial Japan. Walzer, for example, argued that unconditional surrender should have never been demanded.

> Japan's rulers were engaged in a more ordinary sort of military expansion, and all that was *morally required was that they be defeated, not that they be conquered and totally overthrown.* Some restraint upon their war-making power might be justified, but their domestic authority was a matter of concern only to the Japanese people.[21]

I find such a sentiment to be utterly baffling and tinged with a strong Western bias. Japanese terror began well before the 1941 attack on Pearl Harbor, in the period which Asian scholars call the "Fifteen-Year War."[22] While Japanese imperialism had spread already in the beginning of the twentieth century, its colonial aspirations became particularly violent from 1931 with its raid on Manchuria. In this period, we have multiple wars with China, including the infamous "Rape of Nanking" in 1937–38, followed by the "Pacific War," what Westerners refer to as part of World War II. Mass executions, labor camps, rape, and inhuman treatment of POWs were all prevalent.[23] While the number of causalities from Japanese belligerence are hard to calculate, we are clearly speaking in the millions. One doesn't have to claim, like author Iris Chang, that we are dealing with the "forgotten holocaust of World War II" to recognize that this was a form of evil that needed to be dispensed with, with no compromise over conditions of surrender.

Moreover, even toward the end of the war, when their loss to America seemed inevitable, Japanese leaders were holding onto hopes of maintaining control over their mainland territory as well as Korea and Manchuria. They believed that the American fear of a costly land invasion would give them a stronger negotiating position. In the meantime, Japanese *bushido* honor culture led to continued kamikaze suicide-bombings all the way until the end of the war. Almost four thousand Japanese pilots attempted these mass-suicide killings. One in seven successfully hit a ship and inflicted major damage and casualties.[24] (The last kamikaze strike, killing twenty-one soldiers on the USS La Grange, was launched four days *after* the second nuclear bomb hit Nagasaki.) This culture had to be defeated. Conditional surrender was rightly not an option on the table. Such a negotiated settlement might have also prevented the ultimate rehabilitation of Japan and Germany into the stellar countries that they are today. It would also have been seen, with good reason, as a sign of disrespect to all the soldiers who had given their lives to rid the world of this culture. This factor was better appreciated when the dirt over their graves was still fresh, which might explain why more Americans supported the nuclear bombings in 1946 than in 2016.[25]

None of this analysis, however, is meant to demonstrate that the Jewish multivalue framework provides an unambiguous defense of the 1945 area bombings of Germany or Japan.[26] Ethical missteps or bad judgment calls were made. Some are easier to spot in hindsight, while others might have been noticeable then as well. The Allied war machine was a complex organism that was driven by many figures with different and conflicting motivations. Many of these were noble, some less so. Consider, for example, the approach of Curtis LeMay, the American officer in charge of the air strategy against Japan, when he was asked after World War II if he had any ethical qualms.

Killing Japanese didn't bother me very much at that time. It was getting the war over that bothered me. So I wasn't worried particularly about how many people we killed in getting the job done.

I suppose if I had lost the war, I would have been tried as a war criminal. Fortunately, we were on the winning side.

LeMay cynically added how people focus on the nuclear bombings of Hiroshima and Nagasaki without noting that incendiary attacks were launched on every Japanese industrial city. He then went on to say, "Every soldier thinks something of the moral aspects of what he is doing. But all war is immoral and if you let that bother you, you're not a good soldier."[27]

From the perspective of the Jewish multivalued framework, this is a deplorable sentiment. Why? Because he prioritized one value – national victory – to assert that it overrides any other consideration. A strategist who was keeping in mind other values might have determined there were less lethal ways to achieve the same goal. One is thankful that there were other Allied figures who continued to weigh ethical constraints in their strategy.[28] In any case, the morality of Allied (or any other) actions are not judged on intentions alone, for better or for worse. Leaders acting with ignoble motivations might still perform actions that are justifiable under different rationales. Others with noble intentions can still commit egregious moral errors.

Ultimately, we've tried to show how the JMF provides an excellent way of understanding the complex ethical dilemmas that emerge from such a scenario. It allows one to capture the nuance of the debate, both then and now, while understanding the types of arguments that might be launched for and against such strikes. It provides us with a much better understanding of the legitimate disagreements that people have today over the legacy of World War II, something which the rights-based approach does not provide.

For an ethical system to successfully guide people, it must not only allow us to analyze actions in the past, but also assess ethical dilemmas in the present. As we'll now argue, today's leaders can utilize this multivalue framework. In the second half of the book, we'll lay out a broad programmatic statement about when it is justified to fight a war and how to fight it justly. We'll exemplify this approach by focusing on the State of Israel's wars, which have long been used by military ethicists as potent case examples.

As we'll see, Zionist leaders and rabbinic thinkers were themselves divided over many of Israel's decisions. By utilizing the JMF, we'll understand how the different protagonists could all make cogent arguments that are fully comprehensible. Moreover, their outlook could be defined as "Jewish" since they regularly drew on values found in religious sources. The challenge, then, will be to determine which of these cogent Jewish perspectives are most compelling to guide twenty-first-century ethical decision making.

Part II

The Ethics of Going to War: From WWII to Israel's Independence

Chapter 10

World War II and the Fight for Self-Defense and National Honor

FROM BRITISH JAILS TO UNION JACK UNIFORMS

On Saturday, May 17, 1941, Shoshana and David Raziel celebrated Shabbat together in their small Jerusalem apartment. They had married three years earlier in a clandestine wedding on Passover eve. David was still leading the Etzel's reprisal attacks. For a year, they moved from one apartment to another in order to evade the Brits. In May 1939, following repeated Etzel attacks on Arab residents, Raziel was finally captured by the British. Five months later, however, he was released from jail. The British now wanted to use Raziel to buttress support among Palestine's Jewish community for their war efforts against the Nazis.

Raziel had pledged more than just moral support to the British. On that Saturday night, he told Shoshana that he was traveling to Tel Aviv for ten days to help an Etzel activist. In truth, he was traveling to Iraq with a few fellow Etzel members on a mission for British intelligence. Their official mission was to sabotage the fuel supply of German bombers supporting a coup against the pro-Western monarchy. But Raziel also told his commanders that he had additional plans: to kidnap the Etzel's nemesis, the Jerusalem mufti Haj Amin al-Husseini, who had been living in Baghdad for two years after instigating years of attacks on Jews in Palestine.

None of these grand plans would come to fruition. On May 20, following an intelligence gathering mission, the car carrying Raziel was hit by a German fighter bomber. The leader of the Etzel died in a British uniform.

The British attacked Baghdad two days later to depose the pro-Axis leader. Al-Husseini was able to escape and eventually make it to Berlin, where he became an active Nazi collaborator. Before the British took full control of the city, a mob of local Arabs, aroused by local nationalism and Nazi propaganda, attacked their Jewish neighbors. Some 180 Jews were killed over a period of two days known as the *Farhud* ("violent dispossession").

Two weeks later, Shoshana would find out the true fate of her husband. Soon after, she would discover that she was pregnant with their son. He was named David, after his father, but tragically died two days after his birth.[1] Twenty year later, Raziel's remains were finally interred in an official military ceremony in Jerusalem attended by state figures, chief rabbis, and Menachem Begin. Rabbi Tzvi Yehuda Kook, his teacher, eulogized him as the epitome of a dedicated soldier-scholar.[2]

Raziel's remarkable transformation within two years from "public enemy no. 1" in Palestine to British soldier in Iraq highlights how important it was for Jews to join the fight against Hitler. Jews were enraged by the strict immigration limitations placed on Jews by the 1939 White Paper. Yet they held a nearly unanimous opinion that they now needed to join forces with the British to protect Jews in Europe and elsewhere. As Ben-Gurion famously asserted, "We will fight the White Paper as if there is no war, and fight the war as if there is no White Paper."[3]

Another British prisoner-turned-soldier was Moshe Dayan. Despite his previous service under Wingate's Special Night Squads, he had been imprisoned for two years when his Haganah unit was arrested in late 1939 for illegal arms possession. The British were cracking down on underground movements. By the summer of 1941, he was fighting again on the British side, this time as a part of the newly formed Palmach (strike force) division created with British support to fight threats against Palestine. On June 8, 1941, while on a reconnaissance mission in Vichy French Lebanon, Dayan was shot while looking through his binoculars. He lost his left eye and wore his iconic eye patch for the rest of his life.[4]

JEWISH SERVICE IN WORLD WAR II: PATRIOTISM, REVENGE, AND SELF-DEFENSE

During World War II, nearly thirty thousand Jews in Palestine served in the British army. From the very outset, Jews saw the war against Hitler as a battle for Jewish survival. This was a war based on the most basic claims of self-defense: we are under attack and must protect ourselves. Chief Rabbis Uziel and Herzog sent rousing letters of encouragement to all inductees. Rabbi Amiel, whose strong stances against Etzel reprisal attacks were discussed in chapter 4, had no problem urging Jews to emulate the Hasmoneans and take vengeance against the Nazis.[5]

Seeking to repeat the Jewish Legion model from World War I, Jabotinsky, Weizmann, and Ben-Gurion all lobbied for a military unit of Jewish volunteers that would join the British war efforts.[6] They wanted to defeat the Nazis and help the Jews of Europe. But they also had a political agenda: to gain a state as political spoils for their contribution to the eventual victory. Battlefield experience would also prepare Jews to fight on behalf of a future Jewish state. For these same reasons, many British officials resisted the formation of a Jewish fighting unit. They feared that the Zionists would later use their wartime experiences against British interests.

After Jabotinsky suddenly died in 1940, Rabbi Abraham Kook's nephew, Hillel Kook, operating under the alias of Peter Bergson, would continue Jabotinsky's lobbying efforts in America. Only in 1944 did the British assemble a "Jewish brigade," which included five thousand Jews from Palestine. Their members, including Ben-Gurion's son Amos, fought in the latter stages of the Italian campaign under the Zionist flag.

In truth, outside of Palestine, most Jews preferred to fight in the militaries of their countries. As one Jewish GI put it, "There was to be no 'Jewish brigade' in the US Army – nobody wanted that."[7] Surely, Jews wanted to take vengeance against the Nazis. They also felt a patriotic duty to serve their country. Unlike World War I, there was no fear of killing Jews who were fighting on the other side of the battlefield. In total, over 1.5 million Jews served in Allied armies across the globe, 550,000 in the US armed forces, 500,000 in the Red Army, 100,000 in the Polish army, and 60,000 in the British. Britain's chief rabbi, Joseph Hertz, issued strong condemnations of any attempt to shirk the civic responsibility to serve, just as he had done in World War I. Once the United States joined the war, similar calls were made by American rabbis of all denominations. The sentiment was well expressed by R. Soloveitchik.

> [The Jewish tradition] has always wanted to see the Jew committed to all social and national institutions of the land of his birth or choice which affords to him all the privileges and prerogatives of citizenship. Particularly, the halakha emphasizes the duty of the Jew to share in the defense of his homeland in the way in which he is best fitted.[8]

Rabbis across the Jewish denominational spectrum even worked together, in a rare display of unity, to enlist clergy who could provide support for the spiritual needs of Jewish soldiers.[9]

For many Jews, World War II was the first time in which they could fully engage in warfare and believe that they were unambivalently defending both the Jewish people and their country or homeland, wherever that might be. Many also saw World War II as an opportunity to gain acceptance in their broader society and overcome antisemitic prejudices that deemed Jews as either weak or unpatriotic.

The overall approach was well summarized by Rabbi Israel Brodie, then Britain's chief military chaplain, who would later become the chief rabbi of the British Commonwealth. Jewish soldiers, he asserted, have "shown to the world that given the opportunity the Jew as a soldier is the equal of any other man. … [They] enhanced the Jewish name and reputation for gallantry and devotion to duty. They readily deserved the many tributes paid them by statesmen, war leaders and comrades-in-arms."[10] Military service had restored Jewish honor.

SELF-DEFENSE AND THE RESTORATION OF
JEWISH HONOR

One should not underestimate the theological and ethical significance of the restoration of national honor among Jewish leaders. For centuries, Jews had lamented in their prayer supplications how the Jewish nation was scorned by the nations of the world. Their enemies rhetorically taunted, "Where is their God?'" while declaring, "Their hope is lost." As the prayer continues,

> Look down from heaven and see how we have become an object of scorn and derision among the nations. We are regarded as sheep led to the slaughter (*ketzon latevaḥ yuval*) to be killed, destroyed, beaten, and humiliated.[11]

The prayer took on special poignancy during times of persecution, like the massive Russian pogroms in the early 1880s. As Rabbi Chaim Berlin of Moscow (1832–1912) noted, the problem wasn't just that the Jewish people were being killed like sheep. They were being *led* to slaughter with absolutely no control over their fate. The survivors were homeless and driven from one refuge to another.[12] Soon afterward, Jews would leave Russia in masses, many for Western countries like England and America, and some for Palestine.

Now, some sixty years later, Jews had found more welcoming environs in many countries, yet remained under attack. Was the Jewish political condition essentially the same? Yes – unless they would enlist and fight Hitler with their own hands. So declared R. Berlin's younger half-brother, Rabbi Meir Bar-Ilan (Berlin), a leader of the Mizrachi political movement in Palestine. Using his platform as the founding editor of the prominent *Hatzofeh* newspaper, R. Bar-Ilan (1880–1949) repeatedly called on Jews to enlist with those fighting Hitler and redeem the political condition – and reputation – of the Jewish people.

> There is no greater desecration of God's reputation (*ḥillul Hashem*) than the rise of such satanic evil.... There will be no greater sanctification of God's reputation (*kiddush Hashem*) than

the downfall of that evil man and the elimination of Hitlerian impurity from the world.[13]

R. Bar-Ilan's activist approach would later take him in 1943 to Washington, where he lobbied with the Bergson Group for American intervention to stop the slaughter of European Jewry.[14]

On a formal level, R. Bar-Ilan and others argued that the fight against the Nazis was a "commanded war" (*milḥemet mitzva*) of self-defense.[15] The Bible commands, "When you are at war in your land against an aggressor who attacks you, you shall sound short blasts on the trumpets, that you may be remembered before the Lord your God and be delivered from your enemies."[16] The battlefield shofar had been blown. Now was the time to fight. The Sages further demanded universal conscription to fight for these causes. This legal obligation drew from a fundamental moral sentiment well encapsulated by Moses in the Bible: "Are your brothers to go to war while you stay here?"[17] No one may shirk their duty to defend their people.

WAR IS SOMETIMES BETTER THAN APPEASEMENT

The failed diplomatic attempt to appease Hitler highlighted another significant moral teaching about going to war: a nation may elect to defend itself rather than accept a humiliating peace offer that rewards aggression. Rabbinic law, as we saw in chapter 2, calls upon Jews to offer peace deals before going to war. War should be a last resort for dispute resolution. But some humiliating alternative arrangements are worse than warfare.

This point – that war is sometimes preferable to shameful appeasement – was exemplified in a poignant biblical passage when Saul emerged on the national scene to lead the Israelites against the aggressive attack of the Ammonites. The Ammonite leader Naḥash offered the Israelites the option of appeasing them through a degrading relinquishment of the territory of Jabesh-Gilead. "I will make a pact with you," he promised, "on this condition, that everyone's right eye be gouged out; I will make this a disgrace of all of Israel." Despite the humiliation, this might have been tolerable for the Israelites. They had acrimonious relations with the Jabesh-Gilead residents for previously failing to join them in their collective defense.[18] The Israelites could have reasonably made this concession, thereby satisfying the Ammonites and saving themselves from the risk of warfare. Yet Saul, with the support of the prophet Samuel, rejected such accommodation to the "rule of violence." He stood up to evil aggression, bringing salvation and national honor to his people. For this principled stance, the people accepted him as their king.

Chamberlain's appeasement of the Nazis in Europe, along with the British unwillingness to stand up to Arab violence and implement the 1937 partition plan, left the Jewish people homeless and vulnerable.[19] British accommodations to the "rule of violence" had boomeranged against them while subjecting the Jews to violence and discrimination. The inability of Jews to provide sufficient self-defense throughout the generations, moreover, had left them facing a catastrophe in Europe. World War II was a significant turning point in Jewish history in which Jews would no longer abandon their responsibility – the mitzva – to defend themselves and their honor.

Chapter 11

Defending Lives or Honor? Masada, the Warsaw Ghetto Uprising, and the Probability of Success

NATIONAL HONOR AND DEFENSE IN THE "TWO HUNDRED DAYS OF TERROR"

Defending the nation's lives and protecting its honor went hand in hand in the fight over Europe during World War II. Yet what happens if these values conflict? The mandate to defend oneself does not mean that one should never flee or surrender, in spite of the humiliation. An individual might rightfully fight back against muggers. That's not a wise decision if he will certainly fail and lose his own life. The same question must be raised on the national level. Does the communal responsibility to fight in defense ever cease? Or should we always fight, against all odds, to defend our honor?

Over the course of 1942, the Jews of Palestine ferociously debated this question. The Nazi army, led by General Erwin Rommel, roamed through Africa and threatened British control over Egypt. During a period of increased prospects of a German victory in North Africa, later known as "two hundred days of terror," Jewish political and spiritual leaders called for greater conscription while debating what should be done in the case of a Nazi invasion.

The Jews also feared what Arab collaborators might do, particularly if the British abandoned Palestine. Some men began planning the evacuation of their wives and children. A few, more radically, stocked up on cyanide.

Ben-Gurion argued that if the Nazis won in Africa, Jewish fighters must flee Palestine. If the British couldn't stop Rommel in Libya or Egypt, the Jews certainly wouldn't be successful. All fighters should evacuate with British troops so that they could fight elsewhere. Eventually, they'd return to reconquer Palestine.

Opposing him, Yitzhak Tabenkin, a leader of the Kibbutz Movement, argued that any evacuation plan was logistically implausible ("To where will they flee?" "Are there not enough Jewish refugees?"). More significantly, this plan was strategically unwise. Once the land was abandoned, the Jews would never get it back. "If we fall," he continued, "others will come in our place. If we flee, no one will come in our place."[1] Nations that surrender their homeland easily don't get it back so quickly. Perhaps evacuation would save a few women and children, but ultimately, the Land of Israel is the highest priority. We must arm every man and woman and stand our ground against the Nazis. There is no other choice.

Yitzhak Greenboim, who would soon become the head of the Jewish Agency Rescue Committee, went further to assert that any retreat would do irreparable harm to national honor. As it is, we suffer from the fact that European Jewry preferred to be a "beaten dog" rather than suffer a glorified death. That, in his mind, was why Polish Jewry did not fight back against the Nazi invaders. A retreat would spell the end of Zionism. Accordingly, he exclaimed, "If we find ourselves in a state of invasion, we must make sure that, at the very least, we will leave a 'Masada' legend after us."[2]

The Etzel planned to make a final stand in Jerusalem and the surrounding Judean hills. Others plotted to move Jewish residents to Israel's northern, hilly region and prepare for guerrilla warfare. The plan was called "Masada on the Carmel."

Greenboim's statement about Jewish honor outraged the Mizrachi leader Moshe Shapira. If all was truly lost, he asserted, then we would follow the example of the biblical warrior Samson. In the book of Judges, Samson had defeated the Philistines and restored the safety of the Israelites for a period of twenty years. Later, when captured and publicly humiliated in front of a bloodthirsty crowd, he broke the pillars of the public coliseum. He killed himself but also his Philistine enemies with him. Samson's solution – as exemplified in his final words, "Let me die with the Philistines!" – might be brave, but it is ultimately a suicide mission.[3]

Yet as long as there is hope to save some Jews, Shapira continued, we must accept any alternative. Ghettos in Palestine are preferable to death. We'll lose many martyrs, but the survivors will ultimately rebuild our settlement. Jewish honor is found in respecting our ethical imperatives, including those that prioritize saving lives.

R. Maimon attacked Shapira by asserting that Jewish honor cannot be reduced to ethics alone.

> Jewish honor isn't just a question of ethics – there's a question of the honor of Israel… Jewish honor makes it imperative to fight, not to hide in caves like cowards. This is also the meaning of Zionism, which must not be denied when the enemy approaches the borders of our country…. We must not resign ourselves to the fate of downtrodden slaves.[4]

As we saw in chapter 4 regarding his support of the Etzel's reprisal attacks, R. Maimon believed that the Jews must now redeem themselves from their historical downtrodden status, even to the point where it trumps ethical concerns regarding the sanctity of life.

ELEAZAR BEN YAIR VERSUS YOḤANAN BEN ZAKKAI

Looming large over this debate was the legacy of the alleged mass suicide at Masada, a fortress originally built by Herod in the Judean desert. Following the destruction of Jerusalem in 70 CE, some remaining Jewish rebels fled there, only to be surrounded by the Romans some three years later. According to the ancient historian Josephus, 967 Jews chose to kill each other rather than be taken as captives. Their leader, Eleazar ben Yair, allegedly proclaimed,

> We have it in our power to die nobly and in freedom. Our fate at the break of day is certain capture; but there is still the free choice of a noble death with those we hold most dear.

The tale of Masada was lionized by early-twentieth-century Zionists as a symbol for Jewish refusal to accept subjugation to foreign powers. Poets lauded their heroism, youth groups sang songs about their bravery, and all Palmach recruits were taken on treks up its slopes.[5]

In later years, the most outspoken rabbinic defender of the Masada rebels was R. Shlomo Goren.[6] In an extended essay, he noted that suicide is broadly prohibited in Jewish law as a moral wrong. Nonetheless, rabbinic scholars justified it under extreme political conditions on several occasions. Sometimes other values are held higher than life itself.[7] During the times of Roman persecution, for example, a mother and her seven children jumped off a roof rather than commit idolatry. In another tale, four hundred boys and girls jumped into the sea rather than be sold into captivity.[8] Centuries later, some medieval scholars excused persecuted Jews who killed themselves – and even their own children – rather than be forced to convert to Christianity during the Crusades. Perhaps most significantly, the Sages justified King Saul falling on his sword before being captured by the Philistines.[9] For R. Goren, this last case set a precedent to permit committing suicide rather than allowing the desecration of the name of Heaven by allowing an enemy to kill Jews or gloatingly take captives. Defiance of one's enemies and preservation of personal or national honor, it would seem, may sometimes trump the moral obligation to stay alive.[10]

R. Goren would go on to participate in many military swearing-in ceremonies of new IDF soldiers at Masada in which Eleazar ben Yair's final speech was publicly reenacted. In 1969, R. Goren supervised an official military funeral for bones found at Masada allegedly belonging to the rebels. Many archaeologists protested that these were not Jewish remains. Nonetheless, the legend, it would seem, had to be immortalized.[11]

Given this legend's fame, many are surprised that the talmudic Sages never discuss Masada in their vast talmudic literature. One explanation might be that the mass suicide never took place. Several historians have argued that Josephus, whose writings are tinged with inaccuracies based on ideology or personal benefit, is the only source for this myth. There is no substantive archaeological or other evidence to corroborate the story.[12]

Another possible explanation for the Sages' silence is that they disapproved of the rebels' decision and their general strategy. Josephus asserts that the Masada rebels were comprised of members of the Sicarii group, an extremist splinter group that also fought with their fellow Jews and the official Jewish leaders of Jerusalem. These rebels were opposed by the prominent Sage Yoḥanan ben Zakkai, who chose to surrender to Caesar. In return, he received permission to move to the city of Yavne and build up its academy. The ability to rebuild a spiritual center after Jerusalem's destruction allowed Judaism, and its adherents, to live on.

In the words of one prominent historian, "If Judaism has survived, if the Jewish people has survived, it is not by virtue of Masada but by virtue of Yavne; it is not thanks to Eleazar ben Yair, but thanks to Zakkai."[13] There is no honor in sacrificing Jewish lives in a way that threatens the very future of the Jewish people and their religion.

Later talmudic sages, writing from Babylonia following the Jewish exile from the Land of Israel, may have had no interest in memorializing the actions of the uncompromising Masada rebels. This was particularly true after the failed "Uprising of the Diaspora" (also known as the Kitos War, 115–117 CE) in Cyprus and Egypt, and the unsuccessful Bar Kokhba uprising (132–135 CE), which sealed the fate of the Jewish settlement in Judea. Defiance is praiseworthy, but not if it leads to greater death and destruction.

This message, in fact, was already preached by the prophet Jeremiah. He had unsuccessfully warned King Zedekiah, before the First Temple's destruction in 586 BCE, that he should surrender and save the Jewish settlement in the Holy Land.[14] "If you surrender to the officers of the king of Babylon, your life will be spared and this city will not be burned down. You and your household will live."[15] Worried that the masses would see capitulation as act of timidity, Zedekiah did not listen, and all was lost.

The most outspoken rabbinic Zionist critic of the Masada legend was Rabbi Moshe Tzvi Neriya (1913–95). R. Neriya was born in Lodz, Poland, and spent his childhood surviving the political chaos of the post–World War I period. He covertly studied in clandestine yeshivot in the Soviet Union before eventually getting arrested. Because of his age, he was released. His teacher was sent to Siberia and never heard from again. In 1930, through the efforts of Rabbi Kook and his son, R. Tzvi Yehuda, R. Neriya received a visa to immigrate to Israel and study in their rabbinic seminary. He would go on to become a leader of the Bnei Akiva religious youth movement, establish the most prominent network of religious Zionist schools, and serve for a short time in the Israeli Knesset, where he was known for his right-wing views on settling the Land of Israel.

Despite his hawkish worldview, R. Neriya lambasted R. Goren's defense of the Masada rebels as "mistaken and dangerous." King Saul, in his mind, was a unique case of a national symbol whose death had already been foreseen by the prophet Samuel. In general, however, the overarching halakhic ethos is encapsulated by the biblical verse, as interpreted by the Sages, "You shall live by the commandments – and not die through them." This established the principle that we should choose life in order to ensure the future of the Jewish people.[16]

If Jews throughout the generations had followed the model of Eleazer ben Yair – choosing death over political subjugation – then the nation would have never survived. Had the Masada fighters surrendered, some would have been killed or enslaved, but others may have escaped and lived on. In fact, Jewish rebels in the nearby fortress Machaerus were able to negotiate a surrender to the Romans and were ultimately set free.[17] For Jews, heroism means knowing when to fight and when to stay alive. Suicide is not defiance but defeat.

PROBABILITY OF SUCCESS AND "RED VERSUS DEAD"

Part of the debate over the Yavne and Masada paradigms relates to one of the key criteria demanded by just-war theorists to justify going to war: the probability of success. Leaders must recognize the potential harm of the war and ask, "Is this war worth the dangers?" They must weigh the chances of achieving the desired good outcome against the probable evil that may result. Or to put it another way, the positive impact of the ends must outweigh the negative impact of the means. Otherwise, it is not worth going to war, even if there is just cause to do so.

This pragmatic consideration is usually attributed to the Spanish philosopher Vitoria (1483–1546), who wrote, "No war is just the conduct of which is manifestly more harmful to the State than it is good and advantageous." Yet the idea has earlier origins, including in Jewish thought. One famous biblical exegete, Gersonides (1288–1344), made a similar point: "When you start a war with someone stronger than you, do so wisely. That is to say, if you are not sure you'll win, don't endanger yourself."[18] The biblical context of his comment is significant. The nomadic Midianites, alongside Amalekites and other tribes from the east, had been terrorizing the Israelites by plundering their crops and livestock, forcing the Israelites to take refuge in the mountains. "Israel was reduced to utter misery by the Midianites," declares the Bible.[19] Such aggression for seven years constituted a just cause for war, especially when the agitators included the despised Amalekites. Yet Gideon, the leader of the Israelites, sought a divine sign that he'd succeed in his war against this oppression.

Even when acting out of self-defense, one must still act prudently. Of course, in biblical times, one might utilize prophecy to determine one's chances. Today, one must pray – and then make rational calculations. This is a critical moral value that can easily be ignored in the height of nationalist fervor: don't go to war unless you think you can succeed.

Cost-benefit analyses of success, however, are not simple, particularly when one considers not only potential casualties and economic fallout but also the fundamental character of the warring parties.[20] Sometimes defeat means much more than the loss of territory or resources, but a radical transformation of the entire culture of the losing nation. The ideological nature of such warfare, moreover, can have reverberations throughout the world.

This dilemma would become famous in the West during the Cold War. Some philosophers argued that in the event of an initial nuclear strike by the Soviets, the West should not retaliate. Communist domination is preferable to a nuclear holocaust. Others retorted that a conquest by the

Communists would be so horrific on the "hierarchy of strictly moral values" that the Western powers could never surrender to a Soviet onslaught. The West must retaliate in kind, no matter what the consequences. One Catholic just-war theorist put it this way: "There are greater evils than the physical death and destruction wrought in war. And there are human goods of so high an order that immense sacrifices may have to be borne in their defense."[21] As the saying went, "Better dead than red."

This sentiment was endorsed then by a prominent Jewish thinker who argued that the entire religious structure of the West would be in danger. "Being reduced to mere physical existence, being denied the basic moral character of our people ... is not living."[22] In the fight against tyranny, many martyrs must be sacrificed on the altar of freedom. Amalek, as we saw in chapter 2, must not ascend to control the world.

Here, once again, we should use JMF to understand the dilemma. At stake are two different values. Do we pay homage to our core beliefs above the value of life itself? In classic Jewish law, an individual may violate any commandment to stay alive, except for three grave sins: murder, illicit relations, and idolatry. This doctrine inspired many acts of medieval martyrdom. Now, the entire nation was at stake. Do we prioritize the people or the values that they adhere to?

Other rabbinic scholars answered that the notion of martyrdom was premised on individuals sacrificing themselves while others survived elsewhere, a prospect far from guaranteed in a nuclear conflict. The Romans too threatened the existence of the Jewish religion. Yoḥanan ben Zakkai nonetheless surrendered, and Judaism ultimately rebuilt itself. Jews prefer a life of indignity over a glorified death. As painful as it might be, we prefer "red over dead."

In any case, once one takes into consideration the impact on fundamental moral values, then questions of martyrdom for the sake of national honor come into play. One fights not just to protect physical survival, but also to defend the honor of the ideas that they represent and bear moral witness to them. As the philosopher A. J. Coates has argued, communities unwilling to fight for those values that are fundamental to its moral survival – including their very right to exist – have already ceased to be a political community in the fullest sense. In his words,

There may be a victory of a moral kind to be had that transcends military defeat. A war that is fought to defend fundamental human values can be successful even though it ends, *predictably*, in defeat. ... In such a case war is thought to be worthwhile precisely as a vindication of values – a vindication that does not require victory in a military sense, a vindication that may in fact be more complete the greater the certainty of military defeat. To resist in such circumstances would be to witness to a hierarchy of values in which death is not the greatest evil, while not to resist would be to pay obeisance to death, to avoid which no moral price or surrender of values is thought too high to pay.[23]

Death is not the greater evil in our hierarchy of values. The price of sacrificing one's core values is greater than the costs of lost lives.[24]

THE DEBATE OVER THE WARSAW GHETTO UPRISING

This factor of national honor was invoked by proponents of the doomed 1943 Warsaw Ghetto uprising.[25] In the previous year, as Jews in Palestine were trembling over the prospects of a Nazi invasion, three hundred thousand Jews in Warsaw were being effortlessly transported to death camps. Those who remained behind soon wondered whether they had acted foolishly – or even cowardly – to not resist these mass transports. Nonetheless, many ghetto leaders and residents, religious and secular alike, opposed any uprising as a hopeless act that would just hasten their deaths. Several asserted that it was better for Jews to die passively. A few prayed for miraculous salvation.

Ultimately, rebel supporters won the debate. Two of the few survivors later explained their logic. "Death was a given. How to live in the interim was not."[26] In the ghetto, the Jewish Military Organization distributed a courageous flyer, bolding asserting,

Let everyone be ready to die like a man! ...
Know that escape is not to be found by walking to your death passively, *like sheep to the slaughter*. It is to be found in something much greater: in war! Whoever defends himself has a chance of

being saved! Whoever gives up self-defense from the outset – he
has lost already!...
Let the tyrant pay with the blood of his body for every soul in
Israel!...
War for life or death on the conqueror to our last breath![27]

In this remarkable call to battle, the rebels invoke not only notions of
honor, but also declare that the uprising would at least take vengeance
on some Nazis and lead other Jews elsewhere to also stand up and rebel.
Taken together, these factors should trump the normally preeminent
value of preserving life.[28]

Rabbi Menachem Zemba was the most senior rabbinic figure
in the ghetto. In the fateful meeting in which the decision to rebel was
taken, he argued that in times of old, Jews became martyrs by electing
to die rather than convert. Now, however, when the Nazis sought to
annihilate the Jewish people, the only way to sanctify God's name was
to rise to arms and fight to the death. R. Zemba, alongside the rest of
the rebels, would be killed, but only after a remarkably stubborn six
weeks of resistance.

Their *choice* of death through rebellion was the ultimate rejection
of tyranny. It showed that we retain our ability to defy the cruelest forms
of despotism to live, and willingly die, for our values. Usually, protecting our human dignity and the mission of our nation demands staying
alive. On this occasion, it demanded an act of defiance, even at the cost
of lives.[29] The rebellion was ultimately crushed. Yet the Jews were not
led to slaughter with no control over their fate.

MASADA, WARSAW, AND KAMIKAZE DEATHS

After the Nazis torched and liquidated the ghetto, the *Yediot Ahronoth*
newspaper declared, "The Masada of Warsaw Has Fallen –The Nazis
Have Set Fire to the Remnants of the Warsaw Ghetto."[30] Greenboim
exclaimed, "[The rebels] have sanctified the name of their tortured and
downtrodden people with their blood, and renewed the tradition of the
Zealots of Jerusalem and Masada, the heroes of Bar-Kokhba and other
Jewish struggles."

Yet not everyone was so enamored with the rebellion. Rabbinic leaders of the non-Zionist Agudath Israel argued that this was an anti-religious decision which hastened the deaths of Warsaw's Jews and went against the traditional passive response to persecution. (Others would later deny that R. Zemba could ever make such statements in support of the rebellion.) R. Neriya himself had a tempered response. The uprising was defendable, he asserted, because at that stage, when there was no hope to live, one should follow Samson's model of a suicide mission that kills as many enemies as possible. In that situation alone, it was a *kiddush Hashem* to fight and die. Yet he worried that the rebels were becoming dangerously idolized. Our will to exist is our source of honor.[31] The greatest form of heroism is to survive in spite of the persecutions.[32]

Neriya is correct that there is something very dangerous about adulating patriotic "glorious deaths," since it may lead to unnecessary bloodshed. Why kill when you are bound to lose? Why die when you could live on?

The moral futility of an excessive sense of honor was exemplified only a couple of years later by many Japanese soldiers. On August 15, 1945, Emperor Hirohito of Japan finally brought an end to World War II by declaring a cessation of hostilities. After fourteen years of Japanese warfare, he urged his subjects to accept this humiliating loss and "endure the unendurable and bear the unbearable."[33] Nonetheless, several hundred Japanese militiamen, mostly officers, still committed suicide afterward, having been trained over years of war to never surrender.

Hirohito's decision prevented an Allied ground invasion of mainland Japan. It undoubtedly saved tens of thousands of lives, American and Japanese alike. Yet how much better would it have been for him to have made that decision a few months earlier when Japanese defeat was readily apparent. He could have prevented the futile *kamikaze* attacks, the bloody battles at Iwo Jima and Okinawa, and destructive bombings of Japanese cities that took so many lives. Within a few years, all of those people killed could have instead been moving on with their lives. Their never-to-be born grandchildren, in both countries, would have been driving Hondas while listening to Bruce Springsteen songs. National honor can drive people to do horrific things while preventing them from making the correct decisions to preserve life.[34] Generally speaking, one shouldn't fight, or continue fighting, a lost cause.

Yet there are times, as even R. Neriya begrudgingly admits, when fighting to the bitter end is necessary to preserve national honor. This was thankfully not necessary in 1942 Palestine as the British successfully turned back Rommel in El Alamein. Yet there is significant evidence that had the Nazis succeeded in reaching Palestine, they would have killed those Jews as per the "Final Solution," with the help of their Arab collaborators.[35] Shapira's vision of a ghetto in Palestine was wishful thinking, while Ben-Gurion's plans to evacuate soldiers elsewhere were likely unrealistic. Given the undesirable alternatives, the perspective to fight to the end was justifiable and even judicious.

In retrospect, we can see now that the Warsaw rebels were correct that their uprising would inspire Jews around the world to take up arms and defend themselves, during the Holocaust and afterward. As the Mizrachi leadership asserted in May 1943,

> From behind the Warsaw Ghetto's sealed walls rises the muffled cry of the Jewish remnant which fights for its life with wondrous, awe-inspiring bravery…. The sublime holy war for their lives waged by the remnants of Polish Jewry sanctifies the divine name and the name of Israel in an alienated world that stands aloof, revealing the tremendous powers that once animated – and still animate – this proud Jewry.[36]

In the short term, perhaps a few more Jews died than would have otherwise. Or maybe they would have all perished in the death camps. It is impossible to know. But in the long run, the decision to "go down fighting" inspired many more Jews over the coming years to take the necessary actions to protect Jewish lives.

It's harder to take the same positive stance toward the (alleged) mass suicide at Masada. There are certainly examples of rabbinic Sages excusing Jews who took their own lives in the face of centuries of persecution. Yet many other rabbinic figures discouraged or even condemned these acts of defiance, despite their sympathies for the plight of persecuted Jews. They understood that suicide doesn't preserve Jewish lives or inspire Jewish living.[37] To address this problem, some early Zionists, both before and after the founding of the state, tempered their promotion of the "Masada myth" by focusing on their belligerent heroism.[38] Yet it is difficult to suppress the memory of their suicide and their opposition to Zakkai's successful survival strategy while still finding inspiration from their activism and defiance.[39]

Even R. Goren would later admit that Masada was not an ideal model. In a later interview, he would assert about the Masada rebels,

> Under those conditions, they did the right thing. And this was an act of heroism.... But I objected [to the statement] that this would symbolize the heroism of Israel. This was good for the Diaspora. Not after the creation of the State of Israel. Here we have to take as an example the heroism of the Hasmoneans. Kiddush Hashem must be achieved by life, not by death. *The season of Kiddush Hashem by death is finished.*[40]

R. Goren's fascinating statement recognizes that suicidal battles are a better alternative to being led like sheep to the slaughter. Yet suicide alone brings little glory and should not be emulated. To achieve genuine national honor, one needs the nation to live. The just war is about self-defense, not self-destruction.

WHO DECIDES BETWEEN COMPETING VALUES?

What is striking about these debates over Masada, the feared Nazi invasion, and the Warsaw Ghetto uprising is that all of the protagonists make cogent arguments grounded in legitimate values. One can readily argue that one side or another was wrong in the strategic assessment or that their moral calculations were misguided. Yet these were, fundamentally, debates over which legitimate values should take precedence in cases of uncertainty. They highlight the effectiveness of a multivalued framework to understand the different sides within heated and fateful debates.

It's fun to debate these questions over a cup of coffee in Starbucks or in a university classroom while thinking about the dilemmas of the past. Real-time leadership, however, requires someone to make the call. The question then becomes who makes the decision when to fight. This dilemma would consume the next episode in Jewish military ethics: the rebellion against the British and the war for sovereignty.

Chapter 12

The Etzel's Rebellion and the Dilemma over When to Rebel

"FREEDOM OR DEATH": BEGIN'S REBELLION AGAINST BRITISH RULE AND JEWISH TIMIDITY

On February 1, 1944, the Etzel did something which no Jewish group had done since the Bar Kokhba rebellion eighteen hundred years beforehand: they rebelled against the local ruling authorities. Citing grievances over the slaughter of the Jews in Europe and the repeated denial of entry to Jewish refugees into Palestine, the group plastered posters throughout Palestine directed at the "the Hebrew Nation in Zion" which declared,

> The British regime has sealed its shameful betrayal of the Jewish people and there is no moral basis whatsoever for its presence in Eretz Yisrael.… There is no longer an armistice between the Jewish people and the British Administration in Eretz Yisrael which hands our brothers over to Hitler.
> Our people is at war with this regime – war to the end…
> We shall fight – every Jew in the Homeland will fight.

The God of Israel, the Lord of Hosts, will aid us.
There will be no retreat. Freedom – or death.[1]

Eleven days later, the group launched late-night bombings of the British Immigration Department offices. The symbolism was potent, targeting the government organ that prevented Jews from entering the country. The Etzel's new leader, Menachem Begin, further hoped that by avoiding human casualties, his organization would assert its moral superiority over the British, who had mercilessly turned away boats full of Jews fleeing the Nazis.[2] "We fight, therefore we are!" became his mantra.[3]

DOES JEWISH LAW DEMAND OBEDIENCE TO UNJUST RULERS?

Begin also encouraged nonviolent symbolic actions that would demonstrate that the Jews no longer accepted foreign control of their homeland. On Yom Kippur of 1943, the Jewish holy day of atonement, British police officers arrested and beat Jews at the Western Wall. Their crime? They had blown the trumpetlike shofar blasts that mark the end of the fast day. Since the 1929 riots, British authorities had prohibited these customary shofar blasts so as not to offend the sensibilities of local Arabs, who chose to see the sounds as a battle cry. Begin, who was present, was outraged, deeming the Jews "slaves in spirit."[4] The next year, Betar plastered signs around Jerusalem warning against the infringement on the Jewish right to worship.

> The British government – ruling temporarily against the will of the Jewish people it its Homeland – is required not to infringe these principles. Any British policeman who on the Day of Atonement dares to burst into the area of the Wailing Wall and to disturb the traditional service – will be regarded as a criminal and will be punished accordingly.

As Begin tells the story, the warning succeeded. The British police stood down and the shofar blast was loudly blown.[5] At the same time, the Etzel used the threat as a decoy for successful attacks on four police stations around the country. The Jews, as Begin put it, had finally sounded "the trumpet of revolt."

For Begin, the revolt wasn't just against the British. It represented a rejection of the exilic mindset of diffidence to the laws of foreign rulers which was still hampering the Jews of Palestine. After the Etzel published its threatening posters, other Jewish bodies issued warnings against their declaration. One of them was the Chief Rabbinate, which prohibited shofar blowing in deference to the British regulations. Begin mocked rabbinic apologists who declared that the post–Yom Kippur shofar blowing was "only a custom" and that in any case, talmudic law demands that the rule of the land must be followed.[6] "The law of the kingdom is the law" (*dina demalkhuta dina*; hereafter *DDD*) was declared by a third-century Babylonian scholar to help transition Jews to a new reality in which they'd be governed by the centralized Sassanian authorities. For Begin and others, this doctrine was a part of a larger exilic worldview that rendered the Jews as "timid suppliants for protection."[7]

It's not clear that the chief rabbis at the time, Rabbis Herzog and Uziel, were in fact invoking the *DDD* rule. The disputes over shofar blowing at the Western Wall had been ongoing for over a decade. It seemed that the chief rabbis were trying to prevent this ritual from getting entangled in political machinations, or for prayer at the Western Wall to be used as a pretext for Arab violence, as had occurred in 1929. Many politicians, furthermore, felt that strategically it was a mistake to cause unnecessary agitation with the British, particularly just as His Majesty's government was announcing the long-awaited formation of a Jewish brigade in its army.

Nonetheless, Begin was correct that *DDD* could be invoked to support obedience to the attempts of the British to suppress any rebellion. In March 1944, when the British imposed a curfew on the Jews of Palestine as a response to the Etzel's bombings, the lead editorial of the religious Zionist newspaper *Hatzofeh* bitterly complained against the injustice of this collective punishment. Nonetheless, it invoked *DDD* to assert that the Jews must comply with this unjust sanction.[8]

The principle of "the law of the kingdom is the law" undoubtedly played a critical role in shaping Jewish attitudes toward local rulers throughout their centuries of exile. Most directly, the rule mandated that they pay taxes and accept equitable civil regulations imposed by the governing authorities. Over the centuries, the rule came to represent a broader doctrine for how Jews respected the dictates of the societies in which they resided as distinct minorities. It allowed them to live under two systems of law, one Jewish and the other civil, as imposed by the foreign leaders of their residence. To a certain extent, it served as a legal buttress to the sentiment already expressed by the prophet Jeremiah, "And seek the welfare of the city to which I have exiled you and pray to the Lord in its behalf; for in its prosperity you shall prosper."[9] Those who genuinely pray for the welfare of the government do not rebel against the dominion of their kings and princes.

Did the Jews' historic adherence to this principle lead to timid acquiescence to foreign rule? In chapter 1, we saw that Rabbi Samson Raphael Hirsch of Frankfurt contended that Jews must enlist in the German army to protect "the Fatherland." He based this claim on the principle of *DDD*, which he argued must be internalized as a character virtue of "inner obedience." How far does this patriotic duty go?

> This duty is an unconditional duty and not dependent upon whether the State is kindly intentioned towards you or is hard. Even should they deny your right to be a human being and to develop a lawful human life upon the soil which bore you – *you* shall not neglect your duty…. 'Loyalty towards king and country and the promotion of welfare wherever and however you can.'[10]

It is hard to imagine a more problematic internalization of a suppliant attitude toward foreign rule.

Equally problematic was an approach taken by some anti-Zionist Orthodox rabbinic figures who invoked a talmudic passage against rebelling against non-Jewish rulers during the exilic period. According to the legendary account, three oaths were taken when the Jews went into exile:

> One, that the Jews should not ascend to the Land of Israel as a wall (i.e., en masse).
> Another, that the Holy One, blessed be He, adjured the Jews that they should not rebel against the rule of the nations of the world.

And the last, that God adjured the nations of the world that they should not subjugate the Jews excessively.[11]

If one understands this passage as a binding normative directive, then one could claim that illegal immigration and fighting against the British violated the first two oaths of "rebelling against the nations" or "rising up together in force."

Yet, as many Zionist figures retorted, it's more likely that this talmudic passage was a theological or homiletic statement for its era. Moreover, even as a legal directive, the oaths governed only political life outside of the Land of Israel, but did not apply to the Holy Land. Furthermore, the nations of the world confirmed in the 1920 San Remo conference that the Jewish people had rights to Palestine. You can't "rebel against the nations" when the League of Nations is telling you that you are entitled to that territory. Most significantly, the talmudic passage also adjured the nations of the world not to excessively subjugate the Jewish people. One could hardly say that they had upheld their end of the deal, thereby releasing the Jews from any alleged prohibition against rebelling.

Similarly, it's unlikely that any legal proscription of *DDD* was truly holding back the Jews from rejecting British control. Many medieval authorities already recognized that the principle would not be binding on laws which illicitly discriminated against specific people or that infringed upon Jewish ritual life. While generally accepting of British civil law, Zionist rabbinic figures rejected discriminatory immigration policies that prevented Jews from coming to Palestine. They actively supported covert and illegal attempts to smuggle Jews out of Europe.[12] Particularly after the 1939 White Paper, even moderate figures like Moshe Shapiro and Rabbi Amiel came out strongly against the restrictive policy and urged Jews to continue to immigrate, illegally, to Palestine.

Rabbi Herzog delivered a fiery sermon accusing Britain of "betraying the House of Israel" and violating any semblance of justice with its policy. He called out the verse from Isaiah, "Take counsel together and it shall be brought to naught," and then dramatically tore up his copy of the White Paper.[13] Years later, at the onset of the War of Independence, R. Herzog would declare that both the three oaths and the *DDD* principle were only binding in Diaspora lands but had no relevance to Jews in their Promised Land. In Israel, the political authority of foreign leaders would not be respected.[14]

This conclusion was already reached in June 1939 by Rabbi Bar-Ilan, who publicly asserted that the British no longer had a legitimate right to rule over Palestine. In his mind, the White Paper undermined the very premise of the mandate system; as such, they had no entitlements to the territory. He quickly dismissed that such a declaration violated the three oaths, arguing that it was the British government who rebelled against its obligations. In any case, the lives of Jews in Europe and Palestine were at stake. The value of saving Jewish lives trumped the value of civil obedience. The Jews must now rise up in resistance – not through a quixotic open rebellion, but by refusing to cooperate with any British government authorities.[15]

As we previously noted, any such plans ended a few months later with the outbreak of World War II. Ben-Gurion and others, supported by the Chief Rabbinate and the Irgun, felt compelled to work with the British. Only the tiny splinter group of Avraham Stern, the Lehi (Fighters for the Freedom of Israel), chose to attack British targets, until Begin ignited the true revolt against the British.

Ultimately, it may be morally just for a suppressed people to rebel, yet any responsible leadership must recall that most insurgencies have historically failed. That's not only a strategic consideration but an ethical one. As we saw in the previous chapter, "probability of success" has moral force. There's no glory in leading one's people on a hopeless rebellion when other paths to independence may be available.

This, of course, was the rationale of the Jewish Agency leadership. Their decision to continue to cooperate with the British was a political, realpolitik decision, not an ethical statement against a rebellion. The British were not enemies but "bad allies." Their policies went against their better judgment and could be changed, but only through diplomacy and reason.[16] It was precisely this strategy that Begin was now challenging. It was this political revolt against the mainstream Jewish political authority, as much as his active rebellion against the British or the alleged tradition of Jewish timidity, that caused the greatest amount of consternation.

TO REBEL OR NOT TO REBEL? THE GHOSTS OF
BAR KOKHBA

Hovering over the heated debate regarding the Etzel's uprising against the British was the legacy of the failed Bar Kokhba rebellion, the final Jewish rebellion against Roman rule in Palestine in 132–135 CE. The rebels were led by Simeon ben Kosiba, popularly known as Bar Kokhba (Hebrew for "son of the star"). This sobriquet was reportedly given to him by the prominent Sage R. Akiva, one of his many rabbinic supporters who, according to talmudic legend, believed this warrior was the Messiah. His rabbinic opponents, by contrast, gave the rebel leader the moniker Bar Koziba, Hebrew for "son of disappointment." Scholars continue to debate what instigated the rebellion, ranging from economic and administrative decline to a ban on ritual circumcision or the building of a pagan city on the ruins of Jerusalem. Whatever its cause, the result was a strong nationalist movement under the slogan "For the Freedom of Jerusalem."

Although the insurgents had some initial success, the rebellion was ultimately crushed by the Romans. According to talmudic legend, the end of the revolt was particularly grisly, with a river of Jewish blood streaming to the sea over a distance of two and a half miles from Betar, the final rebel stronghold. In one version of the story, Bar Kokhba lost his final battle after he brazenly killed one of his rabbinic opponents – his uncle – who warned him that he was going to fail. The redeemer of the people had turned on his own.

In the coming centuries, the name Bar Kokhba would have a tainted connotation in rabbinic literature, with his rebellion frequently (albeit not universally) associated with dangerous bravado and false messianism.[17] Rabbi Hirsch, for example, deemed his insurgency a "fatal error." It was a lasting reminder for Jews not to restore Jewish sovereignty through "their own force of arms." That aspiration required God's intervention alone.[18]

Early-twentieth-century Zionists, however, rejuvenated Bar Kokhba's legacy by reviving a strand of medieval thought that positively portrayed him as a courageous leader who stood up against the depravity of foreign rule. Poets like Bialik, Tchernichovsky, and Rachel Yanait lauded his bravery in contrast to the timidity of Diaspora Jews. Jabotinsky named his movement Betar, as he saw its self-defense mission continuing in the footsteps of Bar Kokhba. The sentiment was also shared by Ben-Gurion, who later declared during Israel's War of Independence that her soldiers were continuing the legacy of Bar Kokhba and R. Akiva.[19]

Zionists, of course, could not ignore the fact that Bar Kokhba's rebellion ended in miserable failure. Shortly before his death in 1935, Rabbi Kook addressed this problem in a letter to the Bnei Akiva youth group, named for Bar Kokhba's rabbinic supporter. He contended that Bar Kokhba set a model of self-sacrifice toward national redemptions. While he failed in his time, his holy message remains true. Accordingly, he asserted, the day of national liberation will come soon. "Those failures will not repeat themselves. It is not in vain that Israel has always fought for its existence and survived until this generation."[20] For R. Kook and other Zionists, Bar Kokhba's failure did not diminish the justness of his cause or the need to emulate him. In the words of the poet Uri Zvi Greenberg, "Bar Kokhba's teaching is the truth, even with the fall of Betar."

Decades later, in 1982, Rabbi Goren, who we saw had soured on the Masada legacy, initiated a state funeral for bones that were claimed to have been those of Bar Kokhba's rebels. The initiative, not surprisingly, was eagerly supported by then-Prime Minister Begin. Others strongly criticized the ceremony. They saw Bar Kokhba as a dangerous example of unbridled nationalism, both then and now.[21]

THE CHALLENGE OF COMPETENT AUTHORITY AND THE MODEL OF THE AMERICAN REVOLUTION

The rabbinic dispute over the Bar Kokhba rebellion raised the question of who decides when the time is right for war. After all, one may admire Bar Kokhba's courage but recognize that it led to disaster. In the 1940s, a failed insurgency could not be repeated.

These power struggles relate to a much broader requirement in classic just-war theory: competent authority. For warfare to be deemed legitimate, it requires a recognized political ruler to declare the moral rationale for such warfare. They would be expected, for example, to proclaim their grievances and explain why injustice would now be rectified by warfare. Since states have clear, centralized leadership, it is usually not difficult to identify who possesses the authority to declare war.

Competent authority, however, becomes an issue with civil wars and revolts when it remains unclear who has the authority necessary to resort to arms. In classic just-war theory, revolutions were fundamentally unjust because they lacked the support of a sovereign authority.[22] *DDD* was thus far from the only medieval doctrine or perspective that would hamper rebellions against unjust rulers. In fact, some contemporary theorists, stuck in a rigid philosophical framework, still remarkably claim that the American Revolution was unjust because, in part, there was no competent authority to declare their violent rebellion! Others, however, reasonably counter that the colonists basically governed themselves for 150 years. More significantly, the Crown was no longer protecting their well-being.[23]

Ultimately, the American and French Revolutions challenged the medieval paradigm by asserting that each individual, on the basis of their natural rights, could join up in collective defense against the (unjust) sovereign power. Many scholars today further argue that the legitimate authority requirement cannot apply to wars of national independence or succession, since it is precisely the question of public legitimacy that is being contested.[24] The rules of the just-war game, so to speak, cannot be rigged to protect illegitimate British rulers, whether in the American colonies in 1776 or Palestine in 1946.

Irgun sympathizers in America were quick to compare the Jewish insurgency to other revolutionary movements. The playwright Ben Hecht, a member of the Bergson Group, passionately declared, "The few survivors [of the Holocaust] … are making history in the same way as the Maquis, the Partisans, the Irish rebels, and the American revolutionists." The brigade of American volunteers that joined the Irgun was dubbed the "George Washington Legion." Other defenders of the Irgun liked to cite the expression made famous by Benjamin Franklin and Thomas Jefferson, "Resistance to tyranny is obedience to God."[25]

TRENDSETTING PIONEERS OR SECTARIAN SEPARATISTS?

That being said, it is one thing to claim that a rebellion is theoretically legitimate, and another to prove that the alleged beneficiaries support this tactic. Sometimes it is difficult to determine whether a rebel group actually represents their alleged constituency. Many insurgents were historically accused of coercing participation by others in their rebellion.[26] This criticism, as we saw, was leveled against the Warsaw Ghetto rebels.

To win any battle, revolutionary or otherwise, unity and consensus are necessary. As Franklin famously put it regarding the American colonies in a celebrated 1754 political cartoon, "Join, or die."

Yet it takes time to build consensus. Nine years later, the American colonies began collecting grievances against British rule, and it took more than another decade for them to actually declare independence. The "first shots" of the rebellion in Lexington and Concord were taken in April 1775. Yet even two months later, John Adams would write to his wife regarding disagreements among the American colonies to declare independence, "America is a great, unwieldy Body. Its Progress must be slow.... Like a Coach and six – the swiftest Horses must be slackened and the slowest quickened, that all may keep an even Pace."[27]

Begin knew this. Yet with the Nazi killing machine at work in Europe, the pace was too slow for him and his comrades. The Revisionist movement had always had a choppy relationship with the Jewish Agency and other "mainstream" organizations, making the accusation of being a "separatist" somewhat beside the point. They had separated precisely because they didn't think the other organizations understood what it took to save Jewish lives: to fight not only against local Arabs but also against the British rulers who kept Palestine's gates locked.

Begin would also argue that revolutions are different from regular wars as they must break out organically, not through an organized decision. "A revolution is not something you put to a vote. ... The storming of the Bastille preceded the Declaration of the Rights of Man; the Boston Tea Party preceded the Bill of Rights."[28] Recent revolutions in Ireland and Italy succeeded precisely because a small group of fighters was able to successfully galvanize the masses.[29] In politics, an inspiring minority group can quickly become the majority. Or it can splinter the people and prevent a unified front.

For this reason, many rabbis criticized the Etzel because they saw the Jewish Agency as the official representative of Palestine's Jewish residents. It was created to include all Zionist factions and consider all strategic calculations. Any splinter group activity would only cause damage to the broader collective. We've previously seen how figures like Rabbi Maimon, despite his sympathies for the Etzel's tactics, was critical of their sectarianism and urged them to act in conjunction with the larger political group.[30] This was certainly true for figures like Chief Rabbis Herzog and Uziel. They separately wrote academic treatises arguing that Jewish law was compatible with democratic norms while dedicating much time to bringing religious factions into various democratic institutions.[31] They condemned the Etzel not only for their moral sins and political miscalculations but also for violating the dictum of the talmudic Sage Hillel, "Do not separate (*poresh*) yourself from the community." Indeed, Haganah supporters derogatorily called their rivals in the Etzel and Lehi the *porshim* (separatists) to recall the Sages' harsh condemnation of such groups.[32]

THE *SAISON*, THE *ALTALENA*, AND THE THREAT OF CIVIL WAR

Yet calls for unity cut both ways. Therefore, for similar concerns, these same rabbinic critics of the Etzel were also adamantly opposed to the collaboration of the Haganah with the British to arrest Irgun members. In November 1944, following the assassination of Lord Moyne in Egypt by Lehi activists, the British government demanded that the Jewish Agency help them arrest insurgents. Many members of the Haganah were happy to comply, leading to the imprisonment of numerous Etzel activists over several months in a period known as the *Saison* (hunting season). The Haganah justified their collaboration as necessary for the Jewish community to stay in the good graces of the British. They were also using the *Saison* as an excuse to arrest Revisionist figures who had nothing to do with the terror activities, which even British officials eventually realized.[33] Several Irgun members were tortured or exiled to Eritrea.

The chief rabbis were vehemently opposed to any such cooperation with the British. They condemned the *Saison* as "cruel," "abominable," and a grave violation of Jewish legal and moral norms.[34] R. Maimon, for his part, resigned in protest as a member of the Jewish Agency executive committee.

Spurned by their religious colleagues, disappointed Zionist leaders like Ben-Gurion turned to anti-Zionist rabbinic figures for support of their policy. The most strident rabbinic supporter of the *Saison* was none other than R. Hirsch's grandson, Dr. Isaac Breuer. He asserted that the Torah requires handing over the insurgents, who were endangering the entire community.[35] Zionist rabbinic leaders knew better. Despite their opposition to the Irgun's methods, the lesson from the last Jewish insurgencies – against Rome, nearly eighteen hundred years beforehand – was that fratricide would only lead to a self-destructive civil war.[36] Violent factionalism was both a moral and strategic failure.

To his great credit, Begin also internalized this lesson. He ordered Etzel activists not to retaliate against Haganah activists. "Do not raise a hand and do not use a weapon.… They are our brothers…there will not be a civil war, but [we] will approach the big day, in which the nation will rise up – despite the will of those obstructing the way – as one fighting camp."[37] Begin further asserted that despite the instinct to retaliate against the "one-sided civil war" waged on the Irgun, a higher "order" came from the depths of Jewish history to prevent a full-out fratricidal conflict.

> From down the corridors of history, we heard the echo of those other wars, the cursed internecine wars in dying Jerusalem nineteen centuries before.… Not logic, but instinct said imperatively, "No, not a civil war. Not that at any price."[38]

The mixed history of ancient Jewish rebellions, from the successful Maccabean revolt against the Greeks to the dismal failures against the

Romans, highlights how difficult it is to know when a rebellion might succeed. Yet Jewish history clearly teaches that internal violence will always lead to disaster.

The *Saison* would end several months later. For a brief period afterward, the different paramilitary organizations would coordinate acts of sabotage against the British under the united banner of the Jewish Resistance movement. These actions included the blowing up of central railroad tracks ("Night of the Trains") and bridges ("Night of the Bridges") that controlled British military transportation. This coordination was fleeting. The Haganah afterward largely rejected violence against the British out of a combination of moral and pragmatic considerations. They focused more on actions connected to illegal immigration and settlement.[39] Nonetheless, their short-lived collaboration highlighted how the debate ultimately became one of strategy and timing, alongside the ultimate question of who had the authority to make such decisions.

Tragically, the Haganah leadership would make the same mistake of using internecine violence again in 1948, soon after Israel's Declaration of Independence. The Bergson Group had arranged for a boat, the *Altalena,* to deliver badly needed weapons to Jewish fighters in the nascent War of Independence. After a series of disputes and misunderstandings over control of the weapons, compounded by years of mistrust, the newly formed Israel Defense Forces (IDF), under Ben-Gurion's orders, shelled and sank the boat. While historians continue to debate who was to blame for not de-escalating the standoff, the end result was a disaster: sixteen Etzel members alongside three IDF soldiers were dead. Even after a white flag was raised from the boat, soldiers continued to shoot, including at Etzel members swimming in the Mediterranean.

Begin, once again to his great credit, ordered not to shoot back. "It is forbidden that a Hebrew weapon be used against Hebrew fighters." Ben-Gurion, in turn, insisted that the cannon that sank the *Altalena* was so sacred that it should "stand close to the Temple, if it is built" since it helped quash a seditious rebellion. Only twenty years later did he begrudgingly concede, "Perhaps I was mistaken."[40]

Recent archival research has shown that religious politicians like R. Maimon, R. Berlin, and especially Shapira had warned Ben-Gurion in the preceding days that he was overreacting. There was no reason to treat the *Altalena* shipment as a rebellious act.[41] A disaster was bound to happen. Afterward, to their credit, the religious ministers alone resigned in protest from the provisional government. Rabbi Neria would castigate Ben-Gurion for settling political scores in the guise of quashing a rebellion, while Rabbi Tzvi Yehuda called for national reconciliation to prevent further disaster.[42] Alas, Ben-Gurion's errors with the *Saison* and *Altalena* continued to negatively impact internal Israeli politics for decades to come.

You can't call for everyone to come under a "big tent" democratic organization and then shoot those who refuse to obey. There's a danger to disunity, but an even greater danger to civil war. Some had learned the lessons of internal violence that plagued the ancient rebellions. Others had not.

Chapter 13

Central War Authority from King David to Ben Gurion

WHO DECIDES WHEN TO GO TO WAR? THE DILEMMA OF BALANCED WAR POWERS

Notwithstanding the mistake of firing on the *Altalena*, Ben-Gurion was generally correct in asserting that the fledging state had to have a clear chain of military command, with one figure or body making final decisions and others respecting its orders. In addition to requiring the various underground groups to disband and merge into the Israel Defense Forces, he also sought to create a clear structure and organization within the IDF, which necessitated the dissolution of the Palmach.

Who should have the powers to go to war? At its core, the question relates to the proper relationship between a people and its government. Ancient and medieval regimes sought power and glory at the expense of their citizens. Modern democracies seek to prevent such abuse of power.[1] The Founding Fathers of the United States were deeply concerned that the executive branch would endanger its citizens and soldiers through unnecessary warfare. At the same time, they did not want to hamper the government from defending its territory. In the words of Alexander Hamilton,

> We ought to try the novel and absurd experiment in politics of tying up the hands of government from offensive war founded upon reasons of state, yet certainly we ought not to disable it from guarding the community against the ambition or enmity of other nations.[2]

In this spirit, the US Constitution created some balance of powers by making the president the commander in chief, while authorizing Congress to declare war and to raise and support the armed forces. In more recent decades, however, this model has only had limited effectiveness. American presidents regularly launch military strikes and even wars without genuine congressional approval.

As Rabbi Herzog noted, the need to create checks and balances to limit offensive warfare without hampering a leader's ability to provide expedient defense was already perceived by the talmudic Sages.[3] As we saw in chapter 2, a dominant strand within talmudic law, followed by Maimonides and others, distinguished between two types of wars: obligatory or commanded wars, including wars of self-defense and the destruction of the Canaanite and Amalek nations, as opposed to discretionary wars, such as expansionist warfare. Regarding the former, the king could act on his own because the mission was seen as essential and time sensitive, particularly in the face of an attack.[4] For similar reasons, all capable bodies were required to serve to protect the greater collective.

Regarding discretionary wars, however, soldiers could opt out, either because they were recently married or settled in new homes, making them less eager to fight, or simply because they claimed they were fearful of dying in battle or too soft-hearted to kill.[5] According to one Sage, this even included someone who is "a hero among heroes, powerful among the most powerful, but who is at the same time merciful – let him return [from the front lines]."[6] This provision might allow for a certain type of selective conscientious objection for fighters to opt out of unpopular wars. At the very least, it provides, in practice, an important check on monarchal abuse by allowing many soldiers to get out of a war deemed as nonessential.

Equally significantly, the king was required in a discretionary war to first consult with the Sanhedrin, a great assembly of seventy-one Sages. The king was not all-powerful. He needed permission to launch such a war.

Several twentieth-century commentators asserted that the Sanhedrin was central in determining the moral propriety of such warfare. Do the potential national benefits of such warfare justify the costs and risks in human life? [7] Is this step truly necessary? A moral calculation, let alone political, is required to make that assertion. This necessitates the judgment of a great group of spiritual sages, even if – or perhaps precisely because – it entails a prolonged conversation. As many political theorists have noted, this type of ex ante veto power gives outside bodies the most potential impact on military deployments. The inclusion of different voices reduces the effects of groupthink, premature closure, and political exploitation for personal benefit.

Indeed, territory illicitly conquered by a king without the permission of the court is deemed the result of an executive action alone and, for many legal purposes, is not considered part of Israel. The Sages coined such warfare a case of "personal conquest" (in Hebrew, *kibush yaḥid*). This designation places a large symbolic asterisk around the conquest. Judaism recognizes that a military victory might not be a national triumph.

The significance of these limits on discretionary wars should not be overlooked. The philosopher Michael Walzer, in a seminal 1993 article, pointed to the omission of an explicit category of "prohibited" wars as entailing a major lacuna in Jewish ethics. All war is either obligatory or discretionary, but never forbidden. If military exploits were allowed for "greatness and prestige" alone, in Maimonides's words, then the system is problematic. As Aviezer Ravitzky retorted, many rabbinic scholars had, in fact, asserted that wars may be prohibited since our baseline assumption is that all killing is prohibited.[8] Warfare must therefore be justified to become permissible, even if discretionary.[9] We should further recall that there is a strong strand of rabbinic thought which condemned any expansionary warfare even by figures as beloved as King David, as discussed in chapter 2.

"THE SWORD ALWAYS TAKES ITS TOLL": LIMITING EXCESSIVE WAR

Indeed, it is precisely the example of King David that must alert us to the abuses possible when military leaders go unchecked. During such a discretionary war against the Ammonites, in which David achieved a "great name" and much fortune, he became embroiled in his affair with a married woman, Bathsheba. Most significantly for our purposes, he abused his role by sending her husband, a soldier, on a quixotic mission so that he should die.[10] "Place Uriah in the front line where the fighting is fiercest," he ordered his chief of staff, "then fall back so that he may be killed." Uriah died – along with other captains. David dismissed the losses by telling his chief general, "Do not be distressed about the matter. The sword always takes its toll."

The sword does indeed take its toll, particularly when monarchs act out of nefarious motivations. It's precisely for this reason that our moral sentiments – and Jewish law – have progressed to limit such violent imperialism. Spiritual leaders have a duty to tame the natural impulses of many strong leaders and countries.[11] Indeed, a close read of the Bible shows how political leaders regularly consulted with other advisers – spiritual and strategic – before making military decisions in all wars.[12] These included "commanded wars" like the original conquest of Canaan or wars of self-defense. In that respect, the Sages' granting the Sanhedrin such veto powers was revolutionary for its time and remains quite important.[13]

WHICH SYSTEM IS BEST?

Contemporary democracies greatly differ regarding which figures or bodies must be consulted before declaring war and whether they should hold veto powers over any decision. According to a study by the Geneva Centre for the Democratic Control of Armed Forces, roughly twenty democracies grant their parliaments ex ante veto powers. The majority of democracies, however, grant their legislatures oversight roles but do not grant such veto powers, either because they do not think their leaders require such strict limitations (as in the case of Canada), or alternatively because they face regular threats and do not want to limit their executive branch from acting swiftly.

It's difficult to say that there is one correct formula. Each country may need to find its right balance depending on its historical legacy and contemporary threats. To take one example, contemporary Germany lives with trauma from its Nazi past. To cautiously use its growing role on the world stage, it passed in 1995 strict rules that require parliamentary approval of all armed forces deployments and a basic review procedure for "low-intensity" missions.

Israel, which does not have a written constitution, has seen its leaders utilize different approaches, and the question remains a matter of contentious debate. In 1947, Ben-Gurion ran military "seminars" while promoting – and demoting – different military figures to effectively mobilize the six hundred thousand Jewish residents of Israel toward independence and victory. He further appointed himself as defense minister, placing an incredible amount of power in one centralized authority.[14] It worked in that case, but such a centralized model can also come with a price. In any case, formal rules and regulations will not necessarily stop the head of state or defense minister from unilaterally launching many types of military expeditions, particularly when they fall short of full-fledged warfare. Leaders must therefore internalize the importance of this ethical imperative. As we'll see in chapter 18, Israel failed this moral test during the 1982 Lebanon War.

WHO WAS RIGHT, THE ETZEL OR THE HAGANAH?

Whatever system is set up, it's important to stress that increasing the circle of advisers does not at all guarantee the strategic wisdom or military efficiency of the decision. History is full of examples in which the majority of leaders made, collectively, the wrong decision.

In fact, in the case of the uprising against the British, one could argue, as the Etzel did, that had the Jews not made it too costly for the British to stay, they would not have announced their intention to leave in 1947. As Bruce Hoffman has shown, the Etzel succeeded in tarnishing the British prestige and extinguishing any desire to remain in Palestine. This was achieved in spite of the fact that the number of casualties was relatively minimal: Britain lost only 141 soldiers between August 1945 and August 1947, and the number of civilian casualties (Jewish, British, and Arab) also remained very low. Undoubtedly, there were other considerations in the British decision: the granting of independence to India; Britain's postwar economic struggles; the intense pressure of Jewish immigration, particularly from Holocaust survivors; and international pressure to end the mandate. Yet the biggest one, at least in the assessment of the British colonial secretary, was that "terrorism was at its worst and the British public seemed unable to stand much more."[15] Others dispute that opinion, but the very plausibility of the claim highlights that the position supported by the majority (in this case, Jewish Agency leaders) was not the correct decision.

The inclusion of countering powers in democracies, instead, is more likely to succeed in preventing, or at the very least ending sooner, military expeditions which, in effect if not in intent, are imperial overreaches that take the lives of too many soldiers. The possibility of receiving pushback from a legislature, Sanhedrin, or some other independent body increases (but does not guarantee) the chance that there will be voices restraining the use of force that unnecessarily endangers the lives of citizens and soldiers alike.[16]

This, too, we can see from the British-Zionist conflict. The British government realized that their military presence in Palestine was a *milḥemet reshut*. It ended when other powers, like the British parliament, press, and public demanded that the government leave a distant land in which the local residents despised their presence. The mandate was costing too much in blood. British citizens didn't want to die for this cause, and the government had to listen. For the Jews, however, this was a *milḥemet mitzva* for the homeland, worthy of self-sacrifice. As Begin would put it, "When a nation re-awakens, its finest sons are prepared to give their lives for liberation. When Empires are threatened with collapse, they are prepared to sacrifice their noncommissioned officers."[17]

The advice of a Sanhedrin or any other body, however, is only so good as its strategic and moral compass. The challenge for the emerging Jewish state – and any country – is to determine what ethical framework will allow one to judge the morality of going to war. Leaders must determine which wars are essential and which wars are not. It is to these questions which we turn in the following chapter.

Chapter 14

Self-Determination Through Partition Plans and Israel's War of Independence

A TALE OF TWO PAMPHLETS: SHOULD YESHIVA STUDENTS FIGHT IN THE WAR OF INDEPENDENCE?

In April 1948, Shear-Yashuv Cohen, a twenty-year old yeshiva student at the Merkaz HaRav rabbinic seminary, was on a short reprieve from his service in the Haganah. Just months beforehand, the United Nations had voted to partition Palestine following the upcoming termination of the British mandate. The Zionists accepted the plan, but the Arabs rejected it, leading to another period of violent tensions. While it wasn't entirely clear then, this period ultimately became the first stage of Israel's War of Independence.

The Haganah was pushing for widespread conscription. Yet some leading rabbinic scholars, including one of the yeshiva's deans, Rabbi Yaakov Moshe Charlap, protested the attempted enlistment of yeshiva students. They plastered proclamations on Jerusalem billboards that featured quotes from the yeshiva's founder, Rabbi Abraham Kook, who, as we saw in chapter 2, supported draft exemptions for yeshiva students in Britain during World War I.

The proclamations shook the confidence of Cohen. As the son of one of R. Kook's closest pupils, he revered the elder rabbinic figure. And as fate would have it, upon exiting the yeshiva, he ran into R. Kook's son, R. Tzvi Yehuda, and inquired whether he had somehow erred by enlisting in the nascent Jewish army.

R. Tzvi Yehuda was outraged by the publication of the handbills, deeming them a total distortion of his late father's views. In England, the dilemma regarded drafting Russian refugee yeshiva students into an army that was foreign to them; in 1948, the question was of Jews defending their own people and homeland from ongoing attacks. He promised to publish a treatise on why fighting for the Jewish homeland was different. R. Tzvi Yehuda blessed his pupil and sent him back to his post.

Cohen would need that blessing. Over the next month he fought in the besieged Old City of Jerusalem until it capitulated to Jordanian forces. Cohen helped convince the remaining fighters to surrender and not "save one last bullet" for themselves and create a modern-day Masada. Severely wounded, he spent the next nine months in Jordanian captivity until he would be released in a prisoner swap. While recuperating in Jerusalem in 1949, R. Tzvi Yehuda visited him and delivered a copy of the promised treatise defending army service that he had published soon after Israel's declaration of independence.[1] Later, Rabbi Cohen (1927–2016) became the head chaplain of the Israeli air force, serving alongside his brother-in-law, Rabbi Goren. He was ultimately appointed the chief rabbi of the city of Haifa.

In that very same month of 1948, Chief Rabbi Herzog was also receiving queries about mandatory conscription, in his case from a religious youth group and a young religious commander.[2] R. Herzog too supported mandatory conscription, and his treatise even helped a group of non-Zionist yeshiva students enlist into noncombat military units.

R. Herzog's responsum invoked some controversy. One of his senior rabbinic colleagues, himself a Zionist, objected to forcing people to endanger their lives. It is true, he argued, that it is a commandment to dwell in the Land of Israel. Yet do Jews force people to endanger themselves – or kill others – to fulfill a mitzva?[3]

The implications of this question go well beyond the question of conscription. It forces activists to spell out the relationship between nationalism, self-determination, and the justification for violence. In 1948, as we'll now see, religious Zionist ethics were at a crossroads and took two different turns.

JEWISH SOVEREIGNTY: SELF-DEFENSE OR BIBLICAL CONQUEST?

At first glance, the treatises of R. Herzog and R. Tzvi Yehuda are very similar, since they draw the same conclusion: yeshiva students may be conscripted, and these soldiers should see their service as a profound religious act. To reach that conclusion, they even cite many of the same classic rabbinic texts. Nonetheless, the emphasis is quite different. In fact, their treatises are a terrific contrast in choosing competing values within the JMF. As we've repeatedly shown, Judaism recognizes multiple important values and principles, with the primary challenge being which values to prioritize in complex circumstances.

For R. Herzog, the chief justification of the War of Independence was to save Jewish lives. The Arabs had rejected the partition plan and would now slaughter the Jewish residents unless they fought to protect themselves. Following the Holocaust, he further asserted, there was an imperative to create a home for hundreds of thousands of Jewish refugees. A repeated massacre could not take place in the future.

In essence, R. Herzog was adopting the general Zionist view that this was a "war of no-choice." Ben-Gurion and others utilized this phrase to connote that Jews had no alternative to taking up arms for their survival.[4] Accordingly, the War of Independence fulfills Maimonides's most fundamental criterion for a commanded war (*milḥemet mitzva*): this is a war of self-defense, for the present and the future. Jewish survival requires Jewish sovereignty.[5]

R. Tzvi Yehuda also argued that Jews must fight to save lives at risk in Palestine. Yet his primary motivation was that conscription is necessary to fulfilling the biblical mandate of conquering the Promised Land. God commanded the Jewish people, "Take possession of the land and settle in it, for I have assigned the land to you to possess."[6] Maimonides famously did not enumerate any commandment to *conquer* the land, even as he attributed much value in *dwelling* in the land. There's much speculation as to why he didn't include such warfare as a commandment. Did he feel it was redundant because there was already a commandment to wipe out the seven Canaanite nations? Or maybe he felt it applied only during Joshua's initial conquest, or at the very least was dormant in the exilic period? Perhaps he feared the censor would find offense at such a notion?[7] Or perhaps, as R. Tzvi Yehuda speculated, he saw it as so central and overarching to Judaism that it could not be enumerated as a distinct commandment. You can't command the Jewish people to possess the Land of Israel, just as you can't order someone to breathe. It's a natural impulse. Whatever the explanation, Maimonides provided no explicit mandate to fight a war, for its own sake, to conquer the Holy Land.

By contrast, the thirteenth-century Talmudist and mystic Nahmanides asserted that there was a commandment to conquer the Holy Land and not abandon control of it to foreign nations. Rabbi Tzvi Yehuda adopted this position to establish an independent obligation of conquest. He asserted that we are obligated to take advantage of the first opportunity in many centuries to fight for the homeland.[8] The desecration of God's name fostered by our historical downtrodden political condition must end. This is the only true reprieve from Jewish exile.[9]

In this respect, he saw the renewal of Jewish militarism – beginning with the Jewish Legion in World War I and later the Jewish Brigade in World War II – as stages of the messianic redemption. These military developments were equally important stages to the political process begun by the Balfour Declaration.[10] The next stage of this process was to fight for our own territory. Jewish sovereignty – including the display of force necessary to achieve it – is the sanctification of God's name in this world. As such, we must fight.

R. Herzog, of course, was also aware of Nahmanides's view of conquering the homeland. R. Herzog cited this factor as support for his contention that this was a mitzva for which Jews could be compelled to endanger their lives. But for him, it was just an ancillary support to his broader understanding that Jews had to fight for self-defense.[11] Equally important to any such obligation was his belief that the sociopolitical conditions since the Enlightenment had spurred cultural oppression, let alone assimilation, under which Judaism could not thrive.[12] For Jewish life – physical and spiritual – to survive, the Jews required a state. The unwillingness of some yeshiva students to fight for that survival was, in his mind, a terrible *ḥillul Hashem*.[13]

THE 1937 PARTITION PLAN: CAN JEWS RELINQUISH RIGHTS TO PART OF THEIR HOMELAND?[14]

The varying emphases R. Herzog and R. Tzvi Yehuda placed on the issues reflect broader approaches toward territorial disputes and the necessity of independent nation-states. Unique ethnic groups, to survive and even thrive, require a certain amount of autonomy to run their lives the way they see fit. This, however, does not necessarily require the establishment of their own state. That's a good thing, since there are currently over four hundred ethnic or national groups seeking recognition, autonomy, or independence around the world.[15] It would be geographically and economically untenable to grant autonomous territory to all of these groups; moreover, the ensuant breakdown of countries would only lead to fighting and bloodshed.[16] Additionally, even if a people have historical or religious claims to a given territory, other groups may make claims to the same land, leading to interstate or civil war.

As such, we need to create a criterion for determining which groups truly need their own territory while finding alternatives in other cases. The question becomes what type of argumentation a group offers to justify: (a) why their people are entitled to a certain territory, and most importantly for our purposes, (b) why that entitlement allows them to even fight and kill for its cause.[17]

Zionists believed that since the Balfour Declaration and the League of Nations mandate, their entitlement to the Land of Israel was well established. This was challenged, however, when the Peel Commission, created to examine the stability of the British mandate in the wake of the 1936 Arab riots (discussed in chapter 4), came to the following conclusion:

> An irrepressible conflict has arisen between two national communities within the narrow bounds of one small country. About 1,000,000 Arabs are in strife, open or latent, with some 400,000

> Jews. There is no common ground between them.... Their cultural and social life, their ways of thought and conduct, are as incompatible as their national aspirations.

Their solution to this "irrepressible conflict" was to partition Palestine into three different areas: (1) a sovereign Arab state, composed of much of the territory west of the Jordan River, which would be connected to Transjordan on the east side of the river to form one large Arab state; (2) a British-controlled corridor from Jaffa to Jerusalem to protect British interests as well as to keep the peace; and (3) a measly nineteen-hundred-square-mile stretch of land along the coast, the northern valleys, and the Galilee, intended for a Jewish state. The commission also proposed a population transfer between the Arab and Jewish territories. It further suggested that since Jews contributed more per capita to the revenues of Palestine than the Arabs, the new Jewish state would pay a subsidy ("subvention") to the much larger Arab state.

The Zionist leadership was outraged by the proposal. The territory was a pale substitute for the area promised by the Balfour Declaration, which the Jews believed included territory on *both* sides of the Jordan River. Beyond this betrayal, the proposed state was too small to take in the number of European Jews whose lives were in significant danger. As Weizmann put it, "The world for them is divided into two parts – the countries where they cannot live and the countries they cannot enter."

Despite this widespread disappointment, Zionist leaders at the twentieth Zionist Congress in January 1938 sharply debated whether to accept the offer. Opponents to the plan included prominent figures all along the Zionist ideological spectrum, including Jabotinsky, Menahem Ussishkin, and Rabbi Berlin. Weizmann and Ben-Gurion, by contrast, argued that at this stage, any state would be better than no state at all.

In the end, a compromise was reached in which the Jewish Agency declared its willingness to accept a partition, even as it called for negotiations to work out a more suitable land division. The discussion became moot, however, since the Arabs entirely rejected any division and restarted their riots against the Jews. The British, in turn, soon ditched any attempt to resolve the situation following the recommendations of the 1938 Woodhead Commission. The Peel plan remained significant, however, because the Jewish leadership had accepted, in principle, the notion of partition.

It was precisely this concession, which would have long-lasting political implications, that was opposed by much of the rabbinic leadership.[18] Their objections were based on a mix of religious values alongside strategical or political arguments, making it sometimes difficult to distinguish between the two. Their arguments combined Jewish legal and theological claims, in part resting on a biblical prohibition against selling territory (*lo teḥanem*) in the Holy Land to foreigners and in part resting on God's eternal bequest of the territory to the Jewish people.

Rabbi Amiel declared that any political assent by Jews to relinquish their rights to the entire Promised Land would be a massive *ḥillul Hashem* of unprecedented proportions. During these months, we should recall from chapter 4, R. Amiel strongly objected to any revenge attacks against random Arabs as constituting both murder and a mass *ḥillul Hashem*. Yet his opposition to terror didn't mean that he believed in territorial compromise. Nations do not relinquish their homeland.

Rabbi Charlap also stridently prohibited the relinquishing of any piece of territory. It would be better to cut off one's thumbs than sign such an agreement. He further added that he felt this was true even if it could be claimed that some number of Jews would find refuge in this miniscule state. Not surprisingly, R. Tzvi Yehuda strongly supported the position of his senior colleague.[19]

R. Herzog, too, was not a fan of the proposal, and initially published strong remarks against it. Under the pressure of Jewish Agency officials, he backed down from his public opposition. Over time, however, he was influenced by the statements of two leading non-Zionist halakhic decisors. The first, writing from Lithuania, contended that there was no legal prohibition against signing a partition agreement, especially since the territory given to the Arabs was not currently under Jewish control anyway.[20] A political agreement with an Arab state does not represent our signing away of our claim to the Holy Land, which remains eternal.

The second decisor was Rabbi Isser Zalman Melzer, a prominent seminary head in Jerusalem who made an emotional appeal to R. Herzog. "We haven't had a state for nearly two thousand years. If they are offering it to us, even in a small way for now, we shouldn't reject it.

It is a sign from Heaven that this is the beginning of our redemption."[21] When you are homeless, you take whatever home you can get – especially when it's located in your ancestral homestead.

R. Herzog would later furtively testify before the Woodhead Commission, in the contentious summer of 1938, to try to get the British to implement the partition plan. His rationale was very simple.

> If it were not for the terrible hardships of the Diaspora that press upon us, we would never agree to the partitioning of the Land of Israel. The dire situation forces us to agree to the founding of a Jewish state on only part of the land – provided that the state will solve our problems and enable Jewish immigration to the Land of Israel.[22]

Alas, no state was established. The Jews of Europe could find no refuge in their homeland.

THE 1947 UN PARTITION PLAN: WHY DID THE RABBIS CHANGE THEIR MINDS?

When the revised UN partition plan finally won international support in November 1947, the country's religious leadership strongly supported it. What had changed since 1937? The classic halakhic sources remained the same, but the prioritization of values had shifted in light of the political reality. R. Maimon, while still hoping for the ultimate return to the complete biblical homeland, would proclaim, "I love the Land of Israel, but my love for the nation of Israel comes first."[23] R. Herzog would lead celebrations in Jerusalem's synagogues and compose a prayer in honor of the thirty-three nations who voted in its favor. He readily acknowledged the forthcoming bloodshed, but hoped that the war would ultimately usher in peace.

> My heart does not fear the threats of enemies, of Arab leaders, of strangers and tyrants, whose only purpose is to benefit themselves. They eat the flesh of their poor.... We, however, are destined to lift up the stricken, our relatives and neighbors, and rescue them from their travails. Our aim is peace, and our prayer to the God

of all flesh is to crush the evil inclination of our enemies and subdue them. And to pray that tomorrow, a true peace between Israel and the Arab tribes will emerge, which will benefit us and them and all of humanity.[24]

The war would deliver salvation for the Jewish people while hopefully heralding an era of peace.

R. Tzvi Yehuda was now in the clear rabbinic minority against any partition plan. He opposed any territorial compromise – not only in 1937 but even in 1947.[25] He would later admit that he initially cried on the night of the UN vote, weeping for the lost opportunity to take sovereignty over all of the Holy Land. Ultimately, he accepted the will of the nation, and urged them to now fight and conquer whatever holy territory could be captured. In the coming decades, he would become the leading theologian against any territorial compromises for peace, including territories conquered after the Six-Day War.

TWO MODELS FOR NATIONALIST WARFARE: SELF-DEFENSE OR RELIGIOUS CONQUEST

This historical background sheds light on the two models created by these two figures. One model, represented by R. Tzvi Yehuda, cast rabbinic discourse within internal terms that relate to Jewish history, theology, and identity. The Land of Israel is not just the ancestral homeland – it is also the Holy Land and the Promised Land. The territory was sanctified by God and is tied to our destiny. For R. Tzvi Yehuda, the Balfour Declaration and San Remo resolutions were fundamentally the acknowledgment by the world of this God-given truth.

God has commanded us to conquer and settle this territory. This is the primary value that trumps other considerations. Jews have been unable to fulfill this holy deed for many centuries because of political duress. Now that the opportunity has reemerged, we must rightfully fight for the land and take what it ours. The Arabs can remain as residents, he asserted, but only if they recognize our sovereignty and renounce their nationalist aspirations.

R. Tzvi Yehuda's argument is a particularistic claim, but it is far from unique to the Jewish people. As the political theorist Anthony D. Smith has documented, many cultures promote a notion of sacred territory and utilize it to support self-sacrifice and warfare.[26] R. Herzog, by contrast, frames his support for war and conscription in terms of self-defense. This is a choice to adopt a model of halakhic argumentation that resonates with more universalistic, ethical discourse.

His argument for Jewish statehood in 1947 is based on needs and rights. The Jewish people have had the full range of legal minority statuses in their centuries of exile. These arrangements all ended in disaster, stifling our political and cultural survival. The nations of the world have recognized this failure, which is why they supported the UN partition plan. R. Herzog stresses this point not only to show why a Jewish declaration of independence does not violate the talmudic oath against rebellion, but also to stress why the Jews, as opposed to the British or the Arabs, have the best claim to sovereignty under international standards.[27] Accordingly, the Jews have an obligation, and a right, to fight utilizing the most basic universalist claim: self-determination is necessary to overcome persecution and justifies the bloodshed necessary for self-defense.

Significantly, R. Herzog utilized this line of ethical reasoning not just in diplomatic circles, when he was lobbying international figures to support Zionism, but also within internal rabbinic discourse, utilizing the writings of the talmudic Sages and Maimonides. Certainly, R. Herzog was far from indifferent to biblical claims to the Holy Land. Even when speaking before the 1947 UN Special Committee on Palestine, he had no problem invoking Jewish religious and historical claims, among others, to support the restoration of Jewish sovereignty.[28] He too believed that the Land of Israel had been granted by God to the Jewish people, and that, in some way, the restoration of Zion was a part of the redemptive process. Yet his primary mode to justify going to war, in religious terms, remained ethical, not theological.

The self-defense (Rabbi Herzog) versus religious conquest (Rabbi Tzvi Yehuda) distinction creates an entirely different orientation toward the dilemma of going to war. If you are focused on conquering the Holy Land, then you have an almost crusader-like approach to warfare with one major question: Can you win the battle or not? Conquest is an end in itself. If you are focused on self-defense, then your initial question becomes: Is this warfare integral to my self-defense? Victory is a means toward protection.

This orientation also radically changes your approach toward integrating other values, such as finding alternative resolutions to territorial disputes and minimizing the loss of lives on both sides. For R. Tzvi Yehuda, once we've determined that the full extent of the Land of Israel belongs to the Jewish people, then we are the rightful owners entitled to do what is necessary to protect our property.

As such, by the open admission of Rabbi Shlomo Aviner, the primary editor of his writings, R. Tzvi Yehuda was never concerned with addressing questions of military ethics. Bloodshed is unpleasant and undesirable. Yet as long as we are dealing with a *milḥemet mitzva* for the homeland, the only question is whether we have the strength and courage to win.[29] He is willing, therefore, not only to sacrifice the lives of enemies, but also to risk those of his own people, as long as the war can be won, since that is the nation's long-term mission. Fighting for the homeland takes precedence over saving individual Jewish lives (*pikuaḥ nefesh*).[30] In this spirit, R. Aviner regretted that the Israeli army called itself the Israel *Defense* Forces. The goal of the army is not just to defend the people but to conquer the Promised Land.[31]

The weakness of this approach is readily felt when one realizes that R. Tzvi Yehuda has few tools to critique the Arab intransigence to accepting a Jewish state. His claim is theological, not moral. R. Tzvi Yehuda would famously declare after the Six-Day War that within the biblical territory of Israel, "there is no such thing as Arab territory! There is [only] the land of God."[32] This declaration is a conversation stopper. Why should Arabs be bound by the biblical mandate, let alone the British mandate? Moreover, the Arabs have their own internal theological or nationalist claims to the land. It's unclear, under R. Tzvi Yehuda's model, why they aren't equally entitled to fight for their homeland.

The problem with his model is not that it is *im*moral but that is *a*moral. It doesn't provide for any ethical framework to evaluate the claims of Jews or Arabs alike.

R. Herzog's line of reasoning has a basis for critiquing Arab violence: it's not necessary for their self-defense. When unprovoked, the Jews do not represent a physical threat to the Arabs. Moreover, the

Zionists were willing to divide the land peacefully, in spite of their historical connection to Greater Israel. Arab violence against the Jews is unjust because it is unnecessary for their defense.

R. Herzog's self-defense orientation also organically raises other ethical dilemmas, such as whether a given fight or battle is necessary for your protection. You are also likely to recognize that some members of the enemy nation may, out of their own interests for self-defense, have no interests in fighting against you. Indeed, in his responsa regarding conscription, R. Herzog repeated his stance, seen previously in chapter 4, prohibiting reprisal killings of Arab civilians who are not engaged in any warfare. If they aren't threatening you, then you can't target them.[33] It's no longer self-defense.

A self-defense orientation, moreover, might lead you to make territorial concessions from conquered parts of the homeland in order to make peace agreements. In the hierarchy of values, saving lives trumps territorial sovereignty. This question, later known as the "land for peace" dilemma, became famous after the 1979 peace agreement with Egypt and especially the 1993 Oslo Accords with the Palestinians, when Israel agreed to cede territory gained during the Six-Day War. R. Tzvi Yehuda and his students, as we'll see, were adamantly opposed to withdrawing from any territory.

In truth, the "land for peace" dilemma already reemerged after the 1956 Suez Canal War (discussed at length in chapter 18). Under massive international pressure, Prime Minister Ben-Gurion agreed to retreat from the Sinai Peninsula and the Gaza Strip to reach an armistice agreement with Egypt. Some voices in the National Religious Party questioned whether the government could surrender conquered territory, especially Gaza, which was a part of the biblical Commonwealth. In response, the most erudite rabbinic scholar in the Knesset, Zerah Warhaftig, responded that the political reality of security and diplomacy must trump such considerations. This fundamental decision, he declared, was already made in 1947. For the sake of gaining sovereignty, Israelis had reconciled themselves (at least for now) to not controlling central holy cities like Jerusalem's Old City, Hebron, and other famous biblical locations.[34] The safety provided by political sovereignty was more important than any piece of the homeland, however precious it might be.

R. Herzog offers the better model because his model recognizes the need to take into account multiple values found in the Jewish multivalue framework. His orientation, built around self-defense, can integrate ideals like sovereignty, peace, national honor, human dignity, the territorial homeland, and the reputation of the people. It is an ethical model that allows for discourse that helps countrymen debate the merits of going to war while allowing competing nations to understand the competing claims and concerns of their adversaries.

Part III

Preemptive and Preventative Wars: Israeli Warfare, 1956–1982

Chapter 15

The War on Terror: Preemptive or Preventative War?

Sometimes a country must fight because it has been invaded, like Britain in 1940, Israel in 1973, or Ukraine in 2022. On other occasions, a country is under threat but not under attack. This raises difficult moral and strategic questions, as leaders must balance taking preemptive initiatives to protect their citizens while trying to avoid nationalistic zeal that leads to unnecessary bloodshed. The significance of these dilemmas is well demonstrated by Israel's wars between 1956 and 1982, which, as we'll now see, took on great relevance in the beginning of the twenty-first century. For many of the moral debates over the "war on terror" have drawn on numerous examples from the Israeli experience in its dogged fights against Arab states and terrorist groups.

THE DISTINCTION BETWEEN PREEMPTIVE AND PREVENTATIVE WARS

On June 28, 2005, in the midst of the Iraq War, United States President George W. Bush visited his troops stationed at Fort Bragg, North Carolina. Bush wanted to explain why he was sending those soldiers to fight seven thousand miles away from American soil.

> After September the 11th, I made a commitment to the American people: This nation will not wait to be attacked again. We will defend our freedom. We will take the fight to the enemy. Iraq is the latest battlefield in this war.... There is only one course of action against them: to defeat them abroad before they attack us at home.... We either deal with terrorism and this extremism abroad, or we deal with it when it comes to us.[1]

In simple language, Bush was articulating his strategy for the "war on terror": America must go on the offensive to prevent future assaults on her soil. In the past, when the United States faced threats from national armies, a policy of deterrence and containment was sufficient. When facing unconventional threats from nonstate actors, however, America must attack before these terrorists find a way to strike us again. The Bush Doctrine was well encapsulated in the White House's 2002 National Security Strategy paper, in which the president declared, "As a matter of common sense and self-defense, America will act against such emerging threats before they are fully formed."

This doctrine to stop budding threats before they developed – which Bush deemed as "common sense" – was denounced as immoral and dangerous by many of his critics. On a practical level, they asserted that this offensive strategy would lead America into perilous battles against unfounded fears. American soldiers would be chasing ghosts. To this claim, they cited Vice President Dick Cheney's reported statement that when it comes to stopping low-probability but high-impact attacks, we need to act as if they were definitive threats. "If there's a one percent chance that Pakistani scientists are helping Al Qaeda build or develop a nuclear weapon, we have to treat it as a certainty in terms of our response."[2] The "one percent doctrine," critics asserted, would lead the United States to torturing detainees before trial, ordering drone attacks against suspicious but unproven enemy sites, and launching unnecessary wars.

This strategic and moral error, others added, stemmed from the Bush Doctrine's failure to distinguish between "preemptive" and "preventative" wars. Preemptive attacks occur when a country believes that an adversary is about to attack, and that striking first will be better than allowing the enemy to do so. Preventative attacks are launched in response to less immediate threats under the belief that with the alleged adversary, it is better to fight sooner rather than later. Sometimes the attack is instigated, for example, by the belief that the enemy will soon acquire new weapons that will shift the balance of military capabilities in their favor. The window of opportunity to strike victoriously and effectively, so the fear goes, will soon be closed.

In 2003, there was no indication that Iraq was going to imminently attack the United States. The invasion was a *preventative* war meant to stop Iraq from developing weapons of mass destruction (WMD) before she or her allies could eventually use them against the United States. In the end, no WMDs were found. A trillion dollars were spent, hundreds of thousands were killed or wounded, and the region remains deeply, and perhaps more, unstable.

The debates about the Iraq War highlighted the significant risks posed by nonstate actors or rogue states in the twenty-first century. Preemptive strikes, which have arguably become less common anyway in the last two centuries,[3] are usually unfeasible against terrorists who operate in unchartered territories and fight without uniforms. They use weapons that can be easily concealed, delivered covertly, and utilized without warning. Western countries unwilling to strike early against fundamentalist terrorists greatly risk finding themselves under attack at a later date, a point which some of Bush's critics will concede. We should recall that well before 9/11, the Clinton administration launched missile strikes in August 1998 on Al Qaeda targets, hitting a suspected chemical weapons plant in Sudan and a training base in Afghanistan. One wonders how history might have developed had more preventative actions been taken in the ensuing three years.[4]

A CRYPTIC TALMUDIC DEBATE AND THE SPECTRUM OF SELF-DEFENSE INITIATIVES

The morality of taking such anticipatory action, in the name of self-defense against projected aggression, is sometimes questioned because it is premised on a fear that might not be real. [5] Being afraid does not mean that one is threatened. Even when there is a real threat hanging over a nation, such a risk does not necessarily justify initiating a war that will surely bring many deaths. Don't bring upon yourself bloodshed when the threat may not come to fruition. It's a utilitarian calculus focused on the negative consequences of acting hastily.

Many ethicists also raise a more fundamental objection rooted in notions of rights: what gives you the right to kill someone who has not done anything yet against you? They haven't done anything yet to justify killing them.[6]

The complexity of anticipatory attacks was already appreciated by the talmudic Sages. Previously we've seen that imperialist, expansionist battles were permitted by the Sages as "discretionary warfare" but shunned by later figures like Rabbis Kook and Hirschensohn. By contrast, wars to defend the nation from attackers who've crossed over the border were deemed "commanded wars," in which all able-bodied citizens may be conscripted.

Yet there are many in-between scenarios in which Jews are neither expansionist aggressors nor passive victims. One such case is when a country anticipates an upcoming battle and meets the enemy on their side of their border. The motivation for such anticipatory warfare is, in the words of the Sages, "to reduce their enemies so that they will not come and wage war against them."[7] Are these "commanded" or "discretionary" wars? In one presentation of the debate, one prominent Sage deemed *any* anticipatory strike as discretionary.[8] Most talmudic Sages seem to disagree with that clear-cut distinction and render some anticipatory action as "commanded." Unfortunately, they don't specify the circumstances of where to draw the line, leaving later commentators to debate which type of anticipatory warfare was under discussion in the first place.

Are we dealing with a case of an incipient attack with enemy soldiers gathering on the border, akin to what we'd call a "preemptive" strike?[9] Or a more distant threat that is seemingly brewing but somewhat ambiguous at this point?[10] Some alternatively suggest that the debate was over utilizing aggressive military might to deter hostile enemy activity despite the absence of any clear threat, i.e., a "preventative strike."[11]

Emerging from their discourse was an understanding that there's a spectrum of legitimate anticipatory attacks. Some preemptive action may be obligatory, while more preventative actions are discretionary (*reshut*).[12] The latter category of wars, when not done for imperialist expansion, remains permissible.[13] Yet it requires additional deliberation and approval alongside limitations on conscription. Leaders will need to convince their advisory circle that launching a discretionary war is the right move and keep their soldiers believing in the cause. Significantly, the acceptable motivation behind such discretionary warfare remains self-defense, not imperial expansionism.[14]

The difficult question becomes where to draw the line on the spectrum of potential threats to determine if fighting at this stage is truly necessary or more discretionary. The Talmud famously asserts, "If one comes to slay you, rise and kill first."[15] Yet what if it's not so clear that they are coming to slay you – and that if they would attack, it might not happen for some time? Accordingly, the wisdom and morality of an anticipatory attack is greatly contingent on the risk evaluation.

Broadly speaking, one can outline a range of possible threats that may justify anticipatory action. We'll depart from our strict chronological presentation to depict different scenarios along the spectrum of imminent threats of invasion, since imminence is the classic criterion in contemporary ethical discourse. However, as we'll argue, the criterion of imminence is not necessarily the best measure for whether it is necessary – and therefore moral – for a country to launch an anticipatory attack.

Chapter 16

Preemptive Strikes: The Cases of the Six-Day War and the Yom Kippur War

THE RELIGIOUS DEBATE BEFORE THE SIX-DAY WAR

In May 1967, Rabbi Goren celebrated Israel's Independence Day in Australia to support fundraising efforts for the United Jewish Appeal. While abroad, he received word that Egypt had officially closed the Straits of Tiran to all Israeli ships. Israeli officials had long warned that such maritime aggression would be seen as a hostile act. R. Goren raced back to Israel.

In the meantime, IDF Chief of Staff Yitzhak Rabin was under massive pressure. He couldn't convince Israel's cabinet that the IDF must preemptively strike the Egyptians. Prime Minister Levi Eshkol was hesitant, particularly because of significant opposition of ministers from the religious parties, led by Moshe Hayim Shapira. The cabinet debates were fierce. Shapira told Rabin that Israelis must hunker down to defend themselves, yet not take the first shot. As a man of faith, he declared, we cannot bring danger upon ourselves and initiate the warfare, especially without international support. The Bible declares that "Israel will dwell alone" – yet that does not mean that it must fight alone. Already under massive pressure, Rabin snapped and had a nervous breakdown. He was given a tranquilizer and was incapacitated for a day.[1]

By the time R. Goren returned, Rabin had recovered. He urged the IDF's chief rabbi to meet with Shapira and convince him of the urgency to act. After consulting with other military commanders, including the head of the air force, R. Goren concluded that Israel must strike immediately. He spent four hours with Shapira. R. Goren argued that Israel could win if it attacked first. Every day of delay would cost many more Israeli lives. There was no choice but to act since the Arab nations were out to destroy Israel. Shapira was not yet convinced. R. Goren left and began his own preparations for the war, which included preparing military cemeteries and ordering sufficient burial caskets. Around the country, some ten thousand graves were dug.

Soon afterward, the reluctant religious ministers strongly pushed for the expansion of the government to include opposition figures like Begin and the appointment of Dayan as defense minister. Yet until the final moment of the fateful decision to go to war, they remained hesitant. Shapira, citing Ben-Gurion, insisted that the Jewish state should never fight without an international ally. Dayan retorted that by the time Israel found an ally, they wouldn't be alive anymore.

Another religious minister, the legal scholar Zerah Warhaftig, worried that Israel required a clearer *casus belli*, an act of aggression, to justify the war. Warhaftig had three sons serving in the IDF. Nonetheless, he suggested sending a ship through the Straits of Tiran to provoke an Egyptian reaction. The Egyptians would take the first shot. The move would risk soldiers' lives but legitimate the war in the eyes of the world. Most ministers, however, were against such dangerous contrived plots. Israel would inevitably be condemned no matter what it did. If the leadership believed in the justness of their claims, they must act on their own conscience.

By the end of this fateful meeting on June 4, even the religious ministers voted to support the war. The next day, Israeli jet fighters destroyed the entire fleet of the Egyptian air force. Many world leaders criticized their preemptive attack. Yet the conclusive victory was undeniable, with the war becoming the classic case-study in international law of an anticipatory self-defense attack.[2]

SCENARIO 1: IMMINENT, CREDIBLE, AND GRAVE (ICG) THREATS

Israel was morally justified to attack because the perceived threat was imminent, credible, and grave. For short, we'll call this an "ICG threat." In this scenario, there are three key components.

1. Imminence: The threatening country displays active military preparation, like assembling troops near a border.
2. Credible: Its leaders display a highly belligerent attitude through threats or recent past activity, showing that their intentions are genuine.
3. Gravity: The threatened country believes that if not resisted earlier, the attack will become much more difficult or costly, if not impossible, to repel at a later point.

The claim of an "ICG threat" was emphasized by Israeli representatives to the United Nations during the Six-Day War: the Egyptians were long-time enemies whose statements and actions indicated that an imminent and dangerous attack was highly likely. They had closed the Straits of Tiran, kicked out UN peacekeepers, and assembled large forces near the border. We now know, in fact, that in late May 1967, the Egyptian army was hours away from launching forces into the Sinai Desert when the operation was called off under Soviet pressure.[3] Gamal Abdel Nasser, Egypt's leader, preferred to orchestrate a situation where he could blame Israel for being the aggressors. Nonetheless, in the interim week before Israel attacked, Egyptian leader Nasser continued with his hostile threats: "We are ready to settle the problem of Palestine," he triumphantly told the Egyptian Popular Council as he signed a mutual defense pact with Jordan. "It is we who will decide the time and the place of the battle and we will not leave the decision to Israel as was the case in 1948."[4]

Israel calculated that a failure to act first would make its citizens incredibly vulnerable to probable aggression in the immediate future. Conversely, striking first would significantly rebuff this hostility. Many Israeli lives would be saved. By the beginning of June 1967, not everyone in the Israeli cabinet was still sure that an Egyptian attack was imminent. Nonetheless, Nasser's military preparations and belligerent rhetoric made them reasonably confident that an attack would be coming soon enough. The window of opportunity to initiate a war of proactive self-defense would not remain open forever.

The morality of Israel's 1967 preemptive attack may be contrasted with its failure to act before the onset of the 1973 Yom Kippur War. This was a clear case of a war of self-defense by Israel to respond to the coordinated attack by Egypt and Syria. Yet did Israel morally err by not striking first when it had the opportunity to do so?

On the morning of October 6, Yom Kippur day, many Israeli Jews were fasting and getting ready to attend synagogue services. Not Moshe Dayan and David Elazar. Israel's defense minister and chief of staff, respectively, were woken in the wee hours of the morning with impeccable intelligence reports that two of their neighbors intended to attack that day. In truth, the warning signs had been flashing for weeks. Israel's leaders, however, had arrogantly dismissed the possibility of such an attack. By eight in the morning, they were meeting in Prime Minister Golda Meir's office to make a fateful decision.

Elazar wanted to launch a preemptive strike on Syrian airfields and missile launchers while calling up two hundred thousand reservists. The attack, he asserted, would give Israel "a huge advantage and save many lives."[5] Dayan opposed a preemptive strike and favored a more gradual call-up. While acknowledging some operational advantages, he asserted that both of Elazar's proposals would be perceived as acts of war. Given her apparent strength after the Six-Day War, Israel would be labeled as the aggressor. "We should enjoy a sound international standing when the war starts," he asserted. Elazar retorted that a mass call-up might deter the Arab countries from starting the war, and that Israel would still be blamed if it adopted Dayan's proposal for a modest call-up. Most importantly, he concluded, "I prefer that they say we started (the war) and we win."

Meir later testified that she was inclined to act first but decided against out of fear of international isolation. After all, the United States had previously warned her not to strike first again in the event of a war: "1973 is not 1967, and this time we will not be forgiven, and we will not receive assistance when we have the need for it."[6]

Regarding the diplomatic front, her concern was well founded. United States Secretary of State Henry Kissinger had repeatedly warned

the Israelis to never again start a preemptive war. Kissinger would ultimately play a critical role in sending Israel a massive emergency shipment of arms. He would later tell Dayan that had Israel struck first, it
wouldn't have received even a "single nail" of support from the United
States. By the second day of the war, Meir wrote to Kissinger blaming
the Americans for their perilous situation. In his memoirs, Kissinger
denied blame for the decision, arguing that Israeli officials had come to
that decision on their own. In any case, their own military leaders were
skeptical that a preemptive strike would have helped at that stage.[7] In
retrospect, that's a matter of debate. Yet on that Yom Kippur morning,
all the decision makers in that room – Meir, Elazar, and Dayan – who
had responsibility for protecting Israeli lives, believed it would have
been helpful, at least were it not for the likely diplomatic fallout and its
implications for later stages of the war.

DOES THE UN CHARTER ALLOW FOR PREEMPTIVE STRIKES AND DOES IT MATTER?

The critical questions remain whether it would have been fair for the
international community to label Israel as the "aggressor" and whether
Israeli officials should have cared anyway.[8] The answer to both questions is no. The dangers of an Egyptian and Syrian attack clearly met the
criteria of an "ICG threat." Many might have believed that Israel could
"absorb the blow" and defeat its enemies. Yet when "taking the first hit"
means losing additional Israeli lives, how can one justify being derelict
in the basic duty of protecting one's own citizens? The international
community must recognize that primary obligation.

Part of the problem is that international law is somewhat ambiguous regarding the legitimacy of preemptive strikes. Article 51 of the
United Nations charter permits self-defense only in the case of "armed
attack." Some legalists believe that this prohibits any preemptive action
before an enemy physically strikes. Such "strict defense purists," as one
philosopher dubs them, follow the sentiment of a leading medieval philosopher, Francisco de Vitoria, who asserted, "It is quite unacceptable
that a person should be killed for a sin he has yet to commit."[9]

Yet foreign armies threatening grave attacks are not so innocent,
especially in contrast to the hapless members of the victim country who

will suffer from their aggression. Guilt is not solely determined by who took the first shot. If a side embarked on the maneuvers that brought the parties to the brink of conflict, they bear much responsibility. At that stage, the at-risk party does not need to wait for the aggressor to cross the frontier. Moreover, one cannot think simply in terms of whether the aggressor has crossed a line of liability. We also must take into consideration the obligation of self-defense. This factor, as some legalists have acknowledged, grants a country the legal right even under Article 51 to repel attackers in a way that reasonably minimizes the damages inflicted by an aggressive attacker, including through a preemptive strike.[10]

In any case, a country's leadership should act on that *moral* obligation, even if, in the misguided eyes of international bodies, they will be legally deemed the aggressors. Rabbinic decisors considered preemptive strikes "obligatory wars" to stress that this is a duty.[11] The Yom Kippur War became no more of an "obligatory war" of self-defense simply because Israel waited for its enemies to take the advantageous first shot. Many Israeli lives might have been saved by acting earlier.[12] It was a moral failure of Meir and Dayan to have opposed the chief of staff's plan if they had, in fact, believed that it was operationally critical.

None of this is to say that leaders should have not taken into account the strategic importance of international support. Yet that consideration needed to be countered by two additional factors. First, whatever Kissinger's threats, it's not clear that the United States would have stayed neutral as Soviet allies made military gains. One should recall that even before the Six-Day War, President Lyndon Johnson also warned Israel about a preemptive strike ("Israel will not be alone unless it acts alone"). Nonetheless, LBJ still supported her after the war broke out.

Second, whatever the Americans might have thought, one never knows if the enemy will get the strategic upper hand if it is allowed to attack first. This is exactly what the talmudic commentators feared when it permitted preemptive strikes,[13] and this is precisely what happened in the Yom Kippur War. Israel, while perceived to be stronger, turned out to be strategically unprepared to rebut an Arab offensive. After a series of blunders and losses in the first days of the war, many Israeli leaders feared that the country's very existence was at stake. Dayan even told a comrade that the "Third Commonwealth" was in danger. In the end,

Israel recovered, but not before a great number of Israeli lives were unnecessarily lost and its deterrence shattered.

Israel was equally justified to fight in both the 1967 and 1973 wars. The failure of its leadership to attack in 1973, when it thought that it might help, was a moral failure.

Chapter 17

The 1956 Sinai Campaign: A Moral "War of Choice"

Moving along the spectrum of potential risks, the decision to launch an anticipatory strike becomes more complex as the threat of warfare becomes less imminent. To make this point, let's explore another scenario:

SCENARIO 2: PREVENTING A LOW-LEVEL CONFLICT FROM BECOMING A FULL-FLEDGED INVASION

In this scenario, a state of belligerence already exists between two countries. It includes violent confrontations, sometimes overt and sometimes covert, between uniformed soldiers or unofficial agents. The occasional attacks are not an outright invasion. The low-level hostilities could develop into a lengthy war of attrition and even a full-out invasion, or they could dissipate. New factors at play, however, create a credible scenario in which the adversary gains new strategic advantages and increases its chances – and temptation – for a successful invasion.[1]

In this situation, the ongoing hostilities make the potential threat eminently concrete. In fact, one could say that the belligerency has already begun. Yet there's a moral difference between intermittent attacks and constant warfare. In terms of human lives, the status quo is much less costly than an outright invasion. One must then ask: Is an invasion truly necessary? That's a difficult question to answer when there is no sense of an imminent invasion. Since there is no way of knowing for sure, some ethicists argue that it is wrong to kill others in a situation of doubt. Military strategists may retort that acting sooner rather than later will provide significant strategic advantages. A quick anticipatory strike might even prevent more extensive warfare at a later stage. Or it can significantly aggravate the situation. Again, there's no way of truly knowing. The moral life requires decision making in cases of uncertainty.

It was this dilemma that animated the Israeli cabinet in its deliberations before launching its 1956 war with Egypt.[2] By the end of 1955, Ben-Gurion believed that a war with Egypt was inevitable. Nasser continued to insist that his country was in a "state of war" with Israel and repeatedly violated the 1949 armistice agreement. Since 1950, Egypt had not allowed passageway of Israeli ships through the Straits of Tiran. More significantly, since 1954, Egyptian-supported *fedayeen* raids from the Gaza Strip intensified and killed hundreds of Israelis, drawing significant IDF reprisals under Chief of Staff Moshe Dayan's lead (as discussed in chapter 5). Dayan, along with Shimon Peres, then–director general of the Defense Ministry, pushed for an offensive against Egypt. So did opposition leader Menachem Begin. He warned that the Labor government might bring upon the Jewish state another Masada or Holocaust.[3]

Ben-Gurion remained steadfast that Israel should try to preserve the status quo and not launch an offensive attack. This was largely out of pragmatic concerns. Ben-Gurion feared that an Israeli invasion would lead to diplomatic isolation and even an arms embargo. Yet he also made a more fundamental argument. There is no point for Israel to hasten a war with its Arab neighbors. Even if Israel wins, it will remain in conflict and just need to prepare for the next war. "After every war from which we emerge as victors, we will face the same problem, just as we do today."[4]

Two things changed Ben-Gurion's mind. First, there was growing concern that a recent Soviet-sponsored arms deal between Czechoslovakia and Egypt would give Nasser a significant advantage once the weapons were delivered. Attack now – or face a more lethal enemy later.

Second, Egypt had gained some powerful adversaries. Nasser began offering covert support to Algerian rebels and nationalized the Suez Canal, thereby angering both the French and British governments. In a complex secret arrangement reached in the Paris suburb of Sèvres, Ben-Gurion agreed to launch an attack against Egypt with the promise that France and Britain would support Israel's efforts soon afterward. This was a unique opportunity for Israel to fortify both its borders and its international alliances.[5] France and Britain might also help achieve another goal: to drive Nasser out of power.

A couple of cabinet members remained aghast at launching a war. The health minister, Israel Barzilai of the leftist Mapam Party, accused Ben-Gurion of starting a war of aggression. He further argued that "a shaky peace" is preferable to war, even a victorious one, since the latter always brings with it death and destruction and the "loss of a generation." The war, moreover, could take unpredictable turns and quickly become a major conflagration. Barzilai, in essence, offered two of the classic objections to anticipatory strikes. From a utilitarian perspective, the costs are greater than the benefits; and more fundamentally, you are killing when it might not be warranted.

Other ministers responded that maintaining the status quo – a shaky "bad peace" – was worse than going to battle now. A delay made the inevitable war even more dangerous. As one minister opined, "The belt around us is tightening so that the danger for the destruction of the state increases daily."[6] The cabinet, with the support of its religious ministers, approved the Sinai Campaign. They dubbed it "Operation Kadesh" in commemoration of the biblical settlement Kadesh Barnea in which the Israelites stayed after the Exodus from Egypt.

Soon after, Israel would push the Egyptian army out of the Sinai Peninsula and the Gaza Strip. Rabbi Herzog, visiting the troops near the Red Sea, marveled aloud how he was able to pray by the water in which God redeemed the ancient Israelites from the Egyptians.[7] Rabbi Goren, for his part, led a ceremony to "sanctify" the newly conquered Sinai as part of the Holy Land.[8] Even nonreligious leaders found the victory to be of biblical proportions, with figures like Ben-Gurion and the poet Natan Alterman likening it to "standing anew at Sinai."[9]

The Sinai crisis was a diplomatic blunder for France and Britain. World powers chastised them for escalating instability. Arab leaders condemned them as imperialist aggressors. British Prime Minister Eden would resign in disgrace.

Israelis, however, saw the second Arab-Israeli war as a rousing success. It bought the embattled nation a decade of relative quiet on the Egyptian front. Israeli ships could now sail through the Straits of Tiran while the IDF strengthened its military ties with France. The war had proven that the young state would not be so quickly destroyed. Nasser, however, remained entrenched in power with renewed Soviet support. Soon afterward, he vowed that Israel would be destroyed in the "third round."[10]

WAS THE 1956 INVASION A PROPORTIONATE RESPONSE?

Critics of the Israeli component of the war, from within the Jewish state and without, sometimes focus on two bad arguments: (1) Israel had not sufficiently proven Egyptian complicity in the *fedayeen* attacks;[11] and (2) Israel did not receive approval by the UN Security Council, thereby undermining this peacemaking body soon after its inception.

It is hard to take these claims seriously. The *fedayeen* attacks were clearly being supported by the Egyptian government, which was readily acknowledged by Jews and Arabs alike.[12] Israel, moreover, had no alternative to self-help, since both of the major superpowers, the Soviet Union and the United States, had no interests in taking any actions in the UN Security Council that might push Egypt to the other side in the Cold War. This was one of the earliest indications to Israel that the UN would not provide any recourse to either justice or security, a point elaborated on in chapter 3. The Security Council may have some political influence, yet its judgments of Israeli action, driven by national interests, carry very little *moral* weight.[13]

A more serious claim is that Israel's decision to launch a war was a disproportionate response to Egypt's actions. One of the requirements in classic just-war theory in justifying going to war is known as "proportionality," i.e., the negative destructiveness of the war must not be out of proportion to the relative good that will be achieved by the war. Some critics argue that the *fedayeen* attacks were of insufficient "magnitude of damage" to justify an extensive military response.[14] One doesn't go to war to stop raids of bandits.

They further claim that this was a "preventative" war and not a preemptive strike since an Egyptian invasion was clearly not imminent. Israel's anticipatory attack led to bloodshed that was not inevitable. It might have even strengthened Nasser's belligerency that ultimately led to the Six-Day War. More fundamentally, the mere augmentation of Egyptian military weaponry does not make the country, or its representatives, morally liable for attack. One cannot kill Egyptian soldiers when they may not represent a direct threat to Israel's security.

Within Israeli circles, critics accused Ben-Gurion of breaking his pledge to only fight so-called "no-choice wars" (*milḥamot ein bereira*). The concept of a "no-choice war" emerged even before the state was founded to express the notion that Zionists had no alternative to fighting wars that were imposed upon them. To survive, many would claim, Jews were "forced" to fight, or war was "forced upon them." This claim was crucial to the ethos of the Haganah and later the IDF: Jews waged war as an absolute last resort.[15] The 1956 war, critics argue, violated this principle. Israel's existence was not at stake and it could have chosen to take a more defensive posture. The 1956 war was an offensive campaign.[16] Jews should not fight unless they have no other choice which, by its nature, is not the case when an attack is not imminent.[17]

THE MORAL CASE FOR THE SINAI CAMPAIGN

This criticism of the 1956 war – or at least Israel's role in it – is misguided. One may argue that France or Britain did not have sufficient cause to go to war against Egypt. Israel, by contrast, had suffered from dozens of *fedayeen* attacks that led to hundreds of Israeli casualties among civilians and soldiers alike. True, there was no one moment of invasion, like in the 1973 war. Yet accumulated together, the *fedayeen* attacks constituted a magnitude of violent hostility that justified a reciprocal military response.[18] Indeed, a few ethicists deem the 1956 war as a classic defensive war against aggression.[19] At the very least, these attacks provided sufficient grievance for an Israeli offensive.

The Sinai Campaign might nonetheless be deemed a "preventative war." No mass Egyptian invasion was on the immediate horizon, failing the imminence criterion. It is always possible that some diplomatic development could have prevented a war and, critically, also stopped the *fedayeen* attacks. The timing of the attack – before the Czechoslovakian arms delivery would upset the military balance and after European powers agreed to help – was a choice.

This choice doesn't make the war any less necessary or less moral. All strategic decisions are based on imprecise calculations. As many recent just-war theorists have emphasized, the standards of both "last resort" and "proportionality" require judgment calls. After all, there might always be some alternative to war, such as another attempt at diplomacy. Thus "last resort" means that we seek first the least violent method of neutralizing a threat and that we not hastily resort to force.[20] Yet there is no formula for determining the "least violent method" or "hastiness," leaving room for reasonable discretion.

What were Israel's options? Israel had unsuccessfully sought to stop these *fedayeen* raids through diplomacy and military reprisals. Yet IDF raids on select Gazan military bases were not effective in providing protection to Israel citizens. They were also quite deadly. A year before, in February 1955, infiltrators from the Gaza Strip killed an Israeli citizen in the city of Rehovot. In response, IDF paratroopers, commanded by Ariel Sharon, launched "Operation Black Arrow" on an Egyptian military base near Gaza City. Thirty-eight Egyptian soldiers and eight IDF members were killed. Subsequently, more *fedayeen* raids were launched, with even deadlier reprisal attacks by the IDF on Egyptian targets. In this context, it's far from clear that limited reprisals are more ethical or efficacious than an outright invasion.

The status quo, furthermore, remained insufferable. While continuing to sponsor lethal *fedayeen* raids, Egypt would seek a more opportune moment to launch a penetrating invasion into Israel. The threat was credible and grave, even if it was not imminent. The Jewish state has a responsibility to protect its citizens. Israeli leaders reasonably concluded that an invasion of Egypt was the best option at that moment. In the balance of values required in the Jewish multivalue framework, this obligation took precedence.

As with "last resort," it is also impossible to weigh "proportionality." On a quantitative scale, perhaps one can measure body counts and economic expenditures, even as it remains problematic to compare lives with money. Yet this is hardly a sufficient equation, since one must also evaluate qualitative measures like the values of preserving sovereignty and restoring tranquility. In the short-term, more people were killed in the war than from the *fedayeen* attacks and IDF reprisals. That sacrifice doesn't mean, however, that the war wasn't worth it to restore a sense of security to Israeli communities. One must account for both short-time and long-term costs and benefits.[21]

Some ethicists also neglect to properly consider the size and strength of the nation under threat. In 1956, Israel's long-term viability was far from secure. Those living in a tiny country surrounded by larger, hostile nations will feel more risk-averse than, say, powerful America, which has no hostile neighbors and is separated from its rivals by enormous oceans.[22] Critics from the ivory towers of academia and stately capital buildings frequently forget that the gravity of a threat is measured locally.

Must Israel have waited for this actively hostile nation to get the most advanced fighter planes that could more easily strike Tel Aviv and Haifa? It is hard to say why. It wouldn't have been unethical for Israel *not* to act out of hope for some alternative resolution. Yet that doesn't make its ultimate decision to attack any less moral. Israel decided to act first not only to win an eventual war, but to ensure its victory was faster, less costly, and more decisive. An Egyptian invasion might have not been imminent. That doesn't mean an Israeli preventative attack wasn't vital or, at the very least, a reasonable decision. Once one goes to war in self-defense, it is reasonable to use tactics that will not only deter a repeat of past aggression, but further prevent threats from developing in the future.[23] The tactic chosen – an invasion – might have been offensive. Yet the motivation behind it was defensive, seeking to stop continued acts of belligerence and avert more lethal aggression in the future.

THE FLAWED "NO-CHOICE" RHETORIC

Part of the moral confusion stems from the "no-choice war" rhetoric utilized by Ben-Gurion and others. Undoubtedly, there are real practical benefits to such rhetoric, including gaining popular support for the war effort. After the Czech-Egyptian arms deal was announced in 1955, Israeli citizens launched micro-fundraising campaigns for a defense fund for the government to purchase arms. The campaign slogan was "Arms for Israel – our answer to those plotting against us." As Dayan's chief of staff later described it, "Women from all levels of society donated necklaces and rings, children smashed their piggy banks, those without available funds borrowed from friends, unions imposed employee levies, and businessmen opened their pockets."[24]

It's clearly much easier to gather support for patriotic self-sacrifice when one has no option but to fight. Soldiers are certainly more enthusiastic about going into battle when they feel that their homeland is threatened. It's not surprising that President Bush repeatedly asserted that the second Iraq War was a war of necessity. As a sound bite, a "no-choice" war certainly sells better than "best-guess-option-under-the-circumstances" war.

Yet the "no choice" rhetoric distorts the moral framework for debating such decisions. The choice/no-choice dichotomy leads both opponents and proponents of force to overstate their case in absolute terms.[25] As the talmudic Sages understood, in the absence of armed invasion, it's not clear whether one should launch an anticipatory attack. That doesn't mean that going on the offensive is unjust or that it wasn't done for the sake of self-defense. It does require great deliberation. With good reason, preventative attacks are called "discretionary wars."

Indeed, according to one eminent twentieth-century rabbinic scholar, the talmudic Sages were precisely debating whether cases of low-intensity warfare (in his words, "they kill Jews intermittently but do not engage in battle") should be deemed a "commanded" or "discretionary" war. The scholar struggled to understand the Sages who thought this is not a "commanded" war, leaving it as an open question.[26] The answer is that even if there is just cause to initiate a battle, it may still not be necessary or wise. Such decisions require a greater amount of deliberation, including some honesty about risks being taken and the paths not chosen. The choice/no-choice dichotomy is a poor moral barometer. "Discretionary wars" might be a choice, but that doesn't make them immoral.

KEEP HONEST WITH YOUR CITIZENS AND MODEST WITH YOUR GOALS

Discretionary preventative wars also require continued justification for endangering the lives of soldiers and citizens alike. It is precisely for this reason, we argued earlier, that the Sanhedrin's approval was necessary. Their approval gives moral support for enlistment in just causes, while serving as a check on the potential abuse of monarchal power. The necessity of gaining and retaining popular support for anticipatory warfare has only increased in the modern era. As the historian Victor Davis Hanson has argued, democratic societies will not lend support to extensive preventative wars. "A controversial gamble," he notes, "cannot garner continued domestic public support if the attack instead leads to a drawn-out, deracinating struggle, the very sort of quagmire that preemption was originally intended to preclude."[27]

This is not just a strategic consideration but a moral one. When gambling with an anticipatory attack, one must prefer courses of action that prevent the extensive bloody warfare one is seeking to avoid. Accordingly, an optimal preventative strike should be short to quickly incapacitate the threat and hopefully also induce political concessions. The state must focus on eliminating the direct threat and buttressing the immediate security interests of its citizens.

This was an under-appreciated achievement of the 1956 Suez War. Ben-Gurion hoped that Nasser, Egypt's belligerent ruler, would be removed from power. Yet his strategy shifted, as Yitzhak Rabin later noted, to allow for more immediate significant accomplishments: opening the Straits of Tiran, stopping the *fedayeen* attackers, and preventing an Egyptian invasion for a decade. The preventative attack lasted less than two weeks yet directly improved the security of Israelis for almost a decade.[28]

Ultimately, the 1956 case highlights that the criterion of "imminence" is too monolithic to indicate the necessity of anticipatory warfare. Imminence presumes sufficient knowledge to indicate that a "clear and present" danger requires force to stop it. In the real world of international relations, such knowledge is regularly uncertain, forcing us to take other factors into consideration, including the gravity and credibility of the threat.[29] This point will become sharper as we turn to a more classic model of a preventative war in which there is no ongoing belligerency, but one side nonetheless chooses to attack to prevent a change in the balance of power.

Chapter 18

The Raid on Osiraq and the "Begin Doctrine"

Moving further along the spectrum of potential risks, the decision to launch an anticipatory strike becomes further complex when there is clearly no imminent risk of invasion. In this case, a country seeks to prevent the creation of a threat before it develops. To make this point clear, let's see our third scenario:

SCENARIO 3: ATTACKING AN ADVERSARY BEFORE ANY CONCRETE THREAT CAN COME TO FRUITION

Consider country A that is an adversary of country B. Unlike in scenario 2, discussed in the previous chapter, there are no sporadic hostile engagements between the countries, even as they did have armed conflicts in previous decades and remain foes. Due to its stronger position and determination to defend its vital interests, A is confident that it has deterred B despite its continued verbal threats against A. Yet A perceives that B is getting stronger, so that in time B could advance and overwhelm A's resistance or blunt the impact of retaliation. A strategy of deterrence may no longer be sufficient. Country A must choose whether to act at an early stage to prevent that possible threat from developing.

At first glance, there is an intuitive argument to justify an attack. As US Secretary of State Elihu Root stated in 1914, every sovereign state has the right "to protect itself by preventing a condition of affairs in which it will be too late to protect itself." Yet this is an incredibly dangerous model that easily leads to entirely unnecessary warfare. One could use it to justify warfare against any threat that one perceives as possibly developing many years down the line.

Over history, such logic was used by many empires and dynasties to kill potential rivals.[1] Let's take two simple examples. In the beginning of the eighteenth century, Britain attacked France. Why? To ensure that the French would not later join up with Spain and become a rival to the crown's power. Centuries earlier, in 395 CE, Romans slaughtered defenseless foreign aliens in their eastern cities. The motivation? To warn off anyone threatening at the outskirts of their empire. The Romans, Machiavelli asserted, "never postponed action to avoid war, for they understood that you cannot escape wars, and when you put them off, only your opponents benefit." If war is always inevitable, a delay just provides time for enemies to get much stronger. Such an approach has led to much unnecessary slaughter. History has also shown that such wars were frequently unnecessary, because tensions ultimately dissipate without hostilities.

Preventative warfare can also be a strategic disaster. The Japanese attacked Pearl Harbor to limit America's capabilities in a future conflict. Four years later, American air power decimated its cities. In the Bible, it was a similar type of calculation that led the Egyptians to enslave the descendants of Jacob, whose population was increasing exponentially. "Come," they said to themselves, "let us be shrewd with them lest they multiply and then, should war occur, they will join our enemies and fight against us."[2] Besides being morally odious, the strategy ultimately led to the empire's defeat. Many years later, a different generation of Israelites were on the verge of entering the Holy Land. They had pledged not to invade the surrounding nations. Nonetheless, the Moabites convinced the Midianites to cunningly strategize against these newcomers, arguing that "this horde will chew away everything around us as the ox nibbles the grass of the field."[3] Their unfounded fears caused them to make dire mistakes and ultimately led to their downfall.

On a fundamental level, it is hard to justify attacking a rival nation simply because a mightier country fears the economic and political ascent of another country.[4] To concretize this point, let's take a theoretical contemporary example: in 2023, it would be wrong for the United States to invade China because it worries, with good reason, that its rival's increased economic and military power will ultimately threaten American military supremacy. The fear is well-founded, and the potential consequences for political liberty around the world are disturbing. Nonetheless, the perceived threat is so distant that any attack is rightly deemed morally outrageous.

More concretely, Russian apologists sometimes justified its unprovoked 2022 invasion of Ukraine by expressing concerns of an eventual eastward expansion of NATO and even the potential placement of nuclear weapons on Russia's western border.[5] The former option was certainly a possibility, the latter more fantastical. Yet even if that was the case, was there any reason to fear a future NATO invasion of Russia? Not really, and certainly not enough to justify attacking Ukraine. The Russian invasion was much more likely motivated by imperial ambitions and an attempt to restore a modern version of the Russian Empire.

A loose doctrine to allow preventative war, furthermore, also invites rival countries to see each other as actual threats against which they must now consider striking first. War becomes another method in the political toolbox of national rivals. If legitimized, every nation may start to calculate how an adversary could pose a threat that will be more difficult to address at a later point.

The United States invaded Iraq in 2003 because it believed (incorrectly, it turned out) that Saddam Hussein was developing unconventional weapons that he could eventually use to launch an attack on American soil. Following this model could lead to conflagrations between a wide range of rival states: Japan and North Korea, Armenia and Azerbaijan, India and Pakistan, and so on. As Henry Kissinger warned before the Iraq War, "It is not in the American national interest to establish preemption as a universal principle available to every nation." Yet no ethical principle may be applied to allow some states to act while not allowing others to behave in a similar manner. There are, accordingly, good reasons to fear that a permissive doctrine that allows preventative war will lead to very bad consequences.[6]

Yet each nation will – and must – continue to give primacy to its own unique needs and situations.[7] There are clearly times when a nation may quite reasonably fear a growing threat from a rival country. This is particularly true if the feared nation has already displayed ongoing hostility, even as the two countries are not (or no longer) engaged in active hostilities. An adversary's military capabilities can quickly shift to enable it to become both actively belligerent and lethally dangerous. The best and possibly only recourse may be to prevent that scenario from developing. Moreover, as we've previously noted, the existence of weapons of mass destruction, long-range weapons, dirty bombs, and the proliferation of nonstate actors greatly increases the number of threats that must be handled before they become fully developed.

Hence a choice must be made: when is a preventative war justified?

THE 1981 STRIKE ON THE IRAQI NUCLEAR REACTOR AT OSIRAQ[8]

From the day he was elected prime minister in 1977, Menachem Begin felt responsible for preventing the threat of another holocaust – this time nuclear – against the Jewish people. His predecessor, Yitzhak Rabin, warned him about the looming dangers of Iraq's nuclear power plant in Osiraq, located twelve miles southeast of Baghdad. The plant required material support from France and other European countries. Israeli diplomacy, however, was unsuccessful at stopping European support. The Mossad also tried to covertly sabotage the shipment of parts to Iraq. Once again, Israel had limited success.[9]

By 1980, Israeli intelligence believed that the plant would be operational by late 1981 or early 1982. It would take only a couple of years after that for Saddam Hussein to build a nuclear bomb. Israel wasn't the only one fearful of that possibility. Toward the beginning of the Iran-Iraq War, Iran bombed the Osiraq reactor in September 1980 but caused minimal damage.

In the meantime, Iraqi newspapers continued to declare that Iraq would soon vent its anger on the "Zionist entity." Hussein urged

Arab comrades to destroy Tel Aviv once the necessary bombs "become available."[10] Iraq had fought against Israel in 1948, 1967, and 1973 and officially remained in a state of war with the Jewish state. The Mossad had deemed Hussein, known as the Butcher of Baghdad, a cruel megalomanic capable of using a nuclear weapon to destroy Israel and win supremacy over the Arab world. Begin was convinced that Israel must act – now – to avoid another holocaust.[11]

But not all of his cabinet ministers or army intelligence chiefs were convinced this was a wise move. Neither was the opposition leader, Shimon Peres. No pacifist, Peres had been one of the architects of the 1956 Suez War and builder of Israel's own nuclear reactor. In a top-secret letter written toward the end of 1980, he ominously cautioned Begin with one of the classic strategic arguments against preventative warfare: you don't know what you are getting yourself into. A preemptive move can easily backfire. "What is meant to prevent [disaster] can become a catalyst [for disaster].... I am not alone in saying this, and certainly not at the present time under the given circumstances." Foreseeing diplomatic isolation, he cited one of Jeremiah's prophecies of doom, predicting Israel will be "like a thistle in the desert."[12]

Begin nonetheless persisted. His approach was later dubbed "the Begin doctrine": Israel will do everything to prevent its sworn enemies who openly threaten her destruction from developing a nuclear military capacity.[13] After a contentious cabinet debate, Begin, with the support of Defense Minister Ariel Sharon, narrowly won a vote authorizing the strikes. The vote was 10 to 6. On June 7, 1981, eight Israeli fighter jets launched "Operation Opera," a daring raid that decimated the nuclear reactor. Israelis simultaneously celebrated and breathed a sigh of relief.

The international community was harsh and swift with its condemnation. The UN Security Council unanimously passed, with American support, a resolution condemning Israel for violating the UN charter. Margaret Thatcher argued that this was a "grave breach of international law." Begin, for his part, confided to his confidants that he'd never choose between "saving the lives of our children" and getting the approval of the UN or "other fair-weather friends." He wrote to the US secretary of defense that it was easy for him to condemn the tiny Jewish state while his own grandchildren stood comfortably in vast territories far away from any real danger.[14]

Critics of the Osiraq raid, both then and now, launched many of the classic arguments against preventative war. US President Ronald Reagan lamented that Begin should have consulted with him first, as he could have intervened to remove the threat. The strike, in other words, was not truly the "last resort." Others added that there remained time for diplomacy since Iraq would still be a couple of years away from a bomb even if the nuclear reactor had gone live. Israel, in turn, responded that diplomacy had already been given a chance. It would be too dangerous for Israel to attack after the reactor had gone live because of the potential nuclear fallout. Only eight people were killed in the strike, purposely launched on a Sunday when few foreign employees were present. This was far from a disproportionate response to a distant yet very real threat.

Other countries argued that Israel had insufficient proof that Iraq would develop a bomb or use it against her. There was no imminent threat and this was a blatant act of aggression against a sovereign nation. They further warned that if every nation acted similarly, then international law would be replaced by the "law of the jungle."

Over time, many have come to see the wisdom and justice of this preventative strike. This was partly because of the 1991 Gulf War, when the world fully appreciated how dangerous Saddam Hussein was. Richard Cheney, then America's secretary of defense, would thank Operation Opera's chief architect for the "outstanding job on the Iraqi nuclear program in 1981, which made our job much easier."

Attitudes largely shifted because of the growing fear of unconventional weapons being used by rogue states or terrorist groups. During the Cold War, a nuclear attack was partly deterred by each superpower recognizing that any unconventional attack would be met in kind by the other side. With nonstate actors, however, no such deterrent exists, making it an imperative to prevent them from gaining such a dangerous weapon. As Israel argued already in 1981, international norms formulated at the beginning of the Cold War must be rethought in light of new types of weapons and threats.[15]

LESSONS FROM HITLER AND THE CUBAN MISSILE CRISIS

Can one establish criteria that will allow necessary preventative attacks but avoid excessive warfare? Some recent philosophers have tried. Michael Doyle, for example, has proposed a standard of four Ls: (1) lethality, measuring the potential loss of life if the threat is not eliminated; (2) likelihood, calculating the probability that the threat will occur; (3) legitimacy, which includes fostering discourse about the threat, measuring proportionality through cost-benefit analysis, and limiting the violence as much as possible; and (4) legality, arguing that the targeted regime must have violated international law, indicating its hostile intent or nature.

Some thinkers focus on this last point, contending that we should act preventatively to stop rogue states. These are countries with militaristic leaders espousing an ideology of violence, backed up by a track record of brutality, who are now building their capacity for further bloodshed.[16]

It's clear that any standard of preventative war must allow us to stop the next Hitler. In 1936, it should be recalled, Germany remilitarized the Rhineland, violating its post–World War I commitments and making it a greater threat to Western Europe. By 1938, Hitler had annexed Austria and the Sudetenland, Czechoslovakia's German-speaking areas bordering Germany and Austria. Some figures in France and Britain, including Winston Churchill, presciently warned that war with Hitler was inevitable. Now was the time to strike before Germany became militarily stronger and emboldened. Britain's leaders decided otherwise, partly because they believed the military was not ready to strike, but largely because of their strong aversion to another bloody war.[17] Within two years, the Nazis had conquered much of continental Europe.

Yet the legacy of the failure to stop Hitler earlier doesn't mean that we must launch full-throttle invasions against every significant threat. This is exemplified by the Cuban Missile Crisis. In October 1962, a U-2 reconnaissance mission over Cuba photographed Soviet medium range ballistic missiles, nuclear-capable weapons able to reach much of America's east coast. America's military chiefs urged President Kennedy to launch a surprise attack against the missile sites. A strike, they contended, would eliminate the immediate threat and further deter a Soviet-counterstrike through this bold display of firm American resolve. They warned that alternative suggestions, which would prioritize diplomacy and not allow US forces to take the first shot, would only give the Soviets time to hide their missiles while endangering allies in West Berlin. The Air Force Commander, Curtis LeMay – whose callous approach to military ethics during World War II was highlighted in chapter 8 – further warned Kennedy that a failure to strike was "almost as bad as the appeasement at Munich."

The United States was clearly contemplating taking more aggressive preventative action. As its UN ambassador, Adlai Stevenson, declared in a famous speech, "Were we to do nothing until the knife was sharpened? Were we to stand idly by until it was at our throats?"[18]

The answer, in the end, was not to sit by idly but to utilize a less belligerent option. In this case, a limited military response (i.e., a naval blockade) combined with diplomacy sufficiently dissipated the conflict.[19] Preventative action was taken without lives being lost. The Cold War remained on ice. The more hawkish approach might have led to a nuclear holocaust. This is precisely the complexity of anticipatory, preventative action: a wise decision in one historical moment might be perilous at another, and it's not clear which variables determine that outcome.

Opponents of preventative warfare have tried to draw a clear line between preemptive attacks, where the illicit aggression is on the verge of beginning, and preventative attacks, where the threat is more distant. Yet that line is not so easy to draw, as seen by the many arguments over what actions actually indicate that an attack is imminent. Moreover, as long as the attack hasn't started, it might always be stopped. Indeed, as we saw previously, Egypt was only a few hours away from beginning its attack on Israel in May 1967 before Nasser called off the operation. Ultimately, these are questions of probability. The difference between the two kinds of anticipatory self-defense attacks, preemptive and preventative wars, is a matter of degree, not kind.[20]

Accordingly, imminence cannot be the only standard to assess the prudence of an anticipatory strike. One must account for the other variables of ICG scenarios, namely the credibility and gravity of the threat. The character of the adversary and the potential damage from inaction must be examined. If the threated attack would have serious, lethal consequences, and the enemy leaders are the types who would attack if they could, then a preventative military action must remain on the table. Given the gravity and nature of the threat, one doesn't always have the luxury of waiting to act until the last moment, let alone the technical possibility of still mounting an effective preemptive move. What's demanded, therefore, is a high bar of evidentiary standards to assert that this is a grave and credible threat, despite the doubts and uncertainties.

Given the spectrum of possibilities, it's nearly impossible to establish predetermined, definitive rules. There is no perfect system of checks-and-balances to ensure that governments go to war under pristine motivations and with perfect calculations. Instead, we must work with a general standard that allows for analysis of probability and the magnitude of harm. The decision maker is ultimately going to be the country at-risk, who will need to calculate the different variables. Critics, in turn, may give their own assessment and evaluate the country based on the reasonableness of their decision-making process.

Advocates of an international order will find this unsatisfactory. They will continue to insist on approval by an international legal body or, at the very least, through some collective decision-making process to legitimate this action. Yet as we've argued previously, no such body will exist whose judgment won't be tainted by political interests. It's good for a country's leader to consult with allies and others, much as they must seek advice from his or her advisers, as required in all "discretionary wars." At the end of the day, it remains within the discretion – and responsibility – of any given country to defend its own citizens.

For these reasons, anticipatory attacks should remain focused on clear and limited goals to remove the most pressing threats. This was achieved during the Cuban Missile Crisis and later during the Osiraq strike. Israel was not looking for regime change and certainly not a broader war. It had a clear and limited target which, if successful, would be sufficient and minimize the breadth of the war. Of course, it was far from inevitable that the strike would be successful or not lead to a bloody conflict. The justness of the decision lay in the reasonable deliberative process as well as the strategic attempt to limit the scope of the warfare to the most direct threat.

It would be precisely in these two areas which the Begin government would fail soon afterward in its next foray into preventative warfare, Operation Peace for Galilee, later to be known as the First Lebanon War.

Chapter 19

1982 Operation Peace for Galilee and Israel's Gravest Moral Failure[1]

Israel's summer of 1982 invasion of Lebanon had been coming for some time. Violent confrontations between Israel and Palestinian Liberation Organization (PLO) terrorists based in Lebanon had been ongoing for several years. The PLO was founded in 1964 by Yasser Arafat with the explicit aim of destroying Israel. It relocated to Lebanon following its violent eviction from Jordan in the early 1970s. From his Beirut head-quarters, Arafat had ordered many attacks against Jews around the world. His militants also launched raids and rockets on Israeli towns from PLO strongholds in southern Lebanon. In one infamous event in March 1978, later known as the Coastal Road Massacre, eleven Palestinian infiltrators snuck into Israel off the Mediterranean Coast and went on a killing rampage. Thirty-five Israeli citizens were killed. Over seventy more were wounded. In response, the IDF launched the Litani Operation, an invasion of Lebanon to remove PLO strongholds up to the Litani River. This incursion created a roughly six-mile "security belt" from Israel's northern border.

Following a UN-brokered cease-fire, Israeli forces withdrew to their border and were replaced by international peacekeepers. This arrangement had very limited success. In the next three years, the PLO launched fifty missile attacks that killed ten Israelis and wounded nearly sixty more. Israel, in turn, launched over thirty ground operations against PLO operatives and numerous air strikes within Lebanon. In July 1981, the United States brokered another short-lived cease-fire. Israel continued to launch reconnaissance flights over Lebanon and Syria, to the anger of its Arab neighbors. The PLO, more egregiously, insisted that the cease-fire only prohibited border hostilities; attacks on Jews around the world and within mainland Israel, they claimed, remained perfectly legitimate. Between July 1981 and June 1982, the PLO would instigate nearly 150 attacks against Israeli or Jewish targets around the world.[2] In the meantime, they and their Syrian allies upgraded their arsenal with Soviet-supplied weapons, making their threat to Israel even more potent.

In the subsequent year, Israel considered attacking Lebanon on four different occasions. The accumulated years of attacks from Lebanon, repeated failed attempts at diplomacy, and the threat of increasingly potent enemy firepower called for a more serious response than yet another reprisal raid. Each time, however, the invasions were called off. Menachem Begin's government was preoccupied with the attack on the Osiraq reactor, annexing the Golan Heights, and implementing its peace agreement with Egypt, including its withdrawal from the Sinai Desert. Most significantly, there was fundamental disagreement among cabinet members about the necessary action, with several objecting to any extensive incursion.[3]

On June 3, 1982, a small Palestinian splinter group attempted to kill Israel's ambassador to London. Depending on one's perspective, this became the final straw, or the pretense, to put an end to Palestinian terrorism against Israelis around the world.[4] Three days later – one year after the Osiraq raid – the IDF entered Lebanon, launching Operation Peace for Galilee.

BEGIN'S WAR OF CHOICE

Was this a no-choice war? Clearly not. The first to admit this was Begin himself. It's true that the accumulated attacks on Israeli citizens were legitimate cause for warfare. Nonetheless, that doesn't mean Israel had to launch a full-out invasion in response, and certainly not at that moment. As Begin himself put it, in an oft-cited speech two months after the war began, "There is always room for a great deal of consideration as to whether it is necessary to make a *causus* into a *bellum*."[5] That is to say, even when there is a just cause to fight, the nation has to decide if war is the necessary response. He understood Israel was not under a full-fledged attack. Its existence was certainly not at stake. It could reasonably choose to wait. Israel did not need to act at that moment, as it did in 1967 and 1973. The situation was most comparable to the 1956 war, when Israel also suffered from repeated terrorist raids over its border.

So why invade now? Begin saw the PLO as a future existential threat to Israel. He would regularly call the PLO a "Nazi organization" and compare its leaders to "mini-Eichmanns," in reference to the infamous Nazi leader. For some, the comparison was exaggerated; for Begin, that was precisely the point. The West could have dealt with Hitler in 1936. It failed to act, and the world – and especially the Jews – suffered the consequences.[6] Hitler became Hitler precisely because no one stopped him earlier. The purpose of Jewish sovereignty was to prevent a repeat of the moral calamity of inaction.

And if the Holocaust was too distant of a memory for some, Begin would add, the Yom Kippur War served as a sufficient reminder of what happens when Jews wait too long to act. "There is no moral imperative that a nation must, or is entitled to, fight only when its back is to the sea, or to the abyss."[7] To the contrary, responsible states must act so that they do not wait to fight when they have no alternatives. The willingness to act from a position of strength, he further hoped, would not only deter Israel's neighbors from aggression but also bring them to make peace with Israel.

Begin's argument for *some form* of military response is compelling. No nation must live under constant threat from attack, "day after day, week after week, month after month," as he put it. Israel, like any other nation in such a situation, had the obligation to protect its citizens and act when it saw fit.

Yet the critical question was determining the necessary scope of its response that would actually improve Israel's security. In this respect, it's interesting to note the language employed by the medieval scholar Maimonides to describe "commanded wars" of self-defense. In his language, these are wars "to *help* assuage Israel of a persecutor."[8] As one rabbinic scholar noted then, a war is mandated only if you've determined if it will help.[9] Not every war fulfills that goal, even when fought under the genuine motivations of self-defense. Not every enemy, however despicable, represents a genocidal threat. A robust cost-benefit analysis must take place.

THREE OPTIONS AND THE CHOSEN ROAD NOT TAKEN

The ethicist William O'Brien wrote a probing moral and legal analysis of Israel's war with the PLO. He argues that there were three legitimate self-defense rationales for military action.[10] Each argument would justify a significantly different type of proportional response.

1. Israel could aim to prevent continuing PLO terrorist attacks across the border. Yet Israel had tried for a few years to stop border attacks through occasional reprisal/attrition raids on PLO targets, but to no avail. Option 1, therefore, seemed too limited of a goal. In the months before the war, Begin had declared that Israel could no longer focus on retaliation but instead must prevent the PLO's ability to act by striking them on their bases.[11]

This left two more aggressive options:

2. Deny the PLO the ability to utilize its strengthening arsenal in southern Lebanon to threaten northern Israeli cities and make them nearly uninhabitable.

3. Remove the PLO's entire presence from Lebanon.

Option 2 essentially entailed an expanded version of the 1978 Litani Operation, this time with the goal of clearing a fifteen-mile security belt. Option 3 would entail attacks on Beirut, the PLO headquarters, alongside diplomatic efforts. Both options are legitimate aims with various strategic advantages and disadvantages. Each also encompasses different types of risks – military, diplomatic, and ethical. Option 2 was clearly less dangerous, yet it was unclear if it would be sufficient to stop the PLO attacks. Option 3 would accomplish that aggressive goal but it carried greater risks. It is precisely for this type of dilemma that the Sages mandated that discretionary wars require the approval of a wider group of advisers.

The ultimate outcome, in many ways, was the worst of both worlds: the Israeli cabinet voted, in very clear terms, for option 2; in practice, Sharon, the defense minister, implemented option 3.[12] The government, in other words, authorized a limited invasion of limited territorial and strategic goals. The army, in practice, started a war of significantly more extensive ambitions. This was a recipe for disaster.

On a strategic level, the lack of clear government directives led Sharon to guide the IDF in an indecisive manner. If the goal was to remove the PLO entirely from Lebanon, decisive planning to attack Beirut should have been taken immediately. This was, in the words of two distinguished military historians, "one of the greatest blunders in Israel's short military history."[13] More generally, the IDF's generals were making decisions without fully knowing the goals of the operation.[14] While the initial conquest of southern Lebanon had been largely successful, it entailed significant IDF casualties. The cabinet certainly did not desire any protracted bloody struggle for the Lebanese capital – which they had never approved.[15] Israel ended up laying a protracted siege on Beirut that endangered its soldiers, military achievements, and international standing.

On the diplomatic front, Israel was now deemed untrustworthy. Begin had promised President Reagan and other leaders that the Israeli incursion was limited to the fifteen-mile security belt. They now saw him as a liar. Former aides and historians continue to disagree whether Begin was in the loop regarding Sharon's aggressive plans.[16] Most argue that the aging prime minister was not fully aware of Sharon's actual plans. It's clear that the cabinet never approved of them.

All of this led to Israel's greatest moral error: deceiving its citizens and soldiers about the true ambitions of its discretionary war. Over 90 percent of the population initially supported some form of military action. The situation in northern Israel was intolerable. Yet elective surgery requires consent. The medicine can't be more harmful than the ailment, and the patient must know the risks of the procedure. So too with discretionary war. The people must be made aware of the goals and hazards in a war which was motivated by self-defense but could have very different types of strategies. Israel's citizen-soldiers were placing their lives at stake for this war. They were entitled – morally – to an honest explanation for the discretionary decisions of their government. When they didn't, the people took to the streets. For the first time in their history, Israelis openly protested an ongoing military operation, pitting citizen against citizen, and rabbi against rabbi.

THE SURPRISING REVOLT OF RABBI YEHUDA AMITAL

Rabbi Yehuda Amital was not the figure whom one would have expected to lead the religious protest against an Israeli military incursion. A Holocaust survivor, Amital joined the Haganah and later fought in Israel's War of Independence. He penned one of the first halakhic treatises regarding the religious objectives of military service and its spiritual importance. After the Six-Day War, he started a new type of rabbinic seminary in which the students combined army service and yeshiva studies. The yeshiva was in the Judean village of Alon Shvut, one of the new settlements established after Israel took control of the West Bank. Following the Yom Kippur War, much of the country was in despair over the heavy casualties. Despite losing eight of his own students to the fighting, Amital penned an influential treatise arguing that the IDF's ultimate victory was another clear demonstration that Israel was in the midst of national redemption. His words invigorated many religious Zionists, including the leaders of the *Gush Emunim* (Bloc of the Faithful) movement that promoted settlement in Judea and Samaria.[17]

Amital began to break with many of his religious colleagues after the peace agreement with Egypt. Immediately in the wake of the Yom Kippur War, Rabbi Tzvi Yehuda had opposed any territorial retreats from the Sinai Peninsula, even to reach an armistice agreement with Egypt. A few years later, he and his leading students were adamantly opposed to the Camp David Accords. This was, in part, because the Begin government was promising to give Palestinians in the West Bank – the historic biblical territories of Judea and Samaria – some form of "autonomy." Using a play on words, R. Tzvi Yehuda deridingly called this proposal the "anatomy" plan because it dissected and divided the Holy Land.[18]

R. Tzvi Yehuda was not opposed to an agreement with Egypt per se. Yet this could not come at the cost of withdrawing from any conquered territories. This would be a sign of weakness as well as a betrayal of the homeland which included, in R. Tzvi Yehuda's mind, the Sinai Peninsula.[19] When the Sinai settlement strip of Yamit was ultimately evacuated in the spring of 1982, R. Tzvi Yehuda's students led civil disobedience protests at the site.[20] Their efforts failed. They were also without their spiritual leader. R. Tzvi Yehuda had died in February of that year, just four months before the invasion of Lebanon.

R. Amital believed that the opposition to the Camp David Accords was a distortion of Jewish values. Judaism, he asserted, had a scale of priorities.[21] On the top of that list was prioritizing the well-being of the Jewish people. Sometimes this means violating serious ritual laws, like Shabbat restrictions, to provide immediate medical care. At other times, it means withdrawing from conquered territories – including cherished parts of the historic homeland – in order to make peace. The path of national redemption may be achieved through peace, not just war.[22]

R. Amital's statement was an important iteration of the type of multivalued decision-making framework discussed throughout this book. Unlike some figures on the Israeli political left, he did not deny the value of *Eretz Yisrael*, the national homeland. Instead, R. Amital asserted that the value of saving lives (*pikuaḥ nefesh* in Hebrew) trumps other considerations. When we discussed the "dirty hands dilemma" in chapter 5, we noted that the senior Rabbi Kook had once declared that sometimes the Torah's severest precepts may be violated to save the Jewish people. In support, he cited a rabbinic midrash that recorded a conversation between a Sage and his pupil. The pupil asked,

> My master, there are two things in my heart which I love greatly: Torah and the people of Israel, but I do not know which of them takes priority.
>
> [The teacher] replied: People usually say that Torah takes priority over everything else…but I say that the holy people of Israel take priority, as it is written, "Israel is holy to God, the first of His produce" (Jer. 2:3).[23]

The Torah's commandments are precious, but not as important as the people. Now, R. Amital asserted, we must prioritize the people's welfare over preserving the sanctity of the homeland. The people take priority.

Soon after the Yamit withdrawal, the Lebanon War began. R. Amital bade an emotional farewell to his students as they left the yeshiva and deployed to the border. Within a week, one student was dead. Another, Zachary Baumel, went missing after his tank battalion was ambushed in the village of Sultan Yacoub. (His remains were recovered only in 2019.)

Two weeks into the war, R. Amital went to visit the troops alongside two government ministers during an alleged cease-fire period. R. Amital – and the ministers – were shocked to discover that, in reality, the IDF was still shooting. The soldiers were confused while the ministers were dumbfounded. It was clear to R. Amital that Sharon had other intentions and had misled both the cabinet and the people. In the coming weeks, R. Amital would publicly call for an end to the fighting and campaign against the occupation of Beirut. R. Amital's students were shocked by his public stance against the government.[24]

In a dramatic Saturday evening address to his pupils, R. Amital asserted that only defensive wars or preemptive attacks were permissible. The war in Lebanon had exceeded those boundaries. In contrast to R. Tzvi Yehuda, R. Amital asserted, like Maimonides, that there is no independent command to conquer the land. In any case, Lebanon was beyond the biblical borders. The only mandated wars in our times were those to protect the Jewish people. Such unnecessary bloodshed, of Jew and non-Jew alike, had no mandate. He further added that were Israel to have a viable peace partner among the Palestinians, he would even support territorial compromises in Judea and Samaria (in which, it should be recalled, his yeshiva was located).

Sitting in the back of the study hall that evening was R. Hanan Porat, one of the yeshiva's first students and a leader of the *Gush Emunim* settlement movement. In an act of immense intellectual generosity, R. Amital invited R. Porat to rebut his own speech in front of the students. R. Porat respectfully but emphatically denounced his teacher's remarks. Repeatedly citing the approach of Nahmanides and the teachings of R. Tzvi Yehuda, R. Porat asserted that the Bible commands us to conquer the land.[25] Lebanon is, in fact, a part of Greater Israel.[26] We hope our conquest may be done peacefully, but if not, then we must fight for it as long as we have a realistic chance to win.

R. Porat agreed that there is indeed a ladder of Jewish values that should dictate our moral considerations. In his mind, however, conquering the Land of Israel is one of the highest rungs. Any other message is a theological and educational disaster.[27] This is our destiny that began with the biblical forefather Abraham. The continuous divine calling to conquer the land is also a moral mandate, whatever the locals or the rest of the world might say. Our hold on Greater Israel, moreover, cannot be separated from our security. This reality demands the highest form of self-sacrifice.

Many other religious Zionist rabbis joined in condemning R. Amital's remarks. The war in Lebanon was a *milḥemet mitzva* to defend the Galilee and to conquer the Holy Land. Indeed, during the first month of the war, the Israeli Chief Rabbinate Council, under Rabbi Goren's leadership, publicly declared it a "commanded war" to protect Israeli citizens, especially in border cities. They further saluted the IDF for its military restraint and attempt to minimize civilian casualties.[28]

The debate presented a binary choice: either the Lebanon War was a commanded war and therefore necessary (R. Porat) or a discretionary war and therefore wrong (R. Amital). Yet is this the only way to think about it?

FROM COMMANDED WAR TO DISCRETIONARY WAR?

Israeli public opinion about the war greatly shifted after the summer of 1982. The PLO had largely been forced from Beirut. Nonetheless, the popularity of the war soured. Israel had hoped the leader of the Christian Phalangist Party and newly elected Lebanese president Bachir Gemayel would make peace with Israel. But Gemayel was assassinated in September 1982. Soon afterward, Phalangist troops entered the Sabra and Shatila refugee camps and massacred unarmed men, women, and children.

Israelis were outraged that such an atrocity would be committed by their allies with IDF soldiers nearby.[29] An investigative committee found Defense Minister Sharon indirectly responsible. He was ultimately forced to resign. In the meantime, Lebanon descended again into a civil war while Israel no longer had an easy exit strategy.

IDF casualties mounted. Mass protests ensued. By the end of August 1983, Begin would also resign, declaring, "I can't take it anymore." A year after the war began, when R. Goren was no longer chief rabbi, he penned an extensive essay defending his belief that this operation was a *milhemet mitzva* to protect the villages of the Galilee.[30] In the course of his reply, he noted, following the lead of earlier scholars, that a discretionary war could transform into a commanded war. After all, the nation might launch some form of preventative strike, but soon after find its own cities under retaliatory attack. That might have plausibly happened, for example, had Iraq chosen to strike Israel after the Osiraq raid. The tides of war can shift, with anticipatory strikes quickly leading to self-defense battles and even fights for one's existence.

R. Goren went further to argue that once Operation Peace for Galilee had started, it became essential for Israel to win. It would be very damaging for Israel's deterrence and status to not have a decisive victory. As such, even those who opposed the war or questioned its wisdom should now agree that it was a commanded war.[31]

This is a specious argument. Certainly, it is best for a country to win its wars. But sometimes the best option is not to fight until the end, when the human costs of victory may be too great. Instead, one should cease fire and negotiate. If necessary, one might even need to unilaterally retreat. There is no moral obligation to fight only for the sake of victory. For this reason, just-war theorists stress that the proportionality requirement entails an ongoing evaluation, not just a one-off assessment before the battle begins. After all, given the indeterminacies of politics and warfare, one can never know how things will develop. The justness of a war must be constantly assessed.[32]

Nonetheless, leaving aside R. Goren's thesis on how every war becomes a commanded war, his larger point is correct: the moral status of a war can shift. A discretionary war can become a commanded war, but a commanded war can likewise transform into a discretionary one. Once a country under attack has stopped the assault and minimized the chance of its renewal, it no longer needs to fight. It may elect to fight to further weaken its enemy, but that remains a choice. Successful rebuttals of an assault frequently present such opportunities when the attacking army has been sufficiently rebuffed.

Fascinatingly, toward the end of the essay, R. Goren himself hints at this possible interpretation of the current state of affairs. Before 1982, the PLO had been regularly striking at Israel, making the Jewish state's response a classic self-defense war against aggression. A year into the war, the PLO had been greatly weakened. However, the threats from Lebanon were not fully eliminated – nor was it clear that they could be. A continued IDF assault and occupation of Lebanon might lead to even greater loss of Israeli life, thereby making it unjustifiable. Ultimately, that cost-benefit calculation had to be made by political and military leaders to determine the right course of action. The threat from Lebanon remained. Nonetheless, R. Goren admits, Israeli leaders had a choice to make at this stage.[33]

Taking this argument to its logical conclusion, one might declare that this operation started off as a commanded war, but at some point, it became a discretionary one. One might even say, with a flare of rhetoric, that Operation Peace for Galilee was a commanded war, while the Lebanon War was discretionary.[34]

Yet R. Goren's concession seems to point to the fact that Israel always had to make such a cost-benefit decision when it came to fighting in Lebanon. The Israeli cabinet understood that was the case. So did Begin and Sharon. This decision should have been made in June 1982, before the war, and once again, a week or two into the war, when the initial fifteen-mile goal was achieved. Yet no serious deliberation ever took place.

Israel ultimately withdrew from much of Lebanon, but only in June 1985. In the interim period, it lost many soldiers, and at the end of the day, it still needed to occupy a security strip in southern Lebanon until the year 2000.

Six years after its complete withdrawal, Israel went to war against Hezbollah, a terrorist group that emerged during the First Lebanon War and had launched many dozens of intermittent attacks on Israeli targets. In 2006, however, Israel fought for only thirty-four days and then returned to its borders after a cease-fire. It was an imperfectly run war that produced indecisive results; nonetheless, a tense peace held up for over fifteen years, and Israel did not get itself stuck in an extended bloodbath. Lessons had been learned.

The moral tragedy of the Lebanon War was not that it wasn't a war of self-defense; Israel had an obligation to defend its citizens. Instead, it was the unwillingness of its leaders to recognize that in the face of different risky options, one should always prefer the plan that has the clearest objectives and lowest chances of unintended consequences. Most importantly, one cannot lie about these goals to the citizens who will fight – and die – because of that ultimate decision. Begin and Sharon failed in these moral tests. They rightfully lost their positions of power for this moral error.

THE "LAND FOR PEACE" DEBATE, AGAIN

In the aftermath of the Lebanon War, the vociferous debate between R. Amital and the disciples of R. Tzvi Yehuda only escalated. The debate, as we saw, wasn't just over particular policies, but over the theoretical framework around which decisions regarding sovereignty and war should be made. R. Porat could no longer understand R. Amital's argumentation because they did not share a similar moral framework for discourse, let alone a shared ladder of values. R. Porat viewed questions of settlement and self-determination through a prism of conquest. In his rebuttal of R. Amital, he cited the position of R. Tzvi Yehuda and other Zionist leaders who opposed territorial compromise in 1947, let alone in 1967. Settlement takes priority unless it is absolutely impossible for the nation to win the war and retain territorial control.

R. Amital no longer accepted the discourse of conquest. He was now speaking in terms of self-defense, which allows for painful compromises to save lives. To a large extent, he was echoing sentiments made after the Six-Day War by Rabbi Soloveitchik. In a public lecture in New York, R. Soloveitchik declared that the primary triumph of the war was not the liberation of Jerusalem and other biblical territories, but the salvation of millions of Jews endangered by neighboring Arab countries. If those Jews are now best defended by ceding some of those same territories, then that's what must be done. Or, as he stridently put it, "It is prohibited for rabbis or anyone else to declare in the name of Torah that it is forbidden to return any part of land, when stable peace can save the lives of thousands and tens of thousands of our brethren who dwell in Zion."[35]

R. Tzvi Yehuda and his students were outraged.[36]

Yet R. Amital persisted. R. Amital, alongside the co-dean of his rabbinic seminary and R. Soloveitchik's son-in-law, Rabbi Aharon Lichtenstein, founded Meimad, a dovish religious political party that supported the 1993 Oslo Accords with the PLO. The accords were built on the premise that Israel should concede territories from Judea and Samaria (aka "the West Bank") for the sake of a peace agreement with a new Palestinian state. Rabbis Goren, Yisraeli, Porat, and many others adamantly opposed these agreements. Such concessions would endanger Israeli citizens and the Jewish state as a whole. They would also violate our religious covenantal duties to the land.

The polarizing, heated debate frequently confused two topics: theoretical support of "land for peace" deals with the political assessment of this particular agreement. Some theoretically accepted the notion of territorial compromise but believed that Arafat remained a terrorist who utilized his repaired international stature toward political violence. For them, his rejection of Israeli peace offers brokered by US President Bill Clinton in 2000, and the subsequent Palestinian intifada, confirmed their suspicions.

Indeed, the peace camp was initially supported by Rabbi Ovadia Yosef, leader of the Shas political party and Israel's former chief rabbi. R. Yosef had previously written an influential treatise in favor of the "land for peace" agreement that facilitated Israel's treaty with Egypt in the late seventies.[37] Fifteen years later, his party gave support to peace accords with the Palestinians, arguing that saving lives overrides any prohibition against ceding territory. Later, R. Yosef declared it religiously prohibited to cede territory to the Palestinians, not because it was theoretically wrong to withdraw from territories, but because he now deemed it strategically unsafe. As such, such moves were now dangerous – and sinful.

This kind of rhetoric of "sinful" conflates strategic analysis with religious discourse. It obfuscates the moral basis of territorial compromise with hard-nosed political assessment. "Land for peace" deals might be legitimate, yet one still has to determine whether a given proposal will work. This is a discretionary evaluation. One must evaluate the credibility of a potential partner and the dangers of ceding territory or maintaining the status quo.

One might, for example, think that the 1937 partition plan should have been rejected while the 1947 plan embraced; that the military pullbacks to achieve a cease-fire after the 1956 and 1982 wars were wise, but the concessions made to Egypt after the 1973 war and later in the 1979 Camp David accords were excessive; or that the unilateral retreats from Lebanon in 2000 or from Gaza in 2005 were prudent, but that a risky bilateral peace agreement made with the Palestinians to leave parts of Judea and Samaria would be a fatal mistake.

The general pursuit of peace may be a broader religious obligation. The signing of a given peace accord, however, is a discretionary strategic decision.

In this respect, "land for peace" deals are not so different from preventative wars. In both cases, faced with uncertain prospects of continued or renewed hostilities, a state makes a discretionary, strategic move to improve its security. The goal is to prevent a worse situation in the future, whether that be one or five years later. The war or agreement comes with many risks, and you can't know for sure whether it is worth taking them.

These are all strategic questions, not religious ones, and they must be answered at each time and place. This discretionary assessment should be made by elected leaders. They, in turn, should be guided by military and diplomatic experts, while remaining sensitive to the sentiments of the people, as dictated by democratic values.[38] In such a context, there is nothing wrong with a distinguished rabbi – or a celebrated writer, thoughtful columnist, or some other public intellectual – expressing their opinion on these topics. But their authority stems from their wisdom, not their stature as legal decisors. These are not decisions of absolutes, in which we make unambiguous declarations of obligatory and prohibited. In both war and peace, discretionary choices need to be made in a world of uncertainty.

Part IV

The Ethics of Fighting in War

Chapter 20

As the War Starts – Sieges in Lebanon and the Obligation to Let People Flee

THE SIEGE OF BEIRUT AND THE CHALLENGES OF ASYMMETRIC WARFARE

On July 1, 1982, IDF forces laid siege to Beirut.[1] Having taken near-control over much of southern Lebanon, Israeli forces now sought to eradicate the PLO from its headquarters in Lebanon's capital city. A few days later, Israel cut off water and electricity to the city; it restored the supply after two days, however, following heavy American pressure. Israel employed a "fight and negotiate" strategy, using military coercion to pressure the PLO to give in to its demands. It would take two months of American-brokered negotiations until Arafat and some 14,000 PLO terrorists would leave Beirut. Approximately 1,000 PLO fighters and 88 Israeli soldiers died during the siege.

It's hard to know how many noncombatants were killed in Beirut. Estimates from the Lebanese Red Crescent – which was headed by Yasser Arafat's brother, Fathi – were regularly dismissed as propaganda. Most likely, about 5,000 noncombatants were killed in Beirut, with another 20,000–30,000 wounded.[2] Many of the casualties occurred from the end of July till the middle of August, when the IDF utilized heavy air and ground attacks against PLO targets. The pictures were not pretty. World leaders and international media as well as some Israeli figures strongly condemned the raids, deeming them disproportionate and illegal.

By contrast, two military historians who witnessed the attacks, Trevor Dupuy and Paul Martell, accused the media of deep bias in their inaccurate portrayal of the IDF's activity. The experience was undoubtedly horrifying for Beirut's residents. Relative to normal wartime behavior, however, the IDF launched, in their assessment, a "modest bombardment." Regarding the overall war, they further asserted,

> As military historians we can think of no war in which greater military advantages were gained in combat in densely populated areas at such a small cost in civilian lives lost and property damaged. And this despite the PLO's deliberate emplacement of weapons in civilian communities.[3]

These sentiments were shared by two distinguished Israeli military reporters, Ze'ev Schiff and Ehud Yaari. Schiff and Yaari were major critics of the war; their best-selling book documented the Israeli government's defective decision-making process. Nonetheless, they too agreed that Israel "invested great efforts" to avoid civilian casualties.[4] The IDF even made a gigantic master map of all twenty-five thousand buildings in Beirut so that it could issue very precise firing orders. Nonetheless, it was a foregone conclusion that many civilians would die in the tight Beirut quarters. This was especially true, as they noted, because the PLO placed its artillery in apartment courtyards and its antiaircraft guns alongside foreign embassies.

Despite these efforts, Israel was condemned around the world. Israel was learning the hard way that asymmetric warfare can turn into a public relations nightmare in an age of widespread media coverage. The clear, delimited battlefields of the Sinai Desert or the Golan Heights in which Israel battled against formal armies were long gone. Now Israel had to face guerrilla warriors fighting from civilian territory. The battlefield, and the ethical questions that come with it, had now changed.

RABBI GOREN VERSUS RABBI YISRAELI

During the Beirut bombardment, Rabbi Goren dropped his own ethical bombshell.[5] Jewish law, he declared, requires Israel to allow both combatants and noncombatants to flee a besieged city. This stemmed from the opinion of a second-century rabbinic Sage, R. Natan, followed by Maimonides, who ruled that the "fourth side" of a city must always remain open.[6] The logic was twofold. Strategically, this will give combatants an incentive to flee; otherwise, they might fight to the finish, at great cost to both sides. On a humanitarian level, moreover, it is important to show mercy during war, even to our enemies.[7] R. Goren stressed that the "fourth side" was only a one-way exit. No outsiders or supplies needed to be allowed into the city. Yet everyone must be able to run for their lives.

R. Goren's public ruling created a bit of a brouhaha.[8] Who lets terrorists escape from the claws of the siege? Rabbi Yisraeli wrote a public treatise against his chief rabbi. He argued that the ancient sources were offering tactical advice or, at best, humanitarian protections necessary only in cases of expansionist warfare. In a war of self-defense such as Operation Peace for Galilee, however, it was implausible to think we should do anything less than kill or capture the terrorists. R. Yisraeli, however, did agree that noncombatants should be allowed out of the city. Other decisors went further than R. Yisraeli: there is no moral requirement to let *anyone* out of a siege. Wars need to be fought decisively.[9]

The IDF, for its own reasons, followed R. Goren's directive, leaving open two major escape routes from the city. This was, in part, an act of psychological warfare, trying to convince the PLO that they had two choices: leave or die. The IDF had no interest in the terrorists fighting to the last man. They certainly did not desire to harm noncombatants. An estimated one hundred thousand people successfully fled the city.[10] R. Goren would take great pride in this moral behavior, deeming it a wonderful *kiddush Hashem*.[11] Critics would deem this a foolish military move that allowed terrorists to join up with their comrades and fight from other places in Lebanon and Syria. For them, it symbolized the generally bumbled strategy of the IDF's campaign.

Lurking in the background of the Goren-Yisraeli debate was the broader nature of Jewish military ethics. As we saw in our discussion of reprisal attacks in chapter 7, R. Yisraeli believed that Israel was bound only by international practice and binding conventions.

In fact, R. Yisraeli's concession that Israel should allow noncombatants to leave the city is not even mandated by international norms. Customary international law allows a besieging force to deny civilians, let alone combatants, the ability to escape a siege.[12] Historically, force was utilized to keep people from fleeing. From the Roman siege of Carthage (149 BCE) to the Spanish conquest of Mexico and the Nazi barricading of Leningrad, "starve them out" was deemed easier than a frontal invasion. One can argue that it is also more humane. It's better to compel a side to surrender and spare all sides the brutal violence of warfare. Of course, that's easier for the attacking party to assert since they are saving their own while starving the other side. Frequently, moreover, it's the beleaguered civilians who suffer the most, with limited food and supplies given to the besieged soldiers. The siege of Leningrad lasted nearly nine hundred days. Over a million noncombatants died. That's more than those killed in the devastating air strikes on Hiroshima, Nagasaki, Dresden, and Coventry combined.

Where did the Sages get this notion to leave the "fourth side open" from? Biblical narratives make no mention of it,[13] and there is no clear indication of such a requirement in any verses.[14] Some critics further argue that this tactic is totally impractical. Perhaps for these reasons, some ancient Sages did not mandate such a requirement, with others fully endorsing the "starve them out" strategy under certain circumstances.[15] Indeed, ancient siege craft usually involved fully encircling a city.

Yet some first- and second-century Roman writers, such as Polyaenus and Frontinus, advocated facilitating a way for besieged soldiers to flee.[16] Otherwise, they'll fight to the death. It is possible that their stratagem was known by contemporaneous Jewish scholars.

The humanitarian gesture may have also been inspired by the Jewish historical experience. Jews knew well the horror of sieges. The First Temple was destroyed by King Nebuchadnezzar of Babylonia.

Before breaching Jerusalem's walls, he laid a siege for nearly two years. The common people starved to death.[17] The Bible bitterly lamented, "Better off were the slain of the sword than those slain by famine."[18] To survive, many Jerusalemites resorted to cannibalism. Mothers even ate the flesh of their children. Twenty-six hundred years later, Jews today still memorialize the widespread suffering by fasting on the day that the siege began, the 10th of Tevet.

Similarly, the Second Temple in Jerusalem was destroyed in 70 CE after an extended siege. Starved corpses filled the alleyways of Jerusalem. The survivors searched the sewers for old cow dung to eat.[19] The Sages describe that many residents wanted to surrender or flee. The Jewish rebels and the Roman army were not interested in anyone leaving, each for their own reasons. The rebels killed their detractors while burning storehouses of wheat and barley. The Roman general Titus, in turn, ordered his troops to crucify any attempted escapees. According to Josephus, five hundred Jews were crucified daily.[20] The people's fate was sealed. [21]

Might these horrific experiences have contributed to a second-century Sage insisting that if Jews ever regain power, they will be different and allow people to flee? It's a tantalizing conjecture. But this sense of Jewish ethics clearly drove R. Goren to insist that the IDF allow people to flee from Beirut, even if this was not demanded by international standards.[22] Rabbis, he added, bear a unique responsibility to ensure that the Jewish army lives up to Jewish ethical principles.

THE 1983 SIEGE ON TRIPOLI AND THE PRINCIPLE OF "DOING OUR BEST" TO REMOVE CIVILIANS

R. Goren would continue to struggle with dilemmas of fighting enemies in urban settings. A year after the siege on Beirut, many PLO fighters, including Yasser Arafat, made their way back to Lebanon, via Syria, to shore up support for their cause. They were now based in the port city of Tripoli but surrounded by splinter groups who had rebelled against the PLO. The UN, wanting to avoid another Lebanese civil war, negotiated a settlement to evacuate Arafat and his troops. Then, on December 6, 1983, Palestinian terrorists detonated a bomb on a Jerusalem bus. Six Israelis were killed. PLO loyalists and rebels both took credit for the attack.

Israel's new defense minister, Moshe Arens, condemned the international evacuation plan for letting terrorists escape. "If a terrorist committed an atrocity, and a democratic country helped get him to a new location, so he could commit more such acts, that is not something which those of us who accept democratic values can accept." Israel launched a naval blockade on the Lebanese coast and shelled PLO positions in Tripoli. The hope was that the rebel groups would further weaken the PLO. Others dreamed that they would even kill Arafat.

Instead, under immense American and European pressure, Israel opened the blockade. Arafat and four thousand loyalists were taken to safety in Tunisia. They would continue to terrorize Israel in the coming years.

This time, R. Goren was outraged at the Israeli government.[23] In his mind, there was no requirement to allow the PLO fighters to escape since Israelis forces were located on only one side of the siege. The IDF was not responsible for the PLO's predicament. If the PLO wants to flee, he quipped, they should ask the splinter groups for an escape route. The moral burden here does not lie with the IDF. To the contrary, allowing the PLO leaders to leave under these circumstances made no sense. Each PLO terrorist is a "violent pursuer" (*rodef*) whom Jewish law mandates we neutralize before they kill someone else. They are threats to Israel that must be eliminated. This is the law. The Reagan administration's inability to grasp this basic point doesn't change our moral obligation.

As we saw in chapter 7, R. Goren had cited Jacob's censure of his sons Levi and Simeon for destroying the entire city of Shechem because of the atrocities committed by its leaders. Jewish military ethics, he now added, compel us to not only avoid targeting noncombatants but also to allow them to flee beforehand from the battlefield. Yet they also demand from us to unflinchingly act against threatening enemies, like the PLO leaders stuck in Tripoli. If Jacob's sons would have targeted the enemy combatants in Shechem, their actions would have been entirely legitimate. Israel, R. Goren argued, had no moral right to compromise on Israeli security.[24]

That criticism, of course, could also be launched against R. Goren for having supported the IDF in letting PLO terrorists out of Beirut.

Arafat and his comrades were also dangerous "pursuers" in 1982. If we hadn't let them escape then from Beirut, the argument went, we wouldn't have been back in the same place in 1983. When you go to war, your priority must be killing your enemies. Otherwise, don't bother fighting at all. Indecisive actions just drag out a war and its suffering.

Moreover, his argument that the "fourth side open" requirement applies only when the same country (in this case, Israel) besieges all four sides seems overly legalistic. After all, the residents of Tripoli were seemingly also entitled to some humanitarian relief. The "fourth side open" requirement isn't much of a moral rule if it gets waived simply because other warring parties are doing the dirty work. That said, one could argue that the law demands compassionate relief, but there are limits to what we can be obligated to do when we don't fully control the situation. By returning to Lebanon, one might further argue, Arafat and others lost their right to flee again.

R. Goren falls into this legal hairsplitting conundrum because he has overly formalized this disputed rabbinic teaching into a formal law. He's insistent that "fourth side open" is a bona fide law, and not just "advice." Yet it seems more compelling to conclude that we have here a general principle of Jewish military ethics but not a bona fide commandment. Such an approach is a meaningful compromise to the heated disputes over the "fourth side open" rule in ancient, medieval, and contemporary rabbinic sources. The principle asserts that one should do everything they *reasonably* can to reduce the human costs of war, even on the enemy side. This includes allowing noncombatants to escape before the onset of hostilities and, when possible, during the conflict. Even combatants may flee, provided that this doesn't undermine the war efforts. Such a principle pays homage to R. Natan's position. Yet it allows for important critical caveats, including preserving an element of surprise. Ironclad rules undermine other values and goals, such as eliminating the enemy. As always within the JMF, we must consider our full range of principles and determine which factor trumps others in the given scenario.

The "fourth side open" rule might not be absolute, then, but it does highlight that Jewish ethics strongly encourages, when possible, allowing the enemy to clear their people from the battleground. It's sound military strategy and helps reduce unnecessary death.[25] Yet as we'll now see, the steps taken by the IDF to reduce casualties did not alleviate many other ethical dilemmas faced by urban warfare.

Chapter 21

Once the War Starts: Shifting Moral Responsibilities in Urban Warfare

"VICTORY OR DEATH" AT EIN HILWE

The Lebanese port city of Sidon was one of the best-known cities in the ancient Levant. The ancient Israelites never conquered it, and Kings David and Solomon enjoyed friendly relations with its rulers. In fact, the cedarwood used to build the Temple was sent from Sidon. Yet millennia later, as the IDF troops marched up the Lebanese coast, they would find nothing but trouble in the environs of this ancient city.

A few days before the siege on Beirut began, IDF troops fought PLO troops in Sidon and nearby Ein Hilwe, a Palestinian refugee camp established in 1948. PLO troops were shooting at the IDF from a four-story hospital building in Sidon. This is a grave violation of international law. It transforms what should be a protected, neutral civilian resource into a military post. Inside the hospital were not only militiamen, but also hospital staff, patients, and many noncombatants who sought refuge there. The IDF sent in Lebanese negotiators to permit everyone in

247

the hospital to leave, provided that the fighters evacuate without their weapons. The PLO fighters stalled and, through a ploy, escaped overnight, weapons in hand.[1]

Afterward, the IDF sent multiple delegations of Arab residents to negotiate with some 120 PLO fighters who barricaded themselves inside the concrete homes and tin shacks of Ein Hilwe. The local PLO commander had fled. The fighters were now led by an Islamic mullah. In the name of Allah, he declared, "Victory or death!" The PLO fighters condemned the truce intermediaries as "traitors," and shot at their feet. They swore that no one, including civilians, was leaving the camp.

They were dead serious. To make the point, the militiamen shot three children in front of their parents' eyes. Their crime? Their father had suggested accepting a cease-fire and sparing the lives of the little ones. After five attempts, the IDF gave up on negotiations. They went house by house, block by block, bunker to bunker, and with the support of air power, eliminated the last resistance.

Schiff and Yaari, the Israeli military correspondents who documented these negotiations, viciously criticized the IDF soldiers for "pulverizing" the city. They accused them of losing their moral sensitivity. "Sensibilities became dulled; the destruction engendered a chilling tedium."[2] The authors wondered whether the soldiers saw themselves as delivering retribution for Palestinian terrorism, or even vengeance against centuries of antisemitism. They further speculated what "collective fears" would have gripped these soldiers' grandparents had they witnessed this "mayhem." This reference isn't clear. The authors seem to refer to the rounding up of Jews house-to-house during the Holocaust or other horrors of World War II.

This critique is incredulous. Yes, this was a bloody affair. By the IDF commander's own admission, it was vicious battle. War is very unpleasant. Yet one cannot allow disturbing images to cloud one's ethical assessment. Ein Hilwe represented a critical point on the main line of advance. It was militarily necessary to clear the route. In fact, the slowdown, toward the goal of limiting civilian casualties, was strategically costly. In the meantime, Palestinian fighters continued to shoot, in the words of Schiff and Yaari, with "an enormous store of arms and ammunition," including RPGs that were destroying Israeli tanks.[3] Nonetheless, outside assessors have noted, Israel took remarkable steps to minimize civilian casualties: warning civilians in advance over loudspeakers and dropping leaflets, even at the cost of losing an element of surprise; utilizing infantry assaults first instead of heavy artillery bombardments and air strikes; and aiming its heavy weapons at tactical objectives rather than simply leveling the area, as it could have.[4] The distinguished legal scholar and military historian W. Hays Parks, who wrote a monograph on the history of noncombatant immunity, argued that Israeli precautions were "among the highest imposed by any nation in any armed conflict."[5]

More fundamentally, who bears the responsibility for this horrific scene? The commander of the IDF, who tried five times to get his adversaries to surrender, including an offer for the fighters to leave unharmed? Or the fundamentalist cleric who fought under the mantra of "victory or death" while shooting behind the shield of women and children? Those noncombatants could have otherwise fled to safety. Their homes and bodies were turned into military targets by the terrorist leader and his men.[6]

In fact, Schiff and Yaari themselves argued that the Palestinian fighters saw Ein Hilwe as "their Masada," preferring "to die to the last man, deliberately taking many civilians with them."[7] That being the case, it is the PLO, not the IDF, that deserves the primary moral responsibility for the noncombatant deaths. Contrary to Schiff and Yaari, I suspect that the grandparents of the IDF soldiers would have taken pride in their grandchildren's ability to fight against fanatics while doing their best to spare as many lives as possible.

WHO BEARS MORAL RESPONSIBILITY IN URBAN WARFARE?

The shift in moral culpability is critical in moral evaluations of asymmetric warfare. Certainly, we'd like to minimize innocent casualties. Yet guerrilla fighters and terrorist groups like the PLO have little interest in clearing their own people from the battleground. They fight without uniforms and among civilians, making them indistinguishable from noncombatants. The nonstate actors bear responsibility for eliminating a clear, delimited battlefront and blurring the soldier-civilian distinction.

At some point, the guilt, let alone burden of responsibility, for noncombatant deaths now falls on the defender's side.

R. Goren was not the first modern ethicist to adopt Maimonides's teaching regarding sieges, discussed at length in the last chapter. A few years beforehand, the philosopher Michael Walzer cited Maimonides to argue that all sieges must offer an escape route.[8] Sieges and blockades are legal under international law. Nonetheless, they concern many human rights advocates like Walzer because they are a form of collective punishment. Noncombatants will undoubtedly suffer from this tactic; in many ways, that's the point of a siege, to place pressure on the collective and force the hand of the army. For ethicists who prioritize human rights, this is a significant problem. Giving noncombatants an escape route helps alleviate the moral burden.

Beyond the humanitarian benefit of the "fourth side open" strategy, Walzer emphasized an additional ethical benefit: the onus of moral responsibility gets shifted off the besieging country. The noncombatants are given a right of refuge. They can leave for safety. If they don't, the responsibility for their lives now shifts to them, or at the very least to their leaders, who decided not to surrender or to meet their attackers on a battlefield. One can hardly blame the attackers for insisting on capturing the city when it is militarily necessary. By offering an escape route, the besieging country essentially asserts that it will not be held accountable for the fate of anyone who chooses to remain.

R. Goren would second this point by citing the proclamation of the prophet Ezekiel: "If anyone hears the sounds of the shofar horn [i.e., heralding war] but ignores the warning, and the sword comes and dispatches him, his blood shall be on his own head."[9] Don't come yelling later that the innocent were killed alongside the guilty. They chose – or someone chose for them – to stay in a war zone.

COMPETING MORAL RESPONSIBILITIES BETWEEN FORCE PROTECTION AND CIVILIAN IMMUNITY

Yet as the extended fighting in Ein Hilwe highlights, the moral life is not so simple. It's one thing to not be culpable for the deaths of noncombatants when fighting asymmetric wars in urban settings. Yet this doesn't mean that one is absolved of all responsibility to try to avoid noncombatant deaths. When possible, we don't want to kill any of God's creatures unnecessarily.

Restraint might also provide strategic advantages. Bloody attacks, even when justified, can create a blowback effect by aiding terrorist recruitment of young men seeking revenge. In our hyper televised world, the "CNN effect" of high casualty counts is a disaster for public relations and diplomacy. This was Israel's first conflict that was aired live around the world, and led Israeli forces to proceed cautiously.

Yet some Israelis worried, with good reason, that the IDF was being so cautious to avoid civilian casualties that it was overly endangering Israeli soldiers.[10] As the Sages taught, "One who becomes compassionate instead of cruel will ultimately become cruel instead of compassionate," i.e., pity in circumstances which require an attitude of harshness will lead to harsh consequences for those worthy of our pity.[11] Others further warned that Israel was not acting with sufficient decisiveness, thereby allowing the PLO to drag it into a war of attrition. Our moral inhibitions were playing right into the hands of the weaker enemy.

To exemplify this point, let's return back to the streets of the Ein Hilwe refugee camp. After the surrender offers were rejected, the neighborhood could have been conquered through air, artillery, or tank fire. Instead, troops went into the narrow streets and fought house-to-house to minimize civilian casualties. As an American military historian and analyst, Richard Gabriel, wrote, "The Israelis took the Ein Hilwe camp with very small loss of civilian life. *The number of Israeli casualties, however, was considerably higher than it would have been had the IDF brought its firepower to bear.*"[12] This dilemma repeated itself throughout that war. IDF commanders had to decide how much to endanger their own soldiers to minimize enemy noncombatant casualties. As the IDF's body count rose, many questioned whether more should be done to shield IDF soldiers, even at the cost of more enemy noncombatant deaths.

Two prominent students of R. Tzvi Yehuda emphatically argued that Israel must do everything it could to protect IDF soldiers. If this meant more civilian casualties, it's tragic, but that's the price of war. Israel's new chief rabbi, Avraham Shapira, stressed that an IDF casualty was more than just the death of another Jew. It constituted a threat to the entire war effort, as it impacted the army's strategic planning and national morale. Protecting soldiers is the highest priority, even at the cost of the regrettable death of noncombatants. We should not purposely target noncombatants, he agreed. Yet while in the combat zone, we cannot be held responsible for collateral damage.[13]

The rabbi of the Kiryat Arba settlement, Dov Lior, cited the "fourth side open" rule to argue that we display mercy *before* the war. Yet he believed that excessive mercy toward the enemy *during* the battle can quickly become acts of cruelty against our own beloved soldiers. We must always prioritize the needs of the national collective against those of our enemy. After all, war is a battle between two collective nations. "In wartime, there exists halakhic basis *for any action* done to prevent one of our soldiers from being injured, God forbid."[14] Individuals will tragically lose their lives in the battle zone. Better for it to be members of the enemy nation than our own people.

This logic is initially appealing. After all, saving our own people is a high priority. That's the reason we go to war in the first place. This is our primary responsibility.

Upon reflection, however, one recognizes that something is missing: taking into account other values and responsibilities. Imagine we adopt the strategy of prioritizing the lives of our soldiers and permitting "any action," as R. Lior put it, to protect them. We could then conduct massive air or artillery bombardment on military targets without ever taking risks of losing soldiers. True, many more noncombatants would be lost in that type of fighting. But at least we could say that we did *everything* possible, within the context of war, to prevent losing our soldiers. After all, if our soldiers have incommensurate value, then it is never disproportionate to attack any necessary target, whatever the collateral damage on noncombatant life might be.

Missing from their discourse, once again, was a reckoning with other important values found in the JMF. Most prominently absent is the appreciation that all human beings are instilled with divine dignity. A noncombatant may very well be a part of the enemy collective; this doesn't mean that he entirely loses his singular identity of being created in the image of God. One can prioritize victory and saving one's own while still taking action to minimize the loss of all life.

This argument was brought into the heated debate by Rabbi Lichtenstein. R. Lichtenstein was disturbed by the lack of humanitarian consideration given to individual lives within the excessive collectivist discourse espoused by R. Tzvi Yehuda's students. Yes, Jewish law calls upon our boys to fight for the nation. These soldiers, in fact, included R. Lichtenstein's own children and students. Yet we shouldn't rush into any conflict, no matter how justified, without considering how many "divine images" will be lost. Similarly, we cannot forget that God also shed tears, so to speak, when the biblical Egyptians drowned in the Red Sea. Our enemies were also created in God's image. Therefore, we need to think about the proportionality of our military actions, including asking how many of God's creatures we will kill while saving our own.

R. Lichtenstein further warned of losing sight of the corrosive moral impact that bloodshed can have on individual souls. The Bible warns that during wartime, "Protect yourselves from all bad things."[15] This includes developing a callous heart that becomes indifferent to harming others, a real threat during extended warfare. As sensitive thinkers have long noted, fine virtues are critical for the military profession.[16] They are necessary, in part, to foster the discipline, loyalty, and courage to fight for justice. Soldiers also require temperance to make dispassionate decisions on the battlefield. Most critically, they require self-control to display mercy to others, such as prisoners of war or noncombatants. As one medieval scholar noted, many of the Torah's commandments help shape virtuous characters who will display mercy toward all human beings, even when we fight against them. In fact, some even suggest that this was the motivation behind the "fourth side open" rule.[17]

In recent years, the danger of non-virtuous soldiers was evidenced by the abuse of Iraqi prisoners by British soldiers in Basra[18] and American soldiers in the Abu Ghraib prison. As one former British defense official argued, virtues were lacking "to ensure that our service people are good people who deploy the lethal force with which society entrusts them only for the sake of a good end … and that they are able to act thus even amid all the pressures and passions of war."[19] The fighting spirit can turn a brave warrior into a barbarian.

Such risks, R. Lichtenstein warned, increase when we depersonalize all members of the enemy nation into one collective entity.

We cannot forget that they too were individuals born in the image of God. Terrorists, guerrilla fighters, and other nonstate actors may bear moral responsibility for the deaths of noncombatants whom they use as human shields. Yet this doesn't exempt us from trying to minimize noncombatant deaths. Once again, our multivalued system demands that we consider many principles before deciding how to act.

THE MAHARAL OF PRAGUE AND COLLECTIVE WARFARE

R. Lichtenstein, in short, wants us to care for individual enemy lives in the midst of collective warfare. Is that possible, or even desirable?

In this respect, it pays once again to explore the rationales given to justify the eradication of the city of Shechem by the sons of Jacob. As discussed in chapter 7, R. Goren argued, with much support from earlier commentators, that the Bible condemns this indiscriminate killing, as evidenced by Jacob's harsh denunciation of his children.

Other commentators, however, try to justify the sons' behavior. Some plausibly argue, for example, that the sons intended to kill only their sister's attackers. The city residents, however, fought to protect their leaders, thereby forcing the sons to kill them as well.[20] Jacob was nonetheless angry at them because one shouldn't fight wars that can easily entangle your nation in a more dangerous predicament.

However, one sixteenth-century commentator, the famed Maharal of Prague, claimed that the nature of warfare is collective. As such, the sons could take vengeance against the city residents since warfare entails killing between nations. This interpretation – which is not shared by the vast majority of traditional Jewish commentators – is frequently cited by those with a strongly militaristic orientation to the Arab-Israeli conflict since it might allow for collective punishment.[21] For example, the authors of the notorious and radical book *Torat HaMelekh*, which disgracefully allows for indiscriminate killing of an enemy population, cites Maharal's statements as alleged support for their position.[22]

This interpretation is deeply problematic. First, the implications of this idea should frighten any Israeli since it would also justify indiscriminate killing by terrorists. After all, if all members of the collective are legitimate targets, then there's nothing wrong with the PLO launching missiles from Lebanon into Israeli cities.[23] Indeed, perhaps for this reason, sensitive contemporary readers of the Maharal's commentary have argued that he only came to justify incidental killings of Shechem's residents who were indistinguishable from the city's fighters. Targeting random noncombatants, however, would remain prohibited.[24]

Second, even if this was the approach of Jacob's sons, it was not shared by the patriarch, who condemned his children's behavior. His preaching was backed up by his actions. Before dwelling in the Shechem region, Jacob had faced the possibility of going to battle against his vicious brother Esau. Four hundred warriors were accompanying his brother, making "Jacob greatly afraid and distressed."[25] A rabbinic midrash explains that Jacob feared not only his own death but also killing others. This is perplexing, since those four hundred warriors were threatening him. In that circumstance, the rule is "rise up and kill first." It was entirely legitimate for him to kill his attackers.

Some commentators suggest that Jacob was worried that there were less lethal ways of stopping the threat and he'd be accountable for killing unnecessarily. Jacob, it would seem, was concerned that he wasn't doing enough to minimize bloodshed. His actions were entirely legitimate; nonetheless, he worried that he could win the battle with less lethal force. Others argue that Jacob was alternatively concerned that he might kill someone who was forced to join the army. That wouldn't make those fighters into noncombatants. After all, they were still fighting. Yet their deaths would be regrettable because they had no interest in the war.[26]

Most interestingly, the Maharal himself suggests that sometimes fighters are present in battle but would still prefer not to kill. Of course, there would be no way for Jacob to distinguish between the genuine fighters and the disinclined soldiers. He was prepared to fight and to kill. Nonetheless, he still feared the moral stain of inadvertent killing.[27] Jacob – and the Maharal – never lost sight of the individual in the midst of a collective struggle.

The common denominator of all these interpretations is that Jacob felt angst at the prospect of killing unnecessarily. Yes, there was no way for him to know how to identify those truly coming to kill him out of their own free will. Some people were forced to lose their immunity. For this, blame lay with Esau. Nonetheless, Jacob felt he'd be held responsible for killing unnecessarily. None of this stopped Jacob, or should prevent his descendants, from forging ahead with necessary warfare. Yet his moral angst highlights that even as we fight, we should still do what we reasonably can to prevent unnecessary deaths and feel regret for those lives lost anyway.

"ROOF KNOCKING" AND THE ATTEMPT TO
WARN NONCOMBATANTS

The dilemmas of competing responsibilities are well displayed in debates over "roof knocking." Israel's 2008 Operation Cast Lead in Gaza sought to stop repeated rocket launches against Israeli towns in southern Israel. This was the terror method of choice since Israel had withdrawn from Gaza in 2005. Hamas and the Islamic Jihad were utilizing civilian homes, schools, and office buildings in Gaza to store weapons, set up command posts, and cover cross-border tunnel entrances. Morally and legally, these locations became military targets. Yet Israel wanted to avoid unnecessary casualties. In the wars in Lebanon, it would blast warnings over loudspeakers and drop leaflets to give general warnings to flee. In the 2006 Lebanon war, over one hundred thousand noncombatants would flee southern Lebanon alone.

Nonetheless, the IDF pioneered in 2008 a technological method for more pinpoint warnings. Israeli soldiers would call Gazans' personal cell phones and warn, in Arabic, "This is the Israeli military. We need to bomb your home and we are making every effort to minimize casualties. Please make sure that no one is nearby since in five minutes we will attack." Such calls frequently got the residents to leave.

Yet some residents would not go. So the IDF developed the so-called "roof knocking" technique.[28] The air force would drop small, empty missiles over the buildings. Sometimes they would explode above the roof; other times, they blew up upon landing but caused minimal physical damage. Either way, a horrific boom would fill the air. Terrified residents would now flee the building. After waiting a few minutes, the air force would then drop a more powerful missile. The target was destroyed, but casualties were limited.

Morally speaking, "roof knocking" is an updated version of the "fourth side open" imperative to get people to flee. The technique would later earn praise from US military chief Martin Dempsey. Israel, in his mind, went to "extraordinary lengths to limit collateral damage and civilian casualties," despite their enemies not being held by that standard.[29] Subsequently, the US Army employed the strategy in its own asymmetric warfare in Iraq.[30] From the perspective of international law, these types of general warnings are sufficient before opening fire.[31]

Some international jurists, however, attack "roof knocking" and other warning options by arguing that it is morally insufficient. After all, the civilians who remain might have been forced to stay by their leaders. Moreover, even if they do stay in the building or city, that may be because of fear or other emotional factors. Whatever their rationale, it is hard to say that they represent some form of threat to the attackers. As individuals, they have done nothing to shed their right to life. They, and their property, deserve immunity as noncombatants. Thus the 1977 Additional Protocol (AP/1) treaty insists that even after an attacking army delivers a warning, it may still not strike "against the civilian population, civilians or civilian objects."[32] Thus moral responsibility remains with the attacking party. "Roof knocking," to their mind, doesn't fulfill the legal responsibilities to avoid harm to civilians and their property.[33]

Once again, these legalists have turned international law into a weapon for the terrorists. Such a strict interpretation of the AP/1 treaty (which, we should recall, Israel and the United States did not sign) would encourage urban warfare. If civilian buildings that have been turned into terrorist harbors are still deemed a protected "civilian target," then terrorists will always fight under the cover of noncombatants. International law will shield terrorism.

As it is, some military officials criticize "roof knocking" from an opposing angle, as strategically unwise.[34] Many noncombatants undoubtedly escape death. Yet so do terrorists who will flee that building and continue their bombing from a different one. In fact, strong fighters can flee faster than elderly residents or those with families, who might be left behind. Terrorists who know that they can save themselves by working from civilian buildings will not be deterred from fighting. On many occasions, instead of fleeing, they sent (forcibly or voluntarily) human shields onto roofs. Aerial attacks were called off. Terrorists utilize our moral inhibitions as a shield to protect themselves.

Ultimately, the tense debate over "roof knocking" highlights the necessity of utilizing our full set of values and principles to navigate these complex dilemmas.[35] The West cannot allow dangerous enemies with little ethical compunctions to shield themselves behind noncombatants – or our moral inhibitions. This is the lesson which we must internalize if we are going to defeat terrorist groups and other nonstate actors in an age of asymmetric warfare. Decisive victories are necessary, and so is protecting our own soldiers and citizens, even as we desire to minimize all bloodshed.

The IDF, for its part, has argued that if the strike's goal is only to destroy terror infrastructure, a warning and even delay is warranted. Not every target must be destroyed, and certainly not at this moment. Patience is sometimes a tactical virtue. On the other hand, if a significant terrorist target is in the building, they will consider striking without warning, in spite of the collateral damage.

This very distinction between personnel and infrastructure, however, raises the broader question of legitimate targets in warfare, a question which sparks further controversy when fighting occurs within population centers. It is to this question of legitimate military targets that we'll now turn.

Chapter 22

Legitimate Military Targets: Military Necessity and Discrimination in Gaza and Lebanon

BOMBING LEBANON'S POWER PLANTS: "GREATER THAN NECESSARY"?

In July 2006, Israel's chief of staff, Dan Halutz, wanted to send a powerful message to Lebanon. A few days before, Hezbollah killed eight soldiers and abducted two more from the Israeli-Lebanon border. The Israeli government decided to go to war. This was not an obvious decision. After all, a different soldier, Gilad Shalit, had been kidnapped a month before on the Gaza border, but that did not trigger an all-out war. This time, however, Israel elected to respond with an extensive blow that would trigger a counter-response. Israeli citizens and soldiers had suffered from repeated Hezbollah attacks since the IDF had withdrawn entirely from southern Lebanon in 2000. Israel's top brass decided now was the time to act.[1]

Through his spokeswoman, future Knesset member Miri Regev, Halutz publicly (and foolishly) threatened to "set Lebanon back twenty years." He wanted to make this a watershed moment in Israel-Lebanese relations. The former head of the air force, Halutz was convinced of the efficacy of airpower to destroy an enemy. Behind closed doors, he proposed to Prime Minister Ehud Olmert and Defense Minister Amir Peretz an initial strike: bomb all of Beirut's power stations and its civilian airport. "We have to put out all the lights in Lebanon. We can shut off their electricity for a year, damage at a cost of billions."[2] It's a forceful plan – but is such a strategy moral or wise?

Frances Lieber, the pioneer of the US military code during the American Civil War, would ask a simple question to determine the morality of any damaging military activity: Was the destruction "greater than necessary"? This rule seems simple, yet it's far from natural in the context of bloody wars, in which vicious cruelty may reign. Lieber wanted to stop soldiers from inflicting suffering simply for the sake of suffering or revenge, or any other hostile act that would make "the return to peace unnecessarily difficult." An army must seek to do what is indispensable for winning the war, but no more. Soldiers may take up arms, but they must remember that they "do not cease on that account to be moral beings, responsible to one another, and to God." Prohibited acts include torture, maiming, poisoning, perfidy, or the "wanton devastation of a district."[3]

The principle of necessity has iterations in earlier just-war theorists like Grotius but has some of its earliest roots in the Bible itself. In fact, this is probably the clearest biblical injunction regarding the ethics of war:

> When in your war against a city you have to besiege it a long time in order to capture it, you must not destroy its trees, wielding the ax against them. You may eat of them, but you must not cut them down. Are trees of the field human to withdraw before you into the besieged city? Only trees that you know do not yield food may be destroyed; you may cut them down for constructing siege works against the city that is waging war on you, until it has been reduced.[4]

The fruit trees are not your enemies or a threat to you;[5] they are, however, critical for the human diet and take many years to grow. Their destruction can cause immediate starvation and long-term food-supply shortages. The Torah wanted to avoid a punishing "scorched earth" strategy;[6] the long-term viability of the habitat should be preserved. And, a few modern commentators added, if useful but harmless trees deserve special protection, then all the more so noncombatants who do not threaten us.[7]

Yet the Bible does allow the destruction of non-fruit-bearing trees to help battle the besieged city. The Sages expanded this dispensation to establish a general necessity principle: one may destroy anything, including a fruit tree, if it is needed for the war effort. The prohibition is only against "wanton destruction." If the enemy is hiding within a fruit orchard, for example, one can uproot it. Yet one should still seek to inflict the minimum amount of long-term damage, e.g., when possible, uproot a fruitless tree before a fruit tree.[8] Once again, the Sages exemplify an attempt to balance different values, seeking to promote victory while preserving life and the environment.

The converse of the necessity principle is a requirement of discrimination: one should not destroy anything if it is not necessary for the war effort. As such, intentional indiscriminate bombing has no justified place in twenty-first-century warfare, particularly when we have "smart bombs" and other precision weaponry. The aim is to eliminate factors causing military harm.[9]

In practice, this also means we should not aim for civilian targets even for the sake of scaring the people or deterring them.[10] In general, the attempt to "target civilian morale" had a checkered rate of success in the twentieth century.[11] As we noted in chapter 4, attacks on noncombatants frequently harden rather than soften civilian resolve. Even Sir Arthur Harris, the head of the British Air Force whose strategy of strategically bombing German industrial cities during World War II was discussed in chapter 9, would later concede, "The idea...to break enemy morale proved to be totally unsound.... Morale bombing was completely ineffective."[12]

Some military practitioners have argued that a carefully selected, discriminate attack on civilian objects (i.e., not people) like banks or luxury stores may more quickly "break the enemy's will." Such a solution, they argue, is not only effective but also more humane than an extensive and violent barrage against military targets.[13] A similar logic was driving Halutz's recommendation to attack critical Lebanese infrastructure. Immediately before the unplanned war, the IDF had adopted a short-lived "effects-based" strategy to influence the consciousness of the enemy. The goal was to generate a chain of events: destroy symbolic targets which would impact the functioning of the enemy and the psyche of its leadership, making them rethink their use of rockets.[14]

Yet the strategic success of such a policy is questionable and overly hypothetical, especially in light of the extensive, lasting harm to the broader enemy population. Many "break the enemy's will" plans are concocted more out of revenge than in an effort to prevent future attacks. Moreover, noncombatant deaths or damage to civilian infrastructure can have a boomerang effect by pushing civilians closer to the guerrilla warriors.[15] Some Hezbollah warriors, in fact, credited incidental Lebanese casualties from IDF attacks in the early 1990s for strengthening their popular support in later wars.[16]

For these reasons, Olmert and Peretz opposed knocking out the power stations. Instead, they developed an incredibly effective initial strike to attack Hezbollah's long-range Fajr missile supply. Within thirty-four minutes of the war's outbreak, Israeli planes destroyed fifty-nine stationary rocket launchers concealed in homes in southern Lebanon.[17] Sadly, the army almost nixed the operation for fear of incidental casualties.[18] In the end, only twenty civilians were killed, while a massive and lethal arsenal was destroyed. Fortunately, in this case, wiser minds won the debate against both extremes of inaction and targeting willpower.

DUAL-USE OBJECTS, CLUSTER BOMBS, AND THE PROBLEM OF LONG-TERM DAMAGE

It might be theoretically easy to conclude that the army must target combatants and military objectives, not noncombatants and civilian objects. Yet the categories of "combatants" and "military objectives" encompass a wide range of people and objects. Let's begin first with the objects that may be targeted.

Many ethicists, followed by international law, assert that objects may be destroyed if (a) they make an effective contribution to military action, and (b) their destruction or neutralization, in that time and context, will bring a "definite military advantage." As one might expect, there's a considerable amount of debate about what objects fulfill these requirements. It clearly includes weapons, military fortifications and depots, airports and docks utilized by the military, and intelligence-gathering centers (even when not run by the military). It also encompasses power plants supplying the military, industrial plants (even if privately owned) manufacturing weapons and supplies, and transportation routes of strategic importance (e.g., bridges, tunnels, and highways).[19]

Naturally, as a side effect, the destruction of such targets may put psychological pressure on the enemy and its people. The potential deterrence would be a welcome benefit, but this is not predictable, nor is it the goal. The focus remains on the military benefit of these resources.

As one quickly sees from this list, many of these objects could be used simultaneously by both the military and civilians. This causes angst for some human rights advocates, who argue that "dual-use" objects enter into a "gray area."[20] As a matter of ethics (and international law), this is incorrect.[21] If the object is currently being used against you to cause decisive harm, then it may be neutralized. During the 1991 Persian Gulf War, US troops destroyed Iraq's electric grid that supported its air defense system, unconventional weapons research, and telecommunications. In 1999, NATO forces destroyed bridges, railway tracks, electricity plants, and petroleum facilities throughout Serbia. Similarly, during the Second Lebanon War, Israel knocked out many bridges and cellular phone antennas, attacked the Hezbollah television station several times, blasted oil reserves and gasoline stations, and cratered the runways of Beirut's airport. Assuming that these resources were being used to directly support military activity, these are legitimate targets. Protecting one's own people takes priority over protecting enemy civilian objects.[22]

That said, the biblical passage on fruit trees teaches that we should think twice before quickly destroying critical civilian items. Once the hostilities are over, those essential resources take a long time to rebuild. After the Persian Gulf War, for example, water supply and quality were severely hampered because the loss of electricity damaged the functioning of waterworks.[23] Much suffering – and dangerous resentment – ensued. It's to everyone's benefit to minimize the long-term damage of warfare as much as possible in the confines of executing a winning strategy. Nonetheless, there are real immediate consequences to not targeting critical facilities. War will always have some long-term ramifications on civilian infrastructure and life, even as we should try to minimize it.

For the same reasons, armies must prefer utilizing weapons that won't cause casualties long after the shooting stops.[24] Allegedly because of a lack of ammunition, the IDF utilized cluster bombs during the last days of the 2006 operation when the government was racing to make some final strategic victories before a cease-fire.[25] Cluster bombs eject small bomblets over a wide area. Besides being less accurate against their targets, the bomblets will frequently not explode, leaving behind an explosive device that can detonate upon contact later. IDF investigators found that Israel had largely fired the cluster munitions in open areas where Hezbollah forces were operating and not around civilians. On a few occasions, however, they may have been incorrectly utilized, against IDF directives, in civilian areas from where guerrillas were fighting. Whatever the intent, unexploded bomblets continued to detonate after the war, killing civilians.[26]

Beyond the moral gravity of causing postwar casualties, the use of cluster bombs also undermined Israel's well-founded claim that it had taken incredible measures to minimize civilian casualties. Since this controversy, the IDF has asserted it will stop utilizing such bombs.[27] This is the correct decision, irrespective of the fact that Hezbollah did not hesitate to use land mines against the IDF in southern Lebanon or cluster ammunitions against Israeli cities.

THE DEBATE OVER PREVENTATIVE TARGETED KILLINGS

During the so-called second intifada that began in 2000, Israel was under attack from Hamas suicide bombers. Dozens of Israelis were killed and wounded. Intelligence services tried at times to locate the bombers themselves, but it was usually too late to act. In May 2001, the whole country went on alert when intelligence agents realized a "ticking bomb" had infiltrated; by the time they caught up with him, he had blown himself up in a Netanya mall. Five civilians were murdered.

Israel decided that to stop the bombers, it needed to target the entire operational infrastructure behind these attacks.[28] The person who blew himself up was just the last in a chain of attack. There were recruiters, smugglers, couriers, weapons procurers, and commanders who must be stopped. If you can eliminate enough of the critical parts of the system, the attacks will be impossible. Soon after, Israel launched a policy of "targeted preventative acts," popularly called targeted killings, to stop the suicide bombings. Active Hamas military operatives, at all levels, could be killed.

A group of Israeli human rights activists asserted that these assassinations were immoral and challenged the IDF in the Israeli Supreme Court. Hamas operatives, to their minds, were not active combatants. They could only lose their immunity by taking an active and direct part in hostilities, and even then, only "for such time" when their direct participation was ongoing. Once they went home, they regained their civilian status.

Supporting this extremely narrow interpretation of combatants was Antonio Cassese, an international law specialist who served as president of the International Criminal Tribunal for the former nation of Yugoslavia. Cassese argued that a civilian becomes a combatant only in the moment when he is shooting or placing a bomb. If he lays down his weapon, he can't be attacked – even if he is aiding atrocities or sending others to commit them. Last week and next week he may be a combatant; but at this moment, he may not be attacked. This approach, in his mind, was the only way to avoid killing innocent civilians.[29]

Cassese's position represents yet another example of how international law can be utilized to bolster unethical positions. Fortunately, following the lead of several international jurists, the Israeli Supreme Court upheld the theoretical legality of targeted assassinations. This stemmed, in part, from the court's recognition that for an active terrorist, the "rest between hostilities" was simply in preparation for the next act of hostilities. An active Hamas terrorist leader currently "taking a break" between rounds with Israel does not lose his status as an active fighter. He may be killed if Israel reasonably sees him as an ongoing threat who can act at any moment.

From an ethical perspective, Hamas fighters, even without uniforms, are no different than active soldiers.[30] Even when they are not shooting, they are combatants who may be targeted. This remains true even when they are sleeping or bathing (i.e., not currently in fight mode) or in retreat. The United States, for example, was harshly criticized for firing upon over fifteen hundred Iraqi military vehicles retreating from Kuwait City toward the Iraqi city of Basra. The Americans created a massive bottleneck on the highway by bombing the lead vehicles, thereby entrapping the remaining forces. A "turkey shoot" ensued. Estimates suggest that some five hundred retreating soldiers may have been killed on the so-called "highway of death." Yet critics forget that unless these soldiers surrendered, they could regroup and fight again. They remained a part of Iraq's active military effort. Indeed, tens of thousands of troops ultimately fled on foot to Basra. Until a cease-fire was declared, they remained legitimate targets.[31] This certainly remains true of terrorists who, because of their choice to fight in civilian garb, bear the burden of proof to show that they are no longer fighting.

THE FUZZY LINE BETWEEN NONCOMBATANTS AND COMBATANTS

The more interesting question is, what type of activity turns a civilian into a combatant? After all, none of us are born as warriors. We must do something to make us a soldier. Classically, this meant putting on a uniform. Asymmetric warfare has blurred the lines.

Take, for example, the tragic case of "child soldiers." Sadly, in many countries, like Colombia, Sierra Leone, and Iraq, guerrilla warriors utilize minors as warriors. This is a war crime, and rightfully so. Nonetheless, on those occasions, the children are acting as soldiers and represent a real danger.[32] It's possible that they were manipulated to fight; nonetheless, one cannot ignore the duty to eliminate their threat.

During one incident in Iraq, Australian snipers didn't shoot a child who was aiming an RPG toward an Australian army jeep.[33] The child's finger was on the trigger. Fortunately, he didn't shoot, and the jeep drove off safely. The snipers, by their own admission, were lucky. They certainly would have been justified in shooting the child; in fact, had he fired the RPG, the Australian soldiers would have been asking themselves why they didn't fulfill their duty to save their comrades. Their mercy on children can be a grave injustice to their fellow soldiers.

As the case of child soldiers highlights, the distinction between combatants and noncombatants is theoretically sound but complicated in practice. Certainly, a civilian who pays taxes toward the military budget or patriotically flies a flag on their doorpost remains a noncombatant. The same is true for reservists who might eventually be called to the front lines but remain civilians not engaged in any hostilities. Their sympathetic or theoretical support causes no direct harm to the other side or military benefit to their own people; as such, they may not be targeted.

As the jurist Michael Schmitt has compellingly argued, civilians lose their immunity status by directly participating in the hostilities, even if they don't shoot a bullet. They don't need to cause *direct harm to their enemy* in order to *directly benefit the active military effort* of their country.[34] Their functional contributions to their country's war efforts make them culpable. When their actions provide immediate contribution to the war effort, they contribute to the wider nexus of the military threat. As such, they may be pursued because their neutralization will directly save lives.

As noted during the Israeli legal debates over targeted preventative killings, this broader definition of a combatant resonates with the rabbinic law of a "pursuer" (*rodef*).[35] The Sages contended that the verse "You shall not stand idly by the blood of your neighbor" (Lev. 19:16) not only demands saving a friend from drowning or other dangerous situations, but further dictates that one stop an assailant from killing someone.[36] Significantly, scholars broadened the "pursuer" category to also include those who threaten someone indirectly without physical contact (*rodef be-grama*), i.e., their actions will directly lead to someone becoming endangered.[37] Take the following case: person A is threatening to release poisonous snakes to attack person B. Person A will not touch person B. Nonetheless, person A gains the status of a "pursuer" since they trigger events that will directly endanger person B.[38] Indirect threats may also be created without intent. During the Holocaust, for example, families in hiding would sometimes kill a crying baby lest they be discovered by their pursuers. The child, of course, was entirely innocent; nonetheless, their physical actions (e.g., their cries) can cause a clear, direct chain of events leading to the death of everyone. As such, they fall into the category of a "pursuer."[39]

In the military context, the distinction between sympathy, benefit, and harm may be exemplified through a few examples. A truck driver who volunteers to bring firearms to the front lines becomes a combatant, at least while he is fulfilling this mission. He is directly contributing to the military threat. The same, however, would not be necessarily true if he was delivering candy packages from the home front. Soldiers need those weapons to fight; the chocolates, however soothing, are superfluous. A woman who wails at the funeral of a suicide-bomber or pays a visit to the mourning tent of a *shaheed* (martyr) remains a noncombatant. Her public display of sympathy might encourage a culture of martyrdom but doesn't create a direct benefit. If she sews the vest for the suicide bomber or tries to recruit one for the cause, however, she becomes a combatant. A top scientist commissioned by the army to fine-tune a weapon in the middle of the war may be targeted; the janitor of her lab, however, remains a noncombatant, as does her spouse who enthusiastically prepared her a hearty lunch and dinner so she could work late hours. They are not directly benefiting the active military effort.

Many international lawyers argue that workers in a munitions factory do not lose their civilian status, because they are not causing direct *harm* to the enemy. Their work, however, is providing a definitive *benefit* to the ongoing military effort. If these laborers don't show up to work, critical military production is delayed; when they do come to work, on the other hand, the fruit of their labor can be on the way to the front lines within five minutes. One does not need to be irreplaceable to provide direct and proximate contribution to the war machine. I find it hard to see how the workers remain noncombatants. In any case, the factory (or the science lab, for that matter) certainly may be struck as a military target.

NONCULPABLE ATTACKERS: THE "GUSH ETZION 35" AND THE "LONE SURVIVOR"

A more complex example involves the case of a nonculpable attacker. In this scenario, the aggressor has no desire to become a threat. Nonetheless, by accident of circumstances, they end up becoming a threat to someone else. Suppose, for example, a person goes on a psychotic rampage in an elevator and threatens you with a knife. Or, alternatively, a construction worker gets pushed off a roof by a sudden, strong gust of wind. They will fall and crush a passerby, unless the latter quickly pulls out their large umbrella and deflects their body, thereby killing the worker.[40] The psychotic person and the construction worker had no intention to threaten anyone; nonetheless, in practice, these bystanders will die unless they kill them first. Ethically speaking, even "innocent aggressors" may be killed when there is no other choice. For that reason, we mandate aborting a fetus who endangers their mother, or kill a Siamese twin to save their sibling.[41] Unwittingly, the fetus or child is a "pursuer." When necessary, they may be killed.

The dilemma of nonculpable attackers emerged in Israel's War of Independence. In January 1948, the Palmach sent a group of thirty-five soldiers to reinforce the embattled Jewish residents of the Gush Etzion region. Since repeated attempts by convoys to reach the Gush were thwarted by attacks on the roads, the fighters traveled on foot. As the legend goes, when the group was a mere three miles away from their destination, two scouts were discovered by a passing Arab shepherd, whom the scouts subsequently detained. The shepherd had no military role but, if released, would presumably report the whereabouts of the Jewish fighters to the local Arab militia. Nonetheless, the scouts decided to release him since he was not a fighter. Soon afterward, a large band of Arab militiamen from the local village of Surif attacked the group. All thirty-five were killed, with many of their bodies mutilated.

The scouts' decision to release the Arab shepherd was glorified by David Ben-Gurion and immortalized by numerous poems and memorials. Their moral courage was celebrated by the Palmach's commander, Yitzhak Sadeh.

> There can be no doubt that armed Arabs would not have acted in the same way had they encountered a Jew on the road. And that is true not only of Arabs; we know how members of other armies act in similar circumstances. But our fighters are not only courageous; they are also noble and humane in the extreme. They wage war with courage and with love of humanity.

For Sadeh and others, this was, and remains, an example of the "purity of arms" doctrine.[42]

Unfortunately, the tale of the "Convoy of 35" suffers from two deep problems. First, the story with the Arab shepherd may have never taken place. According to reliable reports, the scouts were likely spotted by two female bystanders because the convoy had left too late in the night to reach Gush Etzion before daybreak. No shepherd, or anyone else, was released from their control. It might be that Ben-Gurion was reporting an alternative incident and he found that narrative more convenient for building the Zionist ethos of brave yet humane warriors.[43]

More significantly, even if the legend is true, it's not clear that the scouts acted correctly. The shepherd may have had no intent of getting involved in the hostilities. His accidental discovery of the scouts, however, directly endangered the larger convoy because he would presumedly reveal their location to local militiamen. He didn't intend to do surveillance, but in effect, he became a part of the Arab defense team and could have been killed.[44]

This ethical dilemma was popularized in the movie *Lone Survivor*. In 2005, four US soldiers were on a reconnaissance mission in the Afghani countryside when they bumped into a few local herdsmen. According to the lone surviving soldier, Marcus Luttrell, the American soldiers voted whether to kill the herdsmen. Ultimately, they decided to release them. After all, the herdsmen were unarmed noncombatants protected under international law and American military standards. The decision, however, may have sealed their fates. Soon afterward, local Taliban fighters surrounded the soldiers, killing three of them and wounding Luttrell. Another sixteen American troops were killed while trying to rescue them. Ultimately, Luttrell was saved by local villagers, who themselves had to be relocated later by American troops to protect their safety.

Luttrell would eventually lament that they made a mistake. "I must have been out of my mind. I had actually cast a vote which I knew could sign our death warrant." Others, however, defended the decision as just. Soldiers do not kill unarmed civilians. Period.

In truth, the dilemma is somewhat complicated, since the herdsmen in both cases were not quite "innocent" pursuers. After all, it was their choice to report the presence of the enemy fighters. They didn't choose to be in that scenario. Yet they had to decide what to do once freed. On the other hand, it's also not clear that they were "pursuers." They would likely choose to fulfill their patriotic duties, but they might not. (Recall that in the "lone survivor" case, local villagers risked their own lives to save the life of Luttrell.) Given this uncertainty, the herdsmen might be more akin to "apparent aggressors" whom, under reasonableness standards, the scouts could have deemed pursuers. Ultimately, that's a judgment call which soldiers must make when, in the midst of the "fog of war," conflicting values and uncertainties come into play.

The intricacies of these cases highlight, once again, that many of the complex moral decisions in war are judgment calls. We must provide moral guidelines and principles, yet commanders and soldiers will need to make decisions based on incomplete information. This point will be further highlighted now as we explore questions of proportionality in warfare.

Chapter 23

Proportionality and the Great Missed Opportunity

Imagine you are a head of state with the opportunity to kill in one strike the entire political and military leadership of a terrorist group. Every. Single. One. All of the leaders and commanders who have launched repeated attacks on buses, cafes, and shopping centers would be gone in a flash.

Prime Minister Ariel Sharon had such an opportunity in September 2003 to wipe out the entire leadership of Hamas. Yet he chose not to strike. The commander of the raid on Kibiyeh in 1953 and architect of the First Lebanon War in 1982 was now fearful of TV screens around the world with bloody images of collateral damage alongside accusations of war crimes. The alleged offense? Disproportionate use of force.

The term "proportionality" is one of the most abused terms in just-war theory. The careless use of the term comes with a great cost in innocent lives lost, but not the ones that we usually think of. To correct this moral injustice, we'll need to delineate the proper meaning of the term and understand why so many have lost a sense of why unintended but inevitable deaths in warfare are morally justified.

HOW HUMAN RIGHTS ACTIVISTS UNDERMINED THE
MEANING OF PROPORTIONALITY

If there's one consistent criticism launched by international figures against Israel, it's that its wartime responses to terror groups are disproportionate. Early on in the 2006 war, UN Secretary General Kofi Annan accused Israel of "disproportionate use of force." This was a common refrain proclaimed by human rights groups during the 2006 war and the 2008 operation in Gaza. Such pronouncements have a real impact. Polls showed that well over half of Europe's residents felt Israel acted disproportionately.[1]

Unfortunately, most people don't understand the meaning of the term or its ethical implications. As Walzer noted, for most commentators, including many media figures, "Disproportionate violence… *is simply violence they don't like, or it is violence committed by people they don't like.*"[2] When you don't like a war or the people who are fighting it – or are just plain old upset about the number of people dying – the easiest thing to say is that a response is "disproportionate." Popular misperception of this term is quite regretful. More egregious, however, is the misapplication – or distortion – by senior UN officials and human right activists, as we'll now see.

It is critical to understand the meaning of the term "proportionality," because it helps explain why one may morally fight a war despite the inevitable but widespread incidental killing of noncombatants. "Collateral damage" always occurs, especially in asymmetric warfare where one side purposely fights from the confines of a civilian population. As we saw in chapter 10, before going to war, one must consider whether its destructiveness will be out of proportion to the relative good that will be achieved by the war. So too, during war itself, one must ask whether the benefits of a particular strike or action will outweigh the toll on human lives.

Broadly speaking, this is a healthy moral standard for believers in multi-value moral frameworks. Any ethical commander should take into account their strategic goals alongside humanitarian considerations. As Rabbi Lichtenstein asserted during the First Lebanon War, we must recognize the inevitable side effects of military actions and take those into account before killing God's creatures, even among our enemies.

Warnings, when feasible, may help minimize casualties, but that's not sufficient. One must consider both the military benefits and the harm done to others before acting.

Such notions were well known to early writers of military ethics. They were meant to keep military commanders honest about their intentions. Proportionality demanded the following criteria: (1) the act is militarily necessary, (2) the destruction is effective and not wanton, and (3) the gains are not "grossly disproportionate" to the extent of destruction. If these general principles were met, then, in the words of one writer, "the act can hardly be condemned regardless of the amount of suffering and violence." The principle of proportionality, in a nutshell, is not a separate standard. It is a means to broadly ensure that a military commander did not engage in the intentional killing of noncombatants for which he is morally culpable.[3]

CAN ONE CREATE A MEANINGFUL RULE OF PROPORTIONALITY?[4]

International jurists, however, tried to go beyond these general standards to create definitive rules against any extensive damage to civilians. Beyond forbidding direct targeting of civilians, the AP/1 protocols prohibit:

> An attack which may be expected to cause incidental loss of civilian life, injury to civilians, damage to civilian objects, or a combination thereof, which would be *excessive* in relation to the concrete and direct military advantage anticipated.[5]

Read properly, proportionality remains fairly subjective, as it is based on relative values like "excessive" and "military advantage." It demands that at the time of action, each commander must make a judgment call, based on the information they have. If a target may deliver a compelling or even decisive military gain, severe military losses may be tolerated.

What would be a case of "excessive" collateral damage? The International Red Cross (ICRC), in their widely-cited 1987 commentary to the AP/1 protocols, gave the following case: "For example, the presence of a soldier on leave obviously cannot justify the destruction of a village." That's true, but the extreme example isn't too helpful for real-world scenarios. Giving an *extreme* negative example of a *disproportionate* act doesn't provide clear guidance for what is a permissive proportionate act.

Proportionality serves well as a general guideline, but not as a mathematical equation. There is no "proportionometer."[6] Attempts to quantify such equations produce ridiculous results. In one attempt, a group of assembled legal and military experts were asked to write on a piece of paper how many civilian casualties would be acceptable in a specific case of killing an armed terrorist. The numbers were collected and collated, with the average being 3.14![7] That's a rather convenient number to remember. Yet *pi* (π) tells us the ratio of a circle's diameter to its circumference. It indicates nothing about the significance of the military target or the civilians in his circumference.

Recognizing the difficulty in determining what is a proportionate order, a leading legal historian declared, "Although it may be tricky and embarrassing to define in advance, the reasonable man or woman knows one when he receives one."[8] As we know from other famous legal questions, the "I know it when I see it" criterion cannot be implemented as a legal norm. In the real world, "reasonable" men and women deeply disagree about what's excessive, especially in relating to their judgment of the desired "direct military advantage."

The ICRC, in its commentary, had a different solution to this problem of subjectivity: to change the rule. In their minds, AP/1 means "incidental losses and damages should never be extensive."[9] Note the critical change in language. Not *excessive*, but *extensive*.[10] If the body count is high or the damage too great, then the action is illegal, no matter what the military gain.

Having redefined the meaning of the term, human rights officials could now easily condemn military actions that caused large numbers of casualties, even if it met the classic standard of proportionality. Thus at the beginning of the 2006 war, the UN High Commissioner for Human Rights condemned Israel by declaring, "The bombardment of sites with alleged military significance, but resulting invariably in the killing of innocent civilians, is unjustifiable."[11] Similarly, the Goldstone Commission that investigated the 2008 war in Gaza denounced Israel for killing more than what was considered the "acceptable loss of civilian life." Yet there is no legal quota for the "acceptable" amount of losses. No treaty ever banned "extensive" warfare because no country could abide by such a rule, let alone agree to it.

Every war, especially urban warfare, has extensive noncombatant deaths. This is regretful and even tragic. Yet just as the number of bodies in a morgue doesn't indicate the quality of medical care in the hospital, so too a body count doesn't indicate whether an army acted excessively or immorally.

NO RULES OF PROPORTIONALITY IN ASYMMETRIC WARFARE

The key ethical (and, for that matter, legal) question remains whether the damage is excessive in relation to the military gain. This is an important guideline, but difficult to calculate. Let's understand why.

When it comes to lives lost, it's impossible, on a quantitative level, to measure the necessary ratio of combatant to noncombatant lives. If five enemy soldiers die along with ten noncombatants, is that acceptable? What if it's only four soldiers killed or twenty civilians – does that change things? Clearly, one also needs to calculate the strategic value of the target. The death of a significant terrorist leader may bring significantly more advantages than the killing of twenty of his fighters. Furthermore, as many countries insist, one cannot evaluate proportionality simply based on a specific action alone. Instead, one must evaluate the strategic value based on the general military situation, including factors like the stability of the border, the restoration of a deterrent capability, the protection of military and civilian infrastructures, and so on. Different scenarios justify different actions. Quite simply, anticipated military advantage and expected collateral damage are dissimilar values that are hard to measure.

Let's remember, moreover, that we can only judge commanders based on what they reasonably thought was the anticipated advantage or expected damage. One can learn lessons from twenty-twenty hindsight. It's of little value in real-time decision making.

The use of human shields in asymmetric warfare further exacerbates all these problems of calculating proportionality. Here's why:

officially, the international law codes mandate that the defenders should "avoid locating military objectives within or near densely populated areas," i.e., don't shoot from crowded neighborhoods or behind hospitals. Yet all terrorist or guerrilla groups from around the world – Iraq, Lebanon, Bosnia, Gaza, El Salvador, Somalia, Liberia, Sierra Leone, and Chechnya – violate this rule.[12] They embed their weapon systems within the fabric of their civilian population. Rocket launchers are placed next to hospitals, weapons are stored in schools, and fighters dwell in residential homes.

What's a country supposed to do? The AP/1 treaty – at least as understood by the ICRC commentary and many other rights activists – asserts that the attacker still bears responsibility for causing harm to civilians, because that would be a violation of the latter's human rights. The "golden rule" is to avoid civilian casualties, even if this entirely distorts the proportionality equation.[13] If enough noncombatants are around, even intentionally, the attack must be called off.

This approach is deeply flawed. As the historian and jurist Hays Parks argued, it removes the onus of protecting civilians from the defender, who has greater control of their home field, and places it onto the attacker, who has significantly less control of the battle zone.[14] Furthermore, this provision incentivizes nefarious groups to utilize human shields against their enemies.[15] International humanitarian law becomes a shield against attack. This is another reason why countries like Israel and the United States refused to ratify the AP/1 treaty. They understood it would allow for the laws of war to be manipulated for evil purposes and disproportionately stifle their military operations.

An opposite extreme would assert that we don't care at all about civilian casualties in these circumstances. In this spirit, during Operation Cast Lead, a few outlying rabbinic voices called for Israel to show no mercy on women and children being used as a human shields. Their predicament may be tragic. Nonetheless, they are forcibly being utilized as a part of the war machine against Israel. The Bible teaches that the enemy must be fought "until they are subdued." If this is what is takes, so be it.[16] Occasionally, one hears similar language from legal experts when they speak of the right to full reprisal, i.e., if terrorists shoot indiscriminately, the other side may reply in kind.[17]

The consequence of such a position would, in practice, eliminate the distinction between combatants and noncombatants. This is way too extreme. It's not justifiable to attack indiscriminately, nor is it necessary. In fact, both the "protect human shields" and "kill human shields" approach suffer from the same problem: fundamentalism. They both assert that one value, military necessity or civilian protection, should dominate our reasoning without still trying to take into account other values.

More nuanced thinkers reasonably assert that the systematic use of human shields should be significantly "discounted," so to speak, in the proportionality calculation.[18] This would allow, relatively speaking, for greater acceptance of civilian casualties when attacking a legitimate military target. The United Kingdom manual on the laws of armed conflict makes this point explicit: "The enemy's unlawful activity may be taken into account in considering whether the incidental loss or damage was proportionate to the military advantage expected." The recalibration asserts that the attacking party retains its moral obligation to utilize any information it possesses to minimize civilian casualties, but ultimately culpability lies with the defending party for utilizing human shields as a weapon of war. An attacking party cannot be held liable for the deaths of civilians working in the immediate area of a legitimate target or those placed there by the enemy to shield it from attack.

Now properly understood, one understands why the sheer number of noncombatant deaths – whether they be Palestinian, Lebanese, Iraqi, Afghani, or any other nationality – proves nothing about the proportionality of an army's actions. This point, in fact, was readily acknowledged in a 1987 brief by a leading ICRC lawyer in her analysis of the 1982 Lebanon War. "The Israeli bombardment of Beirut in June and July of 1982 resulted in high civilian casualties, but *not necessarily excessively* so given the fact that the *military targets were placed amongst the civilian population.*"[19] High casualty rates do not indicate excessiveness. Unfortunately, many human rights advocates seem to have lost this nuanced view in the subsequent decades.

Moreover, because the international community has continued to hold attacking parties responsible for the death of human shields, the practice has only expanded to more terrorist groups. As a result, more noncombatants have suffered.[20] This all needs to change. For the West to win just wars, it must internalize the following lesson: body counts are not a moral barometer, and extensive casualties do not indicate excessive behavior.

To exemplify this point, we'll examine the assassination of a senior Hamas leader and its immoral aftermath that led Sharon to make his horrific mistake discussed in this chapter's introduction.

TEST CASE: THE ASSASSINATION OF SALAH SHEHADE[21]

On July 22, 2002, an Israeli fighter jet dropped a one-ton bomb on a three-story apartment building in Gaza City. The target was Salah Shehade, the commander of the al-Qassam Brigades, the military wing of Hamas. Since the outbreak of the so-called second intifada in 2001, Shehade had initiated a series of new combat techniques: explosive devices against tanks, boat bombs, high-trajectory Qassam rockets, and novel ways of deploying suicide bombers, including minors. Over the previous twelve months, Israeli intelligence officials asserted that Shehade was directly involved in attacks that killed 474 people and wounded another 2,650. Israel's defense minister would later claim that Shehade was actively preparing simultaneous mega-attacks in six Israeli towns. He had deservedly become Israel's number 1 wanted man in Gaza. Israel needed to neutralize him.

The bomb instantly killed Shehade along with an assistant. But it also killed thirteen civilians, including his wife and teenage daughter. Over one hundred people were wounded. Fierce international condemnation was quick to follow. At the UN Security Council, a lineup of ambassadors condemned the Israeli strike as disproportionate.[22]

> Action taken in self-defence must be proportionate. Israel *must avoid civilian casualties* and avoid damaging civilian property and infrastructure. (Britain)
> That disproportionate reaction led to the *death of innocent civilians*, most of them children, in addition to considerable material damage. (Guinea)

There can be *no justification* for the missile attack carried out by the Israeli air force in a residential area of Gaza, *which left a high number of individuals, including children, dead or injured.* (Denmark, on behalf of the European Union)

Once again, all of these statements focus on the inevitable collateral damage. They don't ask whether the strike was excessive in proportion to the military advantage of killing, in the midst of an extended war on terror, the lead terrorist commander responsible for thousands of Israeli casualties.

Most incredible, in this respect, was the criticism of US President George Bush, who rebuked Israel for "heavy-handed" action. When asked to distinguish it from cases of civilian casualties in Afghanistan, spokesperson Ari Fleischer explained, "The United States, because of an errant bomb, a mistake in a mission, has occasionally engaged in military action that very regrettably included losses of innocent lives." The Israeli operation, by contrast, "was a deliberate attack on the site, knowing that innocents would be lost in the consequences of the attack." Again, Fleischer makes the common mistake of asserting that knowing a strike will cause the collateral death of civilians makes it inherently illegitimate.

More egregious, however, is his belief that the collateral damage from a well-planned targeted strike is morally worse than the accidental American bombing earlier that month of an Afghani wedding party. Fifty-four civilians were killed. That same summer, moreover, six special US operations raids into the Uruzgan province failed to locate their wanted targets. In the process, eighty Afghans were killed.[23] Over the coming years, an estimated twenty-two thousand Iraqi and Afghani noncombatants would be killed as collateral damage in America's post–9/11 wars.[24] Some of these noncombatants were killed by mistake; at other times, their regrettable but inevitable deaths were known in advance. That doesn't necessarily make them morally wrong. Yet it does make Fleischer's criticism deeply hypocritical.

The Israeli assassination of Shehade was no more excessive than a host of attacks in the "wars on terror" that followed in the coming years or, for that matter, the "humanitarian interventions" in Yugoslavia or Iraq that preceded it. An Israeli commission later justified the strike by asserting that the number of civilian casualties was not foreseeable. An Israeli general apologized on CNN.[25] In truth, there was nothing to apologize for. The deaths were regrettable and tragic. But given the significance of the target, the attack was morally justifiable even if non-combatant casualties were inevitable.

THE MORAL COST OF INACTION: ELIMINATING HAMAS'S LEADERSHIP

In fact, Israel's more egregious error was that it didn't assassinate Shehade earlier. In March 2002, Israel located him within a Gaza apartment but didn't strike because of the number of civilians around. Three days later, a suicide bomber deployed by Shehade blew himself up in Jerusalem's Café Moment, killing eleven Israeli citizens. A similar opportunity was passed up again in June. Two weeks later, a Hamas suicide bomber killed nineteen passengers on a bus in Jerusalem. In fairness, Israel was hoping to find opportunities to eliminate Shehade with fewer civilians around, as it succeeded in doing with other terrorists. For a lower-level operator, that may have been reasonable. Yet ultimately, one must prioritize acting decisively to stop senior enemy operators before they kill your own citizens.

Some critics question the wisdom of targeted killings because they assume that another operative will simply take their place. They fail to recognize that the number of skilled terrorist operators is quite limited. Killing them disrupts the entire organization.[26] The ultimate accomplishment of Israel's targeting killings, despite the regrettable amount of collateral damage, was well summed up by journalist Ronen Bergman: "Thanks to its streamlined targeted killing apparatus, the Israeli intelligence community triumphed over something that for many years had been considered unbeatable: suicide terrorism."[27] The collateral civilian casualties were not excessive in achieving such a triumph.

Israel committed a second moral error by allowing the political and diplomatic fallout from the Shehade killing to stop it from a once-in-a-generation opportunity: the ability to kill the entire Hamas political and military leadership. In September that year, Hamas leader Ahmed Yassin gathered with all of his senior men in a three-story Gaza apartment building. This was Yassin's dream team. Intelligence officials, led by Shin Bet head Avi Dichter, estimated that this was a historic opportunity to cause irreparable damage to the terrorist group.

Yet Israel didn't strike. Fearful of dozens of civilian casualties along with the local and international protests that would ensue, Prime Minster Sharon, at the urging of the army Chief of Staff Moshe "Bogey" Yaalon, called off a massive bomb strike to topple the building. The backlash, they feared, would be even more intense than in the aftermath of the Shehade assassination.

An alternative plan was hastily proposed to shoot a smaller missile to destroy the third floor, where intelligence officials speculated the meeting was taking place. They guessed wrong. The meeting, it turned out, was on the first floor. Immediately after impact, the Hamas men went running out. Israel could have utilized drones to blast every screeching car. The defense minister, however, ruled out that option. "Civilians were likely to be hurt," he said.

Within a few days, sixteen citizens were dead and another seventy-five wounded. These were not Palestinians but Israelis who had been struck by two Hamas suicide bombers. Among the victims were Dr. David Applebaum, head of a Jerusalem emergency room, and his daughter Nava, who was to be married on the following day. Prudence can be deadly.[28]

It would take another several months of Palestinian suicide bombings and Israeli targeted assassinations before Egypt brokered a ceasefire. Hamas survived and rebuilt itself, leading ultimately to its conflict with Israel in 2008 and repeated hostilities since. It would have certainly been justified for Israel to wipe out the Hamas leadership. The collateral damage would have been extensive, but not excessive. Israel's decision not to act cost the lives of many innocent Israelis. Fears of "disproportionate" accusations led Israel to shirk its primary moral responsibility.

Yet it wasn't just concern with the "CNN effect" and the Shehade backlash that led to inaction. In a later interview with the *Washington Post*, Yaalon asserted that two other factors guided his thought process not to strike.[29] Firstly, any action taken had to pass the 'mirror test': at the end of the day, would he be able to look at himself in the mirror? Secondly, his mother, lone survivor of the Holocaust from her family, taught him that, "Jews shouldn't be killed, but it also means that we don't kill others. You need strength to defend Israel, and on the other hand, to be a human."

This is a misguided binary lesson to learn from the Holocaust, placing self-interests against some foggy notion of humanitarianism. Generals and defense ministers have a primary moral claim to protect their own people. This is about ethics and obligations, not just interests. As Dichter, whose father was also the lone survivor from his family, argued, saving the Jewish people is a moral lesson from the Holocaust: "I'm not going to let anyone kill a Jew just because he's a Jew." Deep moral introspection, as reflected in the JMF, recognizes that at some points you need to prioritize certain moral values over others. This is the ethically correct thing to do, even if it fails a *pi* equation for proportionality or does not feel good during the "mirror test."

Yaalon is a seasoned army veteran with many heroic actions under his belt. He dedicated his life to protecting the Jewish nation and deserves much praise for that. Yet Yaalon would not approve targeted killings in which the IDF knew that there would definitely be noncombatant casualties. This was a moral error that cost Israeli dearly. To avoid repeating such mistakes, Israel and other Western countries need to learn anew why inevitable collateral damage is justified in warfare.

Chapter 24

Justifying Collateral Damage in Serbia and the Middle East

Why has the world become overly critical of extensive damage? There are, I believe, two primary explanations. First, it has lost sense of the moral justification for killing in warfare in general and collateral damage in particular. Second, the "CNN effect" from continuous visuals of extensive bloodshed has distorted our moral calibrations. The following two chapters will address these issues.

"TERROR BOMBING" OR "TACTICAL BOMBING"?

Imagine two different scenarios, adapted from an actual incident that took place in 1999 during the NATO bombing campaign to stop ethnic cleansing in Yugoslavia:[1]

1. NATO forces, seeking to frighten Serbian citizens and fighters into submission, order their air force fighters to indiscriminately drop bombs on random gatherings of people in the middle of the night. The fighter pilots drop ten bombs on the village of Korisa. Eighty-seven civilians are killed with another sixty wounded. A

nearby Serbian command post, including an armored personnel carrier and ten pieces of artillery, is also destroyed.

2. In its attempt to systematically destroy the Serbian military machine, NATO forces drop ten precision bombs on a Serbian command post and an armored personnel carrier, and ten pieces of artillery near the village of Korisa. Unbeknownst to the commanders and invisible to the fighter pilots, a group of refugees is also in the vicinity, possibly being used as human shields by the Serbian fighters. Eighty-seven civilians are killed and sixty more are wounded.

What's the difference between these two scenarios? After all, the end result is the same: a legitimate military target is destroyed alongside eighty-seven noncombatants killed and dozens more wounded. Yet the first event we'd reasonably call immoral "terror bombing," while the second we'd deem as legitimate "tactical bombing." The difference is intent. In the first case, the intent of the terror bomber is to kill anyone and everyone without distinction. In the second case, the intent of the bomber is to destroy the legitimate military threat.

Here's another example from the ethicist Helen Frowe. Dropping a bomb on a munitions factory to secure a significant military advantage is legitimate, even if one foresees that many noncombatants in the nearby hospital will be killed as a side effect. Bombing the hospital to kill many patients so that the munitions factory workers won't show up to work, however, is "terror bombing."[2] The key, once again, is intent.

Why does intent matter so much to justify such extensive collateral damage? One cannot utilize the "pursuer" argument (discussed in chapter 21) to contend that these civilians were menacing you. As noncombatants, they don't pose a threat. We would never, for example, justify killing an entire crowd of people to hold off one violent burglar. War, as rabbis and philosophers alike have argued, operates under different ethical rules that somehow justify the widespread killing.[3] Indeed, it's impossible to defend warfare without some theory to explain why it is morally permissible to inevitably kill, even unintentionally, individuals who are not directly threatening you.

"THE DOCTRINE OF DOUBLE EFFECT" AND ITS CRITICS

To address this problem, classic just-war theory utilized "the doctrine of double effect" (DDE). There are many variations to the doctrine, but most go something like this:

1. Intent
   (a) The military act is intended as an act of self-defense
   (b) The collateral damage is not intended
   (c) The collateral damage is not a means to the end of the act, i.e., one does not intend for the collateral damage to serve as a deterrent or provide some other benefit
2. Precautionary Measures
   Efforts are made to avoid or minimize collateral damage
3. Proportionality
   The collateral damage is proportionate to the importance of the mission

As one can quickly see, proper intent is crucial to this doctrine. The UN's international criminal tribunal that investigated the Korisa bombing emphasized this point: NATO forces did not intend to kill civilians and they reasonably did not foresee so many noncombatants in the area. No charges were filed.

The DDE doctrine is also used in other ethical scenarios. For example, most ethicists, Jewish and non-Jewish alike, permit administering morphine to alleviate the suffering of terminally ill patients. We brand such treatment as "end-of-life palliative care." Occasionally, the overall effect of the narcotics might hasten the patient's death; but each dose, gradually administered, is intended to alleviate pain and will not necessarily shorten the patient's life. Purposely delivering a more toxic dose, however, is active euthanasia. That line between care and killing is quite thin in practice; as some researchers have noted, there's a "gray area" between pain relief and mercy killing.[4]

Whether in hospitals or on the battlefield, many philosophers accuse DDE advocates of mental gymnastics. They assert that the only difference between "terror bombing" and "tactical bombing" is how we choose to describe them. At the end of the day, this is a matter of semantics; at the very least, each description is a matter of subjective interpretation.

Good intentions cannot mitigate results that are *foreseen*. On the battlefield, if I know that it is certain – or even highly likely – that noncombatants will be killed, I cannot pretend that their deaths are inadvertent. In light of this critique, some ethicists argue that much collateral damage simply cannot be justified. After all, why is the blood of the attacking soldiers redder than the blood of the noncombatants? These are innocent civilians who have done nothing to surrender their right to life.

With this critique in mind, let's review again the assassination of Salah Shehade, discussed in the last chapter. Again, here are two ways of thinking about this case:

1. Terror Bombing: To inspire fear among Palestinians, the IDF tells its bombers to indiscriminately drop a bomb on a random target in Gaza City in which terrorists occasionally reside. The bomb lands on an apartment building, killing thirteen noncombatants, wounding over a hundred more, and leaving dozens of families homeless. By sheer fortune, the bomb also kills a terrorist group leader and his senior aide.

2. Targeted Bombing: In an attempt to stop a series of suicide bombings, the IDF targets the most senior suicide operator who was purposely taking cover in a civilian area. In a carefully planned strike, it kills the operator and an aide. In the process, thirteen noncombatants are killed along with over a hundred wounded. The strike leaves many families homeless.

According to critics of DDE, the problem with the IDF strike, even according to the second depiction, wasn't just that the deaths were disproportionate – it was that they were inevitable.

In truth, classic Jewish law is quite sensitive to this initial critique of DDE. Here's a rough parallel to the classic case in rabbinic literature: Suppose one Saturday, a person really wanted a deer's head to mount on their wall as a decorative trophy. To do so, however, they would need to slaughter a deer, an action that is prohibited on Shabbat. When they kill the animal, the intent would be just to procure a trophy head. Yet the inevitable effect is that the deer is killed. As the Talmud rhetorically asks, "Can you cut off the head without killing it?" As such, you are liable for violating Shabbat, even though you had no desire to kill the animal. This may be for one of two reasons: (1) The law stipulates that whatever you might say, your intent, in fact, was to kill the animal. (2) Alternatively, the law asserts that intent is fundamentally irrelevant. Since the result is unavoidable, we judge your actions simply based on the inevitable consequences. You killed and must be held liable.[5]

Yet taken to its logical conclusion, this critique of DDE is a short step away from pacifism. For if (a) the unintended but inevitable deaths from collateral damage cannot be justified because they violate inviolable individual rights, and (b) all warfare involves such collateral damage, then (c) all warfare cannot be justified. More moderately, one might conclude, like Frowe, that moral constraints on defensive forces might create occasions in which collateral damage is not justifiable to the point that "it will be impermissible to defend oneself."[6]

Yet such a conclusion is unfathomable to any ethical system, including Judaism, which places a premium value on the moral obligation to defend oneself and one's people. The Jewish multivalue framework does not allow us to dismiss the value of self-defense. As such, it becomes an imperative to either reformulate the DDE justification or to explain why saving one's own people takes priority over the lives of enemy noncombatants.

"DOUBLE INTENTION" AND JEOPARDIZING TROOPS TO AVOID COLLATERAL DAMAGE

To preserve the DDE doctrine, the ethicist Michael Walzer contends that it's insufficient for soldiers to not intend to kill the noncombatants. They must also take proactive actions ("due care") to avoid incidental civilian losses, even if it comes with accepting soldier casualties. The soldiers, in short, require "double intention": to mentally intend to strike only the legitimate target and to display positive intention toward saving civilian lives. In practice, this means that soldiers must take risks for themselves to minimize the harm to enemy civilians. For the human rights of the enemy civilians, like the rights of their own people, must be protected.[7]

To understand the implications of Walzer's thesis, it pays to divide the potential casualties of warfare into four different quadrants.

"Our" Noncombatants	Enemy Noncombatants
"Our" Combatants	Enemy Combatants

It's clear that the highest priority in protecting lives goes with "our non-combatants." After all, the justification for going to war (and to endangering "our" combatants) is to provide defense for our citizens. Inversely, enemy combatants are the lowest on the rung, as they directly threaten us. Yet who takes priority between "our combatants" and "enemy noncombatants?" On the one hand, noncombatants have personally done nothing to make them liable to attack. Yet our soldiers are our comrades. Should brothers take precedence over others?

Walzer's answer is no. The goal of limited warfare is to protect individual rights by distinguishing between combatants and noncombatants. The latter, even if they are a member of the enemy country, have done nothing to surrender their right to life. By contrast, soldiers have lost "their title to life and liberty" because they are fighters. They make themselves vulnerable to danger. We might speak of them as "our boys and girls on the battlefield," but their job remains to protect civilian lives, friend and foe alike, even if this means they must take some considerable risks.[8] As such, whatever risks soldiers are willing to take for their compatriot citizens must also be taken to protect enemy civilians. Soldiers, in short, must jeopardize themselves to avoid enemy collateral damage.

The grave implications of this alleged obligation were made clear during Operation Cast Lead in Gaza in 2008. Walzer and an Israeli philosopher, Avishai Margalit, openly called for IDF soldiers – and all troops engaging in asymmetric warfare, whether in Iraq, Afghanistan, or elsewhere – to take greater risks to avoid collateral damage.[9] As they wrote,

> When soldiers in Afghanistan, or Sri Lanka, or Gaza take fire from the rooftop of a building, they should not pull back and call for

artillery or air strikes that may destroy most or all of the people in or near the building; they should try to get close enough to the building to find out who is inside or to aim directly at the fighters on the roof.[10]

If soldiers aren't willing to protect enemy civilians, they further warned, then complaints about enemy abuse of civilians – whether through terror attacks or the use of human shields – will ring hollow.

In fact, on numerous occasions in 2008 and in other military incursions that decade, it seems that the IDF did take such extraordinary steps to avoid civilian casualties. This usually entailed sending combat soldiers into homes or buildings instead of calling in air strikes or throwing grenades into a room or courtyard with unidentified occupants. These measures saved Palestinian lives, but at a cost, sometimes fatal, to Israeli soldiers. Israel's ambassador to the UN took satisfaction in this moral stance in contrast with that of its terrorist enemies:

> For Israel, every civilian death – Israeli or Palestinian – is a tragedy. In responding to terrorist attacks that show no respect for human life – either Israeli or Palestinian – Israel takes steps to protect both. It takes every possible measure to limit civilian casualties – *even where these measures endanger the lives of our soldiers or the effectiveness of their operations.*[11]

Yet was it morally correct for the IDF to exceedingly endanger its soldiers or compromise their effectiveness in order to protect Palestinian civilians? The answer is an emphatic no, as affirmed by two of Israel's leading ethicists as well as an array of prominent rabbinic figures. Let's understand why.

BROTHER OVER OTHER: FORCE PROTECTION AS A SUPERIOR MORAL VALUE

Walzer's approach is well intentioned but misguided. It repeats the same error that we've seen throughout this work: prioritizing individual human rights to override other values. In this particular example, it errs in two critical ways: (1) neglecting the obligation to protect one's own citizens, combatants and noncombatants alike, from attacks on them; and (2) neglecting the associative duties that a country owes to its own brethren, including its own soldiers. To understand the point, let's focus again on the common dilemma alluded to by Walzer and Margalit:

> Violating international law, Hamas launches mortars from the neighborhood toward a town in Israel. The IDF commander has two options: seek aerial support to bombard suspicious houses in the neighborhood, or order his subordinates to take the neighborhood house by house.

The advantage of the first option, utilizing aerial support, is that it provides not only greater soldier safety, i.e., protection from risk of capture, injury, or death, but also a rapid response. Israel should stop the mortar attacks as soon as possible; otherwise, its civilians will continue to suffer.[12] By failing to immediately halt these attacks with aerial fire, Israel would be prioritizing enemy citizens over its own citizens.

Israel's citizenry, moreover, might not tolerate a high "body-bag count" from house-to-house combat and demand to end it prematurely. Indeed, over the past few decades, heads of leading democracies like Britain, France, and the United States have changed their military plans because of waning popular support following troop casualties. Fighting morale among soldiers, moreover, regularly decreases when the troops feel their lives are being overly jeopardized.[13] As one Israeli soldier lamented, "We're like pizza delivery boys who have to come right to the door of the terrorists' houses."[14] When soldiers feel like they've got the same rules as Pizza Hut drivers, you've got a problem.

The decision to place soldiers at greater risk might also endanger the efficacy of the entire defensive mission. For this reason, countries like Australia, Canada, and New Zealand signed the AP/1 treaty while insisting that "force protection," i.e., actions taken toward protecting troops, must be taken into account when weighing the proportionality of a given action. NATO, in fact, relied primarily on aerial strikes during its intervention in Yugoslavia while flying its planes at higher altitudes to avoid antiaircraft fire. This protected the lives of soldiers – as well as guaranteeing popular support on the home front – but most likely increased collateral damage, including incidents like the one in Korisa described earlier. The decision to "fly high" received much condemnation from philosophers, but was lauded by citizens and soldiers alike.

The IDF's decision to send its soldiers to fight house-to-house, moreover, fails to take into account that those soldiers are also citizens. They are "civilians in uniform," sent on behalf of the state. Yes, we send them to fight to protect their fellow citizens. This makes them liable to attack by the enemy, but that does not mean that the state which sent them can neglect their personal security. To the contrary, the state that sent them to fight must constantly justify why it is endangering them. The state bears *special duties* toward its citizens and agents alike. Force protection, in other words, is a deep moral obligation. There is no compelling reason why the state should jeopardize their lives to save the terrorist's neighbor.

The lead author of the IDF's code of ethics, Professor Asa Kasher, and the former head of the IDF Military Intelligence Directorate, General Amos Yadlin, have repeatedly emphasized this point, including in a pointed exchange with Walzer and Margalit.[15] Israeli forces, they argued, should try to separate enemy noncombatants from fighters. After that, "not only is the state no longer obligated to endanger the lives of its own soldiers in order to attempt to further such a separation, it is forbidden from doing so."[16]

They further argued, compellingly but with great controversy, that the IDF Code of Ethics demanded only that soldiers do "all that they can" to avoid harming noncombatants. This does not include risking their lives and those of their comrades. A very distinguished group of Israeli philosophers lined up to disagree. Yet Kasher – supported by many rabbis – correctly held his ground.[17] When push comes to shove, brother trumps other.

This doesn't mean that we allow the army to protect its soldiers by carpet bombing the enemy nation and indiscriminately killing. That strategy may (or may not) stop the mortar fire, but it would treat the enemy civilians as disposable means to achieving the end of protecting our own. Moreover, it would betray our attempt to balance the values of communal defense and loyalty with respecting the inherent dignity of all humans.

Yet at some point, these values can conflict. Choices must be made. At this stage, we should prioritize the safety of our own brethren at the expense of increased enemy collateral damage. Not because we appreciate the divine image of all human beings any less, but because we value our fraternal responsibilities even more.

WAR AS A COLLECTIVE ENTERPRISE

Ultimately, it is this factor of communal allegiance – our special duty to protect our own – that dictates that we make the necessary moves to provide defense, even at the expense – unintended but inevitable – of enemy noncombatants.[18] This factor has been undervalued by the human-rights approach of Walzer and others who overly focus on one value – individual human rights. We should not forget the individual costs of battle. Yet ultimately, war remains primarily a collective enterprise.[19]

Warfare is not a battle between individuals or groups of people, but rather collective entities. It profoundly challenges an ethical system built on individual rights because it divests people of their individual identity and brands them as a part of a collective. Soldiers are not random fighters but rather representatives of a country. They are meant to kill, or be killed, on behalf of their nation. Citizens of each country are, willy-nilly, a part of these collectives. Some will patriotically support the cause. Others may even enthusiastically join the war effort, thereby shedding their status as noncombatants. Many, on the other hand, will oppose the war or, at the very least, will want to steer clear of the combat. Nonetheless, it is impossible to fully escape our moral identification with the societies in which we reside and the decisions made by our leaders. Our fate – physical and moral – is tied to our people, for better and for worse.

War is one of the best ways in which our collective consciousness emerges. No one in Texas or Oregon was attacked on September 11. Nonetheless, Texans and Oregonians will say, "We were attacked on 9/11." Similarly, we admire those who are willing to fight on our behalf and even die for the national cause, even though we never personally met those soldiers. "They made the ultimate sacrifice for all of us," many will collectively lament. Some will be scared by this identity; others will take pride. Yet we recognize that we do not live on an island.

Our collective moral identification may also be seen from the shame and responsibility people regularly feel for the ethical sins of our fellow countrymen. Even today, many decades after World War II, many Germans and Japanese feel a sense of guilt for the sins of their ancestors, just as many Americans feel a moral stain from the country's Jim Crow days. As citizens who identify with this moral community, we feel responsible for the failed values that characterize our society.

In the deepest sense, this is the implication of *kiddush Hashem* or *ḥillul Hashem*, the concepts of sanctifying or desecrating the reputation of God that have repeatedly arisen over many decades of Zionist warfare. Jews feel a sense of pride or shame for the actions of their compatriots, even if they had nothing to do with those people. This is deeply evidenced, in fact, by the strong reactions that many Diaspora Jews have toward Israeli military actions. Whether this is pride from the Six-Day War, or angst from errant missile strikes in Lebanon, Jews around the world feel that the IDF represents them.

In fact, rebel groups and other nonstate actors feed off this strong sense of collective identity. To succeed, they require the masses to identify with their cause. Guerrilla groups regularly claim to represent the people and depend on popular support and resilience for their unconventional warfare. Take, for example, Hezbollah, which emerged after the First Lebanon War to replace the PLO as Israel's primary nemesis in southern Lebanon. Hezbollah employs a strategy of concealment within population centers to avoid Israeli airstrikes. Utilizing "human shields" is central to its success, including its resistance to Israel in the 2006 war. The UN's humanitarian-aid chief, Jan Egeland, accused Hezbollah fighters then of "cowardly blending...among women and children.... I don't think anyone should be proud of having many more children and women dead than armed men."[20]

For this strategy to work, Hezbollah relies on the masses identifying with their cause. At times, some citizens were even compliant with their methods and even "volunteered" themselves as shields. As one Hezbollah official asserted, their ability to endure against Israel relies upon the mantra of "the people, the army, and the Resistance." In his words:

> Hezbollah has always acknowledged the very important role of the people in the Resistance's actions because when you talk about the Resistance fighters, they are part of the villages, members of the society, and from every walk of life. They are supported by their families, villages, towns, and cities. So really when we talk about steadfastness, it directly leads you to the people.[21]

One might argue that it is legitimate for Hezbollah to utilize popular support for its guerrilla warfare – this, after all, is what rebel groups do. The flip side, however, is that Hezbollah must assume moral responsibility for civilian losses when they fight in their midst. As even Walzer himself wrote, regarding both Lebanon and Gaza, "When Palestinian militants launch rocket attacks from civilian areas, they are themselves responsible – and no one else is – for the civilian deaths caused by Israeli counterfire.... Civilians will suffer so long as no one on the Palestinian side (or the Lebanese side) takes action to stop the rocket attacks."[22]

Yet Walzer mistakenly continues to still require Israeli soldiers to endanger themselves to avoid collateral damage. Ultimately, it is the responsibility of the Palestinian or Lebanese people to stop terrorists from endangering their own people, just as it is the obligation of Israeli soldiers to prioritize protecting their own brethren, citizens, and comrades in arms alike.

To be clear, supporting a rebel cause – or failing to prevent rebels from shooting near your home – doesn't necessarily mean that one loses their noncombatant status. Moreover, there may be many individuals who do not support Hezbollah or other guerrilla groups. They might not be blameworthy for being trapped within urban warfare. Yet neither are their attackers for unintentionally killing them, especially after knocking on their roof to try to allow them to flee from the fate of their people.

SHARED FATE, NOT COLLECTIVE PUNISHMENT

Of course, a sense of responsibility or guilt doesn't make one worthy of criminal punishment. The Germans committed genocide, but only specific individuals were placed on trial at Nuremberg. The post–World War II trials, as the legal scholar George Fletcher has shown, were a remarkable transition point in international justice.[23] For the first time, individuals, as opposed to nations, were held responsible for crimes against the law of nations. This is notable because transgressions like aggression, genocide, and other crimes against humanity are committed by many people acting in the aggregate, leaders and commoners together. There is much to commend in this post–World War II transition. Punishing countries as a whole frequently may lead to widespread resentment and hamper national rehabilitation. This was the lesson learned from German anger following World War I. After World War II, by contrast, Japan and Germany reformed into exemplar countries while their previous leaders were tried, killed, or exiled. Leaders, after all, deserve greater blame given their central role in the chain of command. In any case, later generations of that nation do not need to bear the punishments for the actions of their predecessors. Children should not be punished for the sins of their fathers. This, as we saw, is what Ezekiel taught. "The person who sins – he alone shall die." Similarly, noncombatants should not be punished, let alone targeted, for the mistakes of their leaders or compatriots. As we saw in chapter 4, this is why targeting noncombatants is such a horrible sin, and why we are repulsed by the indiscriminate terror of the PLO, Al Qaeda, and others.

Yet human nature ensures that children do suffer (or benefit) from the decisions of their parents, just as any political order guarantees that citizens face the repercussions of their leaders' decisions. This, too, was a teaching of Ezekiel, who prophesied the destruction of the First Temple. "Thus says the Lord – Behold, I am against you, and will draw my sword out its sheath, and will cut off from you the righteous and the wicked."[24] Jerusalem's citizens, sinners and saints alike, will starve from the siege, and then die at the hand of the sword. The same fate is shared by all. Such is the reality of the human experience.

Ezekiel lays much blame for the Israelites deserving punishment on the moral failings of their leaders.[25] They "shed blood and destroy lives to win ill-gotten gain." Of course, many of these commoners may have not been so innocent. They too sinned by "wronging the poor and needy." Others perhaps may have been complicit in the crimes of their leaders, or culpable for not doing enough to improve society. Some, presumedly, were entirely innocent. But in the end, the righteous and wicked all died together.

More directly, however, it was the political failings of their leaders that sealed the fate of all their people. The Judean kings could have heeded the call of the prophet Jeremiah and surrendered to King Nebuchadnezzar; they decided otherwise, and everyone endured the consequences.[26] The political solidarity of a nation compels them to share the same fate. Even when only soldiers are targeted, noncombatants will die alongside them.

To reiterate, none of this means that one should target enemy noncombatants. The realities and obligations of our shared collective fate, however, dictate that one prioritizes their own soldiers and citizens while worrying less about those who share another people's destiny.

THE "FOG OF VICTORY" AND THE MORAL HAZARD OF INACTION

These two primary factors – our obligation to protect our own citizens and our fraternal duties to our brethren – come together when addressing the dilemma of involuntary human shields. If, at the end of the day, an army won't attack certain legitimate targets because of collateral damage, then the terrorist group will utilize human shields to prevent their defeat. It's hard to achieve a decisive victory when you cannot – or will not allow yourself – to destroy the enemy. Yes, guided missiles and other advanced technologies allow for greater precision targeting. Nonetheless, in the fog of war, it is impossible to achieve "immaculate warfare," especially when the defenders are daring you to kill their human shields.

Take, for example, the case of hospitals. For obvious humanitarian reasons, these should normally never be targeted. Yet precisely because of these moral inhibitions, Hamas leaders hide in bunkers under Shifra Hospital, Gaza's primary medical center.[27] It's challenging for a conventional army like the IDF to decisively stop Hamas if it is unwilling to kill its leadership. This is despite the fact that even international law clearly asserts that hospitals lose their protected status once they are (illegally) used for military purposes.[28]

Of course, any moral person who recognizes the inherent worth of all humans would greatly hesitate before shooting at a hospital, even for high-asset targets. One would need to rule out many other options before taking such a drastic step. Moreover, beyond the ethical considerations, there is a strategic goal to create a wedge between the guerrilla fighters and the civilians upon whom they depend for support and cover. Given the tenuous relationship between nonstate actors and the larger population, one must avoid taking actions that will bring civilians closer to the terrorist groups. To this end, avoiding civilian casualties from collateral damage has strategic importance, because one doesn't want to anger the local population. At some point, however, one might need to act firmly against the enemy leaders, in spite of those consequences, in order to end a war. All options must remain on the table if we want to prevent immoral enemies from using our moral inhibitions as a shield against attack.

Similar questions emerged with American hesitancy about taking decisive action against the Taliban or ISIS for fear of civilian casualties. Critics argued that America should have utilized its asymmetric advantage in air power to deliver a comprehensive, rapid, and simultaneous attack that would kill terrorists. Ultimately, the defeat of these groups is the primary ethical imperative. This will benefit not only America, but also the civilians who suffer longer under their terrorist leaders and the continuous warfare that they breed. There is a moral cost to not acting decisively.[29]

Part of the problem is that many Western countries are unsure of what it means to be victorious in cases of asymmetric warfare.[30] It's hard to act decisively when one doesn't know the ultimate goal. This wasn't a question in most twentieth-century wars, when victors eliminated their enemy's fighting capability and conquered their territory. This is how the Allies won World War II. It is also how Israel won the Six-Day War and the Yom Kippur War. In both cases, it destroyed the Arab armies while making significant territorial conquests. Since the 1973 war, Israel has fought against nonstate actors like the PLO, Hezbollah, and Hamas, who have no official territory to lose. The same is true of many terrorist groups around the world. For them, their very survival and continued ability to operate is seen as a victory against their mightier opponents.

Consequently, a "fog of victory," so to speak, emerges when a decisive victory cannot be achieved on the battlefield.[31] This became clear to Americans after President Bush made his 2003 "Mission Accomplished" speech on a battleship after the initially successful American invasion of

Iraq. Within a couple of years, tens of thousands more American troops were being sent to Iraq to fight a persistent insurgency. The 2021 retaking of Afghanistan by the Taliban following an ignoble American retreat reinforced this point. Analysts continue to debate what went wrong for the United States. Yet it seems clear that one of its failings was an inability to define its goals. Indeed, throughout the war, American strategists shifted terms regarding their goals, moving from "victory" to "winning" and then a deeply ambiguous "success." Whatever the term, they had a hard time depicting the endgame.[32] A dishonorable result followed.

Some Israeli strategists have tried to clear the "fog of victory" in a similar way. They define military success as wearing down the enemy, physically and emotionally, so that they are no longer interested in fighting, even though they retain the ability to do so. This "strategy of fatigue" led many Israeli strategists to stop using the term "victory" (*nitzahon*). Instead, the preferred term became *hakhraa*. The term tellingly does not translate well into English, indicating its murky meaning. It is frequently translated as "decision" to indicate the enemy has chosen to no longer fight, i.e., the will to fight has been decisively broken. The measure is cognitive, not physical. This, they argued, is a better model for Israel since it has no interest in reconquering territories in southern Lebanon or Gaza because of the political, diplomatic, and security imbroglio that it will create.

Many in Israel and around the world worry that such an approach, let alone such rhetoric, is defeatist.[33] For starters, it gives the (correct?) impression to compatriots and enemies alike that the country's leaders lack the will to fully eliminate the terrorists and pay the political price for costly warfare. Sometimes, in fact, a terrorist group may be extinguished or driven from a territory, but only if the military is given sufficient time to defeat it. The biblical command of bravery and courage in warfare mandates the willingness to fight in both swift, robust warfare as well as extended struggles, depending on the demands of the circumstances. Those who believe that "there is no military solution" will suffer quickly from psychological war fatigue, especially against ideological fundamentalists who view death as glorified martyrdom.

Such a mentality also makes one particularly vulnerable to feeling repulsed by collateral deaths. What's the justification for fighting when you aren't going to accomplish victory anyway? Once that's the attitude, it becomes harder to argue for the military necessity of a strike that will incur significant collateral damage. Attacks will always feel disproportionate when you don't understand your goals.

Nuanced strategists have noted that there are alternative but concrete security goals which may be achieved militarily against nonstate actors.[34] Sometimes this may fall short of our conception of "total victory." No celebratory parades will be held. Yet one doesn't necessarily need to "destroy the enemy" or conquer their territory in order to significantly improve one's self-defense. A "sufficient victory" represses terror and discourages terrorists from acting again in the future. To achieve this victory, the political echelon must set a definitive, achievable goal and then give the army a mandate to persistently undertake missions to achieve their aims. This includes the willingness to tolerate enemy noncombatant losses for which one does not bear moral culpability.

The moral implications for this strategic reorientation are wide ranging.

1. Self-Defense, not conquest: First, the goal remains improving one's defense. Territorial conquest might be necessary, but it is a means, not an end. A more limited or expansive operation is dictated by strategic assessments alone. The fact that an area like Gaza or southern Lebanon may include parts of biblical Israel is irrelevant.

2. Military necessity: Related to number 1, clear goals determine the military necessity of different actions. Power and violence are used just when necessary to repel attacks and prevent future ones. By its nature, asymmetric warfare will lead to difficult moral questions of preventative strikes and urban warfare. As we've argued, such actions are justifiable yet require clear thought in determining which actions are necessary and effective in providing greater defense. Especially given their discretionary natures, the focus should be on achieving military, not political goals.

3. Civilian casualties for necessary military actions are justifiable: As with all warfare, noncombatants will suffer. When guerrilla warriors use noncombatants as human shields, they bear

responsibility for making them targets. If a military strike is necessary to achieve a war aim, then it may be launched even in the presence of "human shields." Of course, it's always preferable to perform a strike in a way in which noncombatant casualties will be avoided. This might even mean temporarily delaying a strike. Yet if a critical target is too embedded within a civilian area or must be struck without delay, then the army should act accordingly.

4. Strategic moral assessment: Given the nature of asymmetric warfare and the moral complexities surrounding it, there are bound to be disputable judgment calls as well as tactical mistakes. Targets will be misidentified, precision-guided missiles will still miss targets, commanders will make misguided decisions, and soldiers will panic. Such incidents are regrettable, even tragic. Nonetheless, they remain morally excusable as long as they are undertaken within a broader strategic framework which takes into account the moral values dictated by our multivalued framework. It is impossible to have immaculate warfare. What is necessary is having a strategic goal that dictates military necessity and a moral framework that guides the actions taken to achieving those goals.

5. Ignoring bloody images: Extensive damage does not mean it was excessive.

Many countries fail in this last point because they are overly influenced by unpleasant images from their attacks which instantly appear on televisions and smartphones around the world. It is to this challenge that we turn in our next chapter.

Chapter 25

Public Image and the "CNN Effect" in Qana

SHOULD OUR PUBLIC IMAGE IMPACT OUR MILITARY ACTIONS?

Until now, we've argued that warfare permits the unintended but inevitable killing of noncombatants. Yet don't such scenes constitute a *ḥillul Hashem*? After all, gory pictures of dead civilians on CNN and Facebook serve as fodder for international condemnation, accusations of "war crimes" by NGOs, and uncomfortable water cooler conversations. Moreover, bad publicity negatively impacts a country's so-called "soft-power," i.e., its ability to persuasively influence the global community of the justness of its country and cause. Given our concern for our reputation, should we sacrifice significant military gains to avoid noncombatant casualties or killing human shields?

Generally speaking, the answer is no. The concept of *ḥillul Hashem*, as we've seen, has two different connotations, one political and the second moral.

1. First, God's reputation rests on the *political* state of the Jewish people. Israel's exile is seen, by the world, as divine failure. Its ascent, by contrast, is seen as proof of God's greatness and His

ability to bring justice to the world. Evildoers must fall and a righteous Israel must thrive for the religion to be glorified.

2. Second, God's reputation is impacted by the moral behavior of the Jewish people. Jews represent the values of the Bible. When they act ethically, the Torah is glorified. When they behave badly, the Torah is denigrated. Toward this goal, Israel must, at the very least, maintain basic international standards of civilized military behavior while keeping to its ethical commitments under international agreements.[1]

In general, Rabbi Tzvi Yehuda and his students are associated with the first meaning, while Rabbi Amital and his students are attached to the second.[2] While there is some truth to this perception, both schools of thought actually recognize the importance of both implications of the term. It was Rabbi Yisraeli, co-dean of R. Tzvi Yehuda's yeshiva, who promoted the idea that halakha mandates for Israel to observe international standards of wartime behavior, as discussed in chapter 6. R. Amital, for his part, regularly spoke of the Jewish people's horrific political condition during the Holocaust as the greatest *ḥillul Hashem* and the State of Israel's creation as its antidote.[3] As such, both factors are primary values that need to be taken into consideration. It's important to determine which cases rightly condemn a country's reputation. After all, a country's ethical behavior should not be judged solely on the superficial perspectives of uninformed observers, which are frequently tinged by interests, politics, and other biasing factors.

To illustrate the point, we'll take two well-known examples, once again from Israel's battles in Lebanon.

CASE 1: THE MASSACRE AT SABRA AND SHATILA

On September 1, 1982, PLO fighters were evacuated from Beirut by a multinational force. Lebanon was supposed to now fall under the control of Bachir Gemayel, a Christian Lebanese militia commander of the Phalange Party who had been elected two weeks beforehand as president of Lebanon's National Assembly. Gemayel was supported by the Reagan administration and Israel's government, who saw him as an ally who could sign a peace treaty with Israel. On September 14, however, Gemayel was assassinated. A couple of days later – on the Jewish new year, Rosh HaShana – Phalangist militiamen took revenge for his death by killing or wounding thousands of residents in the Palestinian refugee camps Sabra and Shatila near Beirut. Israel established a government inquiry. It found that Defense Minister Sharon and the IDF chief of staff were "indirectly responsible" for the massacre. They should have known it was going to happen and could have taken steps to stop it once it started.

R. Yisraeli, R. Goren, and one of R. Tzvi Yehuda's premiere students, Knesset member Rabbi Hayim Druckman, were against Israel's investigation and tried to stop it from happening. They believed that Israel was being scapegoated for actions it didn't commit. Accepting any responsibility would only lead to international antisemitism.[4] Where was the international outrage when the Lebanese factions were slaughtering each other during their extended civil war in the 1970s? "Christians kill Muslims and the Jews get the blame," went the refrain.

Yet these weren't random Christians. They were the IDF's allies. For this reason, R. Amital deemed the event an enormous *hillul Hashem* and castigated religious Knesset members for not supporting the government inquiry. His colleague R. Lichtenstein, in an open letter to Prime Minister Begin, asserted that national honor could be restored only through investigation and introspection. This call was echoed in America by R. Lichtenstein's father-in-law, Rabbi Soloveitchik, who pressured religious members of the Israeli cabinet to support the inquiry, as well as Britain's chief rabbi, Immanuel Jakobovits, who deplored the "dishonor done to the Jewish name."[5]

R. Amital and R. Lichtenstein were right, but it's important to understand why. The residents of Sabra and Shatila were noncombatants who could not be directly targeted under Jewish ethics. They were murdered by Israel's allies and under the IDF's noses for the sole purpose of vengeance. The fact that the Christian Phalangists committed the slaughter was a minimally mitigating factor. Israel had chosen them as its allies and they had previously coordinated their actions with the larger IDF assault. As the lead player in the Lebanon conflict, the IDF had the ability – and collective responsibility – to temper the Phalangist behavior. If war is a collective affair, as we've argued, then one must accept some level of responsibility for your ally's behavior.[6]

Moreover, the IDF had just spent many weeks fighting in Lebanon, doing everything possible to avoid civilian casualties from collateral damage. All of its soldiers' restraint, in the name of "purity of arms," was now overshadowed by the unwarranted killing of noncombatants during a cease-fire. Sabra and Shatila not only soiled the reputation of the Jewish people. It desecrated the moral heroism of the IDF's soldiers who made great sacrifices to avoid collateral damage.

The *ḥillul Hashem*, however, was not created just by the images of bloody casualties that were displayed on televisions across the world. This seemed to be the focus of R. Jakobovits, who admittedly had the unenviable task of explaining the war to a hostile European media even as he personally opposed the broader invasion. R. Jakobovits condemned Israel's religious leadership for "ignoring the most agonizing halakhic perplexity posed by the war: its enormous toll of life, both Jewish and non-Jewish, especially among Lebanese civilians unwittingly caught in the bloody conflict." Israel's actions, as well as its poor job of explaining them to the world, represented an "abandonment of the whole concept of *kiddush Hashem* among the nations."[7]

Noncombatant deaths are always tragic. Yet they are not necessarily immoral, not always the attacking army's fault, and certainly not unique to Israel. R. Jakobovits knew this. In fact, he repeatedly condemned the international media for holding Israel to a double standard compared to its coverage of other Western armies which famously killed many more civilians. He further recognized that there were realpolitik considerations and other factors biasing many Western countries against Israel. Nonetheless, he felt Israel should hold itself to a "higher morality" because of our biblical legacy and "Israel's role in moral pioneering."[8]

It's hard to understand why Israel needs to hold itself to a "higher morality" or what that even entails. Jews should set profound moral standards for themselves and articulate them to the world. They should then live by them, but also demand the same from other nations. The universal relevance of these morals is precisely what makes them ethical directives and not just personal preferences. These moral directives, as we've argued throughout, are generated by taking into account multiple and sometimes conflicting values. An attempt to avoid noncombatant casualties for the sake of our public image may endanger other important moral duties such as force protection and defending one's citizens.

Moreover, it's hard to expect a country to act in a supererogatory manner when it is trying to win a fight against enemies who display little ethical inhibition. As discussed in chapter 2, Rabbi Abraham Isaac Kook taught, many decades earlier, that it is difficult for any warring party to rise above the moral standards of its time period; ethical behavior is usually dictated by the side who practices it least. As it was, the IDF's actions in Lebanon showed incredible restraint to avoid noncombatant deaths, even as many were nonetheless unavoidable. Israel should have made greater effort to present its case cogently, as R. Jakobovits urged. Nonetheless, the gruesome TV images of casualties, soldiers and civilians alike, do not tell us anything about the justice of the military action.

Unfortunately, this misperception of both ethics and *hillul Hashem* sometimes drives countries to make costly mistakes in their wars against nonstate actors. This point will be highlighted by our next case example.

CASE 2: NAFTALI BENNETT AND THE BOMBING(S) OF QANA

On April 18, 1996, Naftali Bennett, the twenty-four-year-old commander of the Maglan special forces, radioed in for emergency help from southern Lebanon.[9] Bennett's unit had spent the previous eight days on a reconnaissance mission to locate Hezbollah units, rocket launchers, and other targets. These efforts were a part of Operation Grapes of Wrath, launched by Prime Minister Peres to stop Hezbollah attacks from southern Lebanon that were increasingly fatal for both IDF soldiers and Israeli civilians. Bennett's reconnaissance unit would identify the location of moving Hezbollah targets. The IDF would then launch air strikes or artillery shells to destroy them.

This strategy served two goals: to decrease the number of IDF combat soldiers endangering themselves against Hezbollah guerrilla warriors on their home turf, and to identify targets clearly so that Lebanese civilians would not be caught in the crossfire. As the head of the IDF air force explained, "Extreme precision was required because the apartment buildings [housing Hezbollah operation centers] also housed the families of Hezbollah fighters. We did not want CNN to broadcast scenes of dead women and children."[10]

After eight days, an IDF helicopter was mistakenly sent during daytime hours to provide Bennett's unit with food and supplies. One of the Maglan subunits was exposed. Hezbollah fighters, wearing UN flak jackets, stood in a Lebanese cemetery and shot mortar fire that landed close to the IDF commandos.[11] The Hezbollah men then ran for cover into a UN compound 560 feet away that was sheltering nearly eight hundred Lebanese civilians. (UN peacekeepers were painfully aware that Hezbollah was using their compound to house human shields. Three days before, when a Fijan soldier tried to stop the guerrilla fighters from firing in the vicinity, he was shot in the chest.)[12]

Short on time and left with few options to protect their exposed soldiers, the IDF quickly launched rescue artillery fire at Hezbollah's rocket launchers. Due to a combination of weather factors, imprecise maps, technological limitations, and human error, the artillery fire missed its mark and landed on the UN compound. Tragically, over one hundred people were killed, with another hundred wounded. Images of decapitated children and disemboweled women were soon broadcast throughout the world. In the interim, the IDF commandos were extracted by helicopter to safety. The journalist Robert Fisk, reporting for Britain's *Independent,* filed his report under the headline "Massacre in Sanctuary." The first line began, "It was a massacre. Not since Sabra and Shatila had I seen the innocent slaughtered like this."[13]

The images of Qana and Sabra and Shatila were tragically similar, but the moral responsibility was very different. In 1982, the Phalangists targeted noncombatants when they were under no immediate threat. It was revenge, not self-defense. In 1996, the IDF was trying to destroy rockets that were threatening their fellow soldiers. The noncombatant deaths were unintentional and were caused by Hezbollah shooting next to the UN shelter. As Matan Vilnai, the IDF deputy chief of staff, argued, "Hezbollah are doing their utmost to get civilians killed by sheltering among them and by firing Katyushas and mortars from positions very close to UN or civilian positions." He further noted that there will always be limitations to the accuracy of advanced weapons. A frustrated Bennett, for his part, would later develop as a politician a "no apologies" doctrine to assert that Israel should not hesitate to do what it takes to defeat guerrilla warriors fighting within civilian quarters. Don't go to war unless you are prepared for a certain margin of error and the inevitable deaths of noncombatants.[14]

While Prime Minister Peres was initially sympathetic to the IDF's argument, he cut the operation short. The bloody images from Qana were damaging Israel's international support; he couldn't tolerate such a tarnished image, especially two months before Israeli elections. The IDF bitterly complained. Peres had not only stopped the operation prematurely before the army could complete its mission. He also signed a lopsided cease-fire deal in which both sides promised that they would not "fire any kind of weapon at civilians or civilian targets." Such an agreement would not be observed by Hezbollah; moreover, it could hinder the IDF's future responses since Hezbollah enmeshed itself within Lebanese villages. It further gave the impression that should Israel attack Hezbollah targets within civilian locations, Hezbollah could legitimately retaliate against civilian targets within Israel. Hezbollah had won a strategic victory from the so-called "Qana massacre."

Critical in this regard was the reaction of Rabbi Amital. A few months beforehand, R. Amital had been appointed as a minister without portfolio in Peres's government following the dreadful assassination of Yitzhak Rabin. R. Amital supported Peres's initial resolve to attack Hezbollah but also the decision to end the fighting. He was deeply shaken by the images from Qana. On a trip to England, he deemed the Qana incident an "indescribable *ḥillul Hashem* to the nations of the world."[15] He could not sleep over the fact that he, as a government minister, bore responsibility for this desecration of God's reputation. R. Amital's statement was covered on the front page of the main Jewish newspaper in Britain. His audience, along with some of R. Amital's disciples, would laud this public confession as a *kiddush Hashem*.

R. Amital's moral conscience is admirable, but his reaction was overly emotional and dangerously disproportionate. Yes, the images from Qana were damaging to Israel's public image. But unfortunately, they are also very typical in warfare and should not stop a country from carrying out a just mission. No matter how "smart" bombs might become, and no matter how much intelligence may be gathered, civilians will be killed.

Every attacking party makes mistakes, particularly when the defending party puts their own citizens in harm's way. Yet these gruesome images do not tell us anything about the morality of the particular strike and certainly not the larger mission.

This point was cogently made at a conference in Israel in the year after Operation Grapes of Wrath by US Airforce Colonel W. Hays Parks, arguably the most distinguished legal historian of twentieth-century aerial warfare.[16] Parks noted how just a few years earlier in Operation Desert Storm, Saddam Hussein, who had studied the Israeli experience in Lebanon, purposely used human shields, including foreigners, to deter coalition attacks. The coalition was still largely successful in reducing noncombatant casualties.

Despite these efforts, mistakes were made. On February 13, the United States bombed the Amiriyah bunker in western Baghdad. Built during the Iran-Iraq war, US intelligence believed it was now being used as a command-and-control center. It is possible that this assessment was a mistake. Either way, unbeknownst to the Americans, it turned out that it was a nighttime shelter for local residents. At least three hundred noncombatants were killed. For the first time in the war, foreign journalists were allowed to visit a site without Iraqi censorship; they would broadcast the gory removal of bodies for many days afterward. The BBC declared that its footage of charred bodies was "too grim to show."[17] The journalist Fisk would compare the blast to Hiroshima while detailing how human flesh had become liquified.[18]

Yet as Parks correctly argued, the images from Amiriyah, Beirut, Qana, and elsewhere tell us nothing about who was responsible for these particular casualties or whether the attacking force had generally done a respectable job of distinguishing between legitimate targets and noncombatants. Media spectacles are not moral barometers.

The problem with basing moral judgments on media coverage isn't just that the given journalists may be against the overall war or particularly biased against an attacking army (although this might be true, as is regularly the case with Israel). It's that the very medium itself lends itself to replacing hardheaded analysis with sheer emotion. As Robert Kaplan noted, for many journalists and others, "nothing matters to them except the horrendous spectacle before their eyes – *about which something must be done!*"[19] From their cosmopolitan perspective, one only thinks about the human rights of the victim. What could they have possibly done to deserve this? One stops taking into consideration the behavior of and relationship between the different collectives, including whether one side might be legitimately acting to protect their vital interests.

R. Amital fell into the same trap. He asserted that Hezbollah's firing from civilian areas led to the incident. Nonetheless, he deemed Qana a *ḥillul Hashem,* thereby playing into Hezbollah's misinformation campaign. Unwittingly, the concept of *ḥillul Hashem* was used as a shield for Hezbollah.

THE SECOND ACCIDENTAL BOMBING OF QANA

Alas, the same mistake was made by Israel ten years later during the Second Lebanon War, once again after an unfortunate incident in Qana. American negotiators were on the verge of securing a favorable cease-fire deal between Israel and the Western-leaning Lebanese government. The Lebanese army, backed by an international force with a real peacekeeping mandate, would re-assert control over southern Lebanon. Hezbollah would be displaced and an arms embargo imposed. The militia agreed to the conditions, indicating that they felt militarily vulnerable after two weeks of aggressive Israeli fighting. Hezbollah's fighting spirit seemed to be nearing its breaking point. US Secretary of State Condoleezza Rice arrived in the region to sign the deal.

As Israeli officials were having breakfast with Rice, their cell phones began to buzz. "Incident in Qana in Lebanon. Dozens dead." The IDF had bombed the outskirts of the Qana village from where Katyusha rockets were launched. An apartment collapsed from the impact. Televisions across the world displayed images of bleeding, soot-covered children and rows of bodies covered with white plastic sacks. Twenty-eight people were tragically killed, but initial media reports doubled that number. International condemnation was quick to follow. It didn't matter that Hezbollah had fired over 150 rockets from the area in the previous weeks.[20] Instead of pressing Hezbollah to stop their war crimes of fighting from civilian territories, the UN Security Council held an emergency meeting to lambast Israel. Some members incredulously accused the Jewish state of purposely targeting civilians. Israel also hurt its own case by taking too long to release footage of Katyusha rockets originating in the village.[21] Barred from entering Beirut by the enraged Lebanese government and annoyed by Israel's sloppy handling of the incident, a frustrated Rice realized the cease-fire deal was dead.

Despite the terrible press, the IDF leaders wanted to increase strikes and make clear that notwithstanding Qana, there was no way out for Hezbollah without a political deal. The US national security advisers felt similarly: the war could not stop until there was a fundamental change in the Lebanese reality. Rice, however, demanded Israel issue a forty-eight-hour cease-fire for "humanitarian reasons." She further convinced President Bush that Israel's incursion was now causing more damage than benefit for the region. America successfully applied pressure to get a cease-fire, even without any real political changes. For Hezbollah, as two distinguished journalists would later write, "The killing in Qana was a godsend."[22] Instead of signing a humiliating cease-fire deal, it would continue to fight from civilian locations with impunity. The world's emotional response to bloody images from Qana allowed it to once again win the propaganda war.

For the West to win its asymmetric wars, the "Qana syndrome" must stop. Collateral damage and tragic mistakes are inevitable in these wars.[23] We might be saddened by these deaths, but our moral analysis must remain sober. Good reasoning must overcome our instinctive revulsion to bloodshed. We cannot fixate on body counts or CNN coverage. Instead, we must determine with whom lies the ultimate culpability. In Sabra and Shatila, responsibility fell on the Phalangist militiamen but also, indirectly and secondarily, on those in Israel who could have done more to prevent the massacre perpetrated by their allies. In Qana, responsibility fell on the extremists who ran for cover within their population centers. We should take reasonable steps to avoid collateral damage, but not by taking exaggerated risks with our soldiers or endangering the success of the mission.

Ultimately, the greatest *kiddush Hashem* lies in following our moral principles constantly and consistently despite the protracted conflict against enemies who don't care about any rules.

Final Thoughts on an Uncertain Ethical Future

TECHNOLOGY AND THE FALSE PROMISE OF "PRECISION WARFARE"

There's one more lesson to learn from the Qana incidents: military technology, no matter how sophisticated, will not prevent collateral damage. Night vision, high-resolution satellites, laser designation, and sensors for target identification greatly help in pinpointing a target and avoiding noncombatants in any given vicinity. Yet ultimately, collateral damage remains unavoidable. Technology cannot deliver "pristine warfare." Asymmetric warfare within urban settings won't allow for it, intelligence mistakes regularly occur, unexpected secondary explosions occur because of unforeseen conditions on the ground, and nearly unerring technology still sometimes fails.

Already after the botched 1996 Qana attack, this point was emphasized by the head of the Israel Weapons Development Authority, who led Israel's efforts to develop precise weapons. War, he correctly warned, "will remain bloody and destructive. The dream that...precision firepower will lead to clean, surgical war with little collateral damage and minimal casualties will remain, in most cases, a dream."[1]

Unfortunately, many political leaders have fallen for the allure of "pristine warfare" and promised a precision that cannot be delivered. US President Barack Obama, for example, pledged in 2016, "With our extraordinary technology, we're conducting the most precise air campaign in history." A few years later, the *New York Times* published a devastating report showing that many jet fighter and drone attacks were far from precise.[2] Sometimes, faulty intelligence led to mistaken strikes; on other occasions, civilians were killed because they were in the proximity of legitimate military targets. Thousands were killed, with many more noncombatants wounded and homes destroyed.

One can legitimately debate the morality of each of those strikes and the general campaign. But if you set a standard of precision that's impossible to meet, you aren't setting yourself up for constructive criticism. You are distorting the entire framework of how to discuss the morality of fighting in war. War, no matter how technologically advanced, will always cause extensive damage. The question remains whether it is excessive given the military goals as well as the factors known at the time. Playing Monday-morning quarterback based on gruesome pictures and casualty numbers alone is morally simplistic.[3]

Drones and other unmanned aerial weapons do provide a tremendous advantage because they reduce risks to one's own troops. Some ethicists fear that this might make warfare "too easy" and too impersonal. Drone operators, sometimes located thousands of miles away, might kill their targets with ease and then go off to lunch as if they had been playing an intense video game. There's no doubt that it remains critical to maintain a high level of moral sensitivity to the bloodshed of drone warfare. Nonetheless, the ability not to endanger our own troops must trump that concern. We will still need, of course, to maintain our standards of discrimination and proportionality while keeping in mind the goal of victory against adversaries who do not embrace such ethical standards.

Yet this is no different than it was in the past. New technologies emerge that allow us to fight in powerful ways. The moral principles that must guide us remain the same. Multiple military technological revolutions occurred over the period covered in this book. Yet the ethical categories were sufficiently robust to provide good answers to the moral dilemmas that arose in each period.

Technology, Max Boot has argued, "sets the parameters of the possible." The transformative impact of these new tools, he continues, "depends on organization, strategy, tactics, leadership, training, morale, and other human factors."[4] And, I would add, their moral barometer. The ethical impact of new technology is dependent on how we are willing to use it. It's not that technology is inherently value neutral, as some would argue. It's that societies with strong moral frameworks will have the ability to utilize these tools appropriately. As long as our society continues to take into account the important principles developed in the Jewish multivalue framework, we will be able to handle the technological revolutions.

Here, in fact, lies the greatest concern. Given the ever-strengthening powerful tools in our hands and in the hands of our enemies, are we sufficiently aware of the complexity of moral dilemmas? In the last chapters, we noted how disturbing media images regularly cloud our moral judgment. Thoughtful questions about proportionality and responsibility get overshadowed by knee-jerk reactions. Yet the problem runs deeper.

In November 1948, General Omar Bradley declared, "The world has achieved brilliance without wisdom, power without conscience. Ours is a world of nuclear giants and ethical infants." Much has changed since then, and yet I fear that our moral compass remains insufficiently developed. Some people are simply not thinking enough about ethics in general and the impact of technology in particular. Others are fixated on one value, like human rights or national victory. Yet perhaps the biggest problem is that the world cannot and will not agree on any conventions or ethics.

Peter W. Singer, author of a best-selling book on new military technologies in the twenty-first century, has offered several reasons why the discussion of the ethical implications remains sparse.[5] Part of this has to do with the impact on money in weapons development. There are many people who have incentives not to ask questions. Another part of it is that ethics and science have become disparate fields. That, in and of itself, is a problem, with insufficient communication between the fields. It's particularly problematic when the technology advances exponentially and the ethical discourse cannot catch up.

Yet the biggest challenge is dealing with global conflicts in which different countries have very different views about ethics. On many issues regarding technology, popular attitudes diverge widely over what is acceptable use of technology. The divide is more pronounced when it comes to military technology. And here, no matter how many reservations we may have about a given innovation, we cannot ignore that our adversaries may have no such misgivings. In war, as military strategists like to note, "the enemy has a vote." No matter how much you might want to fight in a certain way, your strategy will be impacted by the tactics of the other side.

No area on the ethical frontier is more controversial than autonomous weapon systems. Once activated, these systems can select and engage targets without human intervention. Their appeal is obvious: they don't endanger your own troops, they don't get tired, and the speed at which they can identity and neutralize a target is unprecedented. They can also be programmed to continue to act when human contact is cut off, like in remote, cavernous areas. And here lies the problem: what code will be utilized for it to make decisions? How will it decide on questions of collateral damage? Who, if anybody, bears responsibility for actions that it will take? For any ethical system that prioritizes case-based decision making, this is a very complex development.

Such "killer robots" are clearly on the way. Russia, China, the United States, the United Kingdom, and Israel are already investing billions in this technology. NGOs like Human Rights Watch are campaigning for a treaty against their use. Here the intentions might be good, yet as we've shown throughout this book, such treaties carry little weight, especially when leading world powers suspect that the other side will utilize them anyway. There is good reason to be worried.[6]

The legal difficulty – who can you hold liable for an action no one planned or performed – is challenging but surmountable: for instance, we might agree, as a matter of convention, that the last human decision-maker bears responsibility. Yet, this legal dilemma reflects another moral problem. In the absence of human control, it may not be possible to explain, after as well as before a decision is reached, exactly what happened and why. To give a moral account of decision making is the ultimate act of ethical discourse. It forces the actor to justify, before and after the act, why he or she prioritized certain values over others in any particular circumstance. It further forces them to learn from those experiences and apply them to future occasions. This form of continuous accounting is a critical part of the moral life.

Autonomous weapons systems are not so much immoral as amoral. That is to say, they don't allow for the type of moral deliberation and reflection necessary to pass ethical judgment. The actions taken by such systems may, overall, be as defensible as decisions made by humans, whose judgments can be deeply flawed. Yet, by replacing human deliberation with a machine, we stop using the moral compass that distinguishes our humanity. "To know good and evil," as Genesis 3:22 puts it, is to be human. Machine decision-making threatens us with the ultimate form of digital dehumanization.

Artificial intelligence can play a critical role in assisting our moral deliberations in many situations. It can help us identify the right targets, clarify the number of non-combatants in an area, and estimate the level of collateral damage. AI-controlled drones can be utilized for early, high-risk surveillance, and play a major role toward disabling enemy air defenses. These are cheaper ways to knock out missile targets that, critically, don't run the mortal risks of piloted planes. In these ways and more, technology can help us fight more efficiently, safely, and even ethically. But moral decision-making with life-and-death consequences must ultimately remain in human hands. Otherwise, there is no moral accountability. And retaining moral accountability is essential for retaining our humanity.

So we'll need to figure out, quickly, how to ethically utilize such powerful technology. We'll need to determine how to take advantage of its many strengths while avoiding its ethical pitfalls. And we'll need to figure this out while recognizing that our adversaries, whether countries like China or nonstate actors like Hezbollah, have very different codes of ethics and honor.

It is my prayer that we'll have the moral courage to handle this task, and my conviction that the Jewish multivalue framework proposed in this book can meet this challenge.

Notes

CHAPTER 1: WORLD WAR I AND THE FALSE PROMISE OF PACIFISM

1   *A Passionate Pacifist: Essential Writings of Aaron Samuel Tamares*, ed. Everett Gendler (Teaneck, 2020), 140. R. Tamares, *Knesset Yisrael UMilḥemet HaGoyim* (Warsaw, 1920), 15–16. Many of R. Tamares's pacifist writings are collected in Aaron Samuel Tamares, *Pacifism and Torah*, ed. Ehud Luz (Jerusalem, 1992) [Hebrew], including a thorough introduction by the editor. See also Ehud Luz, *Wrestling with an Angel: Power, Morality, Jewish Identity*, trans. Michael Swirsky (Yale, 2003), 125–29 and Elie Holzer, *Herev Pifiyot Beyadam* (Shalom Hartman Institute, 2009), 109–64.

2   Churchill, from his *The World Crisis 1911–1918*, as cited in Donald Kagan, *On the Origins of War*, 82–83.

3   Eric Lohr, "The Russian Army and the Jews: Mass Deportation, Hostages, and Violence during World War I," *The Russian Review* 60:3 (July 2001): 404–19.

4   *The Dybbuk and Other Writings*, ed. David Roskies (Yale, 2002), 202.

5   Ibid., 206.

6   Derek Penslar, *Jews and the Military: A History* (Princeton, 2013), 153.

7   *Tel Talpiyot* (Moetzin, 1916), no. 104.

8   Colin Eimer, "Joseph Hertz: A Chief Rabbi at War," *European Judaism* 48:1 (Spring 2015): 23–32.

9   Cited in Pierre Birnbaum, "French Rabbis and the 'Sacred Unity' During the First World War," *European Judaism* 48:1 (Spring 2015), 55.

10 For sources, see J. David Bleich, "Preemptive War in Jewish Law," *Tradition* 21:1 (Spring 1983), 27–28; Shlomo Zevin, *LaOhr HaHalakha* (Jerusalem, 5764), 16–18; and Yehuda Shaviv, "Tokfan shel Milḥamot bein HaUmot," *Teḥumin* 9 (5748), 205–30.

11 Penslar, *Jews and the Military: A History*, 120–44.

12 Zev Leiter, *Shu"t Beit David*, vol 1, no. 71.

13 Rabbi Samson Raphael Hirsch, *Horeb: A Philosophy of Jewish Laws and Observances*, ed. and trans. I. Grunfeld (Soncino, 1962), 462. This passage is further discussed in chapter 12.

14 Hillel Zeitlin, *Davar LaAmim*, 11–12. See Luz, *Wrestling with an Angel*, 123–25 and Oz Bluman, "Ethics on the Border of Two Worlds: The Ethical Dimension in Hillel Zeitlin's Search of God" (unpublished PhD diss., Bar-Ilan University, 2018), 248–63 [Hebrew].

15 See, for example, Donald Kagan, *On the Origins of War and the Preservation of Peace* (New York, 1995), 205–14.

16 Gendler, ed., *A Passionate Pacifist*, 20–21.

17 This paragraph draws from Brian Orend, *The Morality of War*, 2nd ed. (Broadview, 2013), 273–75.

18 Gendler, ed., *A Passionate Pacifist*, 74.

19 Tamares, *Musar HaTorah VeYahadut*, 39.

20 Gendler, ed., *A Passionate Pacifist*, 19.

21 Bleich, "Military Service: Ambivalence and Contradiction," 452–57.

22 See, for example, the opinions of Rabbi Eliezer Shach collected in his *BeZot Ani Boteaḥ*, discussed in Benjamin Brown, "Rabbi E. M. Shach: Admiration of the Spirit, Critique of Nationalism, and the Political Decisions in the State of Israel," in *Dat ULeumiyut BeYisrael*, ed. Neri Horowitz (Jerusalem, 2002), 278–341.

23 Deuteronomy 20:3–4.

24 Micah 4:12.

25 See David Elgavish, "Justification for Warfare in the Ancient Near East and the Bible," *Jewish Law Association Studies* 18 (2008): 37–69.

26 G. E. M. Anscombe, "War and Blood," in *The Collected Philosophical Papers of G. E. M. Anscombe*, vol. 3 (Basil Blackwell, 1981), 53.

27 Exodus 22:1–2.

28 Sanhedrin 72a. For more on this concept, see Shlomo Brody, *A Guide to the Complex* (Maggid Books, 2014), 122–23.

29 For two formulations, see George Fletcher, *Rethinking Criminal Law* (Little, Brown, 1978), 857–58 and Orend, *The Morality of War*, 39–42. For Jewish and general philosophical perspectives on self-defense, see the Association for the Philosophy of Judaism symposium around Shlomo Zuckier's "A Halakhic-Philosophic Account of Justified Self-Defense," available online.

30 Judges 11:27.

31 Samuel Moyn, "Appealing to Heaven: Jephthah, John Locke, and Just War," *Hebraic Political Studies* 4:3 (Summer 2009): 286–303. See also the commentary of Gersonides on Judges, chapter 16, "*toelet dalet.*"

32 Deuteronomy 8:17.

33 Psalms 46:6–7.

34 Zechariah 4:6.

35 I Samuel 17:46–57.

36 I Samuel 18:6–7.

37 *Midrash Tehillim*, ed. Buber 52:3.

38 Avot 4:1, *Avot DeRabbi Natan* 23.

39 For analysis of this form of reinterpretation, see Eliezer Berkovits, *With God in Hell* (1979), chapter 9; Aviezer Ravitsky, *Al Daat HaMakom* (Keter, 1991), 13–33; and Aryeh Edrei, "Divine Spirit and Physical Power: Rabbi Shlomo Goren and the Military Ethic of the Israel Defense Forces," *Theoretical Inquiries in Law* 7:1 (January 2005): 262–67.

40 Gendler, ed., *A Passionate Pacifist*, 194.

41 See Micha Yosef Berdichevsky, "The Question of Culture," in Arthur Hertzberg, *The Zionist Idea* (JPS, 1959), 297.

42 Steven Zipperstein, *Pogrom: Kishinev and the Tilt of History* (Liveright, 2018), 85–90, 115, 133.

43 See Amos Funkenstein, "Passivity as the Characteristic of the Diaspora Jews: Myth and Reality," and David Biale, *Power and Powerlessness in Jewish History* (Schocken, 1986), 72–77.

44 "If You Don't Have the Power to Pay," in *Selected Poems of Shmuel HaNagid*, ed. Peter Cole (Princeton, 1996), 83 (emphasis in original). See also his poem "First War," p. 106.

45 See Steven Bowman, "'Yosippon' and Jewish Nationalism," *Proceedings of the American Academy for Jewish Research*, vol. 61

(1995), 23–51 and Yael S. Feldman, "Not as Sheep Led to Slaughter?" On Trauma, Selective Memory, and the Making of Historical Consciousness," *Jewish Social Studies: History, Culture, Society* 19:3 (Spring-Summer 2013): 139–69.

46 See his letter to Rabbi Tzvi Yehuda Kook, cited in Luz, *Wrestling with an Angel*, 126.

47 Ideas in this paragraph draw from Rabbi Eliezer Berkovits, *With God in Hell*, and Rabbi Shlomo Goren, "Ruaḥ VeKoaḥ BaMishnat HaYahadut" (*Maḥanayim* 100) and "HaGevura BaMishnat HaYahadut" (*Maḥanayim* 120).

48 C. Fink, "The Search for Peace in the Interwar Period," *The Cambridge History of War*, R. Chickering et al, eds., (Cambridge: Cambridge University Press, 2012), 285–309.

49 Paul Mendes-Flohr, *Martin Buber: A Life of Faith and Dissent* (Yale, 2019), chapter 5.

50 The letters from Gandhi and Buber are printed in *A Land of Two Peoples: Martin Buber on Jews and Arabs*, ed. Paul Mendes-Flohr (University of Chicago Press, 1983), 106–26. For the quote from Buber, see p. 125.

51 Maurice Lamm, "After the War – Another Look at Pacifism and Selective Conscientious Objection," in *Contemporary Jewish Ethics*, ed. Menachem Kellner (New York, 1978), 224–25.

52 Interestingly, Buddhists in places like Sri Lanka and Myanmar have begun to reject pacifism because they recognize the vices of powerlessness in the face of Islamic aggression. See Hannah Beech, "Our Duty to Fight: The Rise of Militant Buddhism," *New York Times*, July 9, 2019.

CHAPTER 2: TOTAL WAR, RELIGIOUS FUNDAMENTALISM, AND THE GHOSTS OF CANAAN

1 *Orot*, trans. B. Naor (Maggid, 2015), 95. The original passage may be found in a recently published diary of Rabbi Kook. See *Pinkasei HaRaayah*, vol. 7, Jaffa-Switzerland period (Jerusalem, 5782), entry 241, 242–43. This corrects the claim of the otherwise fascinating article of Hanoch Ben-Pazi, "R. Abraham Isaac Kook and the Opening

Passage of 'The War,'" *Journal of Jewish Thought and Philosophy* 25 (2017): pp. 256–78.

2 Gendler, ed., *A Passionate Pacifist*, 132–40.

3 See his "Teudat Yisrael ULeumiyuto" (Israel's Mission and Its Nationhood), printed in *Azkarah Le-Nishmat HaGaon HaTzaddik HaRav Avraham Yitzhak Hakohen Kook*, vol. 1, ed. Yehuda Fishman (Mossad Harav Kook, 5697–8), 60–61, 69–70, and 89–94. (This work is also printed in *Otzrot HaRaayah*, ed. Moshe Tzuriel, vol. 2 (Rishon Letzion, 5762), 25–65.) See also *Ein Aya, Berakhot*, chapter 1, no. 744. On R. Kook's thought in this period, see Yehuda Mirsky, *Towards the Mystical Experience of Modernity: The Making of Rav Kook, 1865–1904* (2021), 251–59.

4 Kook, "Teudat Yisrael ULeumiyuto," 94.

5 Ibid., 91.

6 *Olat Raayah*, I, 234; emphasis added. The passage draws from *Ein Aya*, vol. 1, no. 77, 69–70. Rabbi Kook's thoughts on the merits and perils of nationalism are also captured in paragraphs 173–76. See also Shtamlar, *Ayin BeAyin*, 194, n. 136.

7 *Kevatzim MiKhetav Yad Kodsho*, ed. Boaz Ofen, vol. 3 (Jerusalem, 2018), *pinkas* 5, par. 43, pp. 96–97 and Kook, *LeNevukhei Dor* (Tel Aviv, 2014), 50–52.

8 Kook, *Orot*, 98.

9 Ibid., 96.

10 *Eder Hayakar*, 52–53.

11 On "total war," see David A. Bell, *The First Total War: Napoleon's Europe and the Birth of Warfare as We Know It* (Boston and New York, 2007); Roger Chickering, "Total War: The Use and Abuse of a Concept," in Manfred F. Boemeke et al., eds., *Anticipating Total War: The German and American Experiences, 1871–1914* (Cambridge, 1999), 13–28; and Talbot Imlay, "Total War," *Journal of Strategic Studies* 30:3 (2007), 547–70.

12 William O'Brien, *The Conduct of Just and Limited War*, 222–34.

13 Johnson, *Just War Tradition and the Restraint of War*, 229–77.

14 See, for example, John Buckley, *Air Power in the Age of Total War* (Indiana, 1999).

15 See II Samuel 8:3–6; Psalms 18:44–48; *Targum to Psalms* 60:1–2; I Chronicles 22:8 and the commentary of Rabbi David Kimchi; the discussion in Goren, *Meshiv Milḥama*, vol. 1, 18–25 and Stuart A. Cohen, "'Unlicensed' War in Jewish Tradition: Sources, Consequences and Implications," *Journal of Military Ethics* 4:3 (2005): 198–213.

16 Michael Walzer, "The Ethics of Warfare in the Jewish Tradition," 636, citing the language of Maimonides, *Mishneh Torah, Hilkhot Melakhim* 5:1. We'll discuss this category more extensively in chapters 13 and 15.

17 Deuteronomy 7:2.

18 See, for example, Deuteronomy 12:29–31 and 20:18.

19 See Joshua, chapters 10–12 and Judges, chapter 2. For analysis, see Nili Wazana, "'Everything Was Fulfilled' versus 'The Land That Yet Remains'" and Schwartz, "Reexamining the Fate of the 'Canaanites' in the Torah Traditions."

20 See Genesis 15:16; Deuteronomy 13:13–19 and Deuteronomy, chapter 28. For ethical qualms about these passages, see Moshe Halbertal, *Interpretive Revolutions in the Making* (Jerusalem, 1999), 122–44.

21 Richard Dawkins, *The God Delusion* (Boston, 2006), 237.

22 See, for example, Reuven Firestone, *Holy War in Judaism* (Oxford, 2012) and the literature cited therein.

23 See *Mishneh Torah, Hilkhot Melakhim* 6:1 and Rabbi Shlomo of Chelm's commentary *Mirkevet HaMishneh*.

24 *Midrash Tanchuma* (ed. Buber), *Tzav* 5; emphasis added. See also Y. Shevi'it 6:1 and Deuteronomy Rabba (ed. Vilna) 5:13. On these passages, see Dov Weiss, *Pious Irreverence: Confronting God in Rabbinic Judaism* (Philadelphia, 2017), 168–79.

25 Proverbs 3:17.

26 See, for example, Simon Federbusch, *Mishpat HaMelukha BeYisrael*, 2nd ed. (Jerusalem, 1973), 218–19 and Zev Gold, *Nivei Zahav*, 509.

27 For various approaches, see the articles of Shalom Carmy and Norman Lamm in *War and Peace in the Jewish Tradition*, ed. L. Schiffman and J. Wolowelsky (New York, 2007); the essays of Menachem Kellner and Dov Schwartz in *The Gift of the Land and the Fate of the Canaanites in Jewish Thought*, ed. K. Berthelot, J. David, and M. Hirshman (Oxford, 2014); and Avi Sagi, "The Punishment

of Amalek in Jewish Tradition: Coping with the Moral Problem," *Harvard Theological Review* 87:3 (July 1994): 323–46.

28 Exodus 20:5.

29 Ezekiel 18:20. The sentiment already appears in Deuteronomy 24:16 and II Kings 14:16. According to one midrash, this change also occurred because of the protest of Moses. See Weiss, *Pious Irreverence*, 173.

30 See, for example, the comments of Rabbi Yosef Babab, *Minhat Hinukh* 604:5, based on Yadayim 4:4 and *Shu"t Avnei Nezer* OH 508.

31 Rabbi Jonathan Sacks, *Not in God's Name: Confronting Religious Violence* (Jerusalem, 2016), 220, 226.

32 For similar conclusions, see Rabbi Shlomo Goren, *Meshiv Milhama*, vol. 1, 14 and Rabbi Neria Gutel, "Lehima BeShetah Ravei Ukhlusiya Ezrahit," in *Tehumin* 23 (5763): 22 n. 16. (Gutel's article is also reprinted in *HaMilhama BaTerror*, ed. Yair Halevi (Kiryat Arba, 2006).

33 See Elliot Horowitz, *Reckless Rites: Purim and the Legacy of Jewish Violence*, 107–46.

34 See, for example, Rabbi Joseph B. Soloveitchik, *Kol Dodi Dofek*, trans. David Z. Gordon (2006), 79, 112–14. Such rhetoric was rejected by Rabbi Tzvi Yehuda Kook. See Rabbi Nahum Eliezer Rabinovitch, *Shu"t Melumadei Milhama*, 22–25.

35 Ronen Luvitch, "Mehiyat Amalek VeHaOyev Aravi," *She'anan* 22 (5777): 43–78.

36 *Iggerot HaRaayah*, vol. 1, no. 108.

37 For a listing of the letters that R. Kook writes to Seidel, see Neria Gutel, *Mekutevei Raayah* (R. Tzvi Yehuda Institute, 5760), 52 and 102–3. Topics include free choice, Darwinian evolution, and intellectual freedom.

38 *Iggerot HaRaayah*, vol. 1, nos. 89–91.

39 Ibid., p. 94.

40 Ibid., p. 100.

41 In *Shemoneh Kevatzim*, vol. 1, 125, no. 444, R. Kook suggests that Saul's error was trying to show mercy to Amalek's descendants when the world was not ready for it. See also his statement recorded in *Middot HaRaayah* (ed. Yuval Carmi, *Ahavah*, no. 6, p. 16) that even

Amalek is worthy of love, at least in the "upper spheres" of the world. His son, Rabbi Tzvi Yehuda, explained that in this world, there are "realpolitik" considerations (his words) that mandate we destroy Amalek. See *Siḥot R. Tzvi Yehuda: Middot*, ed. Shlomo Aviner (Jerusalem, 5773), 29.

42 *Maamarei HaRaayah*, 508–9.

43 For other examples of this line of thinking in R. Kook's thought, see Don Seeman, "Evolutionary Ethics: The *Taamei HaMitzvot* of Rav Kook," *Ḥakira* 26 (2019): 13–55.

44 See his statements in *Responsum Mishpat Kohen*, nos. 44, 145. See also his comments in the twenty-second *derasha* of Midbar Shur. For a similar statement, see Rabbi J. David Bleich, "Preemptive War in Jewish Law," *Tradition* 21:1 (Spring 1983): 6. More broadly, see Aviezer Ravitsky, "Prohibited Laws in Jewish Religious Law," *Meorot* 6:1 (2006): 8–10.

45 See Robert Eisen, *Religious Zionism, Jewish Law, and the Morality of War* (Oxford, 2017), 72–79 as well as R. Eliezer Waldenburg, *Hilkhot Medina*, vol. 2, 119 and R. Yehuda Shaviv, "Le-Mi Mishpat ha-Melukhah?" in *Berurim be-Hilkhot HaRaayah*, eds. R. Moshe Tzvi Neria et al (Beit Harav, 1992), 147–54.

46 *Pinkasei HaRaayah*, vol. 1, 29–30. He adds again a similar sentiment regarding the abolition of slavery.

47 See Deut. 21:10–13 and Kiddushin 21b. For a modern version of this argument, see R. Eliezer Melamed, Peninei Halakha, *Ha-am ve-ha-aretz* 4:18. For a novel "restrictive reinterpretation," see Rabbi Meir Simcha Cohen of Dvinsk, *Meshekh Ḥokhma* on Deuteronomy 21:10 (Jerusalem, 5757), ed. Yehuda Cooperman, vol. 3, 148. See also Walzer, *Just and Unjust Wars*, 133–137; James A. Diamond, "The Deuteronomic 'Pretty Woman' Law: Prefiguring Feminism and Freud in Nahmanides," *Jewish Social Studies* 14:2 (Winter 2008), 61–85; and Shira Weiss, *Ethical Ambiguity in the Hebrew Bible* (Cambridge, 2018), 221–228.

48 *Iggerot HaRaayah*, vol. 1, no. 283, 321. For the basis of this idea, see Makkot 24a and Hayim Angel, *Vision from the Prophet and Counsel from the Elders* (OU Press, 2013), 159–61.

49 *Iggerot HaRaayah,* vol. 1, no. 90. See also Seeman, "Evolutionary Ethics," nn. 48–49.

50 See also Rabbi Shlomo Goren, *Meshiv Milḥama,* vol. 1, 13 and Rabbi Nachum Rabinovitch, *Melumadei Milḥama,* 24–25.

51 The notion of "a developing (halakhic) morality" regarding Amalek is developed by Rabbi Norman Lamm, "Amalek and the Seven Nations: A Case of Law vs. Morality," in *War and Peace in the Jewish Tradition,* ed. L. Schiffman and J. Wolowelsky (New York, 2007), 224–34.

52 See Nili Wazana, "'War Crimes' in Amos's Oracles Against the Nations (Amos 1:3–2:3)," in *Literature as Politics, Politics as Literature,* ed. David S. Vanderhooft and Abraham Winitzer (Winona Lake, IN: Eisenbrauns, 2013), 479–501. See also Federbusch, *Mishpat HaMelukha BeYisrael,* 2nd ed., 190–91.

53 II Chronicles 25:12.

54 Lamentations Rabba, *Petiḥta* 14.

55 See *Iggerot HaRaayah,* vol. 2, 118–20.

56 See the commentary to the Book of Micah in the *Da'at Mikra* series (Mossad Harav Kook).

57 See *Orot Milḥama,* sec. 2, *Midbar Shur, derasha* 29, p. 270; and other sources collected in Hagay Shtamler, *Ayin BeAyin* (Herzog College, 2020), 193–200.

CHAPTER 3: THE LEAGUE OF NATIONS AND THE DASHED HOPE OF INTERNATIONAL LAW

1 *Iggerot HaRaayah,* vol. 3, no. 852, 131–33. See Yitzhak Krauss, "HaTeguvot HaTeologiyot al Hatzharat Balfour," *Sefer Bar Ilan* 28/29 (5761): 81–104.

2 See *Ginzei HaRaayah, Iggerot,* 157–59. See also Ari Shvat, "Sibot Erekh HaGvurah HaFizit VeHaTzvait BaMishnat HaRav Kook," in *Nero Yair* (Mitzpeh Yericho, 5773), 353–394.

3 *Iggerot HaRaayah,* vol. 3, no. 871, 155–59.

4 James Loeffler and Moria Paz, eds., *The Law of Strangers: Jewish Lawyers and International Law in the Twentieth Century* (Cambridge, 2019).

5   See Jeffrey Veidlinger, *In the Midst of Civilized Europe* (Metropolitan, 2021).

6   James Loeffler, *Rooted Cosmopolitans: Jews and Human Rights in the Twentieth Century* (New Haven, 2018), 22–27.

7   Oona A. Hathaway and Scott J. Shapiro, *The Internationalists* (New York, 2018), 298–305.

8   Loeffler, *Rooted Cosmopolitans*, 31–50.

9   Omry Kaplan-Feuereisen and Richard Mann, "At the Service of the Jewish Nation: Jacob Robinson and International Law," *Osteuropa* 58:8/10 (August-October 2008): 164.

10 See Lauterpacht's May 1950 speech given in Jerusalem, cited by Loeffler, *Rooted Cosmopolitans*, 176.

11 *Iggerot HaRaayah*, vol. 2, 54.

12 *Maamarei HaRaayah*, vol. 1, 89–93. See Hagi Ben-Artzi, *HeḤadash Yitkadesh* (Tel Aviv, 2010), 70–73.

13 On the controversy, Mirsky, *Rav Kook*, 167–169, and the introduction to *Orot*, trans. Bezalel Naor (Jerusalem, 2015).

14 *Ḥiddushei HaRav Hayim Hirschensohn LaMasekhta Horayot*, vol. 3, 33a (letter 23). The letter is dated November 1924. On R. Hirschensohn's letter and R. Kook's reply, see Naor's introduction to *Orot*.

15 Luz, *Wrestling with an Angel*, 222, regards R. Hirschensohn as the only religious-Zionist thinker who was systematically engaging in political thinking.

16 Colin Schindler, *The Rise of the Israeli Right: From Odessa to Hebrew* (Cambridge, 2015), chapter 7.

17 Cited in Michael Keren and Shlomit Keren, *We are Coming, Unafraid: The Jewish Legions and the Promised Land in the First World War* (Lanham, MD, 2010), 116.

18 R. Kook's letter to Chief Rabbi Hertz is found in *Iggerot HaRaayah*, vol. 3, no. 859. See Rosenak, *HaRav Kook*, 156–60.

19 *Iggerot HaRaayah*, vol. 3, no. 974. R. Kook further advised Falk on how to maintain standards of dietary law observance.

20 Ari Shvat, *Leharim et HaDegel*, chapter 11.

21 Warren Ze'ev Harvey, "Rabbi Reines on the Conquest of Canaan and Zionism," in *The Gift of the Land and the Fate of the Canaanites*, ed. Katell Berthelot et al. (Oxford, 2014), 386–98.

22 *Malki BaKodesh*, vol. 1, 18–22, 142–63.

23 Hayim Hirschensohn, *Eleh Divrei HaBrit*, 70, 79. R. Kook had also tentatively suggested this idea but ultimately rejected it. See R. Kook, *Tov Ro'i: Sota*, 22. For another openly apologetic attempt to limit the meaning of this commandment to not require annihilation, see Rabbi Tzvi Mecklenberg, *HaKetav VeHaKabbala* on Deuteronomy 20:16.

24 Hirschensohn, *Eleh Divrei HaBrit*, 70.

25 *Malki BaKodesh*, vol. 1, 15–16.

26 Loeffler, *Rooted Cosmopolitans*, 14–15.

27 *Malki BaKodesh*, vol. 2, 5–31 (which includes part of R. Kook's letter), especially pp. 26–28.

28 Ibid., vol. 1, 11.

29 *Iggerot HaRaayah*, vol. 4, 23–25. Also printed in *Malki BaKodesh*, vol. 4, 4–5. On the relation of these passages to the depiction of a future Temple in Herzl's utopian novel, *Old-New Land*, see Eyal Ben-Eliyahu, "Lehakim Binyan Ḥadash?" *Cathedra* 128 (Tamuz 5768), 101–12.

30 *Malki BaKodesh*, vol. 1, 62–64. See also p. 56.

31 Ibid., vol. 4, 8.

32 Ibid., vol. 2, 28. He emphasizes that these holy sites should be utilized for the search for wisdom, not extremism. On the history of Jewish attempts to purchase holy sites in Palestine, including areas around the Temple Mount, see Dotan Goren, *UVa LeTziyon Goel* (Beit El, 2017).

33 This is implied in R. Hirschensohn's follow up letter.

34 R. Hirschensohn, *Eleh Divrei HaBrit*, introduction.

35 Ibid., 8. The importance of reciprocity is made explicit in *Midrash Shoḥer Tov* on Psalms 60:2 regarding the wartime behavior of King David.

36 Hirschensohn, *Eleh Divrei HaBrit*, 13–14.

37 R. Hirschensohn may have in mind the notion of the "standards of civilization" that circulated since the nineteenth century within international legal circles and has made a recent revival. See David P. Fidler, "The Return of the Standard of Civilization," *Chicago Journal of International Law* 2:1 (2001): 137–57.

38 This might even mean upholding agreements made under false pretenses. Following talmudic precedent, he noted that Joshua chose to maintain his peace treaty with the Gibeonites, one of the Canaaanite nations, in spite of the fact they had fooled the Israelites into thinking that they came from distant lands. While the treaty was not compulsory, the Israelites kept their promise since others would think they didn't keep their word. See Hirschensohn, *Eleh Divrei HaBrit*, 71–72.

39 *Malki BaKodesh*, vol. 1, 143–49.

40 *Eleh Divrei HaBrit*, 175–76.

41 Ibid., 37–38.

42 For a similar attitude in more recent writing, see Rabbi Yaakov Ariel, *Halakha BeYamenu* (Ashkelon, Machon HaTorah VeHaAretz, 5770), 378.

43 On the veracity of this final statement and Trumpeldor's broader relationship to Judaism, see Moshe Nahmani, *HaGibbor HaLeumi: Perakim BeHayav shel Yosef Trumpeldor* (2020), 131–256.

44 See Tamares, *Shelosha Zivugim Bilti Hagunim* (Pietrkow, 1930), 9, 40, 60–61.

45 *Malki BaKodesh*, vol. 2, 159–160.

46 *Otzrot HaRaayah*, vol. 1, 393–95.

47 *Iggerot HaRaayah*, vol. 5, 333.

48 As cited in Hillel Cohen, *1929: Year Zero of the Arab-Israeli Conflict* (Brandeis, 2015), Kindle location 1755. See also R. Kook's testimony to the British investigation commission published in *Otzrot HaRaayah*, ed. Moshe Tzuriel, vol. 2, 359–60. On R. Kook's reaction to the 1929 riots, see Yosef Sharvit, "HaRav Kook UMeoraot 5689," *Sinai* 97 (5745): 153–85.

49 Central Zionist Archives, A176/11.

50 Loeffler, *Rooted Cosmopolitans*, 28–30, 49–50.

51 *Iggerot HaRaayah*, vol. 5, 143 and *Maamarei HaRaayah*, 252–53. See also Mirsky, *Rav Kook*, 196–202 and Shtamler, *Ayin BeAyin*, 199–201. R. Kook also told that Zionist Congress that he regretted how the fight over the Western Wall became such a flash point. See Cohen, *1929*, Kindle location 4665–4680, based on documents found in Central Zionist Archives S100/10.

52 Kook, *Ḥazon HaGeula* (Jerusalem, 5701), 46–47.

53 Ibid., 56–57.

54 Jacob Robinson, "International Protection of Minorities: A Global View," *Israeli Yearbook on Human Rights* (1971): 61–91. See Loeffler, *Rooted Cosmopolitans*, 171–201 and Gil Rubin, "The End of Minority Rights: Jacob Robinson and the 'Jewish Question' in World War II," *Simon Dubnow Institute Yearbook* 11 (2012): 55–71. Rubin describes Robinson's later career as one of a "reluctant internationalist." See his article, "A State of Their Own: Jewish Internationalism and Human Rights," *Marginalia*, June 6, 2018.

55 For a survey of positions, see Amos Israel-Vleeschhouwer, "Yaḥas HaHalakha LaMishpat HaBeinleumi" (unpublished PhD diss., Tel Aviv University, 2011).

56 See Soloveitchik, *Kol Dodi Dofek*, 31–32.

57 See Rabbi Hayim David HaLevi, *Dat UMedina*, 21–22, 37–38.

58 Rabbi Shaul Yisraeli, *Amud HaYemini, siman* 16, 195.

59 Michael B. Oren, *Six Days of War: June 1967 and the Making of the Modern Middle East*, 67–75.

60 See, for example, Dore Gold, *Tower of Babble: How the United Nations Has Fueled Global Chaos* (Forum, 2004); Justin S. Gruenberg, "An Analysis of United Nations Security Council Resolutions: Are All Countries Treated Equally?," *Case Western Reserve Journal of International Law* 513 (2009): 41. Gerald M. Steinberg, "The UN, the ICJ and the Separation Barrier: War by Other Means," *Israel Law Review* 38:1–2 (Winter-Spring 2005): 331–47.

61 See, for example, Rabbi Avraham Sharir, "Etika Tzeva'it al pi Halakhah," *Teḥumin* 25 (5765), 436 and Rabbi Avraham Sherman, "HaMishpat HaBeinleumi (BaMilḥama) LeOhr Mishpetei HaTorah," *Torah SheBe'al Peh* 44 (5764), 74. See also Rabbi Yaakov Ariel, *Halakha BeYamenu*, 378.

62 André Nollkaemper, "'Failures to Protect' in International Law," in *The Oxford Handbook of the Use of Force in International Law*, ed. Marc Weller (Oxford, 2015), 439.

63 Paul Kennedy, *The Parliament of Man* (Vintage, 2007), Kindle location 495.

64 See Ana Filipa Vrdoljak, "Human Rights and Genocide: The Work of Lauterpacht and Lemkin in Modern International Law," *The European Journal of International Law* 20:4 (2010): 1163–94.

65 Ben Rhodes, "Inside the White House During the Syrian 'Red Line' Crisis," *Atlantic*, June 3, 2018.

66 "The Ambassador to the UN's Case against the UN," *Atlantic*, Sept 6, 2013; "Samantha Power's Case for Striking Syria," *Washington Post*, Sept 7, 2013.

67 See Natasha Bertrand and Michael B Kelley, "The Startlingly Simple Reason Obama Ignores Syria," *Business Insider*, June 4, 2015.

68 See, for example, Tony Badran, "'Ambassador Samantha Power Lied to My Face about Syria,' by Kassem Eid," *Tablet*, February 27, 2018 and Steve Bloomfield, "The Obama Administration's Misadventures in Foreign Policy," *Prospect Magazine*, November 2019.

69 An exemplar of this idea was Israel's first Ashkenazic chief rabbi, Yitzhak Herzog, who wrote about Jewish law while in dialogue with international norms and ethical standards. See our discussion in chapter 14 as well as R. Herzog's essay on minority rights in Israel, "Zehuyot HaMi'utim Lefi HaHalakha," *Tehumin* 2, 169–179.

CHAPTER 4: REPRISAL KILLINGS, "PURITY OF ARMS," AND THE 1936–1939 ARAB RIOTS

1 For local reports, see "Jew Killed, 2 Wounded in Jerusalem; Troops Hunt Bands Near Nablus," *JTA Bulletin*, October 31, 1937 and "Six Jews Slain in Arab Ambush on J.N.F. Fields Near Jerusalem," *JTA Bulletin*, Nov 10, 1937.

2 "Arab Killed, 5 Injured in Jerusalem Bombing; 5 O'clock Curfew Imposed," *JTA Bulletin*, Nov 12, 1937.

3 Meir Chazan, "The Dispute in Mapai over 'Self-Restraint' and 'Purity of Arms' during the Arab Revolt," *Jewish Social Studies: History, Culture, Society* 15:3 (Spring-Summer 2009): 89–113.

4 During the wave of suicide bombings during the second intifada in 2002, one prominent American constitutional attorney suggested that Israel should immediately kill the immediate relatives of the murderer, unless they renounced the despicable act at once and

refused any financial or other benefit from it. Unethical, you say? His response: "If executing some suicide-bomber families saves the lives of even an equal number of potential civilian victims, the exchange is, I believe, ethically permissible. It is a policy born of necessity – the need to find a true deterrent when capital punishment is demonstrably ineffective." See Nathan Lewin, "Deterring Suicide Bombers," *Sh'ma: A Journal of Jewish Ideas* (May 2002).

5 Daniel K. Heller, *Jabotinsky's Children: Polish Jews and the Rise of Right-Wing Zionism* (Princeton, 2017), 224–27.

6 Rabbi Yehoshua Weisinger, "Rabbeinu VeIrgunei HaMaḥteret," *Shemaatin* 183: 71–103.

7 Raziel, "Hagana Aktivit," in *Be-Harev* (March 1938).

8 Articles 27–28 of the Lieber Code (General order no. 100), available online at https://avalon.law.yale.edu/19th_century/lieber.asp#art27. On the Lieber Code, see John Fabian Witt, *Lincoln's Code: The Laws of War in American History* (New York, 2012).

9 As cited in Patryk I. Labuda, "The Lieber Code, Retaliation and the Origins of International Criminal Law," *Historical Origins of International Criminal Law: Volume 3*, ed. M. Bergsmo et al., (TOAEP 2015), 312–13.

10 Suspicion of reprisal motivations was well expressed by Geoffrey Best: "One of the earliest lessons that a student of the law has to learn is to be on his guard when he hears the word reprisal. Deeper hypocrisy and duplicity attach to it than any other term of the art." See his book *War and Law Since 1945*, 203. On the psychology of revenge in war, see Dave Grossman, *On Killing*, 179.

11 Shane Darcy, "The Evolution of the Law of Belligerent Reprisals," *Military Law Review* 175 (2003): 184–251.

12 Alexander Gillespie, *A History of the Laws of War, Volume 2: The Customs and Laws of War with Regards to Civilians in Times of Conflict* (Oxford, 2011), 81–83. On the status of reprisals in international law at the time, see Olivier Barsalou, "The History of Reprisals Up to 1945: Some Lessons Learned and Unlearned for Contemporary International Law," *Military Law and the Law of War Review* 49:3–4 (2010): 335–67.

13 For different ways in which the various underground groups utilized the image of Gideon, see Hilda Schatzberger, *Meri UMesoret BeEretz Yisrael BaTekufat HaMandat* (Ramat Gan, 1983), 54.

14 Trevor Royle, *Orde Wingate: A Man of Genius 1903–1944* (London, 2010), 114–21, 127.

15 Shapira, *Land and Power*, 250–52. On the controversy over Wingate's legacy, see Michael Oren, "Orde Wingate: Friend Under Fire," *Azure* 10 (Winter 5761/ 001): 33–49.

16 John Berman and Colin Smith, *Fire in the Night: Wingate of Burma, Ethiopia, and Zion* (Random House, 1999), 115–16.

17 Hillel Halkin, *Jabotinsky: A Life* (Yale, 2019), 207–11.

18 Heller, *Jabotinsky's Children*, 234.

19 Bruce Hoffman, *Anonymous Soldiers*, 97.

20 Halkin, *Jabotinsky: A Life*, 211.

21 Additional Protocol I (1977), article 51, par. 6.

22 Michael Walzer, *Just and Unjust Wars*, 3rd ed. (Basic Books, 2000), 207–22. It should be noted that figures like Walzer appreciate the logic that would permit reprisals: "I don't want to claim that those old arguments have no force at all. They correctly point to a certain moral difference between the initial crime and the reprisal-response." As proof, he notes his initial sympathies (but ultimately condemnation) for the French execution of eighty German prisoners of war in retaliation for the execution by the Nazis of eighty French soldiers (organized under the French Forces of the Interior). He further notes that German executions of French POWs ceased afterward, although that may have been for many reasons. See *Just and Unjust Wars*, 215.

23 For a summary of mainstream contemporary legal positions on reprisals, see Yoram Dinstein, *The Conduct of Hostilities under the Law of International Armed Conflict*, 3rd ed. (Cambridge, 2016), 289–96.

24 Frits Kalshoven, *Belligerent Reprisals* (Nijhoff Publishers, 1971), 377.

25 More broadly, see Gary Jonathan Bass, *Stay the Hand of Vengeance: The Politics of War Crimes Tribunals* (Princeton, 2002).

26 For a defense of this policy, see Jeremy Rabkin and John Yoo, *Striking Power: How Cyber, Robots, and Space Weapons Change the Rule of Law*, 76–81, 109–25.

27 For legal and moral debates on this strike, see the special spring 1987 issue of the *Case Western Reserve Journal of International Law.*

28 James Turner Johnson, *Just War Tradition and the Restraint of Warfare* (Princeton, 1981), 20–21.

29 See Schatzberger, *Meri UMesoret*, 73–84. See also Hilda Nesimi, "Mesoret Yehudit UMered HaEtzel: Ezer Kenegdo?", *Cathedra* 121 (Tishrei 5767): 137–70.

30 See Eliezer Don-Yehiya, *Bein Shalom LeShlemut HaAretz* (Ben-Gurion University Press, 2019), 102–4.

31 R. Maimon draws from the commentary of Maimonides, *Mishneh Torah, Hilkhot Melakhim* 9:14. See also Rabbi Isaac Arama, *Akedat Yitzḥak: Bereshit, Vayera*, gate 20, s.v. *uveMidrash and Shu"t Hatam Sofer Likutim* 6:14. For an analysis and rejection of the notion of "responsible bystanders," see Kai Draper, "Self-Defense, Collective Obligation, and Non-Combatant Liability," *Social Theory and Practice* 24 (1998): 57–81.

32 For medieval explanations of this biblical passage, see Menahem Finkelstein, "Tohar HaNeshek: BaYamim HaHahem UBazman Hazeh," *Parashat HaShavua* 235 (*Vayishlaḥ*, 5766). For the use of this passage in contemporary Jewish ethical discourse, see Yaakov Blidstein, "The Treatment of Hostile Civilian Populations: The Contemporary Halakhic Discussion in Israel," *Israel Studies* 1:2 (Fall 1996): pp. 27–45.

33 Hoffman, *Anonymous Soldiers*, 97. Hoffman claims that by the time World War II broke out in 1939, the Etzel had killed more than 250 Arabs over these three years and wounded hundreds more.

34 Bava Kamma 60a.

35 See, for example, Yehoshua Heschel Yevin in *Havlaga o Teguva*, ed. Yaakov Shavit (Ramat Gan, 1983), 91.

36 See Igor Primoratz, "Civilian Immunity in War: Its Grounds, Scope, and Weight" and Colm McKeogh, "Civilian Immunity in War: From Augustine to Vattel," in *Civilian Immunity in War*, ed. Igor Primoratz (Oxford, 2007).

37 Shmuel Katz, *Lone Wolf: A Biography of Vladimir (Ze'ev) Jabotinsky* (Kindle locations 18068–18071) (Plunkett Lake Press, Kindle edition).

38 This sentiment was made clear in a 1938 letter by the Etzel leadership to the National Assembly. They ended the letter with a quote from Isaiah (48:10): "Cursed be he who is slack in doing the Lord's work. Cursed be he who withholds his sword from blood." See Shavit, ed., *Havlaga o Teguva*, 109.

39 This was an allusion to the thirteenth principle of interpretation by the talmudic sage, R. Yishmael, "When two biblical passages contradict each other the contradiction in question must be solved by reference to a third passage."

40 The position of Rabbi Meir Bar-Ilan was somewhat unclear. See Aminadav Yitzhaki, *HaRav Meir Bar-Ilan* (unpublished PhD diss., Bar-Ilan University, 5775), 172–83.

41 Don-Yehiya, *Bein Shalom LeShlemut HaAretz*, 105.

42 Deuteronomy 19:10. See also 21:8.

43 For a recent formulation of the biblical notion of nationalism, see R. Meir Soloveichik, "For Israel to deserve independence, it must remember that it exists for a calling more important than independence itself." See also Uriel Simon, "The Biblical Destinies – Conditional Promises," *Tradition* 17:2 (Spring 1978): 84–90.

44 See, for example, the comments of Rashi and Maharal of Prague to Genesis 32:8. On these traditions, see Yitzchak Blau, "Biblical Narratives and the Status of Enemy Civilians in Wartime," *Tradition* 39:4 (Winter 2006): 12–15.

45 Uziel's positions were recorded in Shavit, ed., *Havlaga o Teguva*, 153–56.

46 Shulamit Eliash, *The Harp and the Shield of David: Ireland, Zionism and the State of Israel* (Taylor & Francis, 2007), 32–48.

47 Shapira, *Land and Power*, 237–38, and Luz, *Wrestling with an Angel*, 204–5.

48 Chazan, "The Dispute in Mapai," 101. On his general approach, see Shaul Mayzlish, *The Rabbinate in Stormy Times*, 51–63 and Don-Yehiya, *Bein Shalom LeShlemut HaAretz*, 94–96.

49 Ezekiel 36:22–36, 28:20–26. See the commentary of Rabbi Yosef Kara on Ezekiel 36:23. See also *Sifre Devarim* 306. On notions of *kiddush Hashem* in antiquity, see the sources cited in Adiel Shremer, "Nekadesh Et Shimḥa BaOlam," *Reishit* 3 (5779), 1–21.

50 See their publications cited in Shatzberger, *Meri UMesoret*, 96–97 and Mordechai Bar-Lev, "HaYesodot HaIdeologim shel Brit Hashmona'im," in *Dat UMaḥteret BeEretz Yisrael BaTekufat HaMandat*, ed. Hayim Genizi (Tel Aviv, 1995), 159–66. After World War II, this group joined the Haganah. See Shaul Avishai, *Brit HaHashmona'im* (Jerusalem, 2007), 124–57.

51 On the different ways that the various groups portrayed the Hanukka story to serve their agenda, see Eliezer Don-Yehiya, "Hanukkah and the Myth of the Maccabees in Zionist Ideology and in Israeli Society," *Jewish Journal of Sociology* 34:1 (June 1992): 5–24.

52 Based on Exodus 32:11–14. See also Joshua 7:9 and Psalms 115:2. This sentiment would be popularized later by R. Tzvi Yehuda who saw the commandment to settle the Land of Israel as an absolute imperative and the mass return to Zion as the beginning of the Messianic Era. The younger R. Kook would assert that the Jewish powerlessness that led to the Holocaust was the greatest *ḥillul Hashem*, while Jewish sovereignty over its land, including its military victories over its enemies, was the greatest *kiddush Hashem*. See Elie *Holzer, Ḥerev Pipiyot BeYadam*, 221–24.

53 For different possible ethical implications of seeking God's honor, see Don Seeman, "God's Honor, Violence and the State," in *Swords into Plowshares: Reflections on Religion and Violence*, eds. Robert W. Jensen and Eugene Korn (Efrat, Israel, 2014): 1015–48.

CHAPTER 5: SUPREME EMERGENCIES AND THE ETHICAL IMPERATIVE OF SURVIVAL, 1938

1 Published in *Teḥumin*, vol. 10, 148. On Amiel's broader worldview, see Holzer, *Ḥerev Pipiyot BeYadam* (Jerusalem, 2009), 183–201. For a contemporary defense of the absolute prohibition against targeting civilians, even in a time of supreme emergency, see C. A. J. Coady, "Terrorism, Just War, and Supreme Emergency," in *Terrorism and Justice*, ed. C. Coady and M. O'Keefe (Melbourne, 2002).

2 Anita Shapira, "Bein Terror LeHavlaga: HaKinus HaYishuvi BeYuli 1938," *HaTziyonut* 6 (1981): 359–425.

3 This perspective has been called "weak realism" by Jeff McMahan, yet the utilization of the term "realism" may be more confounding than

illuminating in this context. See McMahan, "Realism, Morality, and War," in *The Ethics of War and Peace: Religious and Secular Perspectives,* ed. Terry Nardin (Princeton, 1996), 82–83.

4 Thomas Nagel, "War and Massacre," *Philosophy and Public Affairs* 1:2 (Winter 1971–72): 123–44.

5 *Shu"t Mishpat Kohen,* Siman 143. See Nahum Rakover, *Mesirut Nefesh* (Jerusalem, 2000) for further analysis.

6 This formulation follows Kia Nielson, "There Is No Dilemma of Dirty Hands," in Paul Rynard and David P. Shugarman, eds., *Cruelty and Deception: The Controversy over Dirty Hands in Politics* (Peterborough, Ontario, 2000), 139–55.

7 Michael Stocker, *Pluralism and Conflicting Values* (Oxford, 1992), 9–36.

8 Kook, *Shu"t Mishpat Kohen* 144, based on *Tanna Devei Eliyahu Rabba* 14:2. See Neria Gutel, *Hadashim Gam Yeshanim,* 140–44 and Hagi Ben-Artzi, *HeHadash Yitkadesh* (Tel Aviv, 2010), 253–59.

9 See his *Mei Marom,* vol. 9, 254 and vol. 16, 85.

10 See, for example, Ruti G. Teitel, *Humanity's Law,* (Oxford, 2011) and David Luban, "Human Rights Thinking and the Laws of War," *Georgetown Law Faculty Publications and Other Works* (2015), 1474.

11 Avishai Margalit and Michael Walzer, "Israel: Civilians and Combatants," *New York Review of Books,* May 14, 2009.

12 Nagel, "War and Massacre," 59.

13 Antonio Cassese, as cited in Amanda Alexander, "A Short History of International Humanitarian Law," *European Journal of International Law* 26:1 (2015): 109–38.

14 For Jewish perspectives on torture in these cases, see Shlomo Brody, "Does Jewish Law Allow Torture?", *Tablet,* December 12, 2014.

15 Daniel Statman, "Supreme Emergencies Revisited," *Ethics* 117 (October 2006): 58–79.

16 Michael Walzer, "Terrorism and Just War," *Philosophia* 34 (2006): 7.

17 See the articles of Yaakov Shavit and Liat Shtayer-Livni, Daniel Blatman, and Eli Tzur in *Ish BaSaar: Masot UMehkarim al Ze'ev Jabotinsky,* ed. Avi Bareli and Pinhas Ginossar (Be'er Sheva, 2004), 345–416.

18 Rick Richman, *Racing against History* (New York, 2018), 72–75, and Heller, *Jabotinsky's Children*, 226–29. See also Richman's "Could Jewish and Zionist Leaders Have Done More to Rescue the Jews of Poland?" *Mosaic Magazine*, Feb. 5, 2019.

19 Quoted in Benzion Netanyahu, *Jabotinsky's Place in the History of the Jewish People* (Haifa, 1981), 15, emphasis added.

20 See the introduction to Ze'ev Jabotinsky, *Iggrot 1939*, ed. Moshe HaLevi (Jerusalem, 2016).

21 Max Abrahms, *Rules for Rebels* (Oxford, 2018). The claim, it should be emphasized, is referring specially to rebel groups seeking independence, not state armies engaged in general warfare. See also Hoffman, *Anonymous Soldiers*, 472–84.

22 See James Sterba, "Terrorism and International Justice," in *Terrorism and International Justice*, ed. Sterba (Oxford University Press, 2003). In contrast, see Igor Primoratz, "Terrorism in the Israeli-Palestinian Conflict: A Case Study in Applied Ethics," *Iyyun: The Jerusalem Philosophical Quarterly* 55 (January 2006): 27–48, who discusses the 1936–39 hostilities among other incidents in the Arab-Israeli conflict, and concludes that they are not justifiable because they were not effective.

23 Michael L. Gross, *The Ethics of Insurgency* (Cambridge, 2015), 158. See also Avi Kober, "From Blitzkrieg to Attrition: Israel's Attrition Strategy and Staying Power," *Small Wars and Insurgencies* 16:2 (2005): 216–40 and Meir Elran, "Israel's National Resilience: The Influence of the Intifada on Israeli Society" (JCSS, 2005).

24 Soloveitchik, *Kol Dodi Dofek*, 40. R. Soloveitchik delivered this address on April 16, 1956, and from the previous sentence, he seems particularly to be referring to the IDF response to a terror attack on April 11 from Gaza on an Israeli synagogue. "His present desire is that the blood of Jewish children who were slain as they recited the eighteen benedictions of the daily [*Amida*] prayer shall also be avenged" (39–40). On that terror attack and Israel's response, see Benny Morris, *Israel's Border Wars*, 391. (Tragically, R. Soloveitchik's own grandson, Rabbi Moshe Twersky, was murdered by terrorists while reciting prayers in his Jerusalem synagogue on November 18, 2014.)

CHAPTER 6: MUST JEWS FIGHT WITH HIGHER
MORAL STANDARDS? THE DEBATE OVER KIBIYEH

1   Ze'ev Drory, *Israel's Reprisal Policy, 1953–1956* (Frank Cass, 2005), 108.

2   Sharon makes this clear in his autobiography, *Warrior* (New York, 2001), 88.

3   Morris, *Israel's Border Wars*, 244–47. Mordechai Bar-On, *Moshe Dayan: Israel's Controversial Hero* (Yale, 2012), 50–51, claims that Sharon rephrased the general headquarters orders to a more aggressive posture.

4   IDF military historian Benny Michaelson reiterated this point in recent years. See his description of Kibiyeh in *LeNokhaḥ Gevulot Oynim: Tzava UBitaḥon BeAsor HaRishon LeMedinat Yisrael* (Meltzer, 2017), 122. See also Shabtai Teveth, *Moshe Dayan: The Soldier, the Man, the Legend*, Kindle location 4648–4700.

5   O'Brien, *Law and Morality in Israel's War with the PLO*, 101.

6   Moshe Dayan, "Israel's Border and Security Problems," *Foreign Affairs* 33 (January 1955): 261–262.

7   Yigal Alon, *Shield of David: The Story of Israel's Armed Forces*, 235. For articulations of such an approach already in 1950, see Morris, *Israel's Border Wars: 1949–1956*, 176–78, in which Dayan explicitly asserts, "The method of collective punishment has so far proved effective."

8   See Mordechai Bar-On, "Small Wars, Big Wars: Security Debates during Israel's First Decade," *Israel Studies* (Fall 2000): 119. "With the hindsight of forty years, it appears indeed that, between 1953 and 1956, the retaliation policy won for Israel a significant, if temporary, success on the Jordanian border, but failed completely on the Gaza border."

9   Benny Morris, *Israel's Border Wars*, 173, n. 1.

10 Soloveitchik, *Kol Dodi Dofek*, 37–39, emphasis added. The statement was made on April 16, 1956, toward the end of the border war period discussed in this chapter.

11 See the Knesset discussion of the 328th meeting on November 30, 1953.

12 Don-Yehiya, *Bein Shalom LeShlemut HaAretz*, 311–13. He then compared what happened at Kibiyeh to the controversial battle in Deir Yassin during the 1948 War of Independence that allegedly killed many

noncombatants. "We know what happened at Deir Yassin. That happened in the heat of war, but nevertheless, we were all so incensed!... We said that such a path is forbidden from a Jewish point of view.... Jews cannot act thus." As such, Shapira argued, the moral standards of the 1936–39 period should be maintained, with noncombatants never being targeted. Deir Yassin may have been a tragedy in the fog of war, but we cannot excuse Kibiyeh in the same way.

13 See Anita Shapira, "Ben-Gurion and the Bible: The Forging of an Historical Narrative?" *Middle Eastern Studies* 33:4 (October 1997): 645–674.

14 Shapira was referring to the collective punishment that God imposed on the Jewish people to lose in battle at Ai because Achan had illicitly taken spoils. He, his children, and livestock were later stoned by the Jewish people. See Joshua, chapter 7.

15 Yeshayahu Leibowitz, *Judaism, Human Values, and the Jewish State*, ed. Eliezer Goldman (Cambridge, MA, 1995), 188.

16 Leibowitz here seems to reference ideas that he would more fully develop in his opposition to the so-called Israeli "occupation" of disputed territories. See Ze'ev Harvey, "After Kibiyeh," in *Yeshayahu Leibowitz: Bein Shamranut LeRadikaliyut*, ed. A. Ravitsky (2007), 354–65.

17 *Kuzari*, 1:114.

18 Don-Yehiya, *Bein Shalom LeShlemut HaAretz*, 292–343.

19 "Ben Dam LaDam," in his *Tahalikhei HaTemura VeHaGeula* (Mossad Harav Kook, 1959), 139; emphasis added. On the widespread belief that Jordanian and other authorities were supporting such raids, see Morris, *Israel's Border Wars*, 67–69.

20 Sanhedrin 74a.

21 O'Brien, *Law and Morality in Israel's War with the PLO*, 117–25.

CHAPTER 7: MORAL STANDARDS: ETHICS OR CONVENTIONS?

1 R. Shaul Yisraeli, *Amud HaYemini*, siman 16, 3rd ed. (Eretz Hemdah, 5760), 168–205.

2 Ibid., 168 n. 1, where R. Yisraeli assumes that local Jewish villagers raided Kibiyeh.

3 *Midrash Tanchuma, Parashat Pinḥas* 3. See also Numbers Rabba 21:4. The connection between self-defense and the Midianite war was later made by the medieval commentator Menahem HaMeiri (*Beit HaBeḥira* on Sanhedrin 72a). This midrash is also cited by R. Hayim David HaLevi, "HaBa Lehorgekha Hashkem Lehorgo," *Teḥumin* 1 (1980): 344–45; R. Ahron Soloveichik, "Waging War on Shabbat," *Tradition* 20:3 (Fall 1982): 187; and R. Shlomo Goren, *Meshiva Milḥama*, vol. 3, 291–93. (As noted by R. Goren, the invocation of "rise and kill first" in the context of collective self-defense goes beyond the talmudic statements which focused on individual self-defense.)

4 Gutel, "Leḥima BeShetaḥ Ravei Ukhlusiya Ezraḥit," 40, notes that R. Yisraeli thinks reprisals are meant to deter future attacks.

5 *Amud HaYemini*, 202. Translation from Eisen, *Religious Zionism, Jewish Law, and the Morality of War*, 142–43, emphasis added. See also Yitzhak Roness, "Halakhah, Ideology and Interpretation: Rabbi Shaul Yisraeli on the Status of Defensive War," *Jewish Law Association Studies* 20 (2010): 184–195.

6 *Amud Ha-Yemini*, 205. Translation from Eisen, *Religious Zionism, Jewish Law, and the Morality of War*, 147; emphasis added. On the complexity of using the Midianite war as a legal precedent, see Gutel, "Leḥima BeShetaḥ Ravei Ukhlusiya Ezraḥit," 25–26 and n. 30. Gutel cites the position of Rabbi Avigdor Nevenzahl (oral communication) and R. Tzvi Yehuda (in his notes to Federbusch, *Mishpat HaMelukha BeYisrael*, 2nd ed., 242) that the command to kill all the Midianites was a temporary measure and did not set any precedent. Interestingly, Rabbi Moshe Sofer, in his commentary *Torat Moshe* to Num. 31:17, argues that the original plan was not to kill the male children and that Moses got angry because circumstances now dictated that the Israelites would need to kill more than was originally necessary. (I am thankful to Rabbi Dov Lerner for this source.)

7 See the conclusions of Gutel, "Leḥima BeShetaḥ Ravei Ukhlusiya Ezraḥit," 41–43, and Ido Rechnitz and Elazar Goldstein, *Etika Tzeva'it Yehudit* (Yediot, 2013), 116–124. See also R. Yisraeli's position (discussed in later chapters) to allow, when possible, non-combatants to flee a besieged city in his *Ḥavat Binyamin*, ed. Neria Gutel, vol. 1 (Kfar Darom, 2002), 187.

8 George I. Mavrodes, "Conventions and the Morality of War," *Philosophy and Public Affairs* 4:2 (Winter 1975): 117–31.

9 See G. E. Anscombe, "War and Massacre," citing Isaiah 59:7.

10 For critiques of Mavrodes, see Jeremy Waldron, "Deep Morality and the Laws of War," in *Oxford Handbook on the Ethics of War*, and Helen Frowe, *The Ethics of War and Peace* (New York, 2016), 166–81. A similar type of critique against R. Yisraeli is made by R. Yehuda Shaviv, "Tokfan shel Milḥamot bein HaUmot," 229.

11 See Mark Osiel, *The End of Reciprocity*, 49–110 and Eric Posner, "Human Rights, the Laws of War, and Reciprocity" (John M. Olin Program in Law and Economics Working Paper No. 537, 2010). See also Robbie Sabel, "The Legality of Reciprocity in the War against Terrorism," *Case Western Reserve Journal of International Law* 43:1–2 (2010): 473–82.

12 Jeff McMahan, "The Ethics of Killing in War," *Ethics* (July 2014): 730. See also his *Killing in War* (Oxford, 2009), 203–35.

13 Yoram Dinstein, "Comments on Protocol I," International Review of the Red Cross, no. 320.

14 Yitzhak Benbaji and Daniel Statman, *War by Agreement: A Contractarian Ethics of War* (Oxford, 2019), 167–71.

15 See also Michael Ignatieff, "Ethics and the New War," *Canadian Military Journal* (Winter 2001–2002): 5–10 and David Fisher, *Morality and War* (Oxford, 2011), 108–33.

16 Nahmanides, commentary on the Torah, Deuteronomy 23:10. See also his comments on Exodus 15:25 and his addenda to Maimonides's *Sefer HaMitzvot*, negative commandment 11.

17 I Kings 2:5. See the commentaries of *Metzudat David* and Malbim.

18 As quoted in Osiel, *The End of Reciprocity*, 350. The last two chapters of this book explore this type of reasoning.

19 On R. Goren's general approach, see Edrei, "Divine Spirit and Physical Power: Rabbi Shlomo Goren and the Military Ethic of the Israel Defense Forces." On his debate with R. Yisraeli on the latter two issues, see R. Goren's *Torat HaMedina* (Jerusalem, 5756), 416–23.

20 *Meshiv Milḥama*, vol. 1, 26–29.

21 Gen. 49:5–7. This point was also made by Leibowitz in his essay on Kibiyeh. Both draw from the comment of Nahmandies to Genesis

34:8. For the contrary claim that Shimon and Levi made a compelling claim and that Jacob only feared the political dangers from their action, see the midrashim *Peskirta Zutarta* (*Lekah Tov*) and *Sekhel Tov* to Genesis 34:31.

22 *Meshiv Milḥama*, vol. 1, 14–16.

23 Ibid., 3–12.

24 Goren, *With Might and Strength* (Maggid, 2016), 113.

25 Thus when the so-called "Jewish underground" in the early 1980s maimed the mayors of Nablus and Ramallah and killed three students in the Islamic College in Hebron, ostensibly in response to attacks on Jews in that contentious city, the vigilante killings were repeatedly censured by rabbinic figures, even within Israel's right wing. They condemned not only the anarchy created by such vigilantism, but also the murder of those who did not deserve such punishment. See Moshe Hellinger and Isaac Hershkovitz, *Tziyut VeItziyut BaTziyonut HaDatit* (Israel Democracy Institute, 2015), 82–95. Alas, there remained a few figures who defended "price tag" attacks and other acts of vengeance.

CHAPTER 8: THE JEWISH MULTIVALUE FRAMEWORK FOR MILITARY ETHICS

1 See the nuanced formulation of Uriel Tal, "Totalitarian Democratic Hermeneutics and Policies in Modern Jewish Religious Nationalism," in *Totalitarian Democracy and After* (Jerusalem, 1984), 139–40.

2 "Whoever sheds the blood of man, by man shall his blood be shed; for in His image did God make man" (Gen. 9:6).

3 "Blood of the innocent will not be shed, bringing bloodguilt upon you in the land that the Lord your God is allotting to you" (Deut. 19:10).

4 "The person who sins – he alone shall die" (Ezek. 18:20).

5 "And they shall beat their swords into plowshares and their spears into pruning hooks. Nation shall not take up sword against nation; they shall never again know war" (Is. 2:4).

6 "When you are at war in your land against an aggressor who attacks you, you shall sound short blasts on the trumpets, that you may be remembered before the Lord your God and be delivered from your enemies" (Num. 10:10). See also Joshua 24:8.

7   "Hear, O Israel! You are about to cross the Jordan to go in and dispossess nations greater and more populous than you.... Know then this day that none other than the Lord your God is crossing at your head, a devouring fire; it is He who will wipe them out. He will subdue them before you, that you may quickly dispossess and destroy them, as the Lord promised you" (Deut. 9:1–3). See also Exodus 23:31 and Deuteronomy 1:8.

8   "Remember what Amalek did to you on your journey, after you left Egypt – how, undeterred by fear of God, he surprised you on the march, when you were famished and weary, and cut down all the stragglers in your rear. Therefore, when the Lord your God grants you safety from all your enemies around you, in the land that the Lord your God is giving you as a hereditary portion, you shall blot out the memory of Amalek from under heaven. Do not forget!" (Deut. 25:17–19).

9   "When the Lord your God delivers them to you and you defeat them, you must doom them to destruction.... For you are a people consecrated to the Lord your God: of all the peoples on earth the Lord your God chose you to be His treasured people" (Deut. 7:2, 6).

10   Numbers 21:1–3.

11   "Moses replied to the Gadites and the Reubenites, 'Are your brothers to go to war while you stay here?'" (Num. 32:6). See also Numbers 32:20 and Deuteronomy 3:18.

12   "The officials shall go on addressing the troops and say, 'Is there anyone afraid and disheartened? Let him go back to his home, lest the courage of his comrades flag like his'" (Deut. 20:8).

13   This framework was developed in many of his works. See, for example, Baruch Brody, *Taking Issue: Pluralism and Casuistry in Bioethics* (Georgetown, 2003), 31–44. For the utilization of his theory in the context of military ethics, see *Military Medical Ethics: Volume 1*, ed. Thomas E. Beam and Linette R. Sparacino (Washington, DC, 2003), 36–46. My father developed this framework on a normative level. For our purposes, I am using this framework as an accurate description of Jewish ethical discourse.

14   John Kekes, *The Morality of Pluralism* (Princeton, 1996), 19–20.

15   Kekes, *The Morality of Pluralism*, 26.

CHAPTER 9: THE BOMBING OF DRESDEN

1 The best historical account of the Dresden raid is Frederick Taylor's work *Dresden: Tuesday, February 13, 1945* (New York, 2004). See also *Firestorm: The Bombing of Dresden, 1945*, ed. Jeremy Crang and Paul Addison (London, 2006) and Tami David Biddle, "Dresden 1945: Reality, History, and Memory," *Journal of Military History* 72:4 (April 2008): 413–49.

2 See "Canadian Author Malcolm Gladwell Doubles Down on Claim That Bomber Harris Was a 'Psychopath' After WWII Hero's Grandson Brands Writer an 'Armchair Air Marshal,'" *Daily Mail*, May 4, 2021.

3 Bruce Stokes, "70 Years after Hiroshima, Opinions Have Shifted on Use of Atomic Bomb," *Pew Fact Tank*, August 4, 2015.

4 Primoratz, in *Terror from the Sky: The Bombing of German Cities in World War II*, ed. Igor Primoratz, 113. Lackey's essay is also found in that volume.

5 A. C. Grayling, *Among the Dead Cities* (London, 2006). See also Stephen Garrett, *Ethics and Airpower in World War II* (New York, 1993).

6 See the *Times*, June 25, 1943, cited in J. M. Spaight, *Bombing Vindicated* (London, 1944); emphasis added. Garbett continued to assert, "However much we may deplore the sufferings of the civilian population and the destruction of their homes, and of beautiful buildings, we must continue to use our superiority in the air as a means of ending the war as speedily as we can, and then build up some strong central international order which will by force maintain peace until it is willingly accepted by all the nations." His remarks about the extermination of Polish Jews were made in the House of Lords on December 9, 1942.

7 Walzer, *Just and Unjust Wars*, 262, emphasis added.

8 Max Hastings, *Retribution: The Battle for Japan, 1944–5* (New York, 2009), xix. Hastings also asserts, "The myth that the Japanese were ready to surrender anyway has been so comprehensively discredited by modern research that it is astonishing some writers continue to give it credence." See also Niall Ferguson, *The War of the World* (2006), 570. For the use of this line of defense after Hiroshima, which

was later seconded by President Harry Truman, see Karl T. Compton, "If the Atomic Bomb Had Not Been Used," *Atlantic*, December 1946.

9 Walzer, *Just and Unjust Wars*, 263–68.

10 See Richard J. Evans, *Lying about Hitler*, chapter 5.

11 As reported in Biddle, "Dresden 1945: Reality, History, and Memory," 430.

12 Jeremy Rabkin, "Proportionality in Perspective: Historical Light on the Law of Armed Conflict," *George Mason Legal Studies Research Paper No. LS 15–01* (2015), 322.

13 This definition of strategic indiscriminate bombing draws from Geoffrey Best, *Humanity in Warfare* (London, 1980), 266–85. Best defends the reasonableness of the Dresden raid in his *Churchill and War* (2005), 280–84.

14 Taylor, *Dresden*, 148–53, 216–19.

15 Cited in Richard Overy, "Allied Bombing and the Destruction of German Cities," in *A World at Total War: Global Conflict and the Politics of Destruction, 1937–1945*, ed. Roger Chickering et al. (Cambridge, 2005), 277–95.

16 See Victor David Hanson, *The Second World Wars* (New York, 2017), 93–102.

17 Richard Overy, *The Bombers and the Bombed*, 230.

18 On this topic, see Michael Gross, "Saving Life, Limb, and Eyesight: Assessing the Medical Rules of Eligibility during Armed Conflict," *American Journal of Bioethics* 17:10 (2017): 40–52.

19 On this last point, see Rabbi Yaakov Ariel, *Halakha BeYameinu* (Machon Torah Ve-HaAretz, 2012), 378–79.

20 Cited in Hanson, *The Soul of Battle*, 381.

21 Walzer, *Just and Unjust Wars*, 267–268, emphasis added.

22 On Japanese belligerency during this period, see Arnaud Doglia, "Japanese Mass Violence and Its Victims in the 'Fifteen Years War' (1931–45)," *The Online Encyclopedia of Mass Violence* (2011).

23 See Hastings, *Retribution*, 345–68.

24 See Hastings, *Retribution*, 171, 442–62.

25 On this last point, see Victor Davis Hanson, *The Second World Wars*, 526–29.

26 Eliav Shochetman, "Sikun Hayalei Tzahal LeShem Meniyat Pegiya BaEzrahei Eiyev BeShulei Mivtzat Homat Magen," *Netiv* 91–92 (2003): 12, seems to justify the aerial bombardments. See also Rabbi Alter David Regensberg, *Mishpat HaTzava BeYisrael, siman* 15:1–2 (1949), 30–31. By contrast, grave reservations are voiced by Federbusch, *Mishpat Melukha*, 206.

27 As cited in Richard Rhodes, *Dark Sun: The Making of the Hydrogen Bomb*, 22–23.

28 See William W. Ralph, "Improvised Destruction: Arnold, LeMay, and the Firebombing of Japan," *War in History* 13:4 (2006): 495–522.

CHAPTER 10: WORLD WAR II AND THE FIGHT FOR SELF-DEFENSE AND NATIONAL HONOR

1 Hoffman, *Anonymous Soldiers*, 101–18 and Nir Mann, "A Life Underground," *Haaretz* (April 22, 2010).

2 Rabbi Tzvi Yehuda Kook, *LeNetivot Yisrael*, vol. 2, 74–75. On the relationship of R. Tzvi Yehuda to the underground movements, see Rabbi Yehoshua Weisinger, "Rabbeinu VeIrgunei HaMahteret," *Shemaitin* 138 (5773): 71–103.

3 Anita Shapira, *Ben-Gurion: Father of Modern Israel* (Yale, 2014), 115–16.

4 Shabtai Teveth, *Moshe Dayan: The Soldier, the Man, the Legend* (Houghton Mifflin, 1972), chapters 7–9.

5 *Hatzofeh*, December 9, 1942, reproduced in Hava Eshkoli Wagman, *Arevut Yehudit BaMivhan* (Bar-Ilan University Press, 2012), 290. On general rabbinic support in Palestine for enlistment, see her work *Bein Hatzala LeGeula* (Yad Vashem, 2004), 235–47.

6 See, most comprehensively, Yoav Gelber, *HaHitnadvut LaTzava Ha-Briti BaMilhamat Olam HaShniya* (5744).

7 Gottfried Neuberger, "From the American Scene: An Orthodox G.I. Fights a War," Commentary, March 1949. See also Deborah Dash Moore, *GI Jews: How World War II Changed a Generation* (Cambridge, MA: Harvard University Press, 2004).

8 See his letter to Samuel Belkin in Joseph B. Soloveitchik, *Community, Covenant, and Commitment*, ed. Nathaniel Helfgot, 57. While this letter was sent during the Korean War, it originated in discussions

regarding World War II. See Belkin's letter printed in Sidney Hoenig, "The Orthodox Rabbi as a Military Chaplain," *Tradition* 16:2 (Fall 1976): 55–56.

9 Daniel Bronstein, "Torah in the Trenches: The Rabbi Chaplains of World War II, 1940–1946" (PhD diss., Jewish Theological Seminary, 2009).

10 Israel Brodie, "British and Palestinian Jews in World War II," *American Jewish Year Book* 48 (1946–1947), 72.

11 *Taḥanun prayer*, Monday and Thursday version. Translation from *The Koren Siddur*, ed. R. Jonathan Sacks, 152.

12 See the newspaper *Havatzelet*, Year 22, Issue 19, Feb 24, 1882, and discussion in Yael Feldman, "Not as Sheep Led to Slaughter," 150–51.

13 Rabbi Meir Berlin (Bar-Ilan), "LaEzrat Hashem BaGibborim," *Hatzofeh*, August 2, 1942, p. 2. On Bar-Ilan, see Aminadav Yitzhaki, "Rabbi Meir Bar-Ilan: The Leader of Religious Zionism in the Land of Israel, 1926–1949" (PhD diss., Bar-Ilan University, 2009), 199–203. For similar ideas regarding the Holocaust and the State of Israel, see Rabbi Yehuda Amital, *Jewish Values in a Changing World* (Ktav, 2005), 152–56 and Rabbi Joseph B. Soloveitchik, *The Lord Is Righteous in All His Ways*, ed. Jacob J. Schacter (Ktav, 2006), 157–60.

14 Rafael Medoff, *The Jews Should Keep Quiet: Franklin D. Roosevelt, Rabbi Stephen S. Wise, and the Holocaust* (JPS, 2019), 161–73.

15 See Berlin (Bar-Ilan), "LaEzrat Hashem BaGibborim," 2; Pinchas Fishman (Ben-Sirah), "Milḥemet Mitzva – Simḥat Mitzva," *Hatzofeh*, March 3, 1942, 2; Shlomo Zalman Shragai, *Tahalikhei HaTemura VeHaGeula* (Jerusalem: Mossad HaRav Kook, 5719), 254; Rabbi Baruch Epstein (Elitzur), in *BeHitnadev Am*, vol. 1, 36–40; Rabbi Eliezer Silver, as cited in Bronstein, *Torah in the Trenches: The Rabbi Chaplains of World War II, 1940–1946*, 114–15; and Rabbi Herschel Schacter in J. J. Schacter, "'The Voice of Your Brothers' Blood Is Screaming': Rabbi Herschel Schacter's Letter Home," *Tradition* 54:1, 125.

16 Numbers 10:9. See *Sifre Bemidbar* 76; *Sifre Bemidbar Zuta* 10:9; Rabbi Hafetz Gaon, *Sefer HaMitzvot*, ed. Zucker, 50; Rambam, *Mishneh Torah, Hilkhot Melakhim* 5:1 and *Mishneh Torah, Hilkhot Shabbat* 2:23–24.

17 Numbers 32:6.

18 See I Samuel 11:1–13, Judges 21:8–12, and chapter 11 of Amnon Bazak, *Shmuel Aleph: Melekh BeYisrael* (Maggid Books, 2013), 139–47.

19 The criticism of Chamberlain's accommodation to the "rule of violence" draws from Walzer, *Just and Unjust Wars*, 67–73.

CHAPTER 11: DEFENDING LIVES OR HONOR? MASADA, THE WARSAW GHETTO UPRISING, AND THE PROBABILITY OF SUCCESS

1 Assembly comment on July 7, 1942, as recorded in Uri Brennar, *Nokhaḥ Iyum Plisha HaGermanit LeEretz Yisrael* (Yad Tabenkin, 1981), 88.

2 Ibid., 64.

3 Judges 16:30.

4 Shapira and R. Maimon's statements are recorded in Brennar, *Nokhaḥ Iyum Plisha HaGermanit LeEretz Yisrael*, 65.

5 See Yael Zerubavel, *Recovered Roots: Collective Memory and the Making of an Israeli National Tradition* (Chicago: University of Chicago Press, 1995) and Nachman Ben-Yehuda, *Masada Myth: Collective Memory and Mythmaking in Israel* (Madison: University of Wisconsin Press, 1995).

6 Regarding the Goren-Neriya dispute and other rabbinic writings on Masada, see Amir Mashiach, "The Ethos of Masada in Halakhic Literature," *Review of Rabbinic Judaism* 19 (2016): 54–77 and Yaron Silverstein, *Bein Adam LeMedinato* (Magnes, 2021), 225–48.

7 On these sources, see Baruch Brody, *Taking Issue*, 229–64 and Yechezkel Lichtenstein, *VeHaSneh Eineno Ukal* (Yad Vashem, 2015), 29–166, which also includes the most extensive exploration of the Warsaw Ghetto uprising in rabbinic literature.

8 Gittin 57b.

9 I Samuel 31.

10 R. Goren also argued that captured IDF soldiers who may disclose important state secrets or security information, thereby endangering many others, should commit suicide before being tortured into revealing such information. R. Goren likely had in mind the case

of Uri Elan, who was captured in 1955 on a reconnaissance mission in Syria and committed suicide before revealing any secrets. See Silverstein, *Bein Adam LeMedinato*, 242. In a later version of the essay, R. Goren moderated his stance to state it was merely permissible to commit suicide in this case. See Yechezkel Lichtenstein, *HaMe'abed Atzmo LaDa'at* (HaKibutz HaMe'uhad, 2008), 455–458.

11 Ben-Yehuda, *Masada Myth*, 152–55, 241–43.

12 Jodi Magness, *Masada: From Jewish Revolt to Modern Myth* (Princeton: Princeton University Press, 2019).

13 Benjamin Kedar, as quoted in Zerubavel, *Recovered Roots*, 201.

14 On the portrayal of Yoḥanan ben Zakkai in rabbinic literature and its parallels to Jeremiah, see Amram Tropper, "Yohanan Ben Zakkai, *Amicus Caesaris*: A Jewish Hero in Rabbinic Eyes," *JSIJ* 4 (2005): 133–49.

15 Jeremiah 38:17.

16 Yoma 85b. Rabbi Louis Rabinowitz points out that it's possible that the Sages took this attitude after seeing the failed approach of the rebels. See Rabinowitz, "The Masada Martyrs according to the Halakhah," *Tradition* 11:3 (Fall 1970): 31–37.

17 At least according to Josephus, *The Jewish War*, 7.6.1, as noted by other critics of the Masada legend.

18 Commentary on Judges 6:36, s.v. *hatoelet hateshi'i*. (See also Gersonides's comments on I Kings 8:44.) The same idea is also found in Rabbi Meir Plotzki, *Ḥemdat Yisrael: Kuntres Ner Yisrael*, 170, who is approvingly cited by Rabbi Yehuda Gershuni, "On Bravery and Wars," *Teḥumin* 4, 59 [Hebrew], and Rabbi Moshe Tzvi Neriah, *Yisrael Be-Medinateinu: Meorot Neriya*, ed. Reuven Hass (Kiryat Malakhi: Merkaz Neriya, 5758), 299–300. See also R. Shlomo Goren, *Meshiva Milḥama*, vol. 3, 281. A similar assertion was made in retrospect about the Warsaw Ghetto uprising by Rabbi Yehoshua Moshe Aharonson. While the Talmud asserts, "When someone comes to kill you, rise up and strike first," one must nonetheless also ask, "At what cost?" before taking action, since sometimes the wiser move is to flee. See his statement quoted in Lichtenstein, *VeHaSneh Eineno Ukal*, 147–48.

19 Judges 6:6. See Elie Assis, *Self-Interest or Communal Leadership: An Ideology of Leadership in the Gideon, Abimelech, and Jephthah Narratives (Judg. 6–12)* (Brill, 2005), 17–20.

20 One should also not discount the fact that sometimes a spirited, patriotic fight, against the odds, turns into a surprise victory. Most famously, Finland successfully held back the Soviets in the "Winter War" of 1939–40. Many other nations, of course, were not as successful in holding off greater powers during the World Wars.

21 John C. Murray, "Theology and Modern War," in *Morality and Modern Warfare*, ed. William J. Nagle (Baltimore: Helicon, 1960), 80.

22 Maurice Lamm, "Red or Dead," *Tradition* 4:2 (Spring 1962): 194, followed in the same issue by rebuttals by Rabbi Immanuel Jakobovits and the philosopher Michael Wyschograd. On this debate, see Shlomo M. Brody, "Jewish Perspectives on Nuclear Weapons – and Deterrence," *Tablet*, June 26, 2015.

23 A. J. Coates, *The Ethics of War*, 2nd ed. (Manchester: Manchester University Press, 2016), Kindle Edition, locations 3719–3727; emphasis in original.

24 For similar arguments, see also O'Brien, *The Conduct of Just and Limited War*, 31–33; James Turner Johnson, *Morality and Contemporary Warfare* (Yale University Press, 1999), 43; and Harry van der Linden, "Just War Theory and U.S. Military Hegemony," in *Rethinking the Just War Tradition*, ed. Michael D. Brough et al. (SUNY Press, 2007), 56–58.

25 See Isaac Hershkowitz, "Moral Considerations Relating to Criticism of the Warsaw Ghetto Uprising," in *War and Peace in Jewish Tradition*, eds. Yigal Levin and Amnon Shapira (Routledge, 2012), 165–85 and Daniel Statman, "On the Success Condition for Legitimate Self-Defense," *Ethics* 118 (July 2008): 659–86.

26 See Michael Berenbaum, "Some Clarifications on the Warsaw Ghetto Uprising," in *Life in the Ghettos during the Holocaust*, ed. Eric J. Sterling (Syracuse University Press, 2005), 22.

27 "Call to Resistance by the Jewish Fighting Organization in the Warsaw Ghetto, January 1943," available at https://www.jewish-virtuallibrary.org/jewish-fighting-organization-calls-for-resistance; emphasis added.

28 Here I follow Statman, "On the Success Condition for Legitimate Self-Defense," 676, who invokes those and other factors which collectively overcome the "probability for success" requirement to justify the uprising.

29 This formulation draws from Rabbi Yehuda Gershuni, "Berurei Halakha BaInyanei HaShoah," in *Emunah BaShoah* (Jerusalem, 5740), 19–25 as well as Michel Foucault's writings on the uprising. See Blake Smith, "Biopolitics," *Tablet*, June 25, 2020.

30 May 16, 1943.

31 Others would add that one can celebrate the bravery of these rebels without denigrating other models of passive resistance displayed by other Nazi victims. See the remarks of Rabbi Yehiel Yaakov Weinberg (who himself was in the ghetto) in *Yad Shaul: Memorial Volume for Rabbi Shaul Weingart*, ed. Y. Weinberg (Tel Aviv: Merkaz Printing, 5713), 9–10.

32 His writing is reproduced in Wagman, *Arevut Yehudit BaMivhan*, 429–30. See also her work "Religious Zionist Responses in Mandatory Palestine to the Warsaw Ghetto Uprising," *Holocaust and Genocide Studies* 11:2 (Fall 1997): 224–25. In a private interview, Neriah told Wagman that he also believed that more Jews could have survived had they not rebelled. Elsewhere in his writings, Neriah lamented that rebels received all the attention while the real heroes were the educators who continued to risk their lives to teach Torah. See his book *Yisrael BeMedinateinu*, 241. See also Hava Eshkoli, "HaHavlaga HaNiflaa," *Makor Rishon*, April 17, 2015.

33 See chapter 1 of John W. Dower, *Embracing Defeat: Japan in the Wake of World War II* (Norton, 2000), and Hastings, Retribution, 504–40.

34 The critique here is of the institutionalization of the tactic of suicide missions. There are times when soldiers may hurl themselves on the enemy to save others, but this is a spontaneous action. For this point, see Hastings, *Retribution: The Battle for Japan 1944–1945*, 172. For discussion of Israeli soldiers jumping on grenades to save their comrades, see the article of Rabbi Simcha HaKohen Kook in *Bekhol Levavkha: LeZikhro Shel Ro'i Klein*, ed. Rabbi Eliezer Kashtiel (5769).

35 See Michael Mallmann and Martin Cüppers, *Nazi Palestine: The Plans for the Extermination of the Jews in Palestine*, trans. Krista Smith

(New York: Enigma Books, 2010) and Samuel Miner, "Planning the Holocaust in the Middle East: Nazi Designs to Bomb Jewish Cities in Palestine," *Jewish Political Studies Review* 27:3/4 (Fall 2016): 7–33.

36 Resolutions of the Hamizrachi Executive Committee, 26 May 1943, as transcribed in Eshkoli Wagman, *Arevut Yehudit BaMivḥan*, 348.

37 In fact, at the beginning of the Nazi conquest of Central Europe, there was a spike in suicides by Jews in places like Vienna and Amsterdam. Chief Rabbi Herzog sent a letter to their communities to try to strengthen their fortitude to survive. See Lichtenstein, *VeHaSneh Eineno Ukal*, 48–51 and 98–101 and, more generally, Konrad Kwiet, "The Ultimate Refuge: Suicide in the Jewish Community under the Nazis," *Leo Baeck Institute Year Book* 29 (1984): 135–68.

38 Zerubavel, *Recovered Roots*, 76.

39 Tellingly, in the tenth century Book of Jossipon that reworked many of Josephus's stories, it says that the men at Masada killed their families to avoid their capture but then went on to fight the Romans until they fell in battle.

40 Ben-Yehuda, *Masada Myth*, 157–58; emphasis added.

CHAPTER 12: THE ETZEL'S REBELLION AND THE DILEMMA OVER WHEN TO REBEL

1 Menachem Begin, *The Revolt: Story of the Irgun* (Bnei Brak: Steimatzky, 1977), 42–43.

2 Hoffman, *Anonymous Soldiers*, 119–27.

3 Begin, *The Revolt*, 46.

4 Ibid., 89.

5 Eight people, however, were arrested for singing nationalist songs like Hatikvah afterward. See Rabbi Isaac Avigdor Urnstein, *Yoman HaKotel HaMa'aravi* (Jerusalem, 5728), 343–345.

6 Begin, *The Revolt*, 90.

7 Ibid., 40. Ben-Gurion also reportedly saw this principle as a "spineless readiness to accede to Gentile demands." See Shimon Peres, *Ben-Gurion: A Political Life* (Random House, 2011), 82–83.

8 *Hatzofeh*, March 29, 1944, 2. See also Don-Yehiya, *Bein Shalom LeShlemut HaAretz*, 148–51.

9 Jeremiah 29:7. On the principle of *dina demalkhuta dina*, see Shmuel Shilo, *Dina Demalkhuta Dina* (Jerusalem, 5729) and Geoffrey Herman, *A Prince without a Kingdom*, 203–9.

10 *Horeb: A Philosophy of Jewish Laws and Observances*, ed. and trans. I. Grunfeld (London: Soncino, 1962), 462. R. Hirsch's extreme statement also seems to go against the Talmudic statement that *DDD* does not apply when the ruler applies unlimited or whimsical taxes. See Bava Kamma 113a.

11 Ketubot 111a. For various interpretations, see Aviezer Ravitzky, *Messianism, Zionism, and Jewish Religious Radicalism* (Chicago, 1996), 211–345.

12 Hava Eshkoli Wagman, *Bein Hatzala LeGeula* (Yad Vashem, 2004), 111–143.

13 Mayzlish, *The Rabbinate in Stormy Days*, 67.

14 Herzog, *Psakim UKtavim*, vol. 1, 231–32 (Oraḥ Ḥayim 52). See also Chaim Burgansky, "Halakha Tziyonit BaPesikato Shel HaRav Herzog," in *Halakha* Tziyonit, ed. Yedidia Stern and Yair Sheleg (Jerusalem, 2017), 626–629. In this passage, R. Herzog also harshly criticizes British policy toward Zionism. This was a sharp change from his generally supportive attitude that he maintained until 1947. See Shulamit Eliash, "HaRabanut HaRashit, HaTerror, VeHaRevisionistim," in *Dat UMaḥteret BeEretz Yisrael BaTekufat HaMandat*, ed. Hayim Genizi (Tel Aviv, 1995) 116–17.

15 *Hatzofeh*, June 16, 1939, 2. Similarly, in 1940, R. Maimon would argue that Jews had no obligation to hand in their weapons to British authorities since they were necessary for their own self-defense. See Hilda Nisimi, "The Religious Zionist Public and Its Attitude Toward the 'Hagana,' 'Etzel', and 'Lehi': Israeli Unity – Ideal and Reality," in *A Hundred Years of Religious Zionism, Vol. 2 – Historical Aspects*, ed. Dov Schwartz and Avi Sagi (Bar-Ilan University Press, 2003), 295–96.

16 Yehuda Bauer, "From Cooperation to Resistance: The Haganah 1938–1946," *Middle Eastern Studies* 2:3 (April 1966): 182–210.

17 For a survey, see Ram ben Shalom, *Mul Tarbut Notzrit* (Jerusalem, 5767) and Richard Marks, *The Image of Bar Kokhba in Traditional Jewish Literature: False Messiah and National Hero* (Penn State University Press, 1993).

18 See his commentary on Deuteronomy 8:10 in Hirsch, *The Pentateuch: Volume 5 – Deuteronomy*, ed. Isaac Levy (Gateshead, England: Judaica Press, 1989), 147.

19 Zerubavel, *Recovered Roots*, 52–53.

20 *Maamarei HaRaayah*, 202–3.

21 See Zerubavel, *Recovered Roots*, 178–91. For R. Goren's eulogy of the rebels, see his *Mishnat HaGoren*, 230–31.

22 O'Brien, *The Conduct of Just and Unjust War*, 17–19 and James Turner Johnson, *Morality and Contemporary Warfare* (New Haven: Yale University Press, 1999), 54–57.

23 Eric Patterson and Nathan Gill, "The Declaration of the United Colonies: America's First Just War Statement," *Journal of Military Ethics* 14:1 (2015): 7–34.

24 See, for example, the open letter signed in February 2002 by leading theorists like George Weigel, Michael Walzer, Amitai Etzioni, James Turner Johnson, and Robert George entitled "What We're Fighting For: A Letter from America," 18, available online at https://avalon.law.yale.edu/sept11/letter_002.asp

25 Rafael Medoff, *Militant Zionism in America: The Rise and Impact of the Jabotinsky Movement in the United States, 1926–1948* (Tuscaloosa: University of Alabama Press, 2002), 171–200.

26 Michael Gross, *The Ethics of Insurgency*, 51–63.

27 Robert Middlekauff, *The Glorious Cause: The American Revolution, 1763–1789* (Oxford, 2005), 285.

28 Begin, *The Revolt*, 134.

29 Colin Schindler, *The Rise of the Israeli Right*, 212–13.

30 On this larger phenomenon, see Hilda Nissim, "The Religious Zionist Public," 299–301.

31 See Malka Katz, "Rabbi Uziel and the Democratic Way in Religious Zionism during the Pre-State Period: Historic Observations," in *Ben Zion Meir Hai*, ed. Zvi Zohar et al. (Ramat Gan, 2020), 297–328.

32 Don-Yehiya, *Bein Shalom LeShlemut HaAretz*, 129. Some activists, to the right of Jabotinsky, embraced this designation and took on the names of the zealots who fought against the Romans, including "Hooligans" or "Sicarii." See Shapira, *Land and Power*, 197–98.

33 Hoffman, *Anonymous Soldiers*, 191.

34 Hatzofeh, January 1, 1945, 1.

35 R. Breuer, it should be noted, also saw the mandate system as an ideal political system for the Jews. See Amos Israel-Vleeschhouwer, "The Mandate System as a Messianic Alternative in the Ultra-Religious Jurisprudence of Rabbi Dr Isaac Breuer," *Israel Law Review* 49:3 (2016), 339–363.

36 Don-Yehiya, *Bein Shalom LeShlemut HaAretz,*138–44.

37 Hoffman, *Anonymous Soldiers,* 190–91.

38 Begin, *The Revolt,* 152.

39 Shapira, *Land and Power,* 278–96.

40 Jerold S. Auerbach, *Brothers at War: Israel and the Tragedy of the Altalena* (Kindle Version, location 1893).

41 Don-Yehiya, *Bein Shalom LeShlemut HaAretz,* 173–78.

42 Both of their articles were printed in Hatzofeh, July 7, 1948, 4.

CHAPTER 13: CENTRAL WAR AUTHORITY FROM KING DAVID TO BEN-GURION

1 See Jacob Wright, "Human, All Too Human: Royal Name-Making in Wartime," in *War and Peace in Jewish Tradition,* ed. Yigal Levin and Amnon Shapira (London, 2012), 62–77 and Lori F. Damrosch, "The Interface of National Constitutional Systems with International Law and Institutions on Using Military Forces: Changing Trends in Executive and Legislative Powers," in *Democratic Accountability and the Use of Force in International Law,* eds. Charlotte Ku and Harold K. Jacobson (Cambridge, 2009), 39–60.

2 *Federalist Papers,* no. 34.

3 Rabbi Isaac Herzog, *Teḥuka LeYisrael al pi HaTorah,* vol. 1, ed. Warhaftig, 133. See also Rabbi Hayim D. HaLevy, "Sherut Tzevai BaHalakha," *Torah SheBe`al Peh* 13 (1971), 178.

4 He would still be expected, at the very least, to consult with the defense minister and military chief of staff, as was done in biblical times.

5 According to some, this was even if they were fearful that their private sins would make them liable to divine punishment during the course of the war. See Sota 44a and *Sefer HaḤinukh* 526.

6 Tosefta Sota 7:14. See Geoffrey Levey, "Judaism and the Obligation to Die for the State," *AJS Review* 12:2 (Autumn 1987): 189–97.

7 See, for example, Rabbi Eliyahu Rabinowitz-Teumim, "Mitzva Lizkor Ma SheAsa Amalek," *Moriah* 313–315 (Adar II, 5765): 30–31; Rabbi Hayim Hirschensohn, *Malki BaKodesh*, vol. 1, 146–49; Rabbi Aharon Lichtenstein, "Halakha" in *Arakhim BeMivḥan Milḥama: Musar UMilḥama Bere'i HaYahadut*, [no editor listed] (Alon Shvut: Yeshivat Har Etzion, 1985), 18–19; Federbusch, *Mishpat HaMelukha BeYisrael* (Jerusalem, 1954), 199; Rabbi Yehuda Amital, *Resisei Tal* vol. 1 (Alon Shvut 5765), 303–306; Rabbi Uri Cherki, *Berit Shalom*, 101. See also Rabbi Menahem HaMeiri, *Bet HaBeḥira* on Sanhedrin 16a, s.v. *Ein motzi'in*, who directly connects the need for the Sanhedrin's approval to the question of conscription for nonessential purposes. See Reuven Kimelman, "The Laws of War and Their Limits," in *Kedushat HaHayim VeHeruf HaNefesh*, ed. Y. Gafni (Jerusalem, 5753), 236–38. The requirement to consult with a Sanhedrin is found in Sanhedrin 2a.

8 See Walzer, "War and Peace in the Jewish Tradition" and Ravitzky, "Prohibited Wars in the Jewish Tradition," both found in *The Ethics of War and Peace*, ed. T. Nardin (Princeton, 1996), 95–127.

9 For an example of such a statement, see Shlomo Y. Zevin, *LaOhr HaHalakha* (Jerusalem, 5717), 10.

10 See II Samuel 11:1–2, 15–16, 25, and 12:26–31. On the categorization of this war as a *milḥemet reshut*, see Maimonides, commentary on the Mishna, Sanhedrin 1:5.

11 Yair Lorberbaum, *Disempowered King: Monarchy in Classical Jewish Literature* (London, 2011), 72–79.

12 Numbers 27:12–23. See J. David Bleich, "Preemptive War in Jewish Law," *Tradition* 21:1 (Spring 1983): 3–6. See also Rabbi Moshe Feinstein, *Iggrot Moshe*, vol. 7 (*Ḥoshen Mishpat* 78), who argues that all "obligatory wars" require a divine command with the exception of wars of self-defense, when one is compelled to act to protect oneself. R. Yitzhak Soloveitchik (*Griz uBeit HaLevi Al Hatora* #108, p. 62) claims that even war against Amalek should not be waged unless a prophet ordains it. (My thanks to Rabbi Yitzchak Blau for this source.) For examples of different types of consultations, see II Chronicles 20, II Samuel 16:23, and I Chronicles 27:33–34 as well as Hayim Angel, "The Theological Significance of the Urim

ve-Thummim," in his work *Through an Opaque Lens* (New York: Sephardic Publication Foundation, 2006), 195–214.

13 This point was already made, more or less, in Nahmanides's addenda to Maimonides's *Sefer HaMitzvot* (negative commandment 17) found in *Sefer HaMitzvot LeHaRambam im Hasagot HaRamban*, ed. Chaim Chavel (Jerusalem, 1981), 409. Isaac Abarbanel more fully developed the idea that a king is not essential for war-making while stressing the importance of a balance of powers. See his comments on I Samuel 8:4–6 and Deuteronomy 20:10 and the analysis in Aviezer Ravitsky, *Religion and State in Jewish Philosophy* (Jerusalem, 2002), 85–120.

14 David Tal, "The 1948 War: The War of David Ben-Gurion," in *Iyunim BaTekumat Yisrael* 13 (2003): 115–38 and Elliot Cohen, *Supreme Command* (New York, 2002), 133–72.

15 Cited in Bruce Hoffman, "The Rationality of Terrorism and Other Forms of Political Violence: Lessons from the Jewish Campaign in Palestine, 1939–1947," *Small Wars and Insurgencies* 22:2 (2011): 258–72.

16 See also Rabinovitch, *Melumdei Milḥama*, 18, n. 4.

17 *The Revolt*, 290.

CHAPTER 14: SELF-DETERMINATION THROUGH PARTITION PLANS AND ISRAEL'S WAR OF INDEPENDENCE

1 The contents of that treatise, "LeMitzvat HaAretz," were republished in Kook, *LeNetivot Yisrael*, vol. 1, 116–20 and 151–83. Cohen's story is recorded in vol. 2, pp. 611–12. See also Neria Gutel, "Ḥufshat Levnei Yeshivotenu o Mitzva Giyusam," available online at https://www.yeshiva.org.il/midrash/36737.

2 Rabbi Isaac Herzog, *Psakim UKtavim*, vol. 1, *siman* 48.

3 Rabbi Meshulam Roth, *Shu"t Kol Mevaser* 47 (Mossad HaRav Kook, 2020 ed.), vol 1., 208. The previous two chapters include Roth's earlier correspondence with R. Herzog on the topic.

4 See Luz, *Wrestling with an Angel*, 87–88, and the discussion below.

5 Herzog, *Teḥuka LeYisrael al pi HaTorah*, vol. 1, appendix 1, 129–33. (A slightly different version was published in *Teḥumin*, vol. 4, 13–24.)

6 Numbers 33:53.

7 See Herzog, *Psakim UKtavim*, OH 52, 231.

8 Kook, *LeNetivot Yisrael*, vol. 1, 174–77. On R. Tzvi Yehuda's writings during this period, see Holzer, *Ḥerev Pipiyot BeYadam*, 207–10. For a more recent restatement of R. Tzvi Yehuda's basic idea, see Rabbi Shlomo Aviner, "Ḥovat Giyus LeTzahal," in *Halakha Tziyonit*, eds. Yedidia Stern and Yair Sheleg, 221–34. For a compelling alternative interpretation of Nahmanides which advocates establishing control over the land through settlement but denies that there is any inherent commandment to militarily conquer the land, see Rabbi Nahum Eliezer Rabinovitch, *Melumadei Milḥama*, 3–22.

9 Kook, *LeNetivot Yisrael*, vol. 1, 181–83.

10 Ibid., 154–57.

11 R. Herzog's primary reliance on Rambam's orientation to the self-defense claim, as opposed to Ramban, is stated clearly in his letter to Rabbi Meshulam Roth, in Herzog, *Psakim UKtavim*, siman 49, 222.

12 R. Herzog, *Psakim UKtavim*, OH 52, 230–33.

13 Ibid., 230.

14 On the 1937 partition plan, see Itzhak Galnoor, *The Partition of Palestine* (New York, 1995) and Shmuel Dotan, *Pulmus HaHaluka BaTekufat HaMandat* (Jerusalem, 5740).

15 James B. Mininhan, *Encyclopedia of Stateless Nations: Ethnic and National Groups around the World*, 2nd Edition.

16 Amitai Etzioni, "The Evils of Self-Determination," *Foreign Policy* 89 (Winter 1992–1993), 21–35.

17 See Michael L. Gross, *The Ethics of Insurgency*, 21–39.

18 See Itamar Warhaftig, "Emdat HaRabbanim BePulmus Halukat HaAretz (5697)," *Teḥumin* 9: 269–97 and Don-Yehiya, *Bein Shalom LeShlemut HaAretz*, 59–79.

19 R. Tzvi Yehuda favorably cites Rabbi Charlap's statement in *Siḥot HaRav Tzvi Yehuda: Eretz Yisrael*, ed. Shlomo Aviner (Jerusalem, 5771), 283–85.

20 Rabbi Chaim Ozer Grodzinski, as cited in Warhaftig, "Emdat HaRabbanim BePulmus Halukat HaAretz," 23–25.

21 Quoted in Warhaftig, "Emdat HaRabbanim BePulmus Halukat HaAretz," n. 3.

22 Translation from Mayzlish, *The Rabbinate in Stormy Days*, 49. Subtle support for the plan was also offered by Rabbi Maimon. See Don-Yehiya, *Bein Shalom LeShlemut HaAretz*, 63.

23 Cited in Don-Yehiya, *Bein Shalom LeShlemut HaAretz*, 83.

24 Mayzlish, *The Rabbinate in Stormy Days*, 161–62.

25 See Kook, *LeNetivot Yisrael*, vol. 1, 131–37 and Shtamler, *Ayin BeAyin*, 292–304. R. Tzvi Yehuda's essay (alongside those of Charlap and Amiel) was also included in *Kol HaAretz* (Jerusalem, 5707), a small pamphlet distributed by Rabbi Meir Berlin to the twenty-second Zionist Congress in December 1946. Regarding R. Berlin's ultimate acceptance of the partition, see Don-Yehiya, *Bein Shalom LeShlemut HaAretz*, 82–90.

26 Anthony D. Smith, "Sacred Territories and National Conflict," *Israel Affairs* 5:4 (1999), 13–31.

27 *Tehuka LeYisrael al pi HaTorah*, vol. 1, 127.

28 See Mayzlish, *The Rabbinate in Stormy Days*, 148–55.

29 Rabbi Shlomo Aviner, *MiHayil el Hayil*, vol. 1, 217–39, especially 238.

30 The approach of R. Tzvi Yehuda relies, in part, on the statement of Rabbi Yosef Babad, *Minhat Hinukh* 425 that the mitzva of conquering the land requires self-sacrifice of Jewish lives. This contention was disputed by Rabbi Soloveitchik and others. See Rabbi Hershel Schachter, *Nefesh HaRav*, 97–98 and Rabbi Amnon Bazak, *VeHai Bahem – Mivhan Arakhim* (5760), 29–30.

31 Aviner, *MiHayil el Hayil*, vol. 1, 96–97. In this essay, written about the First Lebanon War in 1982, R. Aviner also criticizes Israelis for not recognizing that Lebanon is a part of the biblical homeland that should be conquered.

32 R. Tzvi Yehuda Kook, *Eretz HaTzvi* (1995), 16–17.

33 Herzog, *Psakim UKtavim, siman* 52, 233–34.

34 Warhaftig's statement may be found in *Divrei Knesset*, vol. 22, 1253–54. Regarding the broader debate, see Don-Yehiya, *Bein Shalom LeShlemut HaAretz*, 347–74.

CHAPTER 15: THE WAR ON TERROR: PREEMPTIVE OR PREVENTATIVE WAR?

1 Accessible at https://www.americanrhetoric.com/speeches/wariniraq/gwbushiraq62805.htm.

2   Ron Suskind, *The One Percent Doctrine: Deep Inside America's Pursuit of Its Enemies Since 9/11* (New York, 2006).

3   Dan Reiter, "Exploding the Powder Keg Myth: Preemptive Wars Almost Never Happen," *International Security* 20:2 (Autumn 1995): 5–34.

4   See Steve Coll, *Ghost Wars* (New York, 2004).

5   Some prominent philosophical responses to the Bush Doctrine, taking different sides, include: David Luban, "Preventive War," *Philosophy and Public Affairs* 32:3 (Summer 2004): 207–48; Robert J. Delahunty and John Yoo, "The Bush Doctrine: Can Preventive War Be Justified?" *Harvard Journal of Law and Public Policy* 32 (2009): 843–65; *Preemption: Military Action and Moral Justification*, eds. Henry Shue and David Rodin (Oxford University Press, Oxford, 2007); Jeff McMahan, "Preventive War,"; and Lawrence Freedman, "Prevention, Not Preemption," *The Washington Quarterly* 26:2 (2003): 105–14, who notes the rabbinic discussion discussed below.

6   Walzer, *Just and Unjust Wars*, 79–81. The rights-based approach is rejected for a more consequentialist approach in Luban, "Preventive War."

7   Sota 44b.

8   This is the opinion of R. Yehuda, at least as understood by R. Ḥisda, in Y. Sota 8:10.

9   Meiri, *Bet HaBeḥira*, Sota 42a. See also the ambiguous depiction of Rambam, *Perush LaMishnayot* 8:6 (Kapah edition), 185. (The earlier translation of this text is even murkier and possibly in error.)

10 See Rabbi David Frankel, *Shiyurei Korban*, Sota 8:10, s.v. *Veha de'amar*.

11 Rabbi Avraham de Boton, *Leḥem Mishneh on Hilkhot Melakhim* 5:1 and Rabbi Moshe Margolit, *Pnei Moshe*, Sota 8:10, s.v. *VeRav Ḥisda*.

12 Rabbi Yehiel Michel Epstein, *Arukh HaShulḥan HeAtid, Hilkhot Melakhim* 74:4, indicates that any preventative warfare done for the sake of self-defense would fall into the category of "commanded wars." Most contemporary authorities disagree and assert that some activity clearly falls in the category of "discretionary warfare." Besides the commentators cited in the previous notes, see Zevin, *LaOhr HaHalakha*, 12–13, Rabbi Joseph B. Soloveitchik as cited in Rabbi Schachter, *Nefesh HaRav*, 97–98; and Rabbi Rabinovitch ("Shitat HaRambam VeHaRamban

BeMitzvat Yishuv HaAretz," Tehumin 5, 180, nn. 1–2), who all follow *Lehem Mishneh.* See also *Hazon Ish on Hilkhot Melakhim* 5:1.

13 This is on the assumption that an alternative body (like a legislature or other representative of the people) can replace the ancient Sanhedrin to approve such wars, in contrast to the position of R. Kook discussed in chapter 2. See R. Hayim Hirschensohn (*Malki Ba-Kodesh*, vol. 1, p. 149), R. Isaac Herzog, *Tehuka LeYisrael al pi HaTorah*, vol. 1, 129 and vol 2, 33; R. Shaul Yisrael, *Amud HaYemini*, *siman* 16, and R. Yehuda Gershuni, "Milhemet Mitzva u-Milhemet Reshut," *Torah She-Ba'al Peh* 13 (5731), pp. 149–150. For further discussion, see R. Naftali Bar-Ilan, *Mishtar UMedina BaYisrael al pi HaTorah*, 2nd edition, vol. 4 (Eretz Hemdah, 2013), 1429–1449.

14 Some commentators further assert that even King David's expansionary warfare was really motivated by deterrence, in spite of the implication from Berakhot 3b. See Nachum Eliezer Rabinovitch, *Yad Peshuta, Hilkhot Melakhim* 5:1, 479–80; *Margoliyot HaYam*, Sanhedrin 16:22 (cited favorably by Rabbi Shlomo Aviner in *MiHayil el Hayil*, vol. 1, 127); and Rabbi Schachter, *Nefesh HaRav*, 97–98. Rabbi Yaakov Ariel, *Halakha BeYameinu* (Kfar Darom, 2012), 377–78, asserts that these are international conflicts that began with economic disputes but turned into national threats.

15 As previously noted, this principle originated in domestic criminal law (Sanhedrin 72a) but was also applied on the international level. See *Midrash Tanhuma, Parashat Pinhas* 3; Menahem HaMeiri, *Beit HaBehira* on Sanhedrin 72a, Rabbeinu Bahya on Exodus 14:7; and Hayim David HaLevi, "HaBa Lehorgekha Hashkem Lehorgo," *Tehumin* 1 (1980): 344–45.

CHAPTER 16: PREEMPTIVE STRIKES: THE CASES OF THE SIX-DAY WAR AND THE YOM KIPPUR WAR

1 See Michael Oren, *Six Days of War*, pp. 90–99, 123, and 157; Itamar Rabinovich, *Yitzhak Rabin: Soldier, Leader, Statesman* (Yale, 2017), 60–65; and Don-Yehiya, *Bein Shalom LeShlemut HaAretz*, 377–79.

2 Walzer, *Just and Unjust Wars*, 82–85. For conflicting opinions on the legality of Israel's preemptive action, see John Quigley, "The Six-Day War – 1967," in *The Use of Force in International Law: A Case-Based*

Approach, eds. Tom Ruys, Olivier Corten, and Alexandra Hofer (Oxford, 2019), 131–45.

3 Oren, *Six Days of War*, 119–21.

4 Oren, "Did Israel Want the Six-Day War?" *Azure* (Spring 1999): 71.

5 *Ynet News*, "Morning of Yom Kippur War: Cabinet Rejects Call for Preemptive Strike," June 10, 2010.

6 "Golda Meir: 'My Heart Was Drawn to a Preemptive Strike, but I Was Scared,'" *Times of Israel*, September 12, 2013.

7 Henry Kissinger, *Years of Upheaval* (New York, 1981), 477.

8 On the dilemma, see Steven J. Rosen and Martin Indyk, "The Temptation to Pre-Empt in a Fifth Arab-Israeli War," *Orbis* (Summer 1976) and chapter 3 of Alan Dershowitz, *Preemption: A Knife That Cuts Both Ways* (New York, 2006).

9 Orend, *The Morality of War*, 81. Vitoria's quote is found in Gregory M. Reichberg et al., *The Ethics of War: Classic and Contemporary Readings* (Blackwell, 2006), 325.

10 Regarding Article 51 and international law, see Michael N. Schmitt, "Preemptive Strategies in International Law," *Michigan Journal of International Law* 24 (2003): 513–48 and chapter 7 of Yoram Dinstein, *War, Aggression, and Self-Defense*, 3rd ed. (2001), esp. 172–73. See also Michael W. Doyle, *Striking First: Preemption and Prevention in International Conflict*, 44–98.

11 See, for example, Herzog, *Psakim UKtavim, siman* 52 and Goren, "Milḥemet Mitzva and Milḥemet Reshut," *Mahanyim* 69 (1962).

12 See also Rabbi Yaakov Ariel, "Al Hevel HaAretz HaLevoni," available at https://www.yeshiva.org.il/midrash/5065.

13 See, for example, the formulations in Rabbi Shneur Zalman of Liadi, *Shulḥan Arukh HaRav*, OH 329:6 and Rabbi Simha Rabinowitz, *Sefer Piskei Teshuvot* 329:6, based in part on medieval precedents of protecting Jewish border towns. See Rabbi Moshe Isserles, *Shulḥan Arukh*, OH 329:6.

CHAPTER 17: THE 1956 SINAI CAMPAIGN: A MORAL "WAR OF CHOICE"

1 A rudimentary description of similar conditions is depicted by Rabbi Karelitz as the scenario (discussed earlier) in Sota 44b under dispute

a "commanded war" or "discretionary war." See *Ḥazon Ish* to *Hilkhot Melachim* 5:1 and the discussion below.

2 The events leading to the war are described in Michael Oren, "Escalation to Suez: The Egypt-Israel Border War, 1949–56," *Journal of Contemporary History* 24:2 (April 1989): 347–73 and David Tal, "Israel's Road to the 1956 War," *International Journal of Middle East Studies* 28:1 (February 1996): 59–81.

3 See Amir Peleg-Uziyahu, "'Milḥemet Bereira Musarit': Hashpaat HaShoah al Tefisat HaBitaḥon shel Menachem Begin," *Iyunim BaTekumat Yisrael* 26 (2016): 230–32.

4 Mordechai Bar-On, *Moshe Dayan: Israel's Controversial Hero*, 69. See also his essay "David Ben-Gurion and the Sèvres Collusion," in *Suez 1956*, eds. W. M. Roger Louis and Roger Owen (Oxford, 1989), 146–48, and, more generally, his work *The Gates of Gaza* (London, 1994).

5 J. S. Levy & J. R. Gochal, "Democracy and Preventive War: Israel and the 1956 Sinai Campaign," *Security Studies* 11:2 (2001): 1–49, and Karl P. Mueller et al., *Striking First: Preemptive and Preventive Attack in U.S. National Security Policy*, appendix B (Rand Corporation, 2006), 191–98.

6 Pnina Lahav, "A Small Nation Goes to War: Israel's Cabinet Authorization of the 1956 War," *Israel Studies* 15:3 (2010): 77.

7 Mayzlish, *The Rabbinate in Stormy Times*, 140.

8 Zilberstein, *Bein Adam LeMedinato*, 119–26.

9 Don-Yehiya, *Bein Shalom LeShlemut HaAretz*, 344–59.

10 Benny Morris, *Righteous Victims*, 299.

11 Alexandra Hofer, "The Suez Crisis – 1956," in *The Use of Force in International Law: A Case-Based Approach*, ed. Tom Ruys et al., 36–47.

12 Benny Morris, *Israel's Border Wars* 35, 63–66.

13 Even Brian Orend (*The Morality of War*, 56) concedes that UN authorization is not morally necessary.

14 Kinga Tibori-Szabó, *Anticipatory Action in Self-Defence: Essence and Limits Under International Law* (Springer, 2011), 144.

15 Efraim Inbar, "The 'No-Choice War' Debate in Israel," *Journal of Strategic Studies* 12:1 (1989): 22–37 and Anita Shapira, *Land and Power*, 359.

16 Martin van Creveld, *The Sword and the Olive* (Public Affairs, 2008), 137 and Avi Shlaim's introduction to Motti Golani, *Israel in Search of a War: The Sinai Campaign, 1955–1956* (Brighton, 1998), vi–vii.

17 See Aharon Yariv, "Milḥemet Bereira – Milḥemet Be-Leit Bereira," in *Milḥemet Bereira* (1985), 9–31; and Selwyn Ilan Troen, "The Sinai Campaign as a 'War of No Alternative': Ben-Gurion's View of the Israel-Egyptian Conflict," in *The Suez-Sinai Crisis, 1956*, eds. Selwyn Ilan Troen and Moshe Shemesh, 180–95 and Gavriel Sheffer, "Sharett, Ben-Gurion, and the 1956 War of Choice," *Medina UMimshal* 5 (1988).

18 On the "accumulation of events" doctrine, see Tom Ruys, "*Armed Attack" and Article 51 of the UN Charter* (Cambridge 2011), 168–75 and Barry Levenfeld, "Israel's Counter-Fedayeen Tactics in Lebanon: Self-Defense and Reprisal under Modern International Law," *Columbia Journal of Transnational Law* 21:1 (1982): 1–48.

19 See, for example, Randall L. Schweller, "Domestic Structure and Preventive War: Are Democracies More Pacific?," *World Politics* 44:2 (January 1992): 264–67. Rabbi Shaul Yisraeli clearly believed this constituted an obligatory war of self-defense. See his remarks in *Amud HaYemini, siman 16, perek 5, se'if 23*.

20 Orend, *The Morality of War*, 58; Frowe, *The Ethics of War and Peace*, 64–65; Freedman, "On War and Choice," *The National Interest* 107 (May-June 2010): 9–16.

21 Orend, in *The Morality of War*, 60, deems it "widely improbable" to develop a satisfactory cost-benefit formula. On the complexity of proportionality in the context of discussing Israel's response to Hezbollah attacks, see David Kretzmer, "The Inherent Right to Self-Defense and Proportionality in Jus Ad Bellum," *European Journal of International Law* 24:1 (2013): 235–82.

22 Orend, *The Morality of War*, 58.

23 See Jeff McMahan's comments in Doyle, *Striking First*, 130–34. See also Jeff McMahan and Robert McKim, "The Just War and the Gulf War," *Canadian Journal of Philosophy* 23:4 (December 1993): 501–6.

24 Mordechai Bar-On, *Moshe Dayan*, 71.

25 Lawrence Freedman, "On War and Choice," *The National Interest* 107 (May-June 2010): 9–16. A prominent British military strategist,

Freedman cites rabbinic insights regarding discretionary wars in his article.

26 Ḥazon Ish to *Hilkhot Melachim* 5:1.

27 Hanson, "Epaminondas the Theban and the Doctrine of Preemptive War," in *Makers of Ancient Strategy*, ed. Victor Davis Hanson (Princeton, 2010), 107.

28 Yitzhak Rabin, "Ashlayot Mediniyot UMeḥiratan," in *Milḥemet Levanon: Bein Meḥaa LeHaskama* (5743), 13–14.

29 On the claim that "imminence" is really just a measure for necessity, see David Rodin, *War and Self-Defense*, 40–41.

CHAPTER 18: THE RAID ON OSIRAQ AND THE "BEGIN DOCTRINE"

1 For literature on preventative warfare, see John Vasquez, "Was the First World War a Preventive War?: Concepts, Criteria, and Evidence," in *The Outbreak of the First World War: Structure, Politics, and Decision Making*, eds. J. Levy and J. Vasquez (Cambridge, 2004), 199–224.

2 Exodus 1:10.

3 Numbers 22:4.

4 Walzer, *Just and Unjust Wars*, 75–80.

5 Kelsey Vlamis, "Why is Russia Attacking Ukraine," *Business Insider*, February 25, 2022.

6 This point is stressed in Luban, "Preventative War," 226–28.

7 For various arguments to this effect, see William C. Bradford, "The Duty to Defend Them: A Natural Law Justification for the Bush Doctrine of Preventive War," *Notre Dame Law Review* 79 (2004): 1365–1492.

8 The raid on Osiraq is defended as a defensive *milḥemet reshut* by Rabbi Shlomo Aviner, *MiḤayil el Ḥayil*, vol. 1 (Beit El), 127–28.

9 Dupuy and Martell, *Flawed Victory*, 94–98.

10 Quoted in Beth M. Polebaum, "National Self-Defense in International Law: An Emerging Standard for a Nuclear Age," *New York University Law Review* 59:1 (April 1984): 218–19.

11 Begin's motivations are described in Yehuda Avner, *The Prime Ministers* (Toby Press, 2010), 541–63 and Avi Shilon, *Menachem Begin: A Life* (Yale, 2012), chapter 16.

12 Jeremiah 17:6. The letter is translated in Avner, *The Prime Ministers*, 553.

13 Amos Yadlin, "The Begin Doctrine: The Lessons of Osirak and Deir Ez-Zor," *INSS Insight* 1037 (March 21, 2018).

14 Avner, *The Prime Ministers*, 557.

15 See Lawrence Freedman, "Prevention, Not Preemption," *Washington Quarterly* 26:2 (2003): 105–14 and John Yoo, "Using Force," *University of Chicago Law Review* 71:3 (Summer 2004): 729–97.

16 See Luban, "Preventative Force," and Lee Feinstein and Anne-Marie Slaughter, "A Duty to Prevent," *Foreign Affairs* (January-February 2004): 136–50.

17 Norrin M. Ripsman and Jack S. Levy, "The Preventive War That Never Happened: Britain, France, and the Rise of Germany in the 1930s," *Security Studies* 16:1 (January-March 2007): 32–67.

18 Marc Trachtenberg, "Preventive War and US Foreign Policy," *Security Studies* 16:1 (2007): 8–15.

19 An armed blockade is legally considered an act of aggression. See, for example, UN General Assembly Resolution 3314 (December, 1974).

20 Whitley Kaufman, "What's Wrong with Preventive War? The Moral and Legal Basis for the Preventive Use of Force," *Ethics and International Affairs* 19 (2005): 23–38.

CHAPTER 19: 1982 OPERATION PEACE FOR GALILEE AND ISRAEL'S GRAVEST MORAL FAILURE

1   On the history of the war, see Trevor N. Dupuy and Paul Martell, *Flawed Victory: How Lebanon Became a Culture of War and Hate* along with other sources cited below.

2   See the claim of Israel's ambassador to the UN, Yehuda Blum, as well as other arguments cited in O'Brien, *Law and Morality in Israel's War with the PLO*, 136–40.

3   Ahron Bregman, *Israel's Wars: A History Since 1947* (Routledge, 2016), 162–67.

4   Ariel Sharon (*Warrior: An Autobiography*, 455) asserted that this was the "match that ignited the fuse," but the true *casus belli* was the repeated PLO terror attacks and their arms buildup in southern Lebanon.

5 Begin, "War of No-Choice or War of Choice," *Maariv*, August 20, 1982, as delivered at the National Defense College. Partial translation available at https://www.nytimes.com/1982/08/21/world/excerpts-from-begin-speech-at-national-defense-college.html

6 See Amir Peleg-Uziyahu, "'Milḥemet Bereira Musarit': Hashpaat HaShoah al Tefisat HaBitaḥon shel Menachem Begin," 243–46.

7 Begin, "War of No-Choice or War of Choice."

8 Maimonides, *Mishneh Torah, Hilkhot Melakhim* 5:1; emphasis added.

9 Rabbi Aharon Lichtenstein, "Musar UMilḥama," *Teḥumin* 4, 185.

10 O'Brien, *Law and Morality in Israel's War with the PLO*, 139–45.

11 Aryeh Naor, *Begin in Power: Personal Testimony* (Tel Aviv, 1993), 253.

12 Dupuy and Martell, *Flawed Victory*, 128–29 and Ze'ev Schiff and Ehud Yaari, *Israel's Lebanon War* (New York, 1984), 105.

13 Dupuy and Martell, *Flawed Victory*, 192.

14 Schiff and Yaari, *Israel's Lebanon War*, 109, 163.

15 Ibid., 165–66, 181–88.

16 For a summary of opinions, see Daniel Gordis, *Menachem Begin* (Nextbook, 2014), 203–5.

17 Elyashiv Reichner, *By Faith Alone: The Story of Rabbi Yehuda Amital* (Maggid Books, 2011), 162–65. On the essay "HaMaalot MiMaamakim," see Dov Schwartz, "Milḥemet Yom Hakipurim BaToda'at HaTziyonut HaDatit," *Reishit*, Dec. 23, 2019.

18 Shtamler, *Ayin BeAyin*, 302. For examples of his opposition, see Kook, *LeHilkhot Tzibbur*, 142, 222–23, 230–31.

19 Kook, *LeHilkhot Tzibbur*, 183–85. For a defense of this expansive delineation of the homeland, see Rabbi Moshe Tzuriel, *LeShaa ULeDorot*, 239–42 and Rabbi Eliezer Melamed, *Peninei Halakha: HaAm VeHaAretz – Likkutim*, 2nd ed. (Har Bracha, 5778), 73–83.

20 See Moshe Hellinger and Yitzhak Hershkowitz, *Tziyut VeItziyut BaTziyonut HaDatit*, 52–82.

21 Reichner, *By Faith Alone*, 171. A similar emphasis on the Jewish scale of values is found in the work by Rabbi Lichtenstein, "Musar UMilḥama," 185.

22 Other prominent rabbinic figures supporting the Camp David Accords and permitting territorial concessions included Sephardic Chief Rabbi Ovadia Yosef and Rabbi Hayim David HaLevi of Tel Aviv.

23 *Tanna Devei Eliyahu Rabba* 14:2.

24 Reichner, *By Faith Alone*, 180–95.

25 Hanan Porat, *Et Aḥai Anokhi Mevakesh* (Beit El, 5749), 93–115, particularly 98–101. See also Hagay Huberman, *Hanan Porat – Biographia* (Tel Aviv, 2013), 181–87.

26 See also Rabbi Shlomo Aviner, *MiḤayil el Ḥayil*, 94–98.

27 Porat, *Et Aḥai Anokhi Mevakesh*, 112–15.

28 Goren, *Torat HaMedina*, pp. 400–401. See also Rabbi Ahron Soloveichik, "Waging War on Shabbat," *Tradition* 20:3 (Fall 1982): 180.

29 Rabbinic reaction to Sabra and Shatila is discussed in chapter 24.

30 Goren, *Meshiv Milḥama*, vol. 3, 267–303.

31 See also Goren, *Torat HaMedina*, 399.

32 Frowe, *The Ethics of War and Peace*, 57 and O'Brien, *Law and Morality in Israel's War with the PLO*, 279–80.

33 *Meshiv Milḥama*, vol. 3, 267–303.

34 See also Rabbi Yeshayahu Steinberger, "Mivtzat Shlom HaGalil MiBeḥinat Halakha," *Ohr HaMizraḥ* 31:3–4: 203.

35 In a 1967 letter to Professor Ernst Simon, as reproduced in Yair Kahn and Kalman Neuman, "A Rabbinic Exchange on the Disengagement: A Case Study in R. Aharon Lichtenstein's Approach to *Hilkhot Tsibbur*," *Tradition* 47:4 (2015): 186.

36 R. Soloveitchik's position and the response to it is detailed in Kalman Neuman, "Bein Ortodoxia Modernit BeArtzot HaBerit LeTziyonut Datit BeYisrael: Hashpaat HaRav Soloveitchik al Emdot HaTzibbur HaDati BeYisrael," in *Rabbi in the New World: The Influence of Rabbi J. B. Soloveitchik on Culture, Education, and Jewish Thought* (Jerusalem, 2010), 471–89 [Hebrew].

37 Rabbi Ovadia Yosef, "Ceding Territory of the Land of Israel in Order to Save Lives," *Crossroads* 3 (1990), 11–28. A rejoinder is offered by Rabbi Shaul Yisrael, "Ceding Territory Because of Mortal Danger," 29–46.

38 R. Lichtenstein, "Musar UMilḥama," *Teḥumin* 4, 185, argues that moral decisions in democracies cannot be left to "technocrats and experts."

CHAPTER 20: AS THE WAR STARTS: SIEGES IN LEBANON AND THE OBLIGATION TO LET PEOPLE FLEE

1 See Richard Gabriel, *Operation Peace for Galilee: The Israeli-PLO War in Lebanon* (New York, 1984), 127–70. For ethical analysis, see O'Brien, *Law and Morality in Israel's War with the PLO*, 179–90 and 196–97.

2 Gabriel, *Operation Peace for Galilee*, 164.

3 Dupuy and Martell, *Flawed Victory*, 210, 220.

4 Schiff and Yaari, *Israel's Lebanon War*, 216–17.

5 Goren *Meshiv Milḥama*, vol. 3, 239–65. See also Rabbi Yehuda Gershuni, "He'arot Legabei Milḥemet 'Shlom HaGalil' Bilvanon," *Arakhim BaMivḥan Milḥama*, 151.

6 See the opinion of R. Natan in *Sifre Bemidbar* 157 and Maimonides, *Mishneh Torah, Melakhim* 6:7. Opposing opinions may be found there and elsewhere. See Menahem Kahane, *Sifre Bemidbar*, 1271–72 and Yishai Kiel, "The Morality of War in Rabbinic Literature," in *War and Peace in Jewish Tradition*, eds. Yigal Levin and Amnon Shapira (Routledge, 2011), 129–32.

7 This point is emphasized by Radbaz in his glosses to *Mishneh Torah* 6:7 and is implied by the formulation in the medieval *Midrash HaGadol* (ed. Rabinowitz) on Numbers 31:7, 538. See also Federbusch, *Mishpat HaMelukha BeYisrael*, 205–6.

8 See, for example, the letter printed in *Maariv*, August 11, 1982, 4.

9 IDF Chief Rabbi Eyal Krim, "Kitur HaArim BeMivtzat Homat Magen," in *HaMilḥama BaTerror*, ed. Yair Halevy (Kiryat Arba, 2006), 11–42, based on the position of Rabbi Yehoshua Ehrenberg, *Shu"t Dvar Yehoshua*, vol. 2, *siman* 126.

10 Gabriel, *Operation Peace for Galilee*, 136.

11 Goren, *Meshiv Milḥama*, vol. 3, 264–265.

12 Dinstein, *The Conduct of Hostilities*, 253–57.

13 On sieges in the biblical period, see Jacob Wright, "Warfare and Wanton Destruction: A Reexamination of Deuteronomy 20: 19–20 in Relation to Ancient Siegecraft," *Journal of Biblical Literature* 127:3 (2008), 423–58.

14 Maimonides deems it a "received tradition." See *Torah Temima* on Numbers 31:7, which suggests that the idea originated with Joshua,

who the Talmud (Y. Shevi'it 6:1) asserts always offered the enemy to flee or make peace, as discussed in chapter 2.

15 *Sifre Devarim* 199–200.

16 As noted by Shaul Lieberman, *Tosefta KiFeshutah, vol. 8: Nashim*, 989. See David A. Graff, *The Eurasian Way of War* (New York, 2016), 121.

17 II Kings 25:4. See the commentary of Abarbanel.

18 Lamentations 4:9–10.

19 For sources from Josephus and rabbinic literature, see Gershon Bar-Cochva and Ahron Horovitz, *A Temple in Flames* (Maggid Books, 2014), 86–100.

20 Gittin 56b and Josephus, *The Jewish War*, book 5, chapter 11.

21 The Bar Kokhba rebellion also ended in 135 CE after a siege around the Betar fortress.

22 See Goren *Meshiv Milḥama*, vol. 3, 264–83.

23 Goren, *Meshiv Milḥama*, vol. 3, 283–303.

24 Ibid., 284, 302. In fact, at one point in this essay, he even contemplates whether the "fourth side open" law applies in contemporary times – precisely the position of R. Yisraeli which R. Goren had attacked less than twelve months beforehand. Ultimately, R. Goren rejects that option.

25 This position is also compatible with contemporary international law. Article 57(2)c of AP/1 prescribes that "effective advance warning shall be given of attacks which may affect the civilian population, *unless circumstances do not permit*" (emphasis added).

CHAPTER 21: ONCE THE WAR STARTS: SHIFTING MORAL RESPONSIBILITIES IN URBAN WARFARE

1 Schiff and Yaari, *Israel's Lebanon War*, 139–150.

2 Ibid., 148.

3 Ibid., 149.

4 O'Brien, *Law and Morality in Israel's War with the PLO*, 174–79; Gabriel, *Operation Peace for Galilee*, 94–95; Robert W. Tucker, "A Reply to Critics: Morality and the War," *New York Times*, July 15, 1982.

5 W. Hays Parks, "Air War and the Law of War," *Air Force Law Review* 32 (1990): 166.

6　This was not the first time the PLO utilized human shields. See *PLO in Lebanon: Selected Documents*, ed. R. Israeli (1983), 205–31.

7　Schiff and Yaari, *Israel's Lebanon War*, 142.

8　Walzer, *Just and Unjust War*, 160–70.

9　Ezekiel 33:4. See also I Samuel 15:6.

10　For another recent example of this debate over civilian casualties and force protection, see Carter Malkasian, *The American War in Afghanistan* (Oxford, 2021), 224–226.

11　Ecclesiastes Rabba 7:16. On this version of the midrash, see Eliav Shochetman, "He Who is Compassionate to the Cruel Will Ultimately Become Cruel to the Compassionate: Contemporary Lessons from an Ancient Midrash," *ACPR Policy Paper* No. 124 (2001).

12　Gabriel, *Operation Peace for Galilee*, 95; emphasis added.

13　"Musar UMilḥama," *Teḥumin* 4, 180–183.

14　"Musar UMilḥama," *Teḥumin* 4, 186, emphasis added. This point was reiterated during Operation Protective Edge in 2014 in Gaza, when R. Lior asserted that the IDF could launch aerial or artillery bombardments on any target in Gaza rather than endanger an IDF soldier. The full letter may be downloaded at https://www.haaretz.co.il/news/politics/1.2384726.

15　Deuteronomy 23:10 and commentary of the Ramban, Rabbeinu Bahya, and the Netziv.

16　See David Fisher, *Morality and War: Can War Be Just in the Twenty-First Century?* (Oxford, 2011), 108–33.

17　See Rabbi Yosef ibn Kaspi, *Mishnat Kesef* on Deuteronomy 22:8 (Jerusalem, 5730), vol. 2, 293. (The exception to the rule, he argues, are members of the seven nations because of their bestial behavior.) Rabbi Tzvi Hirsch Ashkenazi, *Shu"t Ḥakham Tzvi* 26, argues that the "fourth side open" requirement is meant to ensure that Jews do not develop callous moral characteristics toward Jews and non-Jews alike.

18　See John F. Burns, "Report Details British Abuses in Iraq," *New York Times*, September 9, 2011.

19　Fisher, *Morality and War*, 129.

20　*Ohr HaHayim* to Gen. 34:25.

21 See Gerald Blidstein, "The Treatment of Hostile Civilian Populations: The Contemporary Halakhic Discussion in Israel," *Israel Studies* 1:2 (Fall 1996): 35–37 and Gutel, "Leḥima BeShetaḥ Ravei Ukhlusiya Ezraḥit," 32–33.

22 Yitzhak Shapira and Yosef Elitzur, *Torat HaMelekh* (Yizhar, 5770), 224–227.

23 Ariel Finkelstein, *Derekh HaMelekh* (Netivot, 5771), 141–42.

24 See Rabbi Yaakov Ariel's approbation to Finkelstein's *Derekh HaMelekh*, 7 and Rabbi Hershel Schachter, *BeIkvei HaTzon* (1997), 206–7.

25 Gen. 32:8 and comments of Rashi, citing Genesis Rabba 76:2.

26 See the comments of Rabbi Shlomo Luria, *Yeriot Shlomo* and Rabbi David Pardo, *Maskil LeDavid*, on Gen. 32:8.

27 Maharal, *Gur Aryeh* to Gen 32:8. See also Radak on I Chronicles 22:8, where he explains that King David didn't get to build the Temple because of excessive bloodshed under his watch, even though his intent throughout was to kill evil combatants.

28 Yaakov Katz, "How the IDF invented 'Roof Knocking': The Tactic That Saves Lives in Gaza," *Jerusalem Post*, March 25, 2021. For rabbinic praise of "roof knocking," see Rabbi Avraham Gisser, *The Just Israel: On War Against Terrorism – Morality and The Law* (Ofra, 5769), written after Operation Cast Lead in 2008, and Rabbi Shlomo Aviner, *Iturei Yerushalayim* (Av 5774), 39–40, written regarding Operation Protection Edge in 2014.

29 Lazar Berman, "Top US General: Israel Protected Civilian Lives in Gaza," *Times of Israel*, November 7, 2014.

30 Adam Taylor, "Israel's Controversial 'Roof Knocking' Tactic Appears in Iraq. And This Time, It's the U.S. Doing It," *Washington Post*, April 27, 2016.

31 Dinstein, *The Conduct of Hostilities*, 172–73.

32 Sec. 57(5). See also 51(8).

33 Janina Dill, "Israel's Use of Law and Warnings in Gaza," OpinioJuris, July 30, 2014. For a contrary opinion, see Laurie R. Blank, "Getting the law right on the Israel-Hamas conflict," *The Hill*, July 14, 2014.

34 Asaf Gibor, "Yorim VeDohim: Assor LeShimush BaNohal HaKash BaGag," *Makor Rishon*, December 9, 2018.

35 Significantly, both the US Department of the Army's *The Army Capstone Concept* (2009) and the UK Ministry of Defense's *Future Character of Conflict* (2010) draw heavily from the Israeli experience for moral direction. See also David E. Johnson, *Hard Fighting: Israel in Lebanon and Gaza* (Rand Corporation, 2011).

CHAPTER 22: LEGITIMATE MILITARY TARGETS: MILITARY NECESSITY AND DISCRIMINATION IN GAZA AND LEBANON

1   In retrospect, many have questioned whether Israel was adequately prepared for this war, raising questions of discretionary wars that we discussed in earlier chapters.

2   Amos Harel and Avi Issacharoff, *34 Days: Israel, Hezbollah, and the War in Lebanon* (New York, 2008), 78.

3   For this passage, see sec. 1, nos. 14–16 of the Lieber Code. For discussion, see Witt, *Lincoln's Code*, 181–84 and Burrus M. Carnahan, "Lincoln, Lieber and the Laws of War: The Origins and Limits of the Principle of Military Necessity," *American Journal of International Law* 92:2 (April 1998), 213 – 231.

4   Deuteronomy 20:19-20. See Jacob Wright, "Warfare and Wanton Destruction: A Reexamination of Deuteronomy 20:19–20 in Relation to Ancient Siegecraft," *Journal of Biblical Literature* 127:3 (2008): 423–58.

5   See Rashi and Ḥizkuni on Deuteronomy 20:19.

6   Rambam, *Sefer HaMitzvot*, negative commandment 57. See *HaKetav VeHaKabbala* on Deuteronomy 20:19 and Federbusch, *Mishpat HaMelukha BeYisrael*, 208–9.

7   Rabbi David Tzvi Hoffman on Deuteronomy 20:19, s.v. *ki haadam*. See also Ido Rechnitz and Elazar Goldstein, *Etika Tzeva'it Yehudit* (Yediot, 2013), 113–14.

8   Ramban 20:19 and his *Addendum to Sefer HaMitzvot*, positive commandment 6 (pp. 246–47 in Chavel edition); *Sefer HaḤinukh* 529, based on *Sifre Devarim* 203–4. For additional sources, see Rabbi Yitzhak Kaufman, *HaTzava KeHalakha* (Jerusalem, 5754), 13–14. Maimonides, however, limits this dispensation. See *Mishneh Torah, Melakhim* 6:9 and *Kesef Mishneh* there.

9   Thus the alleged 2023 Russian bombing of the Kakhovka dam in Ukraine is deeply problematic, even as more details are necessary to make a final judgment. See Aaron D'Andrea, "Ukraine Dam Blast 'Probably a War Crime,' But Not Clear-Cut. Here's Why," *Global News*, June 12, 2023.

10 See Rabbi Yaakov Ariel's statement, available at https://www.yeshiva.org.il/ask/88969, made during the 2014 Operation Protective Edge, apparently against voices who called for reprisal attacks on civilians, such as R. Yisrael Rosen, "Shnei Pagazim Al Kol Raketah," *Srugim* website, Aug. 8, 2014.

11 Hays Parks, "The Protection of Civilians from Air Warfare," *Israel Yearbook on Human Rights*, vol. 27, 77–84; Tami Davis Biddle, *Air Power and Warfare: A Century of Theory and History*, 30; G. Best, *Humanity in Warfare*, 242–85.

12 Arthur Harris, *Bomber Command* (1947), 75–76.

13 Major Jeanne Meyer, "Tearing Down the Facade: A Critical Look at the Current Law on Targeting the Will of the Enemy and Air Force Doctrine," *Air Force Law Review* 51: 143–82.

14 Marcus, *Israel's Long War with Hezbollah*, 214–19 and Harel and Issacharoff, 34 Days, 59–60.

15 Rabbi Avraham Sharir, "Al Kiddush Hashem BeMilḥemet Mitzva," *Tzohar* 31.

16 Marcus, *Israel's Long War with Hezbollah*, 143. For general literature, see Luke N. Condra and Jacob N. Shapiro, "Who Takes the Blame? The Strategic Effects of Collateral Damage," *American Journal of Political Science* 56:1 (January 2012): 167–87.

17 Harel and Issacharoff, *34 Days*, 78–91.

18 Gadi Eizenkot, "Hishtanut HaIyum? HaMaaneh BaZira HaTzfonit," *Tzava VaEstretegia* 2:1 (June 2010): 29.

19 Dinstein, *The Conduct of Hostilities*, 102–11.

20 Steven Coleman, *Military Ethics* (Oxford, 2013), 199–207.

21 W. H. Parks, "Asymmetries and the Identification of Legitimate Military Objectives," in W. H. von Heinegg and V. Epping, *International Humanitarian Law Facing New Challenges*, (Berlin, 2007), 106–7.

22 Rabbi Yaakov Ariel, *Halakha BeYamenu*, 376.

23 Fred Pearce, "Water in the War Zone," *New Scientist*, December 17, 1994.

24 Rabbi Avraham Sharir, "Al Kiddush Hashem BeMilḥemet Mitzva," *Tzohar* 31 (5768): n. 31.

25 Anthony H. Cordesman, Lessons of the 2006 *Israeli-Hezbollah War* (CSIS, 2007), 45–48, 122.

26 "Israeli Military Finds Cluster Bomb Use in Lebanon War Was Legal," *Christian Science Monitor*, Dec. 26, 2007.

27 Virgil Wiebe, "Footprints of Death: Cluster Bombs as Indiscriminate Weapons under International Humanitarian Law," *Michigan Journal of International Law* 22 (2000): 85.

28 Ronen Bergman, *Rise and Kill First* (Random House, 2018), 498–515.

29 "Israel Supreme Court: Public Committee Against Torture in Israel v. Israel," *International Legal Materials* 46:2 (March 2007): 375–408.

30 See Steven David, "Israel's Policy of Targeted Killing," *Ethics and International Affairs* 17:1 (March 2003): 111–26, along with the reply by Yael Stein, and David's rebuttal.

31 Dinstein, *The Conduct of Hostilities*, 117.

32 Sanhedrin 72b and the comments found in *Yad Rama*, as well as *Mishneh Torah, Hilkhot Rotze'aḥ* 1:6.

33 Stephen Coleman, *Military Ethics* (Oxford, 2012), Section 9.4.

34 Michael Schmitt, "Deconstructing Direct Participation in Hostilities: The Constitutive Elements," *New York University Journal of International Law and Politics* 42 (2010): 697–739. For a philosophical explanation (and critique), see Helen Frowe, *The Ethics of War and Peace*, 168–72.

35 See the brief submitted by the Shurat HaDin organization in the 2004 Israeli High Court of Justice case 769/02.

36 Sanhedrin 73a.

37 See Itamar Warhaftig, "Haganah Atzmit BaAverot Retzaḥ UHavala," *Sinai* 81 (5737): 56–62.

38 See Rabbi Meir Simha of Dvinsk, *Ohr Same'aḥ* on *Hilkhot Rotze'aḥ* 1:8. See also *Shu"t Aḥiezer, Even HaEzer* 1:19. More dramatic cases come from eras in which Jews faced discrimination or persecution. Some medieval communities, for example, deemed one Jew a "pursuer" for informing (*moser*) on another Jew to the local authorities. This

was because the alleged offender could be illegitimately prosecuted and killed by the non-Jewish authorities. Several steps are necessary until the accused Jew is killed by the unjust rulers; nonetheless, the informer is still a "pursuer" because he sets off a clear chain of endangering reactions.

39 Yechezkel Lichtenstein, *VeEmunatkha BaLeilot* (Jerusalem, 2017), 165–82. The claim of indirect *rodef* cannot be made against officials whose political views are deemed as "dangerous" by their opponents. The alleged causation is too speculative, theoretical, and indirect. This is especially true for democratically-elected officials who have good intentions. A prime minister who supports a discretionary war, for example, cannot be killed by those who think his decision is misguided, even though such wars are clearly dangerous for the population. On this distinction, which is particularly important in light of the horrific assassination of Yitzhak Rabin, see Eliav Schochetman, "Shilton Yehudi Eino Yahol Lihiyot Rodef," *Tehumin* 19 (5759), 40-50 and R. Yehuda Henkin, *Teshuvot Bnai Banim* 3:33.

40 These examples draw from two well-known philosophical treatises on the topic. See George P. Fletcher and Luis E. Chiesa, "Self-Defense and the Psychotic Aggressor," *Criminal Law Conversations*, eds. Robinson, Garvey and Ferzan (Oxford, 2008) and Jeff McMahan, "Self-Defense and the Problem of the Innocent Attacker," *Ethics* 104:2 (January 1994): 252–90. For rabbinic sources, see Dov Frimer, "HaRodef Lelo Ashama," in *Nediv Lev* (5771), 213–32.

41 See Shlomo Brody, *A Guide to the Complex*, 15–21.

42 See, for example, Benjamin Ish-Shalom, "'Purity of Arms' and Purity of Ethical Judgment," *Meorot* 6:1 (Shevat 5767).

43 See, for example, Uri Milstein, "Takhkir: HaShe'elot Ha-Kashot," *Maariv* Jan. 7, 2018, and Nadav Shragai, "The Legend of Ambushed Palmach Squad '35,'" *Haaretz*, April 27, 2009.

44 Michael Broyde, "Only the Good Die Young?", *Meorot* 6:1 (Shevat 5767).

CHAPTER 23: PROPORTIONALITY AND THE GREAT MISSED OPPORTUNITY

1 https://www.nytimes.com/2006/07/20/world/middleeast/20nations.html.

2 Walzer, "On Proportionality," *New Republic,* January 8, 2009; emphasis added.

3 The quote and commentary is found in W. Hays Parks, "Air War and the Law of War," 168–75. See also Jeremy Rabkin, "Proportionality in Perspective: Historical Light on the Law of Armed Conflict," *San Diego International Law Journal* 16:2 (2015): 263–340.

4 For different theories, see Amichai Cohen, *Proportionality in Modern Asymmetrical Wars* (Jerusalem Center for Public Affairs, 2010).

5 Clause 51(5).

6 As cited in Laurie Blank, "The Application of IHL in the Goldstone Report: A Critical Commentary," *Yearbook of International Humanitarian Law* 12 (2009): 368.

7 Lauren Blumenfeld, "In Israel, a Divisive Struggle Over Targeted Killing," *Washington Post,* Aug. 27, 2006.

8 Geoffrey Best, as cited and criticized in Michael Gross, "The Second Lebanon War: The Question of Proportionality and the Prospect of Non-Lethal Warfare," *Journal of Military Ethics* 7:1 (2008): 4–6.

9 Page 626 of the ICRC commentary, available at https://www.loc.gov/rr/frd/Military_Law/pdf/Commentary_GC_Protocols.pdf.

10 See the criticism of this change in Dinstein, *The Conduct of Hostilities,* 155–64. See also 81–86 for his comments regarding human shields.

11 Warren Hoge, "Attacks Qualify as War Crimes, Officials Say," *New York Times,* July 20, 2006.

12 Michael N. Schmitt, "Human Shields in International Humanitarian Law," *Columbia Journal of Transnational Law* 47:2 (2009): 292–97.

13 ICRC commentary on Articles 57 and 58. This approach and others are discussed in Schmitt, "Human Shields in International Humanitarian Law," 324–32.

14 W. Hays Parks, "Air War and the Laws of War," 137, 161–68.

15 Jeremy Rabkin, "Can We Win a War If We Have to Fight by Cosmopolitan Rules?", *Orbis* 55 (2011): 700–16. See also Noam Zohar, "Risking and Protecting Lives: Soldiers and Opposing Civilians," in *How We Fight: Ethics in War* (Oxford, 2014), 168.

16 Rabbi Shmuel Eliyahu, "Hilkhot Milḥama," 3 Tevet 5769 (January 5, 2009), available at https://www.yeshiva.org.il/midrash/9457.

17 As quoted in Schmitt, "Human Shields in International Humanitarian Law," 327.

18 For a sampling of thinkers, see Amnon Rubenstein and Yaniv Roznai, "Human Shields in Modern Armed Conflicts: The Need for a Proportionate Proportionality," *Stanford Law and Policy Review* 22: 93–127.

19 Louise Doswald-Beck, "The Civilian in the Crossfire," *Journal of Peace Research* 24:3 (Sept. 1987): 257; emphasis added.

20 Richard Rosen, "Targeting Enemy Forces in the War on Terror: Preserving Civilian Immunity," *Vanderbilt Law Review* 42:3 (2009): 683–777.

21 Data here is based on Bergman, *Rise and Kill First*, 516–28; Alon Margalit, "Did LOAC Take the Lead? Reassessing Israel's Targeted Killing of Salah Shehadeh and the Subsequent Calls for Criminal Accountability," *Journal of Conflict and Security Law* 17:1 (2012): 147–73; and Israel's official 2011 report of the Salah Shehadeh Special Investigatory Commission, available online at https://embassies.gov.il/MFA/AboutIsrael/state/Law/Pages/Salah_Shehadeh-Special_Investigatory_Commission_27-Feb-2011.aspx.

22 Emphasis added. Quotes from UN Security Council Meeting, July 24, 2002, available at https://documents-dds-ny.un.org/doc/UNDOC/PRO/N02/494/04/PDF/N0249404.pdf?OpenElement.

23 Carter Malkasian, *The American War in Afghanistan* (Oxford, 2021), 111.

24 Neta C. Crawford, *Accountability for Killing: Moral Responsibility for Collateral Damage in America's Post–9/11 Wars* (Oxford, 2013), 73–158.

25 CNN, "Israeli general apologizes for civilian deaths."

26 Daniel Byman, "Do Targeted Killings Work?", *Foreign Affairs* 85:2 (March 2006): 103–4.

27 Bergman, *Rise and Kill First*, 563.

28 Ibid., 546, and Daniel Byman, *A High Price: The Triumphs and Failures of Israeli Counterterrorism* (2010), 311.

29 Blumenfeld, "In Israel, a Divisive Struggle Over Targeted Killing."

CHAPTER 24: JUSTIFYING COLLATERAL DAMAGE IN SERBIA AND THE MIDDLE EAST

1 https://www.icty.org/en/press/final-report-prosecutor-committee-established-review-nato-bombing-campaign-against-federal#IVB5.

2 Frowe, *The Ethics of War and Peace*, 147.

3 See Netziv, *Haamek Davar* on Genesis 9:5 and Deuteronomy 20:8. See also Gutel, "Leḥima BeShetaḥ Ravei Ukhlusiya Ezraḥit," 34–36 and Yitzhak Roness, "Al Musaryotah Shel HaMilḥama BaSifrut Halakha," *Sefer Emdot* 1 (5770): 182–184.

4 Avraham Steinberg, *Encyclopedia of Jewish Medical Ethics*, vol. 3 (Feldheim, 2003), 1061 and Charles L. Sprung et al., "Relieving Suffering or Intentionally Hastening Death: Where Do You Draw the Line?", *Critical Care Medicine* 36:1 (2008): 8–13.

5 Ketubot 6a. See Rabbi Noam Koenigsberg, "Psik Reisha VeLo Yamut: HaMashal VeHaNimshal," *HaMaayan* 50:2 (Tevet 5770): 31–34 and Rabbi Asher Weiss, "Davar SheEino Mitkaven UPsik Reisha," in his *Minchas Asher: Shemot*, 2nd edition (Jerusalem, 5783), 472–482.

6 Frowe, *The Ethics of War and Peace*, 162.

7 Walzer, *Just and Unjust Wars*, 155–56.

8 Ibid., 136.

9 On the United States' adoption of an approach to prevent collateral damage, see Yagil Levy, *Whose Life Is Worth More?* (Stanford, 2019).

10 Walzer and Margalit, "Israel: Civilians and Combatants," *New York Review of Books*, May 14, 2009.

11 Ambassador Gabrielle Shalev, January 6, 2009, speech to UN Security Council (emphasis added), available online at https://www.gov.il/en/departments/news/statement-amb-shalev-un-ecurity-council-6-jan-2009. See also "Friedman: Siknu Ḥayalim Kedei Lishmor al Palestinim," *YNET*, February 18, 2009; Amnon Lord, "Gantz: Lakaḥnu Sikun BeShejaiya al Ḥeshbon Loḥamei Golani," *Mida*, May 12, 2015.

12 This oft-cited example is discussed by many. See Ziv Bohrer and Mark Osiel, "Proportionality in Military Force at War's Multiple

Levels: Averting Civilian Casualties vs. Safeguarding Soldiers," *Vanderbilt Journal of Transnational Law* 46 (2013): 776.

13 Ibid., 751–52. See also Malkasian, *The American War in Afghanistan,* 224–226.

14 Cited in Yagil Henkin, "Urban Warfare and the Lessons of Jenin," *Azure* 15 (Summer 2003): 56.

15 See Asa Kasher and Amos Yadlin, "Military Ethics of Fighting Terror: An Israeli Perspective," *Journal of Military Ethics* 4:1 (2005): 3–32; Kasher and Yadlin, "Determining Norms for Warfare in New Situations: Between Military Ethics and the Laws of War," *Military and Strategic Affairs* 5:1 (May 2013): 95–117; Asa Kasher, "Operation Cast Lead and the Ethics of Just War," *Azure* 37 (Summer 2009); and the debate between Kasher and Yadlin and Walzer and Margalit, "'Israel and the Rules of War': An Exchange," *New York Review of Books* (July 11, 2009). See also Eyal Benvenisti, "Human Dignity in Combat: The Duty to Spare Enemy Civilians," *Israel Law Review* 39:2 (Summer 2006): 81–109.

16 Kasher, "Operation Cast Lead."

17 See, for example, Eliav Schochetman, "Sikun Hayalei Tzahal LeShem Meniyat Pegiya BaEzrahei Oiyev BeShulei Mivtzat Homat Magen," *Netiv* 91–92 (2003). Rabbinic consensus on this question is highlighted in Amos Israel-Vleeschhouwer, "Nituah Gishot Hilkhatiyot BaDavar Gevulot Shimush BaKoah," *Mishpatim VeAsakim* 17 (August 2014): 605–62 and Elazar Goldstein, "Musar VeDat BeHityahasutam shel Poskei Halakha Tziyonim-Dati'im LaDoctrina shel Hasinut Ezrahim," *Moreshet Yisrael* 18:2 (2020): 357–86.

18 Rabbi Asher Weiss, Minchas Asher: Devarim, 1st ed. (Jerusalem, 5769), 217–222 and Rabbi Yaakov Ariel, *Halakha BeYamenu,* 378–379.

19 See Noam Zohar, "Double Effect and Double Intention: A Collectivist Perspective," *Israel Law Review* 40:3 (2007): 730–42.

20 "UN humanitarian chief blasts Hizbullah," *Jerusalem Post,* July 25, 2006. For greater detail, see Reuven Erlich, *Hezbollah's Use of Lebanese Civilians as Human Shields* (Glilot, Israel, 2006).

21 Raphael D. Marcus, *Israel's Long War with Hezbollah* (Washington, 2018), 205. See also 143.

22 Walzer, "Fair War," *New Republic,* July 31, 2006.

23 George Fletcher, *Romantics at War* (Princeton, 2002), 44–46.

24 Ezekiel 21:8.

25 Ibid. 22:23–31.

26 Here, moral responsibility falls on their leaders for placing citizens in harm's way for a hopeless cause. This is especially true when the leaders had the opportunity to let their people flee for their lives yet instead held them hostage inside the siege. Of course, Nebuchadnezzar and Titus were far from saints. Their imperial conquests were unjust and their tactical methods were brutal. Jerusalem's residents shouldn't have been under attack. Nonetheless, much responsibility lies with the Jewish leaders who could have prevented their people's deaths. Indeed, as we noted earlier, one of the criticisms of the Warsaw Ghetto rebels was that they'd be endangering the ghetto residents by rising up against the Nazis. In their case, however, the deaths of the ghetto residents were fairly inevitable. The same is not at all true for Lebanese civilians, with whom Israel has no gripes.

27 Amos Harel, "Hamas Leaders Hiding in Basement of Israeli-Built Hospital in Gaza," *Haaretz*, January 12, 2009; Steven Erlanger, "A Gaza War Full of Traps and Trickery," *New York Times*, Jan. 10, 2009; and "Violating Int'l Law, Hamas Uses Hospital Patients as Human Shields," *The Tower*, July 23, 2014. On Israel's unwillingness to bomb this target, see Amnon Lord, "Gantz: Lakaḥnu Sikun BeShejaiya al Ḥeshbon Loḥamei Golani," Mida, May 12, 2015. Israel would bomb a rehabilitation center once its occupants were cleared. See "Watch: IDF Targets Hospital Used as Hamas Command Center," *Times of Israel*, July 23, 2014.

28 Rosen, "Targeting Enemy Forces in the War on Terror," 741–743, 761–769; Laurie Blank, "Was the U.S. Attack on the Kunduz Hospital a War Crime?", *Washington Post*, October 8, 2015; and Kevin Jon Heller, "Don't Blame IHL for Attacks on 'Hospital Shields,'" *OpinioJuris*, October 21, 2016.

29 See "Obama Administration Micromanagement Hamstrings Air Command in ISIS Fight," *Washington Times*, September 13, 2016 and Charles Dunlap, "The Moral Hazard of Inaction on War," *War on the Rocks*, August 19, 2016.

30 See William C. Martel, *Victory in War* (Cambridge, 2011) and Azar Gat, *Victorious and Vulnerable* (Lanham, 2010).

31 Gabriella Blum, "The Fog of Victory," *European Journal of International Law* 24:1 (2013): 391–421.

32 Craig Whitlock, "The War in Afghanistan: Promises to Win, but No Vision for Victory," *Washington Post*, April 14, 2021.

33 See, for example, John David Lewis, *Nothing Less Than Victory* (Princeton, 2010) and Victor Davis Hanson, *The Father of Us All*, 105–22, 161–87.

34 Yaakov Amidror, "Winning Counterinsurgency War: The Israeli Experience," Jerusalem Center for Public Affairs (2008) and Yagil Henkin, "A High Price for Our Blood: Israel's Security Doctrines," Jerusalem Institute for Strategy and Security (2018).

CHAPTER 25: PUBLIC IMAGE AND THE "CNN EFFECT" IN QANA

1 On the role of *kiddush* Hashem in warfare, see the debate between Rabbi Yitzhak Roness, "She'elot al Musar Milḥama Yehuda VeAmanot Beinleumiyot," *Tzohar* 29: 1–10, and Rabbi Avraham Sharir, "Al Kiddush Hashem BeMilḥemet Mitzva," *Tzohar* 31 (5768). See also Goldstein, "Musar VeDat BeHityaḥasutam shel Poskei Halakha," 364–367.

2 Rabbi Ronen Luvitch, "Kiddush Hashem VeHillul Hashem BeHagut shel HaTziyonut HaDatit," *She'anan* 16 (5771): 113–46. See also Rabbi Yuval Cherlow, "She'elot al Musar Milḥama," *Tzohar* 11 (5762): 97–104 and the response of Rabbi Yisrael Rozen in the following issue.

3 Rabbi Yehuda Amital, *Jewish Values in a Changing World* (Ktav, 2005), 152–56.

4 See Rabbi Eliezer Malemed, "Bosariyut Musarit VeTotzaoteha," *BaSheva* 23, December 26, 2002. Many ultra-Orthodox figures, including Rabbi Eliezer Shach, also opposed the national inquiry.

5 Sir Immanuel Jakobovits, *If Only My People: Zionism in My Life* (London, 1984), 109–10.

6 See Rabbi Yisrael Schepansky, "Shlom HaGalil VeShalom Akhshav," *Ohr HaMizraḥ* 31:3–4 (Nissan, 5743): 195–97.

7 Jakobovits, *If Only My People*, 109–10.

8 Ibid.

9 Akiva Bigman, "Naftali Bennett UKfar Qana," Mida, January 5, 2015 and Lazar Berman, "Bennett Defends Actions During 1996 Lebanon Operation," *Times of Israel*, January 5, 2015.

10 Marcus, *Israel's Long War with Hezbollah*, 145.

11 US Captain David Williams, "A Most Painful Lesson: The 1996 Shelling of Qana, Why It Matters Today," April 22, 2016, available online at https://www.army.mil/article/166556/a_most_painful_lesson_the_1996_shelling_of_qana_why_it_matters_today.

12 Letter from the UN Secretary General to the Security Council, May 7, 1996.

13 *Independent*, April 18, 1996.

14 Quotes from Marcus, *Israel's Long War with Hezbollah*, 146–47.

15 "Qana Wrong – Top Rabbi," *Jewish Chronicle*, May 3, 1996. See also Rabbi Mordechai Breuer, "Kiddush Hashem KeTohen shel Ḥayim," *Daf Kesher* 738 (1 Shevat 5760) and Reichner, *By Faith Alone*, 285.

16 W. Hays Parks, "The Protection of Civilians from Air Warfare," *Israel Yearbook on Human Rights*, vol. 27 (1997), 65–112.

17 See Nora Boustany, "Bombs Killed Victims as They Slept," *Washington Post*, February 14, 1991, 1.

18 Robert Fisk, *The Great War for Civilization*, 627.

19 Robert Kaplan, *Warrior Politics*, 125; italics in original.

20 Benjamin S. Lambeth, *Air Operations in Israel's War against Hezbollah*, 167–74.

21 Gil Hoffman, "Delay in Screening Kana Footage Causes PR Disaster," *Jerusalem Post*, July 30, 2006.

22 Harel and Issacharoff, *34 Days*, 166.

23 Ordre F. Kittrie, "A War Crime at Qana?" *Wall Street Journal*, August 5, 2006.

FINAL THOUGHTS ON AN UNCERTAIN ETHICAL FUTURE

1 Marcus, *Israel's Long War with Hezbollah*, 147.

2 Azmat Khan, "The Human Toll of America's Air Wars," *New York Times Magazine*, December 19, 2021.

3   Lieutenant Colonel John Cherry, Squadron Leader Kieran Tinkler, and Michael Schmitt, "Avoiding Collateral Damage on the Battlefield," *Just Security*, February 11, 2021.

4   Max Boot, *War Made New* (New York, 2006), Kindle Edition Location 287.

5   P. W. Singer, "The Ethics of Killer Applications: Why Is It So Hard to Talk about Morality When It Comes to New Military Technology?", *Journal of Military Ethics* 9:4 (2010), 299–312.

6   Kai-Fu Lee, "The Third Revolution in Warfare," *The Atlantic*, Sept. 11, 2021 and Michael Hirsch, "How AI Will Revolutionize Warfare," *Foreign Policy*, April 11, 2023.

Acknowledgments

When I told a colleague that I was writing a book on Jewish military ethics, his initial response was, "That's going to be a very short book." This colleague, deeply knowledgeable about rabbinic literature and moral political discourse, was skeptical about how much insight can be found in Jewish military discourse. I hope this book –which could have been longer to cover more topics – shows the wisdom that Torah offers for these dilemmas while highlighting the fact that our tradition can provide insights into every facet of the contemporary life.

I admit that I submit this work for public consideration with a bit of trepidation. Given that we are dealing with matters of life and death, the thought of "getting something wrong" is terrifying. It is my prayer that I have not grossly erred in these deliberations, and my belief that the presented moral framework can help guide our conversations, even if people will reasonably disagree with some of my conclusions.

It was a pleasure to collaborate with Maggid Books once again. Many thanks to Matthew Miller, Rabbi Reuven Ziegler, Caryn Meltz, Alex Drucker, Aryeh Grossman, Tani Bayer, Ita Olesker, and Debbie

Ismailoff. Special thanks to my good friend Rabbi David Silverstein for his encouragement and advice throughout this project. Rabbi Yitzchak Blau reviewed the entire manuscript and provided many insightful comments. Thanks as well to Neal Kozodoy, Jeremy Rabkin, and Michael Broyde for their insights on some initial ideas of the book.

The book was written while I was a post-doctoral fellow at Bar-Ilan University Law School. My thanks to Prof. Yitzhak Brand for his support of my fellowship and to the law school faculty and library staff for their assistance.

This publication was made possible through the generosity of many friends listed in the beginning of the book. Many thanks for their commitment to my scholarship, with a special thank you to our friends from Houston for their commemoration of my father's legacy. I have much gratitude to Daniel Bonner, Gidon Halbfinger, and Talia Katz of the Paul E. Singer Foundation for their interest and support of this project.

As always, my writing proceeds only with the unfailing encouragement of my family. I am deeply grateful for the loving support of my mother Dena Brody, her husband Rafi Shvil, my in-laws Irv and Lynn Shapiro, and my siblings Todd and Ellen Brody, Jeremy and Rocky Brody, Mikey and Tova Perl, Sammy and Debbie Shapiro, and Aaron and Mirit Shapiro.

My beloved wife, Rocky, has been a consistent source of strength and fortitude throughout while providing so much love to our home.

The writing of this book was completed as my two oldest kids begin the initial process of enlisting in the Israel Defense Forces. The subject matter of this book is thus far from theoretical for me. Throughout writing the book, I've asked myself what types of moral standards I'd want them to live by as soldiers and, equally important, what types of ethical considerations should be guiding their commanders and our country's leaders. The book includes much praise of the ethics behind Israeli warfare as well as some pointed questions about some of the standards set over the years. As a Zionist, rabbi, citizen, and parent, I consider it to be both an honor and responsibility to think deeply about these moral questions. It is my hope that the book will spur serious discussions about policies and maneuvers. It's also my prayer that my beloved children – Gila, Amichai, Maayan, Amalia, and Shaked – will not need to implement these teachings in battle, and if they do, that they'll find our tradition to be a source of wisdom and insight into these great dilemmas. May God bless them and protect them alongside all of our soldiers. I received final proofs of the manuscript soon after Israel was brutally attacked by Hamas terrorists on Shabbat Simḥat Torah, October 7th, 2023. Our leaders, citizens, and soldiers – including four of my nephews and countless neighbors and friends – will need a tremendous amount of physical and moral fortitude to remove this evil from our midst. I hope the ideas in this book will help provide the tools necessary to explain to ourselves, and to others, how we can ethically fight this just war and emerge victorious.

The writing of this book commenced shortly after my beloved father, Baruch Brody *a"h*, passed away. To others, my father was a renowned ethicist, celebrated teacher, *talmid chocham*, and Jewish communal leader. To me, he was, first and foremost, a loving father. Those roles became intertwined during college when I began asking my father for feedback on numerous papers. This would continue through many years of pursuing advanced degrees. Our last in-depth conversation, before he died in the summer of 2018, was about revisions to a particularly complex chapter of my doctorate.

In this book, I utilize a philosophical model that he developed as a normative model for how all thinkers, Jews and non-Jews alike, should think about complex ethical cases. I have utilized it as a descriptive model for how Jewish ethics operates. I recognize that I might be biased in my evaluation. Nonetheless, I am convinced that his framework is an accurate description of Jewish moral discourse and offers much to global thinking about military ethics.

Throughout the writing of the book, I have constantly wanted to call him for advice: Am I applying this ethical appeal wisely? What do you think of this argument? Am I reading this talmudic passage correctly? Alas, it has been a one-way conversation, bereft of his important insights and corrections. חבל על דאבדין ולא משתכחין

I hope that he would be proud of this book, and I offer it as a tribute to his memory. יהיה זכרו ברוך

Modiin, Israel
October 2023

The fonts used in this book are from the Arno family

Maggid Books
The best of contemporary Jewish thought from
Koren Publishers Jerusalem Ltd.